Radical Gotham

Radical Gotham

Anarchism in New York City
from Schwab's Saloon
to Occupy Wall Street

EDITED BY TOM GOYENS

UNIVERSITY OF
ILLINOIS PRESS
Urbana, Chicago, and Springfield

© 2017 by the Board of Trustees
of the University of Illinois
All rights reserved
1 2 3 4 5 C P 5 4 3 2 1
♾ This book is printed on acid-free paper.

Library of Congress Cataloging-in-Publication Data
Names: Goyens, Tom, 1972– editor.
Title: Radical Gotham : anarchism in New York city
 from Schwab's saloon to occupy Wall Street / edited
 by Tom Goyens.
Description: Urbana : University of Illinois Press, 2017. |
 Includes bibliographical references and index. |
Identifiers: LCCN 2017007713 (print) | LCCN
 2017020906 (ebook) | ISBN 9780252099595 () |
 ISBN 9780252041051 (hardback : alk. paper) | ISBN
 9780252082542 (paperback : alk. paper)
Subjects: LCSH: Anarchism—New York (State)—New
 York. | BISAC: POLITICAL SCIENCE / Political
 Ideologies / Anarchism. | HISTORY / United States /
 State & Local / General. | HISTORY / United States
 / 20th Century.
Classification: LCC HX846.N7 (ebook) | LCC HX846.N7
 R33 2017 (print) | DDC 335/.83097471—dc23
LC record available at https://lccn.loc.gov/2017007713

In Memory of Nunzio Pernicone (1940–2013)
and Judith Malina (1926–2015)

Contents

Introduction 　*Tom Goyens*	1
Johann Most and the German Anarchists 　*Tom Goyens*	12
Saul Yanovsky and Yiddish Anarchism on the Lower East Side 　*Kenyon Zimmer*	33
Fired by the Ideal: Italian Anarchists in New York City, 1880s–1920s 　*Marcella Bencivenni*	54
Times of Propaganda and Struggle: *El Despertar* and Brooklyn's Spanish Anarchists, 1890–1905 　*Christopher J. Castañeda*	77
From Union Square to Heaven: Dorothy Day and the Origin of Catholic Worker Anarchism 　*Anne Klejment*	100
New Wind: The Why?/Resistance Group and the Roots of Contemporary Anarchism, 1942–1954 　*Andrew Cornell*	122

Poetic Tension: The Aesthetic Politics of the Living Theatre   142
Allan Antliff

Up against the Wall Motherfucker: Ideology and Action in a "Street Gang with an Analysis"   161
Caitlin Casey

Gordon Matta-Clark's *Anarchitecture*   180
Erin Wallace

ABC No Rio as an Anarchist Space   201
Alan W. Moore

The Influence of Anarchism in Occupy Wall Street   221
Heather Gautney

Contributors   241

Index   245

Radical Gotham

Introduction

TOM GOYENS

On May 30, 2012, the Greenwich Village Society for Historic Preservation dedicated a plaque to Justus H. Schwab, who died in 1900, at the site of his Liberty Hall saloon at 50 East 1st Street on the Lower East Side.[1] Born in 1847, Schwab was a German American mason by trade and one of the first anarchists in New York. He opened his saloon in 1875 or 1876, and it quickly became a "headquarters for anarchists," as the *New York Tribune* phrased it.[2] Today, the former barroom is a small art gallery. Only a short walk away, on Allen Street, is Bluestockings, one of the few remaining radical bookstores, which sells publications on some of the famous anarchists who once lived in the neighborhood. A bit further away, on Rivington, is ABC No Rio, "a venue for oppositional culture" founded in 1980.[3] Countless other notable venues from more than a century ago have long vanished, replaced by parking garages and high-rises. The physical past is fast disappearing. "We don't always know when we pass buildings the incredible history that happened there," said Andrew Berman, executive director of the Society for Historic Preservation, standing in front of what had once been Schwab's anarchist watering hole.[4]

Eight months earlier, social activists, including anarchists, occupied Zuccotti Park in Lower Manhattan to protest global social and economic inequality and inaugurating what came to be known as the Occupy Wall Street movement. There is no direct connection between the two events, but the symbolism and juxtaposition are noteworthy. The two events are connected by the largely hidden 130-year history of anarchism in the largest U.S. city. While Occupy Wall Street was never wholly an anarchist movement, it is clear, as Heather Gautney's chapter in this volume shows, that anarchist principles were practiced.[5] Meeting places such as Schwab's were conceived by anarchists of the 1880s as alternative, autonomous spaces where anticapitalist activists sought to "occupy" at least a small sliver of the urban capitalist landscape. Indeed, in the depression year of 1874, a crowd of unemployed New Yorkers effectively occupied Tompkins Square. Among the protesters walked Justus Schwab, holding a red flag, until he was arrested.[6] Both the patrons at Schwab's and the Zuccotti protesters were internationalists in the sense that their ideas and practices could transcend national borders. A little looking shows that anarchist ideas and practices have endured, and this story is worth telling.

Never a monolithic bloc, anarchism is distinct from socialism and communism though all three have DNA in common. Anarchism, communism (the Marxist-Leninist version after 1917), and democratic socialism (in Europe, Social Democracy) all developed out of nineteenth-century socialism. A detailed exploration of the nuances of these ideologies is beyond the scope of this volume, but several key philosophical components distinguish anarchism. Anarchists' most sacred tenet is anti-authoritarianism, and they accordingly defend individual autonomy against any form of coercive authority. During the 1860s and 1870s, anarchism (although the term was not yet common currency) began to drift away from so-called state socialism, which followed a Marxist line. Within the emerging labor movement, anarchists believed that the emancipation of the working class—indeed, of all of society—should proceed from the bottom up, without the formation of revolutionary parties or governments. Anarchists condemned the principle of authority and power itself. Marx, of course, strongly believed that the most advanced workers must conquer political power. In contrast, anarchists vehemently rejected the state, even as a vehicle for emancipation, because it was based on authority. Socialists saw political participation as a core strategy for curbing the excesses of capitalism, whereas anarchists believed any participation in "change from above" to be futile and unnecessary. The vilification of anarchists as schemers and nihilists dates from this time, and Marx and his allies are to a great extent responsible for it.

Radical Gotham begins with the premise that anarchism is and has been a distinct, resilient, transnational, and significant political philosophy and movement that deserves to be studied on its own turf. Liberal and Marxist historiography has not always taken this approach. The success or failure of anarchism, for example, is often judged by socialist or Marxist criteria. Those who search the past for or expect from the future a successful "anarchist state" or "anarchist party" fundamentally misunderstand the movement: anarchists never set out to accomplish such a project. As sociologist Irving Horowitz, compiler of one of the first anthologies on anarchism, realized in 1964, "The anarchist does not live in terms of criteria of success and neither should his views be judged in such terms."[7] Even after the launch of the "new social history" during the 1960s, anarchist history remained on the margins. As late as 1983, labor historian Paul Buhle urged a reassessment of American working-class anarchism, stating that "syndicalist and anarchist themes have remained a hidden text, awaiting the unraveling of the political knot bound up in the Russian Revolution and the generations of Cold War that have followed."[8]

Though this fact is seldom recognized, despite its alleged organizational weakness, anarchism soldiered on with a message of vigilance toward the false comfort and security of hierarchical systems. Like a reliable compass, anarchists point to the dangers of statist projects that invariably lead to the concentration of power, even within a democratic system. For example, Mikhail Bakunin, one of the pioneers of the anarchist movement and Karl Marx's rival in the 1870s, predicted with eerie foresight what could (and did) happen in Russia forty-one years after his death: a dictatorship *over* the proletariat, "all the more dangerous because it appears as a sham expression of the people's will." Further anticipating the Soviet Union, Bakunin characterized life in a "workers' state" as "a barracks regime for the proletariat, in which a standardized mass of men and women workers would wake, sleep, work, and live by rote."[9]

Radical Gotham not only professes anarchism's distinctiveness but also demonstrates its endurance as a political and cultural ideology and movement in New York for nearly a century and a half. Such an innovative approach necessarily challenges the conventional periodization of anarchist history, which identifies—not without some truth—a "classical" period from the 1870s to 1920 (for the United States) or until the end of the Spanish Civil War in 1939 (on a global scale). From the 1940s on, anarchism is presumed to have disappeared, deprived of adherents, who turned instead to communism. Such a view gives the false impression that anarchism lacks continuity, that it is ungrounded and therefore ineffective and irrational. In fact, anarchism never quite disappeared. Before 1940, anarchism was overwhelmingly a working-class and immigrant movement that certainly differed from contemporary anarchism, but ideas and practices lived on, though perhaps under a dimmer spotlight. The 1940s saw the founding of anarchist federations in Cuba, Mexico, Bulgaria, France, Italy, Germany, and Japan, while the following decade saw the creation of such organizations in Uruguay and Argentina. In 1962, historian George Woodcock astutely described anarchism as "a strong underground current, there gathering into a swirling pool, trickling through crevices, disappearing from sight, and then re-emerging where the cracks in the social structure may offer it a course to run. As a doctrine it changes constantly; as a movement it grows and disintegrates, in constant fluctuations, but it never vanishes."[10]

This collection is not the first to present anarchism on an extensive time scale with a topical focus. Jesse Cohn's *Underground Passages: Anarchist Resistance Culture, 1848–2011* (2014) offers an impressive synthesis of global anarchist culture spanning 160 years.[11] The late Paul Avrich's monumental *Anarchist Voices: An Oral History of Anarchism in America* (1993), while not limited to one geographic location, captures the personal experiences and generational dimension of anarchism in America.[12] Only a few urban studies that deal with anarchism over many decades exist. New York's Lower East Side, one of the most significant urban enclaves for radical history, has been the subject of a broad, interdisciplinary study, *Resistance: A Radical Social and Political History of the Lower East Side* (2003), edited by community activist Clayton Patterson and others.[13] A more recent contribution, *Art Gangs: Protest and Counterculture in New York City* (2011), by critic and media artist Alan W. Moore (who is a contributor to this volume) focuses on countercultural groups in the same neighborhood.[14] Jennifer Guglielmo's pathbreaking study, *Living the Revolution: Italian Women's Resistance and Radicalism in New York City, 1880–1945* (2010), demonstrates the benefits of a multigenerational approach to immigrant radicalism in an ever-changing metropolis.[15] In *A Fire in Their Hearts*, Tony Michels finds that Yiddish-speaking immigrants' socialism grew primarily out of their New York experience and was less a remnant of their Old World lives.[16] Kenyon Zimmer (another contributor to this volume), finds a similar dynamic among the city's substantial Jewish and Italian anarchist communities.[17] Chris Ealham's *Anarchism and the City* (2010) presents a social and cultural history of four decades of anarchism in Barcelona.[18]

A thorough look at New York City illustrates that anarchism must be taken seriously as a philosophy and movement precisely because it endures. Each chapter presented here picks up elements from the previous one, linking together a string of seemingly isolated projects to form a long, unbroken conversation or transference of anarchist ideas and practices. The anarchist movement in New York began as an overwhelmingly immigrant and working-class story. Before the word *anarchist* was a self-conscious designation, French and German radical immigrants embraced an anti-authoritarian socialism. Johann Most embodied this dynamic when he came to New York in 1882 and transformed the German movement with the help of Schwab's financial and recreational resources. Most forged friendships with French American radicals such as Victor Drury and Edmond Mégy as well as with a growing anarchist movement in Chicago, London, and Vienna.

The Haymarket bombing in Chicago in 1886, resulting in the execution of four anarchists after a controversial trial, was a seminal event in radical history. Most had already mesmerized early Jewish socialists with his "oratorical fire," as Kenyon Zimmer explains in his chapter, and although it tempered Most's often-violent rhetoric, it also inspired younger activists such as Emma Goldman and Saul Yanovsky to join the movement. Despite the tragedy, Haymarket inspired the founding of the first Jewish anarchist group, which frequently invited Most to speak. Many Jewish and Italian immigrant radicals worked in low-paying jobs in the garment or construction industries. As both Zimmer and Marcella Bencivenni show, many in both groups radicalized after their arrival in America. Spanish anarchists in Brooklyn also appropriated the tragic symbolism of Haymarket and drew inspiration from Most, whose lectures were announced in *El Despertar*, one of the premier Spanish anarchist journals in the United States. New York's immigrant anarchist communities were sometimes connected by personal bonds. Most's relationship with Goldman did much to launch her career as America's most vocal anarchist until her deportation in 1919. Italian feminist anarchist Maria Roda shared a home with Pedro Esteve, the leading Spanish anarchist. A large gathering held in New York's Grand Central Palace on Lexington Avenue to commemorate Most's 1906 death featured eulogies by Goldman, Yanovsky, Esteve, and others in a total of five languages, with music provided by a German anarchist band, the Carl Sahm Club.[19]

The U.S. entry into the First World War, the Red Scare, and the immigration restriction that followed certainly diminished the movement. The outbreak of war in 1914 forced anarchists to take a position, leading to a crippling divide in the movement between those who opposed the war on principle and Peter Kropotkin, Yanovsky, and others who took the side of the Allies. The Bolshevik Revolution led many radicals to embrace communism, although by 1921, the anarchists, who had initially supported the Bolsheviks, turned against the party of Lenin and Trotsky. Despite these convulsions, anarchist ideas persevered throughout the 1920s among Italian and Jewish radicals, who sustained some of their precious periodicals. As Anne Klejment's chapter highlights, anarchist ideas welled up again with the Catholic Worker movement in the 1930s, centered in the same ethnic neighborhoods of Lower Manhattan and speaking the same language of social revolution and nonviolent direct action.

In many respects, Andrew Cornell's chapter bridges two seemingly separate periods: "the prewar American anarchist movement rooted in working-class immigrant communities and the circles of younger artists, writers, and intellectuals that carried anarchist ideas and practices into the New Left of the 1960s" (p. 122). While not a mass movement in the 1940s, anarchism was passed on through personal connections and by the activities of small circles of activists. Cornell profiles Audrey Goodfriend, who combined roots in the remnants of the old Jewish movement and a desire to steer a new anarchism through the crucible of the Second World War.[20] The Why? Group, one of the key anarchist circles during the war years, engaged in joint pacifist street action with Catholic Workers. Allan Antliff's chapter places the politics of the Living Theatre within the anarchist context of the postwar years: Judith Malina and Julian Beck, the founders of the Living Theatre, attended anarchist meetings during the 1940s. Caitlyn Casey describes the countercultural activism of the Motherfuckers on the Lower East Side during the 1960s, including visual and performing arts—in fact, the Living Theatre introduced the Motherfuckers to anarchism. Both the Living Theatre group and radical artist Gordon Matta-Clark were influenced by French anarchist Antonin Artaud, as Erin Wallace reveals. And finally, the quest for autonomous spaces and meaningful community activism is evident in the more recent manifestations explored by Alan Moore and Heather Gautney.

Not all of these activists explicitly labeled themselves *anarchist*, even though their writings and practices are certainly anarchist. The label declined in usage during the 1930s, 1940s, and 1950s before making a comeback in the 1960s. A host of celebrated personalities whose names are well known today espoused anarchist principles but did not always trumpet those views. For example, renowned French artists Camille Pissaro, Gustave Courbet, Paul Signac, and Marcel Duchamp all embraced anarchist ideas. Similarly, Americans such as composer John Cage and artists Donald Judd, Barnett Newman, and Mark Rothko were inspired by anarchism. Such French *chansonniers* of the 1950s and 1960s as Georges Brassens and Léo Ferré and Belgian singer-songwriter Jacques Brel had unmistakable anarchist tendencies, as did a string of politically engaged punk bands from the 1970s and 1980s, such as Crass and Chumbawamba in Britain and MC5 and the Dead Kennedys in the United States.

Prefigurative politics is another consistent element in the history of anarchism: in other words, anarchists believe that the actions, methods, and organizations of revolutionaries should prefigure the kind of society that is desired. Anarchists take this view because their enduring critique of authoritarian (revolutionary) organizations as a means to build a future society commits them to an ethical balancing of ends and means. Power structures should not be part of the efforts to transform an unequal society into a free one. Anarchists believe that the desire for transformation and resistance can and should be consummated in the here and now. Revolution happens in the daily subversion of the normal and unjust. Rather than building parties, immigrant anarchists in New York and elsewhere congregated in small groups that adhered to anarchist principles of decision making and solidarity. After 1940, when anarchism became somewhat detached from the labor movement, anarchist activists still emphasized "living anarchist lives," as was the case with members of the Why?/Resistance Group and to some extent the Occupy movement's General Assemblies. During the 1950s, the Living Theatre's attempt to dramatize the concept of alienation (in society and between audience and actors) was inspired in part by Paul Goodman's notion of "drawing the line" and "refusing to submit to the demands of any oppressive or destructive authority," as Antliff writes (p. 144). More than other radicals, anarchists have been open to experimentation on a number of cultural fronts. A recognition of the liberating and consciousness-raising potential of cultural rebellions has been one of the reasons that anarchist ideas began to reemerge and infuse many youth movements of the 1960s and 1970s such as the Motherfuckers—a "recurrence of defiance," as Terry M. Perlin wrote in 1979.[21]

Anarchism in New York is unthinkable without its many cultural and artistic manifestations, and this aspect is on display in *Radical Gotham*. The extraordinary creativity and experimentation of anarchistic artists stands in sharp contrast to socialist or communist practitioners of art. The notion of revolution in the here and now has inspired or served as the catalyst for a wide array of avant-garde art. But are any anti-authoritarian practices, including in art, anarchist? Scholars have debated how best to delineate anarchism's past and contemporary manifestations. In 2009, sociologist Lucien van der Walt and journalist Michael Schmidt argued for a narrower definition of what constitutes an ideologically coherent anarchist movement. In their impressive synthesis, *Black Flame*, the authors specifically anchor anarchism and syndicalism within the context of class-based mass politics and revolutionary anticapitalism, beginning with Bakunin.[22] Their approach excludes a sizable number of premodern, philosophical, and cultural anarchist personalities, and I have deviated from it in some important respects. While definitional demarcations are useful, anarchism is and has been much richer than a purely political movement born in the 1860s. I agree with Robert Graham's recent observation that *Black Flame*'s "'genealogical' or 'historicist' approach conflates anarchism as a body of ideas with anarchism as a movement."[23] Indeed, anarchist ideas lie at the root of a variety of small-scale, autonomous cultural projects and acts of resistance. Political and cultural anarchism are two sides of the same coin. Theater in one form or another was as important to the German and Jewish anarchists of the Gilded Age as it was to Judith Malina and Julian Beck or the Motherfuckers.

Art, humor, and performance are as integral to New York anarchism as are pamphlets, strikes, and mass demonstrations. As Cohn has recently argued, "What anarchists *did* demand from art, by and large, was what they demanded from all the forms and moments of their political lives: i.e., that it should, as much as possible, embody the idea in the act, the principle in the practice, and end in the means."²⁴

Radical Gotham underscores not only anarchist culture but also biography and print culture as part of the connective tissue of long-term New York anarchism. While movement building was a key objective for immigrant anarchists, the same did not necessarily hold true for later anarchist manifestations. Small groups and tireless individuals that flew under the radar were frequently responsible for transmitting anarchist ideas and practices from one period to the next. Most and Goldman acted as transmitters from one ethnic group to another or to the wider American public. Dorothy Day was inspired by the antiwar activities of anarchist and socialist groups. Cornell describes Goodfriend, who died in 2012, as one of the crucial links between the prewar movement and the activists who inspired the New Left. The significance of the anarchist press as the lifeblood of the movement cannot be overstated. Circles of activists cohered and sustained themselves around the movement's numerous periodicals, some of them short-term ventures, others lasting for decades. It would be wrong to point only to the long-lasting papers such as *Fraye Arbeter Shtime* or *Freiheit* as illustrations of anarchism's modest success. Small and irregular papers often kept anarchism alive in periods of decline simply by denying mainstream society a monopoly on (official) opinion.

The interaction between anarchism and the social space of the city is another common theme that runs through the collection and that is facilitated by the unique approach of *Radical Gotham*. On one level, the story of anarchism in New York parallels the city's rise since the 1870s. Three major urban themes can be identified: First, the city as a cultural and artistic center that superseded Boston during the Gilded Age. Second, the city as the point of arrival for and residence of millions of newcomers. And third, the city as the hub of industrial and finance capitalism. Physical and social space is as much a player in the story of anarchism as are Most and Day. New York is not merely the concrete backdrop for anarchism and other social movements; an interplay takes place between human actors—even ideas—and urban space. The spatial environment is fluid, contingent, and contested. The stories told in this volume did not merely occur in New York City by chance; rather, the cosmopolitan space allows (or perhaps necessitates) these radical expressions to exist and flourish. Conversely, New York anarchism contributes to the formation of the city's identity as a fluid, democratic (with a small *d*), and "unfinished" place, as urban historian Thomas Bender has phrased it.[25] In other words, anarchism cannot be detached from its environment.

Every chapter in *Radical Gotham* is in some way an investigation of radical space: the spatial dimension is particularly relevant for anarchists because they practiced a prefigurative politics. Anarchists searched for, occupied, and conceptualized spaces as suggestive of the future society they envisioned. This is an essential activity—even mission—for anarchists, especially in light of the fact that anarchists (unlike socialists) as a matter of principle repudiate politics, capitalism, and any form of coercive authority. All the immigrant anarchist groups—political, educational, and cultural—met regularly in saloon back-rooms, restaurants, and other locales designated as alternative spaces. Schwab's saloon, for example, was explicitly a radical hangout, decorated and conceptualized as a free, anticapitalist space. So, too, were many meeting places of Italian, Jewish, and Spanish anarchists in Manhattan, Brooklyn, and Paterson, New Jersey. For large commemorations attended by thousands, New York anarchists of the 1880s and 1890s rented well-known venues such as the Cooper Union, Thalia Theater, or Germania Assembly Rooms. During the worst years of the Great Depression, Catholic Worker anarchists carved out alternative spaces throughout the Lower East Side to help the needy, sometimes in conflict with city authorities, as in the later case of the ABC No Rio space. Public space was routinely transformed into a stage for radical politics—in labor demonstrations during the Gilded Age and Progressive Era, the street theatrics of the Motherfuckers, and the occupation of Wall Street. Matta-Clark and other radical artists literally reconfigured urban structures to convey their critique of private property, waste, and homelessness during the 1970s.

New York City is also a conspicuous locale for observing the transnational dimension of the anarchist movement, one of the most exciting directions of contemporary scholarship on anarchism. In *New York Intellect*, Bender describes the city's regenerative and unfinished nature bound up in transatlantic connections: "The presence of Europe is fundamentally important to the culture and society of New York."[26] It was indeed easy for transnational and multilingual New York radicals to acquire an Atlantic identity rather than an American one. For each of the immigrant anarchist communities, the city was but one node in a global network reinforced by the anarchist press and traveling speakers. Local and regional anarchist movements were linked to other hubs or individuals in different countries. New York was just such a hub. Nevertheless, this "transnational turn" in anarchist studies should not substitute for analyses at the local or regional levels but should constitute one of several "scales of analysis" that help to produce a more holistic picture of the anarchist movement.[27]

For all these reasons, *Radical Gotham* repositions the significance of anarchism by documenting the evolution of anarchist ideas and practices in one place so that the movement's endurance and continuity come into sharper view. This collection adds to existing methodologies and perspectives by emphasizing and thereby reasserting spatial, biographical, and cultural dimensions within the field of anarchist history.

Notes

1. Serena Solomon, "Former Saloon of Radical Thought in East Village Honored with Plaque," *DNAinfo New York*, May 31, 2012, http://www.dnainfo.com/new-york/20120531/east-village/former-saloon-of-radical-thought-east-village-honored-with-plaque; Bonnie Rosenstock, "E. First St. Plaque Recalls Bar That Was Totally Rad," *The Villager*, June 7, 2012, http://thevillager.com/2012/06/07/e-first-st-plaque-recalls-bar-that-was-totally-rad/. See also Jared Malsin, "Where Radicals Once Drank, a Search for a Mild-Mannered Tenant," *Local East Village*, February 6, 2012.

2. *New York Daily Tribune*, September 10, 1901. Schwab's saloon was originally located at 84 Clinton Street, but he moved to 1st Street sometime in the late 1870s. He died of tuberculosis in 1900 (*Trow's New York City Directory for the Year Ending May 1, 1877* [New York: Trow City Directory Company, 1876], 1233).

3. See ABC No Rio website, http://www.abcnorio.org/about/about.html.

4. Quoted in Solomon, "Former Saloon of Radical Thought."

5. See also Heather Gautney, *Protest and Organization in the Alternative Globalization Era: NGOs, Social Movements, and Political Parties* (New York: Palgrave Macmillan, 2009).

6. See Herbert G. Gutman, "The Tompkins Square 'Riot' in New York City on January 13, 1874: A Re-Examination of Its Causes and Its Aftermath," *Labor History* 6:1 (1965): 55.

7. Irving L. Horowitz, ed., *The Anarchists* (New York: Dell, 1964), 11.

8. Paul Buhle, "Anarchism and American Labor," *International Labor and Working Class History* 23 (Spring 1983): 21.

9. Mikhail Bakunin, *Selected Writings*, ed. Arthur Lehning (New York: Grove, 1974), 268, 259.

10. George Woodcock, *Anarchism: A History of Libertarian Ideas and Movements* (1962; New York: New American Library, 1975), 17–18.

11. Jesse Cohn, *Underground Passages: Anarchist Resistance Culture, 1848–2011* (Oakland, Calif.: AK, 2014).

12. Paul Avrich, *Anarchist Voices: An Oral History of Anarchism in America* (Princeton: Princeton University Press, 1995).

13. Clayton Patterson, Joe Flood, Alan Moore, and Howard Seligman, eds., *Resistance: A Social and Political History of the Lower East Side* (New York: Seven Stories, 2007).

14. Alan W. Moore, *Art Gangs: Protest and Counterculture in New York City* (Brooklyn, N.Y.: Autonomedia, 2011).

15. Jennifer Guglielmo, *Living the Revolution: Italian Women's Resistance and Radicalism in New York City, 1880–1945* (Chapel Hill: University of North Carolina Press, 2010).

16. Tony Michels, *A Fire in Their Hearts: Yiddish Socialists in New York* (Cambridge: Harvard University Press, 2005).

17. Kenyon Zimmer, *Immigrants against the State: Yiddish and Italian Anarchism in America* (Urbana: University of Illinois Press, 2015), 1–2.

18. Chris Ealham, *Anarchism and the City: Revolution and Counter-Revolution in Barcelona, 1898–1937* (Oakland, Calif.: AK, 2010).

19. *Freiheit* (New York), March 24, 1906.

20. See also Andrew Cornell, *Unruly Equality: U.S. Anarchism in the Twentieth Century* (Berkeley: University of California Press, 2016).

21. Terry M. Perlin, ed., *Contemporary Anarchism* (New Brunswick, N.J.: Transaction, 1979), 3.

22. Michael Schmidt and Lucien van der Walt, *Black Flame: The Revolutionary Class Politics of Anarchism and Syndicalism* (Oakland, Calif.: AK, 2009).

23. Robert Graham, *We Do Not Fear Anarchy, We Invoke It: The First International and the Origins of the Anarchist Movement* (Oakland, Calif.: AK, 2015), 2.

24. Cohn, *Underground Passages*, 16–17.

25. Thomas Bender, *The Unfinished City: New York and the Metropolitan Idea* (New York: New Press, 2002), with a dedication to the victims of 9/11.

26. Thomas Bender, *New York Intellect: A History of Intellectual Life in New York City, from 1750 to the Beginnings of Our Time* (New York: Knopf, 1987), xiii. In the same year, Alan Wald wrote his more specific *The New York Intellectuals: The Rise and Decline of the Anti-Stalinist Left from the 1930s to the 1980s* (Chapel Hill: University of North Carolina Press, 1987).

27. Constance Bantman and Bert Altena, eds., *Reassessing the Transnational Turn: Scales of Analysis in Anarchist and Syndicalist Studies* (New York: Routledge, 2015).

Johann Most
and the German Anarchists

TOM GOYENS

Johann Most's arrival in New York started with an accident. In the morning darkness of December 14, 1882, Most and his fellow passengers on board the steamer *Wisconsin* were jolted by a crash; they rushed on deck to see what had happened. The steamer had collided with a bark some 250 miles from New York. The bark was eventually repaired, but the accident and the heavy seas of the preceding ten days considerably delayed the transatlantic voyage. Johann Most, the only German on board, finally disembarked on the morning of December 18 and was warmly greeted by saloonkeeper Justus Schwab and a small crowd of smiling, red-ribboned comrades.[1] Schwab had immigrated to the United States in 1869 and joined the German section of the Workingmen's Association. In the midst of the 1874 depression, he was arrested for marching in Tompkins Square while holding a red flag. Shortly thereafter, he married and opened a tiny basement saloon at 50 East 1st Street on the Lower East Side, and it soon became a watering hole for immigrant radicals of all stripes.[2]

The evening after Most's arrival, thousands of men and women—some bringing their tired children—crowded into Cooper Union's Great Hall for a welcoming reception organized by the city's radical groups. Most began to speak in broken English before switching to German. The spirit of revolution was rising, he thundered, and the workers of the world must be ready to act. To this end, he would undertake an American speaking tour before sailing back. In the end, Most never again saw Europe—he, like thousands of other

Justus Schwab's saloon at 50 East 1st Street.
New-York Daily Tribune, September 10, 1901.

newcomers, became a New Yorker. Who was this slender man with a scraggly beard who had for years wielded the sharpest pen against the rulers of Europe?[3]

A bookbinder by trade, Most had since 1868 made a name for himself as an orator and editor in first the Austrian and then the German socialist movement. As a child he had suffered two major traumas: his mother died of cholera when he was nine, and at age thirteen, he underwent a jaw operation that saved his life but left him with a deformed face that he later hid by growing a beard. He discovered a gift for speechmaking and popular prose, endured several stints in prison, sat in Parliament for a while, and by 1878 found himself exiled from his native Germany. The Reichstag's October 1878 passage of a draconian antisocialist law opened the door for a sweeping Red Scare. Socialist meetings were prohibited and the movement's press was quashed. Hundreds of activists, like Most, were arrested or expelled.[4] Socialist legislators, however, were allowed to retain their seats, and they resolved to sit out the Red Scare. Most fiercely criticized what he perceived as the party leaders' shameful docility.

Expelled from Berlin and shunned by the party, Most moved to London in December 1878, where he found an exile community that was a storehouse of revolutionary ideas well to the left of social democracy. Without party approval, Most started a new socialist paper, *Freiheit* (Freedom), which was delivered to German readers via an elaborate smuggling operation. Socialist Party leaders set up a rival paper the following year and then unceremoniously expelled Most from the Party in August 1880.

All of these events radicalized Most and his circle of friends. With the socialist labor movement in Germany crippled, *Freiheit* emerged as the voice of social revolution and opened its pages to a variety of opinions. Most published excerpts of Mikhail Bakunin's writings and printed Sergei Nechaev's 1869 pamphlet, *Catechism of a Revolutionary*, as well as his own ideas on secret societies. In December 1880, when German police arrested key activists in a dragnet operation, *Freiheit* published one of the first discussions of terroristic action against the state.[5] After the news of the March 1881 assassination of Czar Alexander II, Most printed a front-page article, "Endlich!" (At Last!), glorifying the killing of the monarch. Most was promptly arrested, tried, and sentenced to sixteen months of hard labor. In addition, police confiscated (possibly illegally) a trove of material, including composition materials, personal papers, and most disastrous of all, address lists, which were allegedly handed over to German and Austrian authorities prompting the arrest of several activists there.[6] The prosecution of Most and his paper was not without controversy in Britain or the United States. Indeed, the extensive coverage of the trial and the concomitant debate over free speech introduced many New Yorkers to "Herr Most."[7] Undeterred, two *Freiheit* typesetters and then Swiss comrades continued to publish articles on insurrectionary methods and explosives. Toward the end of his sentence, in October 1882, Most was invited to undertake a speaking tour of the United States. Refusing to abandon his beloved newspaper, Most decided to move it to New York.

The tour idea came from the New York Social-Revolutionary Club (Sozial-Revolutionäre Klub), founded on November 15, 1880, in a Lower East Side beer hall by a group that included Schwab and Moritz Bachmann. The club soon grew to nearly one hundred members, who openly discussed direct action, insurrection, and self-defense—the same topics Most was dishing up to his subscribers.[8] The club maintained close ties with established French radical groups led by Victor Drury and Edmond Mégy, a close friend of Schwab's.[9]

What united these revolutionaries was a hostility to electoral socialism, its hierarchical party structure, and its eagerness to compromise. The radicals wanted a more combative program of resistance such as the formation of self-defense groups. They discussed extrapolitical means to achieve the goal of a new society, including propaganda by the deed. At a congress of social revolutionaries held in London in 1881, while Most was in prison, the International Working People's Association, or Black International, was formed along federalist principles, and propaganda by the deed, violent or not, was codified in the gathering's final document.[10] In the United States, the fight over armed defense and educational groups (*Lehr-und Wehr Vereine*) caused Schwab and many other social revolutionaries to break with the party in 1880.

By the summer of 1881, two German anarchist groups existed in New York: the Social-Revolutionary Club and New York Group 1 (mostly radicalized former Socialist Labor Party members, like Schwab). A German diplomatic envoy in Washington saw the writing on the wall. "Several hints coming from that region," he wrote, "lead me to suspect that New York threatens to become a headquarters of Anarchists."[11] In Chicago, however, social revolutionaries supported self-defense and opposed elections and reformism but embraced trade unionism as a vehicle for revolutionary change—violent insurrection and "propaganda by the deed" were hardly mentioned. One labor paper wondered "how the Eastern revolutionaries who ridicule trade unions as well as 'politics' will agree with the Chicago malcontents who advocate trade unions first and politics next, and in their published call profess to be opposed to dynamite schemes."[12] As an Atlantic gateway, New York had always been a dumping ground for displaced European radicals—the city was, in the words of the historian Ronald Creagh, the "cosmopolitan metropolis of the avengers."[13]

This was the radical landscape of industrial America in which Most made his prominent entry. With no regular income other than peddling his newspaper, Most took an upstairs apartment at 167 William Street, near the financial district, and set up the *Freiheit* editorial office as well as his living quarters. He was single, was prison-hardened, called himself an anarchist, and was bent on resuming the war against the Bismarcks of the world. As editor of the foremost German-language revolutionary paper, he focused on Europe, where he expected a revolution to soon begin and where a precarious smuggling network continued to supply his subscribers. A settled life for Most was out of the question, since the coming revolution demanded vigilance and possibly a quick return to Europe. "I'm ready at any moment," he wrote to a friend in 1885, "I have no one to leave behind, and there is nothing in the world that particularly interests me apart from the preparation for the social revolution."[14]

Most's influence on the anarchist movement in New York and other eastern cities was unquestionably profound and lasting. His two speaking tours during the spring of 1883 were by all accounts successful, and he continued to undertake such excursions until his death in 1906. At an 1883 conference of American revolutionaries in Pittsburgh, Most emerged as the leading East Coast delegate and authored the conference's proclamation. The International Working People's Association was reaffirmed as a federation of autonomous groups. As a result, dozens of groups sprang up along the industrial East Coast. The proclamation declared that the people had a right to overthrow an oppressive government and that through "organization and unity," propaganda by the deed should coexist with propaganda by the word.[15]

Most was certainly a master at propaganda by word, both printed and spoken. Most had adored the stage since he was a child, and as an orator he was keenly aware of the theatrics of power. His listeners attested to the mesmerizing ferocity of his words. "I hear in my ears his mighty voice," recalled Jewish anarchist Chaim Weinberg, himself an exceptional speaker, "which used to enchant me and all the workers present, exhorting and calling to the struggle against all forms of oppression."[16] A young Emma Goldman remembered that "the rapid current of his speech, the music of his voice, and his sparkling wit, all combined to produce an effect almost overwhelming. He stirred me to my depths."[17] Throughout 1884 and 1885, Most published numerous articles on explosives, chemistry, and insurrectionary tactics, synthesizing them together in a July 1885 booklet, *Revolutionary War Science*. When speaking or writing about politics and revolution, Most relished a provocative style with witty sarcasm. "Herr Most writes a peculiar style in German," one anarchist free-love magazine explained, "his paper can be understood and appreciated only by one who adds to a knowledge of German, a knowledge of New York life, and both German and American slang."[18]

There is no record of Most ever committing a violent crime, but his words could have a nefarious effect on others.[19] Most firmly believed that against a terror regime, more terror must be applied: it is a "holy cause of the peoples of the world."[20] For much of the 1880s, he openly praised assassins who targeted police officials and businessmen in Austria and Germany. He was at least indirectly involved in the October 1883 bombing of a Frankfurt police station, with

Freiheit claiming responsibility because it wanted to test dynamite.[21] In the fall of 1884, Most obtained a job in a New Jersey explosives factory under a false name, assuring a friend, "I can obtain from this factory ready-made materials and in considerable quantities."[22] A month later, Most shipped a "large ration of poison" (blue acid) to Europe.[23] To dispel any ambiguity on the subject, Most declared in 1885 that "not much more needs to be said today about the significance of modern explosives for the social revolution of the present and the future.... [R]evolutionaries of all countries strive more and more to obtain them and learn the art of applying them practically."[24] He also warned the ruling classes of his adopted country, "Where America is concerned, one day the people will similarly learn to understand that playing around with ballot boxes will need to come to an end, and that it would be better to hang fellows like Vanderbilt, Jay Gould, etc. from the nearest lamp post."[25] At the same time that Most was purloining explosives, some of his anarchist associates were setting fire to their Manhattan tenements intending to collect insurance payments for the cause. This scheme worked well until 1885, when a mother and two children were killed. Most never directly participated but refused to condemn the perpetrators, a decision that cost him several friendships.[26]

But Most and his fellow revolutionaries were not merely apostles of destruction, as the press frequently branded them. Most had considerable experience in and appreciation for organization and discipline, going back to his days as labor editor in Germany in the 1870s. The vast majority of activists were not terrorists but members of a variety of clubs—propaganda groups, discussion circles, rifle clubs, musical or theatrical associations—that formed in the wake of the 1883 Pittsburgh congress and that had anywhere from a few dozen to nearly two hundred members. Whereas the country had only thirty German groups in August 1883, by the spring of 1885, eighty such organizations met regularly, with a total estimated membership of three thousand and an additional four thousand sympathizers (including one thousand in New York alone), according to a Chicago anarchist paper.[27] In 1886, one German anarchist estimated that the United States had ten thousand resident anarchists: five thousand in Chicago, twenty-five hundred in New York, and the rest dispersed among other industrial cities.[28] A closer look at New York City reveals the anchors that connected the German anarchist movement to its physical meeting places—mostly backrooms of saloons and rented lecture halls. Some seventy-eight German anarchist groups existed at one time or another in the New York–New Jersey area between 1880 and 1914. Some groups existed only for a few weeks; others persisted for much longer, in some cases briefly suspending activities during times of economic hardship. Nearly half of German anarchist groups in New

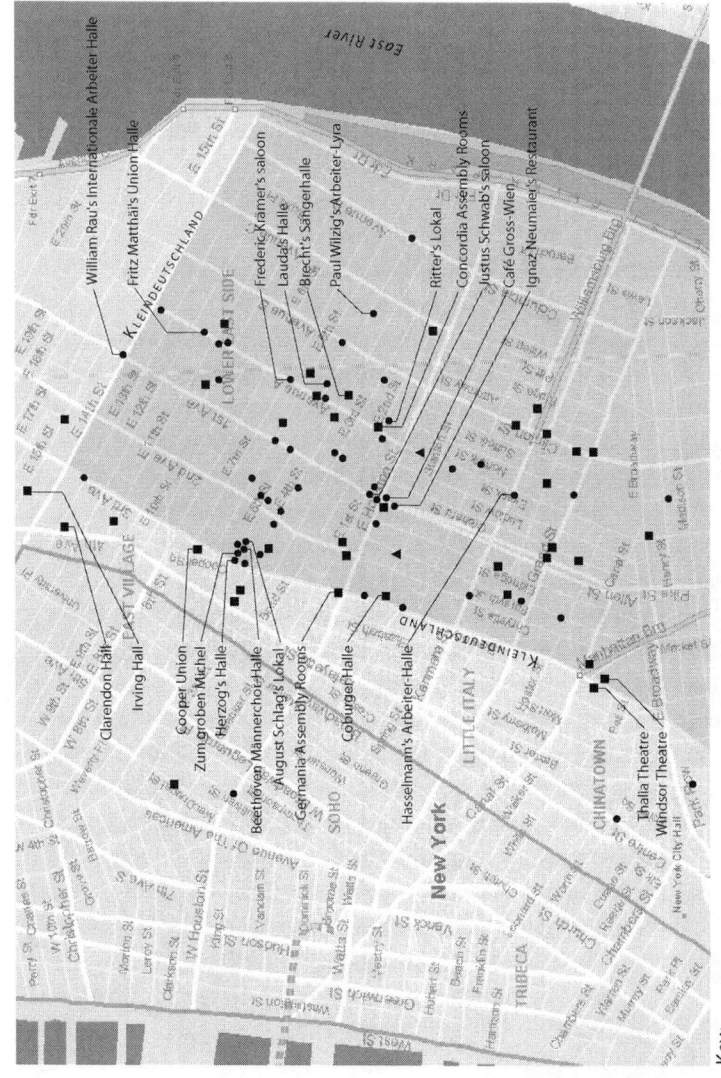

German anarchist meeting places in Lower Manhattan, 1880–1914. Map by Heather Harvey.

York were founded in Manhattan, and more than a third were established in northern New Jersey. Half of all groups were active during the tumultuous 1880s, while more than a third lasted into the 1890s.[29]

The cornerstone of weekly anarchist group activity was the lecture evening, held in the back room of a beer hall or sometimes in a larger venue. Public speakers played prominent roles, with Most, Franz Wiesinger, Carl Wölky, Wenzel Führer, Fritz Fuhse, August Lott, Moritz Schultze, Phillip Kennel, and others promoting the movement and turning lethargy into militancy.[30] Topics ranged widely, encompassing subjects such as "Darwinism and Socialism," "Modern Marriage," and "Clericalism and Bigotry in America." Some radical New Yorkers found beer-hall-based clubs too recreational to pass for proper revolutionary agitation. "If a group or club occupies a saloon as a favorite pub with hall," complained one Milwaukee anarchist, "the money is usually spent on drinking, smoking, and gaming, whereas half of it would otherwise have been allocated to agitation."[31]

But to German anarchists, all recreation was political and provided the opportunity to practice their anarchist philosophy in the here and now. Beer halls were not merely drinking places: they were conceived and experienced as autonomous anarchist spaces. In 1892, reporter John Gilmer Speed visited Zum groben Michel (Rough Mike's Place), an anarchist bar located at 209 East 5th Street, and saw a beer hall where men played music and pool while "files of anarchistic papers" were strewn around; "portraits of the anarchists that have been executed for their crimes" adorned the smoke-stained walls.[32] American writer James Gibbons Huneker stumbled into Schwab's saloon on 1st Street and found "no bombs, though there was plenty of beer." He remembered, "the discussions in German and English betrayed a culture not easily duplicated on the West Side.... Before Nietzsche's and Stirner's names were pronounced in our lecture-rooms they were familiarly quoted at Schwab's."[33] Anarchist beer halls combined an egalitarian informality with political seriousness. In 1896, a *New-York Tribune* reporter with some knowledge of German noticed that unlike in typical American saloons, men and women at Schwab's mingled freely and addressed each other with the informal *Du*. The reporter further grasped the political atmosphere amid the flow of beer and tobacco: "On the tables where there is no card-playing may be found copies of newspapers in German and Russian. The saloons are unlike others, because one rarely hears laughter there, and the men are always, even in their cups, serious."[34]

Even the frequent outdoor excursions organized by German anarchist groups reveal a synergy between politics and relaxation. As many as hundreds of families gathered in New York's parks and groves (though apparently not in

Central Park). Activities held at gardens owned by breweries, such as in Fort Wadsworth on Staten Island, included not only drinking beer but also children's games, shooting practice, speeches, parades, and music. At one time or another, the New York City area boasted forty-two German singing societies affiliated with the anarchist movement.[35] "Everywhere groups of comrades who came with their families lay down on the vast park grounds," read one anarchist review, "in order to combine the relaxation of the outdoors with serious discussions about current events."[36]

The city's anarchist movement remained largely out of sight for most New Yorkers despite the forays of a handful of reporters and intellectuals into what Alan Trachtenberg has called "forbidden and menacing spaces."[37] A major exception occurred when urban anarchists held large commemorative gatherings in rented venues such as the Great Hall at Cooper Union, Concordia Assembly Rooms (28–30 Avenue A), Germania Assembly Rooms (291–93 Bowery), Clarendon Hall (114–18 East 13th St.), and the Brooklyn Labor Lyceum (67 Myrtle St.). A mainstay on the anarchist calendar was the Commune Festival, held around March 18 each year to celebrate the 1871 Paris Commune. It was jointly organized by German, French, Bohemian, and Italian anarchist groups and typically attracted thousands of paying attendees. Halls were decorated with banners, flags, and portraits. Orators delivered speeches in four or five languages, interspersed with musical and theatrical pieces, before partygoers danced into the night at a large ball. Here again, politics, recreation, and fundraising were on display—a show of oppositional strength for the movement.

The 1886–87 Haymarket tragedy devastated the German movement in New York. In the midst of a campaign for an eight-hour workday, Chicago anarchists staged an outdoor rally on May 4, 1886, to protest police violence against strikers. When police appeared and ordered the crowd to disperse, an unidentified person hurled a bomb into the police ranks, instantly killing one officer and horribly wounding others. In the ensuing melee, police shot and killed an unknown number of workers, while a total of seven policemen died. In retaliation—and in light of some anarchists' history of advocating violence and of the fact that some Chicago anarchists had been manufacturing bombs in the days before the rally—officials rounded up anarchist leaders, including some who had not even been present at the rally. On August 20, 1886, eight men accused of being part of an anarchist conspiracy that led to the bloodshed were convicted, with seven sentenced to death; four were hanged on November 11, 1887. The subsequent annual commemoration of the Haymarket martyrs would become the most important mass public event of the anarchist movement worldwide, with socialists, labor activists, and progressive New Yorkers in attendance.[38]

The shock of Haymarket changed Most's views on revolutionary tactics. He now rejected indiscriminate violence, partly because he feared for his life. On May 11, eleven days before the bombing, Most had been arrested after he delivered a speech in which he urged workers to arm. Although the incident was unrelated to the events at Haymarket, prosecutors attempted unsuccessfully to persuade New York authorities to hand over Most.[39] Most realized that lone wolf attacks were futile and counterproductive, almost cultish, and he now proposed a sort of Jacobin struggle: "Confiscation of all Capital by the soldiers of Revolution acting as a kind of world conquerors."[40] Indeed, the arming of workers in self-defense or in preparation for social revolution was a favorite topic of Most's. "Probably the best thing," he wrote in 1885, "would be that all organized workers of the civilized world could be persuaded to acquire good rifles ... and a good amount of munitions, to train militarily and then mobilize themselves for the coming social war."[41] When confronted by reporters, Most invariably invoked the Second Amendment to the U.S. Constitution.

By 1888, the forty-two-year-old Most, was revising his anarchist philosophy yet again. Convinced that terrorist actions were futile, he refused requests to republish his explosives manual.[42] He felt that anarchists should use print and oratory and insisted that "propaganda by deed has by no means become for us an exclusive hobby-horse that we ride constantly and forget all other propaganda. We work by the printed word wherever and whenever we can."[43] Most lamented the anarchist's prevailing image as a knife-wielding bomb thrower though he had helped to create that image.[44] Though he did not entirely renounce forceful resistance, Most further refined his position in 1892: "There is no greater error than to believe that we as anarchists need only to commit *any* deed, no matter *when, where* and against *whom*. To have a propaganda effect, every deed needs to be *popular*; it must meet with approval by an important part of the proletariat. If that is not the case, or if it actually meets with *dis*approval of the very part of the population it is intended to inspire ... anarchism makes itself unpopular and hated."[45]

In the wake of the Haymarket Affair, younger activists entered the movement. Two of them—Alexander Berkman, who came in February 1888, and Emma Goldman, who arrived in August 1889—became disciples of Most at the same time he was rethinking his views. Whereas Most and the older comrades had been shocked—even chastised—by Haymarket, Goldman and Berkman seemed emboldened. When Berkman shot but failed to kill industrialist Henry Clay Frick to protest his handling of the July 1892 Homestead steel strike, Most condemned the assassination attempt, arguing that such actions would not work in America: "In a country where we are so weakly represented and so little understood ..., we cannot afford the luxury of assassinations.... In countries like America, where we still need solid ground to stand on, we must limit ourselves to literary and verbal agitation."[46] Goldman, a close friend of Berkman who had helped him procure a gun, was furious. When Most mounted the podium at a December 1892 meeting of Jewish anarchists at 98 Forsyth Street, Goldman horsewhipped him in front of the audience.[47]

Deeper rifts in the German anarchist movement explain the Most-Goldman confrontation. In 1890, Goldman and Berkman had joined the Autonomists, a new group of Austrian and German anarchists founded in London in 1885 by Josef Peukert. Autonomists espoused communist-anarchism, a new philosophy developed primarily by Peter Kropotkin and critical of Bakuninism. Communist-anarchists believed that the collective fruits of labor should be distributed according to need and that all instances of authority and inequality must be eliminated. Most and other Bakuninists believed that distribution had to proceed according to deed. Most's anarchism was in fact considerably more eclectic, incorporating not only Bakunin but also elements of Marx and of Auguste Blanqui, a French revolutionary who advocated secret revolutionary organizations. As late as 1887, Kropotkin commented that *Freiheit's* brand of anarchism was full of Blanquism.[48] And until the 1890s, Most continued to ridicule what he saw as Kropotkin's pie-in-the-sky vision of human goodness and spontaneity.

Beyond these academic differences, Most had come to despise the Autonomists and especially Peukert, who remained Most's archenemy for life. Autonomists in London and New York challenged Most's position as the leading opinion maker of German anarchism through what they saw as his authoritarian control of *Freiheit*. Most viewed these challenges as attempts to undermine his efforts to build a united anarchist front in the United States. Personal enmity and the emotions that come with operating in a movement rife with police spies exacerbated the situation. When Belgian police arrested Most's friend and key smuggler, Johann Neve, in 1887, the editor bluntly accused Peukert of betraying Neve. This rivalry between Mostians and Autonomists suffused much of the anarchist atmosphere on both sides of the Atlantic during the 1880s and 1890s.[49]

Most had always felt ambivalent about his adopted country and kept open the possibility of returning to Europe. Early in 1890, he learned that the Reichstag had refused to renew Germany's antisocialist law, which then lapsed in October. According to the *New York Times*, Most at that point contemplated relocating his newspaper to London, but he could not return to Germany because of the indictments against him there.[50] In any event, Most remained in the United States, where Max Baginski, a young anarchist sympathetic to Most, sensed a feeling of alienation: "In the United States Most was out of his element, without the inspiration and impetus that come from the life and struggle of the masses. Most, of course, had considerable German support in the country, but it is only the native element in a country that can bring about fundamental change. It must have been the helplessness of his position in America and the absence of a native anarchist movement that caused Most to turn against 'propaganda by deed' and, with it, against" Berkman.[51] This "helplessness" was perhaps not so uncommon among immigrant anarchists, who resided in urban America yet found native-born Americans unreceptive to the anarchist ideology. An 1887 *New York Times* editorial noted that "to all intents and purposes [Most's supporters] are living in Europe yet, and are as far from being assimilated to the American people as Anglo-Indians are from having become Hindus." The writers consequently recommended restrictions on the granting of U.S. citizenship.[52]

One of the more constructive consequences of the rivalries within the German anarchist movement in New York was the proliferation of periodicals. Since anarchists rejected a party structure, they had no need for an official party organ. However, sustaining any anarchist periodical was expensive, and Most wondered about draining resources or diluting the message. He was well aware of the power and responsibility of an editor, and he had of course not forgotten what could happen when a liberal state such as Britain went after an obscure paper like *Freiheit*. Most believed that the only way to ensure that his paper remained afloat was for him to retain absolute control over his "beloved daughter."[53]

Debate over the diversity of the German-language anarchist press had begun as early as 1884, when members of the Social-Revolutionary Club openly questioned the need for an editor who could reject contributions at will. Most simply dismissed the idea.[54] That same year, comrades in Philadelphia launched *Die Zukunft* (The Future), and the following year, New Haven, Connecticut, radicals purchased the *New England Anzeiger* (New England Advertiser) and transformed it into an anarchist organ. Most apparently sought to co-opt this effort by taking over the paper and publishing it in New York.[55] A similar incident occurred across the Hudson River where anarchists set up the *New Jersey Arbeiterzeitung* (New Jersey Workers' Journal), and Most responded by denouncing the project.[56] In 1886, Wilhelm Hasselmann launched the *Amerikanische Arbeiter-Zeitung* (American Workers' Journal) with the explicit goal of competing with *Freiheit*. While the *Amerikanische Arbeiter-Zeitung* lasted just six months, the paper focused on American conditions, and in contrast to

Most's paper did not employ an editor or manager. In an unmistakable jab at Most, the *Amerikanische Arbeiter-Zeitung* stated that "every worker can, without censorship and with responsibility for the content, publish relevant articles, space permitting, in the columns of this paper."[57]

Freiheit's most successful challengers came from the Autonomists, starting with Peukert's London-based *Die Autonomie* in 1886. The paper found ready subscribers in New York because the Autonomists had been building their own groups, meeting places, and festivals such as the Vintage Harvest Festival (Weinlesefest) and the Austrian Peasants' Ball (Österreichischen Bauern Ball). The most important Autonomist circle was the Radical Workers' Association (Radikale Arbeiterbund), which frequently met at Zum groben Michel. One of the first communist-anarchist newspapers published in the United States was *Der Anarchist*, which first appeared in 1886 in Chicago but relocated to New York in 1891 under the editorship of Karl Mazur, who urged his readers to "prevent any personal authority or tutelage within our own ranks"—another reference to Most.[58]

Sometime in the summer or fall of 1888, Johann Most met Helene Minkin, a Russian Jewish immigrant twenty-six years his junior, but the two did not become close friends until 1892. The following year, possibly in the summer, Most and Minkin, who had become an anarchist, sealed their bond by common-law marriage.[59] This event not only opened a new chapter in their lives but exposed a gendered and even sexist dimension within the German anarchist movement. When Most and Minkin moved in together, the German anarchists loyal to Most expressed their disapproval. "These comrades," remembered Minkin, "considered it a terrible misfortune for the movement that Most had started a family," even though, as she pointed out, they had families. According to Minkin, the other anarchists objected to "a young wife, a child, and perhaps more children! That's not for Most. . . . That's not for a revolutionary."[60] From this viewpoint, family life softened (male) movement leaders and harmed the cause.

Implicit in this attitude was the assumption that women could not be trusted or could play only supporting roles in the movement. It is likely that most wives of German anarchists were indeed confined—happily or not—to a domestic role, even though many attended mass meetings and recreational activities. Goldman, who arrived in New York in August 1889 after a brief and unhappy marriage, was especially attuned to the politics of gender and sexuality. She quickly noticed the male-centered nature of the German movement and the outdated and hypocritical nature of members' views on gender and "expressed contempt for the reactionary attitude of our German comrades on these matters."[61] In a 1929 letter to Berkman, she charged that the Germans "remain stationary on all points except economics. Especially as regards women, they are really antediluvian."⁶²

Goldman's brief but intimate relationship with her mentor Most confirmed for her the underlying conservatism of many male activists.⁶³ Most sought domestic comfort and security and assumed that she would provide it. Goldman would not, and she told him as much. Instead, she chose the path of a liberated woman revolutionary and looked down on other women, like her roommate, Minkin, who accepted some domestic role. In Goldman's view, "a home, children, the care and attention ordinary women can give, who have no other interest in life but the man they love and the children they bear him—that was what he needed and felt he had found in Helen."⁶⁴

The topic of women and feminism remained awkward for Most and probably for most older activists. Most could not see that gender equality was intrinsically linked to economic freedom. Sexual politics and the issue of free love, which became central for many anarchists, including younger Germans, appeared to Most to constitute frivolous distractions. In December 1899, Sarah Comstock, a young Stanford-educated reporter for the *San Francisco Call*, tracked down Most on a lecture tour in California. When asked for his views on women, he responded, "I had troubles, I do not like to get into the woman question." Then he continued with a typical analysis that put off the question of feminism: "The woman of the future will have a different life from the woman of the present, and so she will be a different creature. She will no longer be a mere housewife, but she will enter all fields which are open to man, and she will be his companion in art and science and labor. She will not need to marry that she may be supported. There will in the happy future be no unfortunate marriages."⁶⁵

Minkin and Most remained together until Most's death and had two children, John Jr., born on May 19, 1894, and Lucifer, born on July 22, 1895. Their relationship had moments of discord and was strained by their constant financial worries, but according to Minkin's account, they shared a mutual respect as well as a commitment to the anarchist cause. Minkin, who was not a public speaker, became instrumental in the daily operation of *Freiheit*. During the late 1890s, when the paper nearly died and Most was close to giving up, Minkin kept it afloat when many (mostly male) comrades failed to step up.⁶⁶ "Of the few who stood faithfully beside [Most] during these tough months," wrote biographer Rudolf Rocker, "his brave life partner Helene Most deserves special mention because time and again she helped him keep up his work, and took care of almost the entire dispatching of the paper."⁶⁷

Minkin admired Most's principled—others might say, obstinate—position as a leading figure in the movement. Life in urban America for all committed anarchists always involved balancing a revolutionary anticapitalist movement and the practical realities of a modern, commercial metropolis. For example, shortly after Lucifer Most's birth, Joseph Pulitzer's *New York World*, one of the nation's largest dailies, offered Most a weekly Sunday column on whatever topic he chose with a fee of fifty dollars per week. When he and Minkin discussed the idea, "we both laughed." According to Minkin, "I knew very well that he would never do it, and he knew that I would never want him to.... We both had tears in our eyes, and laughed off the *World*'s offer. It was better this way: our souls remained pure."[68]

Most's troubles with the law were another way ordinary New Yorkers learned, albeit in a biased way, about the anarchists in their midst. The *New York World* and other dailies were all too eager to get a scoop on anarchist antics and courtroom drama. Most stood trial in New York on three occasions, and in all three instances, he was convicted and imprisoned on Blackwell's Island (now Roosevelt Island) in the East River. The New York Police Department and its detective bureau employed several bilingual German American lawmen who attended meetings where Most was scheduled to speak.[69]

Most's first two trials, in May 1886 and November 1887, resulted from speeches he delivered in small anarchist venues that led to his arrest on charges of unlawful assembly and inciting to riot. The surveillance and arrests in both cases were conducted by officers under the command of Irish-born precinct captain John McCullough and chief inspector (and later superintendent) Thomas F. Byrnes.[70] Both trials took place in New York's Court of General Sessions. Represented by William Howe and Abraham Hummel, a high-profile New York law firm with a well-earned reputation for defending all manner of crooks and celebrities, Most appealed his 1887 conviction to the Court of Appeals in Albany, which found against him.[71]

Most's third U.S. arrest occurred in 1901 and was reminiscent of the 1881 *Freiheit* libel case. Most had reprinted an 1849 article in which German revolutionary Karl Heinzen praised tyrannicide. Unfortunately for Most, the article appeared on September 6, 1901, the same day that President William McKinley was shot by a self-styled anarchist. Most was arrested several days later, charged with inciting to riot, convicted, and sentenced to one year on Blackwell's Island even though he proved that the article and the shooting were unrelated. Again, the appeal failed. Now aged fifty-five and frail, Most was visibly shaken by the sentence, and as he was led away, Minkin quietly said good-bye before attempting to explain events to her sons.[72] These events received copious attention in the mainstream press, obsessed with filling their pages with lurid details, including excerpts of Most's incriminating speeches and articles. Minkin continued to bear responsibility not only for her children but also for publishing *Freiheit*.

By this time, the German anarchist movement had lost much of its energy. On January 1, 1904, the Germans and others gathered at the Bronx Casino to celebrate *Freiheit*'s twenty-fifth anniversary, a significant accomplishment for a proud but worn-down Most. The occasion represented a last hurrah for the German movement. Many of the new immigrants from Italy and Eastern Europe became radicals after arriving in the United States and started building their own anarchist, socialist, and syndicalist movements. Most and other leading German anarchists were not involved in the founding of the Industrial Workers of the World in Chicago in 1905. Most continued to travel on lecture tours, and he died in Cincinnati on March 17, 1906. Four days earlier, in what would be his last letter to his wife, Most wrote, "I hope that your health is better than mine. In the next issue of the paper (*Freiheit*), you'll be able to see how my trip went. Give my best to the dear boys. Yours, Hans."[73]

By 1900, the anarchist movement in New York, while still heavily immigrant and working-class, was no longer dominated by Germans. When five thousand men and women had gathered to welcome Most in 1882, no one minded that the evening proceeded in German with perhaps a few lines in French and English. But when the anarchists of New York gathered on April 1, 1906, to commemorate Most's death, "many nationalities" were represented, and speeches were given in five languages. Putting aside any grudges, Emma Goldman spoke in English, Pedro Esteve spoke in Italian, and Saul Yanovsky spoke in Yiddish.[74]

Notes

Some of the material in this chapter previously appeared in Tom Goyens, *Beer and Revolution: The German Anarchist Movement in New York City, 1880–1914* (Urbana: University of Illinois Press, 2007).

1. "The Bark Ella's Signals: Wrong Lights Cause a Crash at Sea and Help to Delay the Steamer Wisconsin," *New York Sun*, December 19, 1882; "A Bearer of the Red Flag: Cooper Union Overflowing at the Reception of Herr Most," *New York Sun*, December 19, 1882; "Arrival of Herr Most," *New York Times*, December 19, 1882; "Notizen," *Der deutsche Correspondent* (Baltimore), December 19, 1882. The vessel was supposed to arrive on December 14, but the accident caused the landing to be postponed until Sunday, December 17. After further delays at the quarantine station, it finally docked the following morning.

2. Paul Avrich, *The Haymarket Tragedy* (Princeton: Princeton University Press, 1984), 50; *Freiheit*, December 22, 1900; *New York Times*, January 14, 1874.

3. For a detailed narrative of German radicals in New York, see Tom Goyens, *Beer and Revolution: The German Anarchist Movement in New York City, 1880–1914* (Urbana: University of Illinois Press, 2007).

4. Wilhelm Liebknecht, a key figure of German social democracy, gave a speech in the Reichstag on March 17, 1879, reminding his colleagues that the Socialists were a reform party, not a revolutionary one, and that all laws must be obeyed, including the antisocialist law. Many rank-and-file activists were disillusioned by the law and drifted to the social-revolutionary camp. See Heiner Becker, "Johann Most," in *Internationale wissenschaftliche Korrespondenz zur Geschichte der deutschen Arbeiterbewegung* 41:1–2 (2005): 38–41.

5. "Durch Terrorismus zur Freiheit," *Freiheit (London)*, December 11, 1880. See also Andrew Carlson, *Anarchism in Germany*, vol. 1, *The Early Movement* (Metuchen, N.J.: Scarecrow, 1972), 277 n. 15.

6. Becker, "Johann Most," in *Internationale wissenschaftliche Korrespondenz*, 47 n. 136. See also "The Government and the 'Freiheit,'" *Times of London*, April 2, 1881. This episode left an indelible mark on Most. He felt responsible for the safekeeping of sensitive information, especially subscription lists, and was enraged by the conduct of the British authorities. Two years later, Most's opponents viciously attacked him for allegedly handing over sensitive documents to Austrian authorities in return for payment. See Becker, "Johann Most," in *Internationale wissenschaftliche Korrespondenz*, 49–50. German and French social revolutionaries in New York made (but did not publish) similar speeches and declarations without being arrested. See "In New York City: Consular Flags at Half Mast—Revolutionists Calling a Meeting," *New York Sun*, March 15, 1881; "The Assassination Defended," *New York Sun*, March 16, 1881. See also "The Liberty of the Press: Prosecution of Johann Most," *New York Tribune*, June 6, 1881.

7. The *Times of London* (April 1, 1881) regretted the decision to prosecute, wishing the government had treated "Mr. Most and his inflammatory articles with silent contempt." *The Nation* (April 21, 1881, 271) was sure the prosecution would fail: "There is hardly any doubt that the prosecution will be a failure. The jury will either acquit the prisoner or disagree, and nothing will come of the affair but great notoriety for Most."

8. August Sartorius von Waltershausen, *Der moderne Socialismus in den Vereinigten Staaten von Amerika* (Berlin: Bahr, 1890), 171; Dirk Hoerder, ed., *Plutokraten und Sozialisten: Berichte deutscher Diplomaten und Agenten über die amerikanische Arbeiterbewegung 1878–1917* (Munich: Saur, 1981), 107.

9. French radical groups in New York may have been the first revolutionary anarchists in the United States. Such organizations included the Society of the Refugees of the Commune, the Société Communiste Révolutionnaire, and the Cercle Socialiste. One reporter counted two thousand French communists at an 1881 gathering in New York. As late as 1896, a *New-York Tribune* reporter noted the remarkable brotherhood between French and German radicals a decade after the Franco-Prussian War: "Their French fellow-Anarchists fraternize with them as though there had never been a Sedan or a confiscated Alsace." See *New-York Tribune*, March 21, 1881; "Under the Red Flag: The New-York Anarchist and His Ways," *New-York Tribune*, November 1, 1896. See also *New York Sun*, March 21, 1880.

10. For more on the London congress, see Goyens, *Beer and Revolution*, 75–80.

11. Diplomat's report, April 22, 1881, quoted in Hoerder, *Plutokraten und Sozialisten*, 94.

12. *Leader Review*, October 1881, quoted in Ronald Creagh, *L'anarchisme aux États-Unis*, 2 vols. (New York: Lang, 1983), 1:629.

13. Ibid., 638.

14. Johann Most to Victor Dave, January 13, 1885, Most und Neve, Briefe deutscher Anarchisten, 1884–1887, Aus Victor Dave's Nachlass, Herausgegeben von Max Nettlau, October 12, 1925, Internationaal Instituut voor Sociale Geschiedenis, Amsterdam.

15. Goyens, *Beer and Revolution*, 102–09. The German text of the proclamation can be found in Rudolf Rocker, *Johann Most: Das Leben eines Rebellen* (Berlin: "Der Syndikalist," 1924), 146–49. For the English version, see Richard T. Ely, *The Labor Movement in America* (New York: Macmillan, 1905), 358–63; Albert Fried, ed., *Socialism in America from the Shakers to the Third International: A Documentary History* (New York: Anchor, 1970), 208–12.

16. Chaim Weinberg, *Forty Years in the Struggle: The Memoir of a Jewish Anarchist*, ed. Robert Helms, trans. Naomi Cohen (Duluth, Minn.: Litwin, 2008), 7.

17. Emma Goldman, *Living My Life* (New York: Knopf, 1931), 1:6.

18. *Lucifer, the Light-Bearer* (Chicago), December 12, 1901, quoted in Goyens, *Beer and Revolution*, 100.

19. An 1885 police raid of a San Francisco apartment, for example, found dynamite, wires, fuses, and blasting caps, along with Most's manual. See Timothy Messer-Kruse. *The Haymarket Conspiracy: Transatlantic Anarchist Networks* (Urbana: University of Illinois Press, 2012), 115.

20. [Johann Most,] "Zur Propaganda der That," *Freiheit* (New York), February 16, 1884.

21. Becker, "Johann Most," in *Internationale wissenschaftliche Korrespondenz*, 52; Eduard Müller, *Bericht über die Untersuchung betreffend die anarchistischen Umtriebe in der Schweiz an den hohen Bundesrath der Schweiz: Eidgenossenschaft* (Bern: Wyss, 1885), 58, 69; J. Langhard, *Die anarchistische Bewegung in der Schweiz von ihren Anfängen bis zur Gegenwart und die internationalen Führer* (Bern: Stämpfli, 1909), 280 n. 1.

22. Johann Most to Victor Dave, July 8, September 19, 1884, Most und Neve, Briefe deutscher Anarchisten.

23. Ibid., October 2, 1884.

24. Johann Most, *Revolutionäre Kriegswissenschaft: Ein Handbüchlein zur Anleitung betreffend Gebrauches und Herstellung von Nitroglycerin, Dynamit, Schiessbaumwolle, Knallquecksilber, Bomben, Brandsätzen, Giften u.s.w., u.s.w.* (New York: Internat. Zeitungs-Verein, 1885), 1.

25. [Most,] "Zur Propaganda der That." Most elsewhere condemned the lynching of blacks as evidence of the violent nature of ordinary Americans. See Johann Most, "Attentats-Reflexionen," *Freiheit* (New York), August 27, 1892.

26. "The Beast of Communism," *Liberty* (Boston), March 27, 1886; "A Chapter on Anarchism: Is Most's Arson Doctrine in Practice Here?" *New York Sun*, May 3, 1886; "The Facts Coming to Light," *Liberty* (Boston), May 22, 1886. *Liberty*, an individualist anarchist paper, broke the story, specifically linking named individuals to Most's circle. Subsequent stories in the *Sun* and *Liberty* provided further details. The children's death occurred in the Henry Kohout case (1885–86). See "Under Arrest for Arson," *New York*

Tribune, November 24, 1885; "Fires in the Kohuts' Room," *New York Tribune*, January 23, 1886; "Current Events," *Brooklyn Eagle*, February 4, 1886. On Schwab's break with Most, see Goyens, *Beer and Revolution*, 120.

27. August Sartorius von Waltershausen quoted in Goyens, *Beer and Revolution*, 108.

28. *Freiheit* (New York), June 12, 1886, quoted in ibid., 147.

29. Ibid., 148. For detailed lists and tables of anarchist groups, see Tom Goyens, "Gemeinschaft and Revolution: The German Anarchist Movement in New York City, 1880–1914" (Ph.D. diss., University of Leuven, Belgium, 2003).

30. Most speakers were men, but Johanna Greie, Martha Krause, and Helene Wilmann also lectured.

31. *Freiheit* (New York), May 29, 1897.

32. John Gilmer Speed, "Anarchists in New York," *Harper's Weekly*, August 20, 1892, 798–99.

33. James Gibbons Huneker, *New Cosmopolis: A Book of Images* (New York: Scribner's, 1915), 5.

34. "Under the Red Flag: The New-York Anarchist and His Ways," *New-York Tribune*, November 1, 1896.

35. Goyens, *Beer and Revolution*, 169.

36. *Freiheit* (New York), June 18, 1887. The original text for "relaxation of the outdoors" reads "Erholung im Freien," which carries the double meaning of "outdoors" and "in the wild."

37. Alan Trachtenberg, *The Incorporation of America: Culture and Society in the Gilded Age* (New York: Hill and Wang, 1982), 126.

38. See "They Mourn Their Dead," *New York Times*, November 11, 1888: "Over 3,500 men and women were crowded into the hall that is calculated to seat only half as many."

39. Hoerder, *Plutokraten und Sozialisten*, 150.

40. Johann Most, *Die Anarchie* (New York: Müller, 1888), 13.

41. Most, *Revolutionäre Kriegswissenschaft*, 50; translation by author.

42. Becker, "Johann Most," in *Internationale wissenschaftliche Korrespondenz*, 56.

43. [Johann Most,] "Die Stellung der Anarchisten gegenüber anderen Arbeiterparteien," *Freiheit* (New York), November 30, 1889; translation by author.

44. Johann Most, *Der kommunistische Anarchismus* (1889; Frankfurt a.M.: Edition AV, 2000), 2.

45. *Freiheit* (New York), April 23, 1892, translation quoted in Becker, "Johann Most," in *Haymarket Scrapbook*, ed. David Roediger and Franklin Rosemont (Chicago: Kerr, 1986), 139.

46. Johann Most, "Attentats-Reflexionen," *Freiheit*, August 27, 1892; translation by author.

47. Emma Goldman, "Warum ich Most durchpeitschte," *Der Anarchist* (New York), December 31, 1892; Helene Minkin, *Storm in My Heart: Memories from the Widow of Johann Most*, ed. Tom Goyens, trans. Alisa Braun (Oakland, Calif.: AK, 2015), 72; *Der deutsche Correspondent* (Baltimore), December 21, 1892.

48. Max Nettlau, *Anarchisten und Sozialrevolutionäre: Die historische Entwicklung des Anarchismus in den Jahren 1880–1886* (Berlin: Asy, 1931), 384.

49. Peukert was eventually cleared of all charges, but Most never accepted the findings. Neve died in 1896 in the "lunatic" section of a German prison.

50. "Most Wants to Leave America," *New York Times*, October 16, 1890.

51. Emma Goldman quoted in Goyens, *Beer and Revolution*, 131.

52. "'American' Anarchists," *New York Times*, November 30, 1887.

53. Minkin, *Storm in My Heart*, 113.

54. Johann Most to Victor Dave, October 7, November 8, 1884, Most und Neve, Briefe deutscher Anarchisten.

55. This charge was made by individualist anarchists—no friends of Most—in *Liberty* (Boston), January 3, April 25, 1885.

56. *Freiheit* (New York), April 12, 26, 1884, February 5, 1887.

57. *Amerikanische Arbeiter-Zeitung* (New York), January 2, 1886; translation by author.

58. *Der Anarchist* (New York), August 8, 1891; translation by author. Two other New York periodicals launched by Autonomist anarchist Claus Timmermann, a close friend of Goldman, include *Die Brandfackel* (The Torch, 1894–95) and *Sturmvogel* (Storm Petrel, 1897–99).

59. Most had been married from 1873 to 1880 to Clara Hänsch, the daughter of a constable. The union was apparently unhappy, and they had two children, both of whom died before their first birthdays. Years later, Most attributed this failure to his rise in the socialist movement and his hectic schedule that left no time for family. See Becker, "Johann Most," in *Internationale wissenschaftliche Korrespondenz*, 27 n. 89; Johann Most, *Memoiren: Erlebtes, Erforschtes, und Erdachtes* (1903; Hannover: Kobaia, 1978), 3:27.

60. Minkin, *Storm in My Heart*, 91, 90.

61. Goldman, *Living My Life*, 1:151.

62. Emma Goldman to Alexander Berkman, February 20, 1929, in *Emma Goldman and Alexander Berkman, Nowhere at Home: Letters from Exile of Emma Goldman and Alexander Berkman*, ed. Richard Drinnon and Anna Maria Drinnon (New York: Schocken, 1975), 145.

63. Most's attitude toward women and women's rights resulted partly from his childhood traumas, which he later described to Goldman as the "deepest tragedy of my life." She was convinced that he possessed "what would now be called an inferiority complex" (Emma Goldman, "Johann Most," *American Mercury*, June 1926, 159, 160).

64. Goldman, *Living My Life*, 1:77. Minkin published her memoirs to rebut Goldman's *Living My Life*.

65. Sarah Comstock, "Why Herr Most Likes California," *San Francisco Call*, December 24, 1899.

66. Helene Minkin, "An die Leser der 'Freiheit,'" *Freiheit* (New York), April 21, 1906.

67. Rudolf Rocker, *Johann Most: Das Leben eines Rebellen* (1924; Glashütten im Taunus: Auvermann, 1973), 387.

68. Minkin, *Storm in My Heart*, 96.

69. "Two Socialists Arrested: Police Kept Quiet at the Meeting and Took Notes for Future Use," *New York Times*, May 1, 1886; "What Most Really Said," *New York Times*, November 24, 1887.

70. See J. North Conway, *Big Policeman: The Rise and Fall of Thomas Byrnes, America's First, Most Ruthless, and Greatest Detective* (Guilford, Conn.: Lyons, 2010).

71. Cait Murphy, *Scoundrels at Law: The Trials of Howe and Hummel, Lawyers to the Gangsters, Cops, Starlets, and Rakes Who Made the Gilded Age* (New York: Smithsonian, 2010), chapter 7; "The People v. John Most," *The New York State Reporter: Containing All the Current Decisions of the Courts of Record of New York State* (1891): 829–34.

72. Minkin, *Storm in My Heart*, 113.

73. Ibid., 131.

74. *Freiheit* (New York), March 24, 1906; *New York Sun*, April 2, 1906.

Saul Yanovsky and Yiddish Anarchism on the Lower East Side

KENYON ZIMMER

Between 1880 and 1924, two million Eastern European Jews migrated to the United States, and more than half of them made their homes in New York City. They crowded into the deplorable tenement houses of Manhattan's Lower East Side, where most found employment in the hyperexploitative sweatshops of the city's booming garment industry. These factors proved ideal breeding grounds for radicalism. But Jewish immigrants did not bring anarchism with them from Europe. In fact, no anarchist organizations existed within the Russian Empire until after the turn of the twentieth century. As Russian Jewish immigrant Leon Moisseiff recalled in 1925, "Anarchism as a popular movement was alien to us." Moisseiff read the works of Mikhail Bakunin and other anarchists only after coming to America in 1891, "and their principles were to me a new phenomenon."[1]

Although Alexander Berkman and Emma Goldman are better remembered today, no anarchist of their era had as large an impact as Saul Yanovsky, who was instrumental in founding Yiddish-speaking anarchist movements on both sides of the Atlantic and edited New York's weekly *Fraye Arbeter Shtime* (Free Voice of Labor) for twenty years. Yanovsky and the Yiddish anarchist movement for which he spoke were pioneers of New York's Jewish labor movement and instrumental in fostering the working-class Yiddish culture of the Lower East Side. Anarchist historian Herman Frank has noted that Yanovsky "occupied a dominant position not only in the Yiddish anarchist press, but in all of Yiddish journalism in America. For a few continuous decades he was the spiritual trailblazer for innumerable Jewish journalists, writers, actors, trade union organizers and community leaders in Jewish society, and hence in the social life of millions of immigrant Jews in their new home."[2]

Saul Joseph Yanovsky was born in Pinsk in 1864, the son of a cantor and grandson of a rabbi, and in 1880 he began attending a gymnasium (secondary school) in Bialystok, the epicenter of Russia's growing Jewish labor movement. He studied Russian literature and wrote a few articles for a Russian-language radical paper before migrating to New York in 1885.[3] Yanovsky was a member of the *inteligentn*, a small minority of secular Jewish intellectuals who had attended secondary schools and universities in Russia during the relaxation of anti-Semitic restrictions on Jewish education and residency in the decades preceding the 1881 assassination of Czar Alexander II.[4] Like other transplanted *inteligentn*, Yanovsky initially found employment alongside other Jewish immigrants as a dishwasher, shirtmaker, cloakmaker, capmaker, and sheet-metal worker. Like thousands of fellow Jews, he quickly discovered that, as Yiddish anarchist poet David Edelstadt put it, "in the free republic / something is only free on paper, / and there the factories are full of slaves, and every boss—a vampire."[5]

Sweatshops and tenements were crucibles in which declassed intellectuals and needleworkers came together to forge Jewish radicalism. Romanian Jewish immigrant Marcus Ravage recalled his surprise when he "suddenly realized that everybody I knew was either a socialist or an anarchist."[6] These ideologies reached the Lower East Side's Jewish community through two routes: the neighborhood's preexisting German radical movement, and London's burgeoning Jewish labor movement.

In the 1880s and 1890s, the Lower East Side was home to dynamic German socialist and anarchist communities, as Tom Goyens describes in this volume. The close phonetic similarity between German and Yiddish allowed most Jewish immigrants to understand at least some spoken German, and no German immigrant could rival the oratorical fire of Johann Most, who entranced German and Jewish listeners alike. Many radical Jewish immigrants learned German before English so that they could read Most's pamphlets and his newspaper, *Freiheit*, for which Berkman worked as a compositor.[7] Meanwhile, London's East End, where Jewish immigrants were similarly crammed into dilapidated housing and sweatshop labor, gave rise to the world's first radical Yiddish newspapers. In 1884, socialist poet Morris Winchevsky founded *Der Poylisher Yidl* (The Little Polish Jew), which he replaced the following year with *Der Arbayter Fraynd* (The Worker's Friend), a paper "open to all radicals," including a growing number influenced by anarchism.[8] These papers and other radical Yiddish literature published in London circulated in New York, and some Jewish migrants who became anarchists in England continued on to the United States.

These two sources drew a small nucleus of Jewish workers and intellectuals into the anarchist orbit. However, the Haymarket Affair precipitated the formation of New York's first Jewish anarchist group. Eight of Chicago's leading anarchists were tried and convicted, on highly suspect evidence, of conspiring with the unknown assailant who hurled a bomb at police during an anarchist-organized rally off of that city's Haymarket Square on May 4, 1886.[9] Seven were sentenced to death (though two had their sentences commuted to life in prison), and on October 9, 1886, following the announcement of the date of execution, a group of five workers on the Lower East Side founded the Pioneers of Liberty, the first Jewish anarchist group in America and the first exclusively anarchist group of Jews in the world. The Pioneers affiliated with the anarchist International Working People's Association and immediately organized a fundraising ball and concert that collected one hundred dollars for the Haymarket defense fund.[10] The injustice of the Haymarket verdict radicalized hundreds of Jewish immigrants, including Yanovsky, Edelstadt, medical students Michael A. Cohn and Hillel Solotaroff, and seventeen-year-old Emma Goldman. Before this travesty, in Yanovsky's opinion, "To even think of a Jewish labor movement was crazy."[11]

The Pioneers of Liberty soon boasted an impressive array of speakers and writers, including Yanovsky, Cohn, Solotaroff, Berkman, Moyshe Katts (Berkman's former classmate in Vilnius), and famed "sweatshop poets" Edelstadt and Joseph Bovshover. One of the group's only female members was Anna Netter, described by Goldman as an "ardent worker" who "made a name for herself by her untiring activity in the anarchist and labour ranks." However, Netter soon contracted cancer and lived her remaining years as an invalid, cared for by her husband, Michael Cohn, until her death in 1920.[12] Another woman close to the Pioneers was Katherina Yevzerov, who had received an extensive religious and secular education in Russia before earning a medical degree from New York University in 1893. Yevzerov soon married fellow anarchist physician Jacob A. Maryson and distinguished herself as a writer on "the woman question" for the Yiddish radical press.[13]

Members of this group were initially steeped in notions of imminent revolution and "propaganda by the deed." Cohn later described the Pioneers of Liberty as "impractical, naive, lyrical dreamers, convinced that presently the social revolution will come and at last bring a new, a free world." The group was originally organized like a revolutionary cell, with a secret "inner membership" of a few dozen individuals who met as an "underground" body. Yanovsky

35

described the first meeting he attended in the back room of a saloon as having "the appearance of a true conspiracy."[14]

The Pioneers' headquarters was located at 56 Orchard Street, a tenement building in the bustling heart of the Jewish ghetto that was the home of Netter and her father, A. Jacob Netter, a former Talmudic scholar turned grocer and "ultraradical socialist." Their apartment was an "oasis for the radical element" of the Lower East Side where socialists, anarchists, and atheists read and debated the works of Marx, Bakunin, and Kropotkin.[15] However, the radical *inteligentn* literally had to learn how to speak to the city's Jewish working classes.

Unlike the majority of Jewish immigrants, most educated intellectuals arrived as Russian-speakers who viewed Yiddish as a jargon unfit for serious literature. Prior to Haymarket, most had either belonged to the vaguely socialist Russian Progressive Union, of which Yanovsky was a member, or participated individually in German anarchist circles. Few could speak Yiddish fluently, and the earliest meetings of the Pioneers of Liberty were conducted in Russian. Edelstadt, the father of modern Yiddish poetry, had to be tutored in the language by Katts, and Berkman "really learned Yiddish in America, through association with my many Yiddish friends and comrades."[16] Yanovsky's mother had spoken Yiddish, but Russian was his first language, and after joining the Pioneers, he discovered that his Yiddish "reeked strongly of German."[17] By 1889, however, Cohn was telling critics of Yiddish, "Our broad literature on socialism will serve as fair proof that we are able to express all we want in our Jewish tongue, or, as you prefer to call it, jargon."[18]

Once committed to the language, the Pioneers of Liberty organized an endless succession of Yiddish mass meetings, lectures, and educational groups.[19] They also began writing for and circulating the *Arbayter Fraynd* before beginning the world's first explicitly anarchist Yiddish-language periodical, their weekly *Varhayt* (Truth), on February 15, 1889. The group recruited Joseph Jaffa, a former rabbinical student who had become an anarchist and wrote for the *Arbayter Fraynd*, to come to New York from London to edit the publication. While awaiting Jaffa's arrival, Yanovsky, who proved to be "a conqueror of languages" and emerged as a leading Yiddish anarchist agitator, was elected the interim editor.[20] Although its founders intended *Varhayt* to communicate in "the people's speech," most of the articles published were written in a pretentious, Germanized form of Yiddish derisively known as *daytshmerish*. Much of the paper's content was also too theoretical for its audience. The exceptions were the poems by Edelstadt and Morris Rosenfeld that graced the front page of nearly every issue, which viscerally articulated the miseries of the Jewish ghetto and exhorted readers to revolt. *Varhayt* reached a circulation of around twenty-five hundred, but its finances were so poor that some of the Pioneers of Liberty used their rent money to keep it afloat and slept in the basement on Suffolk Street where the paper was produced. The enterprise folded after just four months.[21]

The Pioneers' next periodical, *Fraye Arbeter Shtime* (a name suggested by Yanovsky), was backed by thirty-two Jewish anarchists' and workers' groups from throughout the Northeast and debuted on July 4, 1890. But Yanovsky had left the county by the time the first issue appeared, having been invited to London to take over the editorship of the *Arbayter Fraynd*. He threw all of his energies into that paper, transforming it into "an outspoken anarcho-communist organ" and driving the recalcitrant social democrats from the Arbayter Fraynd Group.[22] During his sojourn in London, Yanovsky honed his skills as a publisher, translator, polemicist, and debater, developing his trademark caustic sense of humor and becoming, in Frank's words, a "gifted and cunningly sarcastic writer and editor." "Lightning-fast in his thinking," according to one comrade, Yanovsky "was a masterful coiner of epigrams, and his speeches were a startling blend of pathos and satire. He was short and slight, always unkempt, and in spite of his Vandyke beard, almost boyish in appearance."[23] London's cosmopolitan anarchist movement also brought Yanovsky into contact with internationally renowned figures such as Errico Malatesta, Max Nettlau, and Peter Kropotkin, with whom he maintained a regular correspondence after returning to the United States.

London was also a hotbed of syndicalist ideas, which contributed to a major shift in Yanovsky's thinking. He had arrived an ardent disciple of Most and proponent of propaganda by the deed, but as early as 1890, Yanovsky also argued "a union could be the vanguard of the workers' army in its fight against the capitalist class." As he put it, the anarchists "are not entirely opposed to unions, they are, however, opposed to the unions as they are now."[24] Then, in 1893 Spanish anarchists bombed a crowded theater in Barcelona, killing around twenty people and provoking a fierce wave of repression. The brutality of the act as well as its counterproductive results caused Yanovsky to reverse his stance on individual acts of violence. "A revolution," he subsequently argued, "is a mass act" that could not be artificially induced through such deeds. This stance caused such controversy within the Arbayter Fraynd Group, however, that Yanovsky was forced to resign as editor of the paper.[25] When he returned to New York in 1895, he found a much more receptive audience for his new vision of "constructive" anarchism—or, in the more affirmative formulation that he preferred, libertarian socialism.

During Yanovsky's absence, the Yiddish anarchist movement had flourished and then withered. The *Fraye Arbeter Shtime* cycled through a number of editors before winding up under the direction of Edelstadt and Katts. With them at the helm, the paper enjoyed moderate success and reached a circulation of between three thousand and four thousand copies a week, prompting the Pioneers of Liberty to consider making it into a daily.[26] By all accounts, anarchism was the leading current within New York's Jewish labor movement in these years. In the early 1890s, anarchist lectures at 56 Orchard Street attracted hundreds of listeners, while larger events held at Cooper Union or Union Square drew thousands. Affiliated Yiddish anarchist groups formed in Baltimore, Boston, Chicago, Cincinnati, Milwaukee, New Haven, Paterson, Philadelphia, Pittsburgh, Providence, and St. Louis.

Anarchists' prominence within Jewish garment unions conflicted with the movement's Mostian notions of imminent, violent revolution. According to an early issue of the *Fraye Arbeter Shtime*, unions presented a field in which to "spread dissatisfaction, plant the seeds of freedom and equality, [and] to bring unconscious workers to their class consciousness" but not a sphere for practical action. To the contrary, many Yiddish radicals believed that more desperate conditions would more quickly spark revolt.[27] Yet both Yanovsky and Edelstadt were fired from multiple jobs after organizing for better conditions, and Berkman believed he had a "duty to stand up for the others in the [cigar] shop" where he worked.[28] In 1886, during New York's first Jewish cloakmakers' strike, young radicals from "a group of Russian students" aided the strikers

"A Jewish anarchist meeting in Military Hall on the Bowery, New York."
Harper's Weekly, August 20, 1892.

in organizing the first Jewish cloakmakers' union. Soon thereafter, anarchists organized a knee-pants workers' union and a Jewish musicians' union, and Anna Netter participated in several strikes conducted by the Knights of Labor.[29] Pioneers of Liberty members Katts and Roman Luis became prominent union organizers, pressuring their comrades to reassess their approach to the labor movement. Anarchists went on to play leading roles in the cloakmakers' strikes of 1890 and 1893.[30]

The Yiddish social democrats of the Socialist Labor Party, however, were eager to supplant the anarchists at the head of the budding Jewish labor movement. They formed rival unions and campaigned against anarchist influence. There followed several years of bitter infighting, boycotts of rival newspapers, mutual slanders and recriminations, and fistfights that drove garment union membership down to "between a few dozen and a few hundred." These events, combined with the economic downturn of 1893, resulted in the closure of the *Fraye Arbeter Shtime* the following year.[31] The anarchist movement also lost many of its leading figures, including Luis, who became a social democrat in 1892 and later a Democratic assistant district attorney in Chicago; Edelstadt, who succumbed to tuberculosis in 1892 at the age of twenty-six; and fellow poet Bovshover, who was institutionalized in 1899 with a severe mental illness.[32] Simultaneously, anarchists were consumed by a dispute over revolutionary tactics sparked by Berkman's attempted assassination of Pittsburgh steel magnate Henry Clay Frick in July 1892, with a majority subscribing to Johann Most's surprising stance that such tactics were impractical in America.[33]

When Yanovsky returned in 1895, the anarchist movement was marginalized, shrinking, and divided against itself. Its only sign of life was *Di Fraye Gezelshaft* (The Free Society), a thick, intellectual journal edited by Moisseiff that reached a limited readership. Yanovsky immediately campaigned to revive the *Fraye Arbeter Shtime* as a popular anarchist labor paper, but four years of patient work and partisan infighting—particularly against the supporters of the *Fraye Gezelshaft*—would pass before a national Jewish anarchist convention in the Brownsville area of Brooklyn voted in favor of Yanovsky's proposal.[34] The *Fraye Arbeter Shtime* was resurrected in October 1899 with Yanovsky as editor. Though a small man "with a feeble physique," Yanovsky labored tirelessly on the paper, which was described by his Yiddish biographer as his "first and final love."[35]

The reappearance of the *Fraye Arbeter Shtime* coincided with the explosive growth of the American Yiddish press and the revival of the Jewish labor movement. Already high literacy rates among Jewish immigrants climbed in the 1890s and 1900s, and by 1902, according to Hutchins Hapgood's study of the Lower East Side, radical Yiddish newspapers had "largely displaced the rabbi in the position of teacher of the people." These papers were read individually and in groups, passed from hand to hand, read aloud, and debated at meetings and in cafés.[36] The new *Fraye Arbeter Shtime* embraced a simpler style that one thankful reader praised as "a plain, flowing Yiddish," and its circulation doubled from four thousand to eight thousand within a year. By 1910, the paper was printing between fifteen thousand and twenty thousand copies a week, one-third the circulation of Abe Cahan's socialist *Forverts* (Forward), the most popular Yiddish daily in the country.[37] In 1900, surviving Jewish garment unions united under the umbrella of the International Ladies' Garment Workers' Union (ILGWU). Although anarchists played second fiddle to the more numerous social democrats in the organization, their role as organizers and rank-and-file militants should not be underestimated. In particular, young anarchist women made a major contribution to the shop floor activism that led to 1909's "Uprising of the Twenty Thousand," a general strike of female shirtwaist makers that swelled the ranks of the ILGWU. Between a third and half of the Yiddish anarchist movement's members were women, far more than any other segment of American anarchism, in part as a result of the more balanced sex ratio among Jewish immigrants. Men, however, monopolized most public positions.[38]

The revived *Fraye Arbeter Shtime* endorsed a three-pronged, evolutionary approach to social change based in day-to-day engagement with cooperatives, education, and labor unions. Cataclysmic social revolution was seen as an increasingly distant prospect; until then, North America's annual Yiddish anarchist convention resolved in 1910, "we recognize the necessity of taking part in all present political, economic and social problems of city and country, and working for their solution in the direction which is the nearest to our goal."[39] Yiddish anarchists experimented with numerous worker, consumer, agricultural, and residential cooperatives designed to free participants from capitalist exploitation. They also founded worker self-education circles and were major backers of the Francisco Ferrer Center, a multiethnic radical venture established on the Lower East Side in early 1911 and relocated to Jewish Harlem the following year. Named for martyred Catalan anarchist educator Francisco Ferrer i Guàrdia, the Ferrer Center offered evening classes and lectures for adults as well as a "Modern School" for children, designed to nurture individual personal development as well as anti-authoritarian values.[40] The *Fraye Arbeter Shtime* also espoused a moderate version of syndicalism that supported the general strike as a nonviolent means of toppling the existing order, albeit after a long period of labor organizing and consciousness-raising. Yanovsky admired the

Industrial Workers of the World, but because the Wobblies never established a foothold among the city's Jewish workers, he gave conditional support to the ILGWU while regularly criticizing its socialist leadership.

By contrast, the *Fraye Arbeter Shtime* firmly renounced propaganda by the deed. After President William McKinley was shot by novice anarchist Leon Czolgosz in 1901, Yanovsky disavowed the action on the grounds that "the benefits that such an attempt can bring to the propaganda for our ideas are very questionable, the damage however is certain and sure." Nevertheless, on the night of September 16, three days after Yanovsky's words saw print and a day after McKinley succumbed to his wounds, a mob of "Jewish school boys" ransacked the offices of the *Fraye Arbeter Shtime* at 185 Henry Street and chased down and beat its editor.[41] In his 1902 pamphlet, *Der olef beys fun anarkhizmus* (The ABCs of Anarchism), Yanovsky reiterated that "Anarchism is not a doctrine of assassination and the anarchists are not murderers." Rather, its foundational principle is "peace between men [*menshen*]."[42]

Although not all Yiddish anarchists adhered to Yanovsky's ideas, the *Fraye Arbeter Shtime* ushered in a dramatic expansion of the movement. At least ten new Jewish groups formed in New York between 1899 and 1914, several of them in the growing communities of Harlem and Brownsville.[43] In 1906 Yanovsky founded a daily anarchist paper, *Di Abend Tsaytung* (The Evening Newspaper), to compete with the *Forverts*, but the understaffed experiment lasted only two months. More successful was Yanovsky's revival of *Di Fraye Gezelshaft* as a literary supplement to the *Fraye Arbeter Shtime* in 1910–11 and the formation of an accompanying network of fifty "Fraye Gezelshaft Clubs" across North America.[44] In 1914, the *Fraye Arbeter Shtime* reached its peak circulation of 30,000 copies per issue, six times that of Most's *Freiheit* and ten times the regular circulation of Goldman's *Mother Earth*. Estimates put the number of readers of the *Fraye Arbeter Shtime* as high as 150,000.[45] When historian Max Nomad arrived in the United States in 1913, he discovered that "anarchism still had a mass following among the Jewish sweatshop workers of New York."[46]

Anarchism was also woven into the cultural and social fabric of New York's Jewish community. Yanovsky tenaciously adhered to his own editorial line but opened the pages of the *Fraye Arbeter Shtime* to a wide range of radical viewpoints. The newspaper therefore had an influence far beyond the anarchist movement. Historian Joseph Chaikin counts Yanovsky among the six most influential editors of the North American Yiddish press, and socialist poet Abraham Liesin described Yanovsky as "one of the most talented pioneers of Yiddish journalism in England and America."[47] If his "biting sarcasm and too-often venomous epithets did not lead to great friendship," they did delight tens

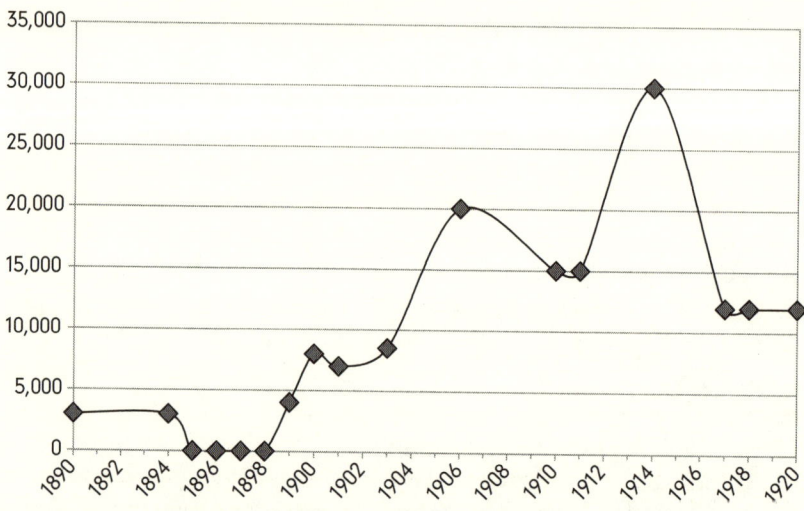

Circulation of the *Fraye Arbeter Shtime*, 1890–1920
Sources: Ronald Sanders, *The Downtown Jews: Portraits of an Immigrant Generation* (New York: Harper and Row, 1969), 112; Abba Gordin, *Sh. Yanovsky: Zayn lebn, kemfn un shafn, 1864–1939* (Los Angeles: Sh. Yanovsky Odenk Komitet, 1957), 249, 314; Hutchins Hapgood, *The Spirit of the Ghetto: Studies of the Jewish Quarter of New York*, new ed. (New York: Schocken, 1966), 192; Hertz Burgin, *Di geshikhte fun der idisher arbayter bevegung in Amerike, Rusland un England* (New York: Fareynigte Idishe Geverkshaftn, 1915), 651; *N. W. Ayer & Son's American Newspaper Annual and Directory* (1910–11, 1917–18, 1920).

of thousands of readers and supporters.[48] Moreover, under Yanovsky, the *Fraye Arbeter Shtime* became "a central tribune for Yiddish literature in America."[49] The cantankerous editor developed an unparalleled reputation for discovering new literary talent and was an early champion of the modernist Di Yunge and In Zikh schools of Yiddish poetry. Prominent poets whose first published work appeared in the anarchist paper include Mani Leib, A. Glanz-Leyeless, Jacob Glatstein, and Leon Feinberg. Yanovsky also championed the work of such female writers as Celia Dropkin, Fradel Stock, Yente Serdatzky, and Anna Margolin (who at one point worked as the paper's secretary).[50] In his classic study of the American immigrant press, sociologist Robert E. Park observed that the *Fraye Arbeter Shtime* was "the peculiar organ of the Yiddish intellectual. To be able to say 'I have written for Yanovsky' is a literary passport for a Yiddish writer."[51] Contributors, however, risked Yanovsky's barbed wit if he judged their work substandard; his rejections—published in a special section of the *Fraye Arbeter Shtime* to entertain and scandalize readers—ranged from the concise ("Not a spark of talent") to the merciless ("What did you scribble there? It seems to us, that not an editor, but only a doctor can help you, if it is already not too late for the latter").[52]

Yanovsky, Jacob Maryson, Katerina Yevzerov, Hillel Solotaroff, literary critic B. Rivkin, and other public anarchist intellectuals contributed to a wide range of other Yiddish publications, including the rival *Forverts*. Furthermore, as Romanian Jewish writer Konrad Bercovici noted, the Lower East Side anarchists of his youth "believed that people could be educated to a degree that would make every form of constraint superfluous. To achieve that, these anarchists published the best literature, translated the best books from a dozen languages, and organized amateur theatricals, concerts, and lectures. They were saints without knowing it." Through these activities, anarchists helped create a "Yiddish public culture" strongly colored by working-class and radical values.[53] Anarchists were ubiquitous figures on the Lower East Side's bustling café culture. In the 1880s and 1890s Sachs' Café on Rutgers Square was "the headquarters of the East Side radicals, socialists, and anarchists, as well as of the young Yiddish writers and poets." Later, Schmuckler's Café at 167 East Broadway Street became "the mecca of the radicals," including the staff of the *Fraye Arbeter Shtime*, who for a time worked out of offices on the second floor of the same building. Sholem's Café, on the corner of Canal and Division Streets, likewise became a hotbed of radical and literary discussion.[54]

The Yiddish stage was central to Lower East Side culture; Hapgood observed "all the ghetto classes—the sweatshop woman with her baby, the day laborer, the small Hester Street shopkeeper, the Russian-Jewish anarchist and socialist, the ghetto rabbi and scholar, the poet, the journalist," crowded into the theaters. Bovshover and Katts were successful playwrights, and theatrical performances were a major source of funds for radical causes. Acclaimed Yiddish actor Jacob Adler made his 1899 New York debut in a fund-raiser for the *Fraye Arbeter Shtime*, and in December of that year, he performed in a benefit for a "legal appeal" for Berkman (though the money actually financed a failed attempt to tunnel Berkman out of prison).[55]

Although anarchists stood aloof from the parochial mutual benefit societies known as *landsmanshaftn*, they were active within the Workmen's Circle (Arbayter Ring), a socialist federation of mutual aid societies founded in 1900. The Workmen's Circle provided anarchists with both an organizational structure and access to a large working-class constituency. New York's Fraye Arbeter Shtime Group and multiethnic International Group became official branches of the Circle, the first of some two dozen anarchist affiliates by the end of the 1920s, including Harlem's Ferrer Center Group and the Bronx's Amshol Group, Friends of Arts and Education Group, and Fraye Gezelshaft Group.[56] Other

Workmen's Circle branches included strong anarchist sections, such as Branch No. 2 in Harlem, which hung Bakunin's portrait on the wall of its headquarters alongside those of Marx and Lassalle. In Rivkin's opinion, the Workmen's Circle and other mutual aid societies "helped to convert the socialistic dream future into a tangible, practical reality."[57]

Anarchists also constructed a subculture centered around a variety of invented traditions, among them regular anarchist picnics, "excursions" to parks or the countryside, *vetcherinkas* (dinner parties), and balls, a category that included *boyernbeler* (peasants' balls), *arestatnbeler* ("arrested balls" to raise funds for political prisoners), and, most controversially, Yom Kippur balls, where anarchists feasted and danced while observant Jews fasted on Judaism's holiest day.[58] The *Fraye Arbeter Shtime* also held an annual two-day "bazaar" featuring entertainment, food, and the sale of donated and handmade items.[59] Such gatherings infused leisure time with radical politics, raised money for anarchist causes, and provided Jewish immigrants with a sense of community.

This community was unapologetically Yiddish. Anarchists redefined their Jewish identity in terms of *yidishkayt*—literally meaning both "Yiddishness" and "Jewishness" but expressing an entire worldview in which language and working-class culture rather than race, religion, or tradition were the essential features of group identity. This allowed anarchists to celebrate their Yiddishness and help build Yiddish culture without resorting to chauvinistic claims of superiority over other cultures. The anarchist variant of *yidishkayt* rejected both Judaism and Zionism and instead celebrated Jewish diasporism as a positive good.

The scope of the Jewish diaspora dispersed the *Fraye Arbeter Shtime* far beyond New York. The paper quickly overtook London's *Arbayter Fraynd* as the worldwide organ of the Yiddish anarchist movement, which by 1910 extended to Canada, Argentina, France, Germany, Austria-Hungary, Egypt, South Africa, and the Ottoman Empire. Anarchist groups also appeared in the Russian Empire beginning in 1903 and relied largely on Yiddish and Russian literature smuggled from abroad; Yanovsky's *Der olef beys fun anarkhizmus* became a local favorite in Bialystok, home of Russia's first anarchist group.[60] The failed Russian revolution of 1905, in which this newborn anarchist movement took an energetic role, thrilled New York's Yiddish radicals, who rushed to aid their comrades or returned to Europe to fight alongside them. Within less than a month, the *Fraye Arbeter Shtime* had collected five hundred dollars for Russian revolutionaries, and at the 1907 International Anarchist Congress in Amsterdam, Goldman reported, "Hundreds of thousands of dollars have been sent from America to assist our Russian brothers. . . . Scores of our Jewish comrades have also returned to Russia to aid by word and deed the heroic struggle against Tsardom."[61]

The Russian Revolution of 1917, however, proved a disastrous turning point. After the February Revolution toppled the czar, thousands of Russian-born radicals returned from America, including hundreds of anarchists who would play a crucial role in Russia's bourgeoning anarchist movement over the next few years. Among them were the members of Brownsville's Bread and Freedom Group, who departed en masse and took their printing press.[62] Anarchists initially embraced the Bolsheviks as like-minded revolutionaries: in January 1918, the *Fraye Arbeter Shtime* hailed "Our Trotsky" as a hero, and the following year Goldman reported that returning anarchists had left the United States "with the determination to help the Bolsheviki."[63]

Yanovsky was one of the few anarchists who did not share in this enthusiasm, instead insisting that the Bolshevik dictatorship was "not anarchistic" and "not kosher" and labeling Lenin a deceitful "Mephistopheles." Watching the stampede of returning anarchists, Yanovsky lamented, "I have raised a generation of idiots."[64] But the editor's credibility within the movement had plummeted following his reversal on World War I. Before 1917, Yanovsky, like most anarchists, had opposed American intervention in the war. Support for the Allies was impossible for Jewish radicals as long as the coalition included czarist Russia. Some Yiddish anarchists, including Cohn, even declared their support for Germany, believing that a German victory might end czarist rule.[65] But Yanovsky's central objection disappeared with the overthrow of the czar, and he soon joined Kropotkin in arguing that a victory for the Western democracies was much preferable to German imperial rule.[66] Yanovsky's about-face mirrored a general shift in American Jewish opinion but discredited him in the eyes of antimilitarist anarchists. By 1919 the *Fraye Arbeter Shtime*'s circulation had dropped to less than half of its prewar height, and Yanovsky was forced to resign as the paper's editor after two decades at the post. Jacob Maryson was appointed as his replacement, but Maryson was also skeptical of the Bolsheviks and was discharged a few months later. Beginning in July 1920, the *Fraye Arbeter Shtime* was edited by communists Haim Kantorovitch and Mosheh Kats (not to be confused with former anarchist Moyshe Katts), briefly losing its anarchist identity.

Anarchist opinion, however, soon turned decisively against the Bolsheviks, and in 1921 the *Fraye Arbeter Shtime* discharged its communist editors and recruited Philadelphia anarchist Joseph J. Cohen to take over. That year, Cohen oversaw the formation of the Jewish Anarchist Federation of America and Canada, which had twenty-five chapters at its founding and guaranteed the *Fraye Arbeter Shtime* a stable base of financial and organizational support. The federation maintained a high level of activity, and members in New York opened the Free Workers' Center on 2nd Avenue, which "always buzzed with activity" such as lectures, meetings, and dances and housed a vegetarian diner run by Cohen's wife, Ida.[67] In the mid-1920s the *Fraye Arbeter Shtime* maintained a circulation of around seven thousand, still among the highest of any American anarchist periodical.[68]

Immediately after leaving the *Fraye Arbeter Shtime*, Yanovsky was recruited to edit the ILGWU's new newspaper, *Justice*, and its Yiddish-language edition, *Gerekhtigkayt*. The invitation was arranged by Morris Sigman, an anarchist garment worker and former Industrial Workers of the World organizer who joined the ILGWU in 1907 and had worked his way up to the position of secretary-treasurer, one of many anarchists within the union's hierarchy. Yanovsky was given nearly complete editorial control, and when a communist "Left" faction emerged within the ILGWU and vied for control of the union, he denounced it as a "cancer that is devouring the innards of the union" and needed to be excised "with a strong, fast hand."[69] As the factional struggle between the communists and the social democratic leadership worsened, Sigman was elected president of the union in February 1923. His selection came with an unofficial mandate from his anarchist comrades and socialist backers to quash communist influence, and he lost little time in ejecting individual communists from the union and dissolving or reorganizing communist-controlled locals.[70] While Yanovsky railed against the communists in *Gerekhtigkayt*, an ad hoc Anarchist Group of the ILGWU published its own newspaper, *Der Yunyon Arbayter* (The Union Worker), to combat both the communist insurgency and the union's entrenched socialist leadership. In 1925, under pressure from the powerful *Forverts* to bring conflict to an end, Sigman negotiated a truce that allowed expelled communists back into the union, prompting Yanovsky to resign rather than condone concessions to "the worst enemies of the union."[71]

The cease-fire ultimately fell apart, and by 1928 the ILGWU's civil war had decimated the union's treasury and membership, leaving "several dead and hundreds injured and maimed."[72] Sigman resigned the presidency, and the communists founded an ill-fated dual union, leaving the ILGWU's leadership in the hands of the increasingly moderate social democrats. The remaining anarchists within the union, including Yanovsky's successor at *Gerekhtigkayt*, former *Yunyon Arbayter* editor Simon Farber, became part of its "progressive" bloc, but anarchism as a movement had lost its independence and most of its influence within the Jewish labor movement. Yanovsky received a regular labor column in the *Forverts* but left after clashing with his old rival, Cahan.[73]

By the end of the 1920s, Yiddish anarchism had entered a period of crisis and decline from which it would never recover. Tens of thousands of radical Jews, including a small number of former anarchists, flocked to the new Communist Party; thousands more embraced Labor Zionism following the 1917 Balfour Declaration, in which Britain expressed its intention of forming "a national home for the Jewish people" in Palestine. Both movements competed with anarchism for support within a dramatically shrinking pool of Jewish immigrants. World War I had interrupted more than three decades of mass migration from Eastern Europe, and the Immigration Acts of 1921 and 1924 put into place the most sweeping immigration restrictions in American history, aimed specifically at limiting the entrance of Southern and Eastern Europeans. Geography and demography further worked against the anarchists. The tight-knit immigrant enclave in which their movement was based was unraveling: by 1916, only 23 percent of New York City's Jews still lived on the Lower East Side as opportunity and economic mobility carried increasing numbers to better housing in Brooklyn and other new suburbs.[74] (Ironically, Moisseiff was chief engineer for the Manhattan Bridge, one of the routes that facilitated this exodus from Lower Manhattan.) A generational divide also emerged between Jewish immigrants and their American-born children, who overwhelmingly chose English-language literature and motion pictures over the Yiddish newspapers and theater of their parents.

The Great Depression took a heavy toll as well. Yanovsky was suspicious of Franklin Roosevelt's New Deal, which the editor viewed as an attempt to combine a capitalist economy with a socialist form of government, creating what he called "private socialism."[75] A number of older Yiddish anarchists, however, "voted (for Roosevelt) for the first time" even while accepting Yanovsky's critiques.[76] By 1931 the *Fraye Arbeter Shtime* was thousands of dollars in debt, and two years later, Joseph Cohen resigned as editor amid accusations by some critics that he was too moderate and others that he was too soft on communism. He was temporarily replaced by an editorial committee that included movement veterans Cohn and Yanovsky. However, according to Cohn, Yanovsky was "getting old and more cynical" and could not tolerate the arrangement, "cussing and abusing everybody who dares to differ with him." In late 1934, Mark Mratchny, an anarchosyndicalist refugee from the Russian Revolution who came to New York in 1928, was appointed the paper's sole editor. By that time its circulation had dropped to five thousand.[77]

The movement's last hurrah came with the Spanish Civil War. The *Fraye Arbeter Shtime* raised funds for the Spanish anarchists and publicized the accomplishments of revolutionary Spanish workers' collectivized factories and farms.

Jewish anarchists protested the American embargo against aid to Spain, while a few men traveled to Spain to fight or otherwise aid the struggle and several women went to work as nurses. The fervor evoked by the struggle also temporarily doubled the *Fraye Arbeter Shtime*'s circulation.[78] The Fascist victory in Spain, however, shook many anarchists' faith that their ideal was realizable. Mratchny recalled the outcome as "a crushing disappointment to me. I had also become disappointed with my work. I felt like a rabbi in an empty synagogue. So I resigned from the *Fraye Arbeter Shtime* and from the anarchist movement."[79] Yanovsky was spared such disillusionment: a heavy smoker, he died of lung cancer on February 1, 1939, two months before the conflict's end.

During World War II Yiddish anarchists strayed far from their antimilitarist roots, with nearly all endorsing the Allied fight against Hitler. In the wake of the war and the trauma of the Holocaust, most Yiddish anarchists made peace with Zionism and supported the new state of Israel as a necessary measure to ensure the survival of Europe's Jews. Few seriously attempted to reconcile these stances with anarchism's core principles of antistatism and antimilitarism. In 1961, North America had at least ten surviving Yiddish anarchist groups, and Fraye Arbeter Shtime Groups persisted in London and Buenos Aires. The Jewish Anarchist Federation lasted until 1966, and the *Fraye Arbeter Shtime* limped on until 1977, when its circulation fell to an untenable seventeen hundred copies.[80]

Yiddish language and culture were the foundations on which anarchism was built on the Lower East Side, and *yidishkayt* presented Jewish immigrants with an alternative to both Old World traditions and Americanization. But these characteristics also walled the movement off from the world outside the Jewish ghetto and doomed Yiddish anarchism to wither away once the stream of Jewish immigrants was choked off. Nevertheless, at its height, this vibrant movement constituted one of the largest segments of American anarchism, helped launch some of America's most important labor unions, played a vital role in developing New York's working-class Jewish culture, and supported revolutionary movements across the globe. Yanovsky and his comrades, whatever their flaws or errors, left a rich legacy of struggle in pursuit of a better world.

Notes

Some of the material in this chapter previously appeared in Kenyon Zimmer, *Immigrants against the State: Yiddish and Italian Anarchism in America* (Urbana: University of Illinois Press, 2015).

1. Leon Moisseiff, "M. Katts—der faraynigender element in der bavegung," in *M. Katts Zamelbukh*, ed. A. Frumkin and Khaym Faynman (Philadelphia: Merts, 1925), 39–40.

Unless otherwise noted, all translations by the author. Transliterations follow YIVO guidelines except in the case of personal names, which are rendered in the more familiar forms that appear in the catalog of the Library of Congress.

2. Herman Frank, "Anarkho-sotsialistishe ideyan un bavengungen bay yidn," in *Geklibene shriftn* (New York: Dr. Herman Frank Bukh-Komitet/Bialistoker Historishe Gezelshaft, 1954), 280.

3. Sh. Yanovsky, *Ershte yorn fun yidishn frayhaytlekhn sotsializm* (New York: Fraye Arbeter Shtime, 1948), 5–35.

4. Steven Cassedy, *To the Other Shore: The Russian Jewish Intellectuals Who Came to America* (Princeton: Princeton University Press, 1997).

5. *Varhayt*, March 29, 1889.

6. M. E. Ravage, *An American in the Making: The Life Story of an Immigrant*, ed. Steven G. Kellman (New Brunswick, N.J.: Rutgers University Press, 2009), 106.

7. Abe Cahan, *The Education of Abraham Cahan*, trans. Leon Stein, Abraham P. Conan, and Lynn Davison (Philadelphia: Jewish Publication Society of America, 1969), 227; Emma Goldman, *Living My Life* (1931; Salt Lake City: Smith, 1982), 9; I. A. Benequit, *Durkhgelebt un durkhgetrakht* (New York: Kultur Federatsie, 1934), 2:52–55; Chaim Weinberg, *Forty Years in the Struggle: The Memoirs of a Jewish Anarchist*, ed. Robert P. Helms, trans. Naomi Cohen (Duluth, Minn.: Litwin, 2008), 5–9; Helene Minkin, *Storm in My Heart: Memories from the Widow of Johann Most*, ed. Tom Goyens, trans. Alisa Braun (Oakland, Calif.: AK, 2015), 30.

8. William J. Fishman, *Jewish Radicals: From Czarist Stetl to London Ghetto* (New York: Pantheon, 1974), 138–59.

9. The best studies of the case remain Paul Avrich, *The Haymarket Tragedy* (Princeton: Princeton University Press, 1984); James R. Green, *Death in the Haymarket: A Story of Chicago, the First Labor Movement, and the Bombing That Divided Gilded Age America* (New York: Pantheon, 2006).

10. *Varhayt*, March 1, 1889.

11. Yanovsky, *Ershte yorn*, 91.

12. Goldman, *Living My Life*, 54–55, 672.

13. Zalman Reisen, *Leksikon fun der yidisher literatur, prese, un filologye* (Vilnius: Kletskin, 1926), 2:469–70.

14. Michael Cohn, "In Neters keler," in *Dovid Edelshtat gedenk-bukh: Tsum zekhtsikstn yortsayt, 1892–1952*, ed. B. J. Bialostotsky (New York: Dovid Edelshtat Komitetn, 1953), 183; Sh. Yanovsky, "Genose H. Zolotarov der frayhayts-pioner in der idisher arbeter bavegung in Amerika," in Hillel Solotaroff, *Geklibene shriftn*, ed. Joel Entin (New York: Dr. H. Solotaroff Publication Committee, 1924), 1:28; Yanovsky, *Ershte yorn*, 84.

15. Cohn, "In Neters keler"; Goldman, *Living My Life*, 55.

16. M. Katts, "Zayn geshtalt," in *Dovid Edelshtat gedenk-bukh*, ed. Bialostotsky, 178–79; Ori Kitz, *The Poetics of Anarchy: David Edelshtat's Revolutionary Poetry* (New York: Lang, 1997), 42; Alexander Berkman to Zalmen Reisen, February 1931, Alexander Berkman Papers, Folder 65, International Institute of Social History, Amsterdam, Netherlands.

17. Yanovsky, *Ershte yorn*, 85.

18. Tony Michels, *A Fire in Their Hearts: Yiddish Socialists in New York* (Cambridge: Harvard University Press, 2005), 63.

19. *Varhayt*, March 1, 1889; Y. A. Merison, "Der ershter period fun der anarkhistisher bavegung," in *M. Katts Zamelbukh*, ed. Frumkin and Faynman, 31.

20. Abba Gordin, *Sh. Yanovsky: Zayn lebn, kemfn un shafn, 1864–1939* (Los Angeles: Sh. Yanovsky Odenk Komitet, 1957), 131–32.

21. *Varhayt*, March 29, May 3, 1889; Elias Schulman, "Di 'Varhayt,'" in *Zamlbukh likhvoyd dem tsvey hundert un fuftsiksn yoyvl fun der yidisher prese, 1686–1936*, ed. Jacob Shatsky (New York: Amopteyl fun YIVO, 1936), 197–98; I. Kopeloff, "M. Katts's tetigkayt in der anarkhistisher un sots. revolutsionerer bevegung," in *M. Katts zamelbukh*, ed. Frumkin and Fineman, 22–23.

22. Gordin, *Sh. Yanovsky*, 192; Fishman, *Jewish Radicals*, 197–201.

23. Herman Frank, "Anarchism and the Jews," in *Struggle for Tomorrow: Modern Political Ideologies of the Jewish People*, ed. Basil J. Vlavianos and Feliks Gross (New York: Arts, 1953), 280; Lucy Robins Lang, *Tomorrow Is Beautiful* (New York: Macmillan, 1948), 112.

24. Sh. Yanovsky, *Vos vilen di anarkhisten?* (London: Arbayter Fraynd, 1890), 15–18; Fishman, *Jewish Radicals*, 197–201.

25. Yanovsky, *Ershte yorn*, 203–10; Gordin, *Sh. Yanovsky*, 193–201.

26. Ronald Sanders, *The Downtown Jews: Portraits of an Immigrant Generation* (New York: Harper and Row, 1969), 112; Kitz, *Poetics of Anarchy*, 68.

27. *Fraye Arbeter Shtime*, December 25, 1890.

28. Yanovsky, *Ershte yorn*, 51–58; Kitz, *Poetics of Anarchy*, 31; Goldman, *Living My Life*, 54.

29. Abraham Rosenberg, *Di klokmakher un zeyere yunyons: Erinerungen* (New York: Klok Opereytors Yunyon Lokal 1, 1920), 8, 22; Elias Tcherikower et al., *The Early Jewish Labor Movement in the United States*, trans. Aaron Antonovsky (New York: YIVO, 1961), 239, 290–91; Goldman, *Living My Life*, 26.

30. Rosenberg, *Di klokmakher*, 23–24; Goldman, *Living My Life*, 54–56; Hertz Burgin, *Di geshikhte fun der idisher arbayter bevegung in Amerike, Rusland, un England* (New York: Fareynigte Idishe Geverkshaften, 1915), 335–38; Louis Levine, *The Women's Garment Workers: A History of the International Ladies' Garment Workers' Union* (New York: Huebsch, 1924), 51–54; Paul Avrich and Karen Avrich, *Sasha and Emma: The Anarchist Odyssey of Alexander Berkman and Emma Goldman* (Cambridge: Harvard University Press, 2012), 112–15.

31. Burgin, *Di geshikhte*, 331–35; Melech Epstein, *Jewish Labor in U.S.A.: An Industrial, Political, and Cultural History of the Jewish Labor Movement* (New York: Ktav, 1969), 1:210; Levine, *Women's Garment Workers*, 59–83.

32. Burgin, *Di geshikhte*, 329–30; Benequit, *Durkhgelebt un durkhgetrakht*, 71; Kalmon Marmor, *Yosef Bovshover* (New York: Kalmon Marmor yubiley-komitet, 1952), 64–70.

33. Joseph J. Cohen, *Di yidish-anarkhistishe bavegung in Amerike: Historisher iberblik un perzenlekhe iberlebungen* (Philadelphia: Radical Library, Branch 273 Arbeter Ring, 1945), 79–90.

34. Ibid., 104–5.

35. Thomas B. Eyges, *Beyond the Horizon: The Story of a Radical Emigrant* (Boston: Group Free Society, 1944), 82; Gordin, *Sh. Yanovsky*, 315.

36. Hutchins Hapgood, *The Spirit of the Ghetto: Studies of the Jewish Quarter of New York* (New York: Schocken, 1966), 177; Michels, *Fire in Their Hearts*, 113–15.

37. *Fraye Arbeter Shtime*, October 13, 1899; *N. W. Ayer & Son's American Newspaper Annual and Directory* (1910).

38. Kathy E. Ferguson, *Emma Goldman: Political Thinking in the Streets* (Lanham, Md.: Rowman and Littlefield, 2011), 268.

39. Epstein, *Jewish Labor*, 1:218.

40. Paul Avrich, *The Modern School Movement: Anarchism and Education in the United States* (Princeton: Princeton University Press, 1980).

41. *Fraye Arbeter Shtime*, September 13, 20, 1901; Gordin, *Sh. Yanovsky*, 258–9.

42. Sh. Yanovsky, *Der olef beys fun anarkhizmus* (New York: Radikal Riding Rum, 1902), 3.

43. Paul Avrich, "Jewish Anarchism in the United States," in *Anarchist Portraits* (Princeton: Princeton University Press, 1988), 190–91.

44. Joseph Chaikin, *Yidishe bleter in Amerike: A tsushteyer tsu der 75 yoriker geshikhte fun der Yidisher prese in di Fareynikte Shtatn un Kanade* (New York: Sklarski, 1946), 197–98; Cohen, *Di yidish-anarkhistishe bavegung*, 185–86, 258.

45. *N. W. Ayer & Son's American Newspaper Annual* (1894–1909); Ferguson, *Emma Goldman*, 100; Cohen, *Di yidish-anarkhistishe bavegung*, 479; Israel Shenker, "Anarchy's the Rule as Anarchists Gather for a Banquet in New York," *New York Times*, June 5, 1977.

46. Max Nomad, *Dreamers, Dynamiters and Demagogues: Reminiscences* (New York: Waldon, 1964), 153.

47. Chaikin, *Yidishe bleter*; "Yanovsky, Sh.," in *Leksikon fun der nayer Yidisher literatur*, ed. Samuel Niger and Jacob Shatzky (New York: Alveltlekhn Yidishn Kultur-Kongres, 1956).

48. Cohen, *Di yidish-anarkhistishe bavegung*, 92.

49. Moshe Starkman, "80 yor 'Fraye Arbayter Shtime,'" in *Geklibene shriftn* (Tel Aviv: Cyco, 1979), 1:111.

50. Norma Fain Pratt, "Culture and Radical Politics: Yiddish Women Writers, 1890–1940," *American Jewish History* 70 (September 1980): 76–85.

51. Robert E. Park, *The Immigrant Press and Its Control* (New York: Harper, 1922), 100.

52. *Fraye Arbeter Shtime*, November 20, 1909, September 17, 1910.

53. Konrad Bercovici, *It's the Gypsy in Me: The Autobiography of Konrad Bercovici* (New York: Prentice-Hall, 1941), 50; Michels, *Fire in Their Hearts*, 61.

54. Goldman, *Living My Life*, 5; Eyges, *Beyond the Horizon*, 127–28; Bercovici, *It's the Gypsy in Me*, 50.

55. Hapgood, *Spirit of the Ghetto*, 118, 141; *Fraye Arbeter Shtime*, December 8, 1899.

56. Daniel Soyer, *Jewish Immigrant Associations and American Identity in New York, 1880–1939* (Cambridge: Harvard University Press, 1997), 84–85; Avrich, "Jewish Anarchism," 190.

57. Jeffrey S. Gurock, *When Harlem Was Jewish, 1870–1930* (New York: Columbia University Press, 1979), 61–62; Hannah Kliger, ed., *Jewish Hometown Associations and Family Circles in New York: The WPA Yiddish Writers' Group Study* (Bloomington: Indiana University Press, 1992), 56.

58. Rebecca E. Margolis, "A Tempest in Three Teapots: Yom Kippur Balls in London, New York, and Montreal," in *The Canadian Jewish Studies Reader*, ed. Richard Menkis and Norman Ravvin (Calgary: Red Deer, 2004), 141–63.

59. Audrey Goodfriend, interview by author, July 11, 2011.

60. Rudolf Rocker, *The London Years*, trans. Joseph Leftwich (1956; Oakland, Calif.: AK, 2005), 7, 97–98; Paul Avrich, *The Russian Anarchists* (Princeton: Princeton University Press, 1967); *Anarquistas de Bialystok, 1903–1908*, 2nd ed. (Barcelona: Furia Apátrida and Ediciones Anomia, 2011), 25, 127.

61. *Fraye Arbeter Shtime*, February 4, 1905; "The Situation in America," *Mother Earth*, November 1907, 386.

62. Kenyon Zimmer, "Premature Anti-Communists? American Anarchism, the Russian Revolution, and Left-Wing Libertarian Anti Communism, 1917–1939," *Labor: Studies in Working-Class History of the Americas* 6:2 (2009): 48–49; Cohen, *Di yidish-anarkhistishe bavegung*, 336.

63. *Fraye Arbeter Shtime*, January 19, 1918; *Freedom* (New York), October–November 1919.

64. Cohen, *Di yidish-anarkhistishe bavegung*, 240; Lang, *Tomorrow*, 112.

65. *Fraye Arbeter Shtime*, October 24, December 12, 1914.

66. Gordin, *Sh. Yanovsky*, 329–32.

67. Frank, "Anarchism and the Jews," 282; Paul Avrich, *Anarchist Voices: An Oral History of Anarchism in America* (Princeton: Princeton University Press, 1995), 350; Clara Freedman Solomon, *A Memoir: Some Anarchist Activities in New York in the 'Thirties and 'Forties* (Los Angeles: Clara Freedman Solomon Memorial Gathering, 2001), 5.

68. *N. W. Ayer & Son's American Newspaper Annual and Directory* (1923–25).

69. *Gerekhtigkayt*, June 9, 1925, quoted in Gordin, *Sh. Yanovsky*, 374.

70. Levine, *Women's Garment Workers*, 357ff.

71. Gordin, *Sh. Yanovsky*, 375–76.

72. Cohen, *Di yidish-anarkhistishe bavegung*, 424.

73. Gordin, *Sh. Yanovsky*, 376–80; Cohen, *Di yidish-anarkhistishe bavegung*, 416–19.

74. Moses Rischin, *The Promised City: New York's Jews, 1870–1914* (Cambridge: Harvard University Press, 1962), 87.

75. Sh. Y., "Prezident Ruzvelt un der Amerikaner mitlklas," *Tsukunft*, April 1935.

76. Avrich, "Jewish Anarchism," 196; Cohen, *Di yidish-anarkhistishe bavegung*, 506.

77. Michael A. Cohn to Rudolf and Milly Rocker, March 23, 1933, Michael A. Cohn to Rudolf Rocker, July 12, 1933, both in Rudolf Rocker Papers, Folder 78, International Institute of Social History; Michael A. Cohn to Max Nettlau, February 8, 1935, Max Nettlau Papers, Folder 307, International Institute of Social History.

78. Cohen, *Di yidish-anarkhistishe bavegung*, 520; David Koven, "On Hanging In," unpublished manuscript, 1986, 8, David Koven Papers, Folder 131, International Institute of Social History; *N. W. Ayer & Son's Directory of Newspapers and Periodicals* (1940).

79. Avrich, *Anarchist Voices*, 384.

80. "Sent Invitations to the Conference to Be Held, January 13 & 14, 1961," Records of the *Fraye Arbeter Shtime*, Record Group 763, Box 3, Folder 49, YIVO Institute for Jewish Research, New York; "Oldest Yiddish Paper in U.S. Is Closing," *New York Times*, November 29, 1977.

Fired by the Ideal

Italian Anarchists in New York City, 1880s–1920s

MARCELLA BENCIVENNI

On September 16, 1920, a bomb exploded across from the office of the J. P. Morgan firm at 23 Wall Street in Manhattan, killing thirty-eight people and wounding hundreds more. It was the worst terrorist attack in New York City until 9/11. Authorities immediately denounced the incident as part of a "gigantic plot" to overthrow capitalism. A frantic investigation followed, hundreds of individuals were questioned, and a number of suspects were detained, but the bomber was never found. The culprit, however, was almost certainly Mario Buda, an Italian anarchist seeking revenge for the indictment of Nicola Sacco and Bartolomeo Vanzetti, two comrades accused of a robbery and murder in South Braintree, Massachusetts, a few months earlier despite inconclusive evidence.[1]

Buda had embraced anarchism at a very young age in Italy. He migrated to the United States in 1907, at the peak of the "New Immigration" wave from Europe, settling in Roxbury, Massachusetts, near Boston. While working at a variety of jobs, he became active in the local Italian anarchist movement, distinguishing himself for his unrestrained insurgency. "A short man with a little mustache, nicely trimmed," he "was a real militant, capable of anything," recalled a friend.[2] Arrested in 1916 for taking part in an antiwar demonstration, he served five months simply for refusing to swear on the Bible. After his release, he went to Mexico with a group of other militants to avoid the draft; angered by mounting U.S. government repression of radicals, he crossed the border again in October 1917, plunging into an underground existence devoted to "war against the enemy"—including a deadly bomb attack in Milwaukee in 1917 and a rash of bombings in 1919–20 culminating with the Wall Street blast. Suspected also of participating in the South Braintree holdup, Buda eluded authorities by sailing for Naples a few weeks after the Wall Street explosion, never to return to the United States.[3]

Buda's story offers an important window into the history of Italian immigrant anarchism, particularly its diasporic, transnational, and militant roots. In fact, Buda's terrorist campaign was the culmination of more than three decades of Italian transnational anarchist activities. Long before the Wall Street attack, Italian anarchists had earned international notoriety as dangerous conspirators and revolutionary zealots. No fewer than four European heads of state were killed by Italian anarchists during the repressive fin de siècle: President Marie François Sadi Carnot of France (1894), Prime Minister Antonio Cánovas del Castillo of Spain (1897), Empress Elisabeth of Austria (1898), and King Umberto of Italy (1900).[4] Umberto's assassination caused a particular sensation in the United States because his assailant, Gaetano Bresci, had been born in Italy but emigrated to Paterson, New Jersey, before returning to his native country and killing the king. Italian silk weavers had established an anarchist haven in Paterson in the 1890s, and in the murder's aftermath, the press reveled in lurid details of presumed international plots, declaring the city "the capital of world anarchism" and Italians "a caste of cutthroats and bandits."[5]

The assassinations of this period were most likely the work of lone individuals but forever associated Italians with anarchist violence in the American public eye.[6] As the *New York Times* commented after Bresci's *attentat*, the words *Italian* and *anarchist* had become "more or less synonymous." "No matter where one hears of the life of some ruler or some royal personage being attempted," echoed the *New York Evening Journal*, "one may always be certain to find that the assassin bears an Italian name."[7]

Behind this distorted characterization of Italian anarchists as a social menace stood a dynamic movement and culture rooted in Italian events and linked to transatlantic revolutionary networks. As the late Nunzio Pernicone has documented, anarchism dominated and largely defined the early history of the Italian socialist movement: "During their heyday in the 1870s, the Italian anarchists, together with their Spanish comrades, were the most active revolutionaries in all western Europe." They led the Italian section of the International Working Men's Association (the First International) and exercised a major influence over the early labor and socialist parties. Perhaps more important, Italian anarchism supplied a cadre of revolutionary leaders whose notoriety transcended ethnic boundaries, giving the movement an international reputation.[8]

Italian anarchism also sustained itself over a long period. Despite systematic government repression and arrests, the movement did not vanish under the blows of the state. Rather, as Davide Turcato has written, when the movement was beheaded in Italy, it moved elsewhere, like a many-headed hydra. Indeed, Italian anarchism was truly "a transnational movement stretching around the Atlantic Ocean and the Mediterranean Sea"—an international network of militants "fired by the Ideal" and closely connected through intense organization, correspondence, newspapers, and physical mobility.[9]

In keeping with patterns of Italian migration and political exile, New York City became an important center of such transnational networks starting from the late nineteenth century. As the largest American metropolis and the most cosmopolitan and heterogeneous city in the world, New York offered a dynamic setting not only for persecuted Italian anarchists but, as this volume illustrates, for radicals from all over the world. While Italian anarchists shared many characteristics of the city's anarchist milieu, three distinctive elements set them apart: their large number vis-à-vis the socialists, the persistence of anarchist ideas, and their extreme devotion to their beloved "Ideal," as they commonly referred to anarchy.

As Paul Avrich has noted, Italians "comprised one of the largest and most militant of the ethnic groups which made up the immigrant anarchist movement" in the United States, peaking at about ten thousand activists nationwide during World War I.[10] Whereas in Italy and most of the rest of the world, anarchism declined dramatically by the late nineteenth century and was eventually eclipsed by socialism, anarchists remained a major component of the Italian American Left until World War II, when the radical movement as a whole faded. Finally, Italian American anarchists tended to be more intransigent than other ethnic anarchists, proclaiming over and over their "manet immota fides"—their unchanging and unshakable commitment to anarchism. Most openly opposed organization and disdained conciliatory measures, instead glorifying acts of reprisal and preaching militant tactics based on direct action, insurrectionary violence, and armed retaliation.

Removed from the mainstream of both American labor and Italian immigrant life, these anarchists built a revolutionary movement and thriving culture all their own, pursuing the creation of a new anarchic society with a passion and vigor that remained undiminished for more than fifty years. This chapter details the social and historical context out of which this particular community emerged in the Little Italies of New York City, providing an overview of the movement's main leaders, geopolitical spaces, and distinctive subculture.

Anarchist Roots

The spread of Italian anarchism in Gotham closely followed the pattern of Italian emigration, which began in the late 1870s, after the country's unification, and grew rapidly up to World War I. Although the United States was not at first the preferred destination of Italian immigrants, five million Italians (about a third of Italy's total migration) eventually settled there. By 1920, Italians had become the largest bloc among new immigrants to the United States, accounting for more than 20 percent of the total.[11]

The overwhelming majority of Italian newcomers settled in northeastern cities, particularly New York. Increasingly resembling an "Italian city outside of Italy," New York by 1920 had almost four hundred thousand Italians—as many as Rome had and nearly equaling Gotham's foreign-born Irish and German populations combined.[12]

From the start, these waves of emigrants included a sizable number of radicals seeking to escape Italian government persecution. The first anarchist militants to reach American shores were more likely political refugees fleeing the repression that destroyed the First International in Italy around the end of the 1870s. A steady diaspora of anarchists followed thereafter, as political repression intensified, reaching a fevered pitch in the 1890s, after the uprisings of the Fasci Siciliani and the infamous Fatti di Maggio (May Events), a series of riots and popular protests violently suppressed by the police. Anarchists were hit particularly hard because of an 1880 legal ruling that "any group of five or more anarchists constituted an 'association of malefactors' under the penal code."[13]

Outlaws in their homeland, all of Italy's most prominent anarchists—Francesco Saverio Merlino, Pietro Gori, Giuseppe Ciancabilla, Errico Malatesta, and Luigi Galleani—traveled to the United States, where they propagated their radicalism, providing a strong foundation for the embryonic anarchist movement.[14] According to Carl Levy, "Exile shaped the lives of three generations of leaders and followers; it circulated new ideas and forms of labour organization back home; it allowed Italians to play a major role in the formation of other national socialist and labour movements."[15]

But while the propaganda of these pioneering leaders was essential to the development of Italian anarchism in the United States, Italian immigrants were also radicalized by the conditions they faced in America. . In fact, a large number of Italian immigrants became activists *after* they arrived in America.[16] Bartolomeo Vanzetti, among others, left no doubt that conversion to anarchism was triggered by the suffering experienced in the "Promised Land." Vincenzo Ferrero, a prominent San Francisco anarchist, similarly noted that "the American experience of struggle" made most of his comrades become anarchists in the United States. His friend Dominick Sallitto, a Sicilian active in Brooklyn, New York, who was arrested and held for deportation along with Ferrero in the 1920s, agreed that for the most part, the anarchists were young immigrants whose "hopes for a better life, a better society in America were disappointed."[17] In anarchism they found a new ideal, a community, and, most important, faith in a better tomorrow when, as Vanzetti wrote, there would be "a roof for every family, bread for every mouth, education for every heart, light for every intellect."[18]

The Movement in New York

Although Italian anarchists could be found from coast to coast, with industrial towns like Paterson, New Jersey; Barre, Vermont; and Tampa, Florida; among the largest and most active centers, New York City—the nation's major port of entry and home to the country's largest Italian population—naturally became the heart of the movement. Its history and experiences are therefore quite representative of Italian anarchism in the United States as a whole.

Aldino Felicani, the treasurer of the Sacco-Vanzetti Defense Committee, claimed that when he arrived in 1914, the city's population of around three million included about five thousand Italian anarchists.[19] They "came from every corner of Italy," but southerners, especially Sicilians, dominated the movement. Most were artisans and semiskilled workers—tailors, barbers, masons, waiters, shoemakers, and carpenters.[20] Though small, the movement was visible and solid as a consequence of members' passion, militancy, and unshakable faith in their "Beautiful Ideal."[21]

Italian anarchists banded together in small, autonomous *circoli* (circles or clubs) that reflected particular schools of thought. An Italian section of the American Federation of the First International was formed in New York as early as 1871, though it soon disappeared. In 1885, however, exiled members of the International on Thompson Street in downtown Manhattan created the Italian Socialist-Anarchist-Revolutionary Group Carlo Cafiero, named after a famous nineteenth-century Italian anarchist. Three years later, seeking "to express and give voice to their ideas," the group launched *L'Anarchico* (The Anarchist), the first of more than eighty Italian-language anarchist newspapers published in North America. Reflecting growing support for the emerging anarchist movement, its second issue listed the names of eighty-eight contributors, including six women, with donations totaling $26.50.[22]

By 1904, New York was home to at least six new groups: the Bresci group (originally based in Brooklyn but later moved to East Harlem), the Gruppo

Socialista-Anarchico Rivoluzionario (Revolutionary Socialist-Anarchist Group), the Club Indipendente Bassa Città (Independent Club of Lower Manhattan), the Circolo Libertario (Libertarian Circle), La Nuova Civiltà (The New Civilization), all in Manhattan, and the Circolo di Studi Sociali (Circle of Social Studies) in Yonkers.[23] Dozens of others, among them the Club Avanti (Forward), founded by Sicilian anarchists in Bushwick, Brooklyn, and the downtown group Il Risveglio (The Awakening), subsequently flourished in all of the city's major Italian neighborhoods as well as across the Hudson River in Paterson, Orange Valley, West Hoboken, and Newark, New Jersey.[24]

Reflecting the overall demographic patterns of their communities, the real centers of anarchist action were East Harlem and Lower Manhattan, the two most densely populated Italian neighborhoods until the 1920s. In particular, the area stretching from 8th to 23rd Streets and 2nd to 5th Avenues was home to a large number of Italian radical groups, social clubs, newspapers, and unions. The Italian Chamber of Labor, Local 48 of the Amalgamated Clothing Workers Union, Local 89 of the International Ladies' Garment Workers Union, and the offices of most radical newspapers clustered in this district.[25]

Many American socialist schools and social centers, among them the Manhattan Lyceum, Webster Hall, the Thalia Theatre, and the People's House, were also located there, providing radicals of all stripes and nationalities with places to hold conferences, concerts, and other performances. Finally, a multitude of Italian cafés and restaurants offered cheap meals and distraction, serving as important social and political centers. Founded in 1908 by John Pucciatti, an immigrant from Umbria, John's on East 12th Street was legendarily known as "the favorite meeting place of free thinkers of all nationalities." Other popular anarchist hangouts included Albasi's grocery on East 106th Street and the Vesuvio restaurant on 3rd Avenue near 116th Street in East Harlem, where for one dollar radicals could enjoy a cheap meal while debating politics and socializing.[26]

As Italians relocated in search of better-quality housing and homeownership, anarchist activities gradually shifted away from Manhattan to other neighborhoods. For example, Williamsburg and Bushwick in Brooklyn and Belmont in the Bronx, emerged as major centers of the clothing industry in the early twentieth century and hosted several important Italian anarchist groups and newspapers after World War I.

Lacking a central party or organization, these political groups formed the cornerstone of the movement. Most were small and insular, with between twenty and forty members, but Paterson's Bresci and Diritto all'Esistenza (Right of Existence) each counted a few hundred comrades, were multiethnic, and persisted for almost two decades, until the Red Scare. One 1914 police report put the membership of the Bresci group at nearly six hundred and described them as "a cosmopolitan lot" who "met regularly in the basement of a building at 301 East 106th Street, a shabby house in a shabby district east of the New York Central tracks."[27] As these groups dissolved, others formed, among them Il Martello (The Hammer), a group headed by Carlo Tresca on the Lower East Side; the Circolo Volontà (The Will Circle) of South Brooklyn; and East Harlem's more militant I Refrattari (The Refractories) and Berneri group, named after Camillo Berneri, an Italian anarchist murdered by Stalinists in 1937 during the Spanish Civil War.

Most of these groups centered on male activism, but, as Jennifer Guglielmo has shown, women made important contributions to the anarchist movement and labor and organized groups that sought economic equality and women's liberation. As early as 1897, led by the fiery Maria Roda (see Christopher J. Castañeda's chapter in this volume), anarchist women in Paterson became exasperated by the chauvinist attitudes of their male comrades and launched the Gruppo Emancipazione della Donna (Emancipation of the Woman Group) to show that "women also have a heart and brain; a soul that must be free." Other feminist clubs quickly followed in other anarchist strongholds across the nation. In 1900, following a series of meetings at her home at 338 East 22nd Street in Manhattan, Maria Raffuzzi and fifteen other *compagne* (female comrades) announced the formation of a "Group of Feminist Propaganda" to defend women's rights, advance the cause of women's emancipation, and "educate the new generation in the sublime principles of anarchism."[28]

Questioning the power relations that relegated them to subordinate roles, Italian anarchist women hosted lectures on women and labor radicalism and published provocative articles on the "woman question" and feminism.[29] But their activism for the most part remained not only "distinct from men's but also largely invisible or insignificant to them." Nevertheless, women played important roles at the local level, particularly as community organizers and fundraisers, helping "to run the stores, publishing houses, boarding homes and other spaces that knit together the community and provided the foundation for the movement." And while men attended the political meetings, women organized lectures, festivals, dances, picnics, and theatrical performances, often acting in them as well. For example, Elvira Catello, who had migrated from Apulia in 1910, led a popular East Harlem theater group that produced plays written and performed by women and ran a radical bookstore at 1946 1st Avenue that was renowned for its collection of anarchist books and periodicals.[30]

Italian anarchism, indeed, centered on family and kin networks, using culture to reach out to the immigrant communities. In addition to forming the center of political organizing, anarchist groups served as social clubs and schoolhouses, with members and other radicals dropping by daily to chat, organize, and relax.[31] Each group held weekly propaganda meetings restricted to its core members and larger open meetings on Sunday afternoon that often "drew as many as 150 people."[32] Hundreds more participated in the frequent performances, dances, and picnics they sponsored.

The ambience of these circles suggests their importance as cultural spaces. Offering a rare glimpse into the life of Italian anarchist organizers, the *New York Times* described the office of Il Diritto all'Esistenza in 1900 as "a little dingy room decorated with pictures of prominent Socialists, among them being that of the notorious Count Enrico Maletesta [sic]." "Two big medallion busts of Michile Angiolello [sic], the assassin of Canovas of Spain," hang on the walls, and "big pictures of him" were scattered around the room."[33]

Such spaces often contained small libraries with an assortment of anarchist and socialist classics as well as social novels and dramas that were typically advertised in anarchist newspapers and sold for a few cents. When federal agents raided the Paterson office of *L'Era Nuova* (The New Age) in 1920, they were stunned by the size of the group's "Modern Library." Established in 1903 and run by Firmino Gallo and his wife, Ninfa Baronio, it was said to be "America's richest storehouse of extreme radical literature." The couple's son, Bill, recalled that "people wrote in from all over the country to order books by mail."[34]

Connected by railroads and ferries, members of the various Italian groups maintained contact with other ethnic anarchist circles through occasional open meetings, cultural events, and above all the press. Comrades came with their children, spouses and friends from all over New York, New Jersey, and Connecticut for the annual fall Festa della Frutta (Fruit Festival), for May Day, and for other anarchist celebrations.

But despite close interaction and occasional cooperation, Italian American anarchists were far from united. Functioning as a loose network of tiny enclaves of propaganda and action, the movement was irremediably divided by internecine personal rivalries and doctrinal disputes, many of which had originated in Italy and continued through the movement's demise. Most Italian anarchists subscribed to the form of anarchist-communism popularized by Peter Kropotkin and Errico Malatesta, advocating the destruction of the state and capitalism and the creation of an egalitarian and free society of voluntary associations. Despite sharing this goal, activists split over strategy and methods of struggle, debating endlessly whether to organize to conduct revolutionary activities.[35]

In New York disagreements between the *organizzatori* and *anti-organizzatori*, as supporters and opponents of organization were known, coalesced around the movement's two most important U.S. leaders, Luigi Galleani and Carlo Tresca. Born in 1861, Galleani emerged as one of the most charismatic figures of the post-International generation of Italian anarchists, distinguishing himself for his fanaticism and uncompromising positions, particularly his opposition to all forms of organization, including labor unions and anarchist federations, and his endorsement of terrorism. Arrested and detained for several years in prison and on the island of Pantelleria, off the coast of Sicily, he escaped in 1899, traveling first to North Africa, then to London, and finally to the United States in October 1901. He originally settled in Paterson but soon relocated to Barre, Vermont, a town dominated by stone and marble cutters from the northern Italian city of Massa Carrara, which had a strong anarchist tradition. Until his deportation in 1919, Galleani's fierce and eloquent voice roared through the pages of his paper, *Cronaca Sovversiva* (Subversive Chronicle) and his countless propaganda tours, attracting dedicated militants throughout the United States (including Buda, Sacco, and Vanzetti) as well as in Europe and Latin America.[36]

In stark contrast, Tresca was the least sectarian of all Italian radicals, "a rebel without uniforms" who believed in the need to organize and when necessary to forge important coalitions with the broader labor movement. Born in 1879, he came to the United States in 1904 to escape a prison sentence stemming from his activism in the local union in his hometown in Abruzzo. After briefly editing *Il Proletario* (The Proletarian), the official organ of the Italian Socialist Federation, his political views became increasingly anarchistic, eventually culminating in anarchosyndicalism. In 1907 he began publishing his own newspaper, *La Plebe* (The Populace), first in Philadelphia and then in Pittsburgh, winning many converts especially among mine workers. The 1912 Lawrence Strike propelled Tresca almost overnight into national prominence, transforming him from an obscure agitator of the Little Italies into the country's foremost Italian radical leader.[37]

In 1913, after falling in love with revolutionary socialist Elizabeth Gurley Flynn, Tresca abandoned his wife and daughter and moved to New York, which remained his home and main battleground for the rest of his life. He published there first *L'Avvenire* (The Future) and, after it was suppressed by American authorities in 1917, *Il Martello* (The Hammer), which remained the main platform for his ideas until his murder in 1943.

Like Galleani, Tresca acquired a large personal following among Italian immigrants, with a close-knit entourage of friends and collaborators, most notably Pietro Allegra and Luigi Quintiliano, who assisted with the publication of the newspaper and other political activities. But, unlike Galleani, Tresca cooperated with the unions, particularly the Industrial Workers of the World, often playing a key role in the industrial disputes of his time. Galleani consequently

"Sympathy Labor Parade—1916" in support of Carlo Tresca and other World War I political victims. Library of Congress.

considered Tresca a traitor and seized every opportunity to discredit him. After Galleani's deportation, his disciples, faithful to the antiorganizationalist principles of their teacher, continued to undermine Tresca's leadership through their paper, *L'Adunata dei Refrattari* (The Call of the Refractories). The rift between the *galleanisti* and *treschiani* seriously undermined the movement, compelling other anarchists to align with one or the other faction or to completely distance themselves from the movement.[38]

A third group, anarchist individualists, also had small but visible presence in the movement in New York, as demonstrated by *Il Novatore* (The Innovator) by Massimo Rocca (alias Libero Tancredi), Cesare Stami's *La Rivolta degli Angeli* (The Angels' Revolt), Enrico Arrigoni's *Eresia* (Heresy), and other periodicals. Inspired by the ideas of German philosopher Max Stirner, anarchist individualists emphasized personal freedom and individual action over everything else and rejected rigid, orthodox doctrines and dogmas, including socialism.

Arrigoni (1894–1986) was probably the most interesting Italian anarchist individualist, living illegally in New York under the pseudonym *Frank Brand* from 1924 until his death. Arrigoni declared himself an anarchist at the age of fourteen and endured the first of his many arrests in 1912 for selling anarchist papers. A fierce antimilitarist, he left Italy in 1916 to escape the draft, beginning a long clandestine exile that took him from Germany to Moscow, Vienna, Buenos Aires, France, Cuba, and ultimately the United States. While working as a bricklayer in New York, he became involved in the city's anarchist movement, becoming a close associate of Brooklyn's Circolo Volontà, the Road to Freedom Group, and the Spanish Cultura Obrera (Workers' Culture). In addition to contributing to various Italian-, Spanish-, and English-language anarchist newspapers, Arrigoni founded *Eresia* in 1928. With a circulation of two thousand, the paper featured articles by such well-known Italian anarchists as Ugo Fedeli. Although Arrigoni mixed well with all other kinds of anarchists, he remained a Stirnerite to the end, convinced that "freedom is the greatest good and that with freedom we make no compromise."[39]

Italian anarchists occasionally tried to overcome their differences and band together. The most ambitious effort to achieve unity occurred at the end of 1939, when a general conference sought to establish "harmony" within the movement and launch a new anarchist paper, *Intesa Libertaria* (Libertarian Accord). But the project failed miserably, and *Intesa* suspended publication after only four issues. The *galleanisti*, led by Raffaele Schiavina (alias Max Sartin), who had illegally returned to the United States in 1928 to edit *L'Adunata dei Refrattari*, boycotted the conference. Tresca and his followers initially cooperated but soon backed out after mounting polemics with *L'Adunata*.[40]

But while disagreeing about doctrine and the proper methods of struggle, all Italian anarchists shared a distinct worldview and sensibility, a set of common values and beliefs grounded in the socialist political culture of nineteenth-century Europe and its struggle for social justice and equality. Pursuing an internationalist, cosmopolitan vision of global humanity, they rejected religion and government and opposed all wars. Perhaps most important, they all aspired, in Galleani's words, to establish "a society without masters, without government, without law, without any coercive control—a society functioning on the basis of mutual agreement and allowing each member the freedom to enjoy absolute autonomy." Refusing to give up their anarchist dream, Italian American anarchists persisted in attempting "to kindle in the minds of the proletariat the flame of the idea: to kindle in their hearts faith in liberty and justice: to give their anxiously stretched out arms a torch and an axe."[41]

The Anarchist Subculture

Italian anarchists were to a large extent "a colony within a colony."[42] On the one hand, they were an integral part of the broader *colonia italiana*, with whom they shared a language, history, experiences, and neighborhoods. On the other hand, anarchists were separated from the larger Italian community by their distinctive lifestyle and political views. The values advocated by anarchists—anticlericalism, antinationalism, free love, anticapitalism, the abolition of the government and all other forms of authority, and especially violent revolution—offered a "world turned upside down" that contrasted markedly with the traditional beliefs of most Italian immigrants.[43] As Kenyon Zimmer has noted, "In form anarchists' social and cultural institutions often mirrored those of their larger immigrant communities, but in content they were antithetical."[44]

Striving to refashion the world according to their moral and political values, Italian anarchists created a rich web of organizations, institutions, and traditions that shaped and sustained their oppositional culture. On Sundays, public lectures provided a substitute for religious Mass. Revolutionary holidays replaced traditional celebrations. Marriages were supplanted by "free love" unions, and newborns were baptized to the rhythms of revolutionary songs with the names not of Catholic saints but of revolutionary martyrs such as Spartaco and Cafiero or with names taken from libertarian nouns such as Libero (Free), Ateo (Atheist), and Alba (Sunrise).

Inspired by Spanish anarchist Francisco Ferrer's Escuela Moderna (Modern School), Italian American anarchists formed alternative schools to counter "the perverted education of the priests" and help children become "champions of free thought." Italian anarchists also had orchestras and dramatic societies, *filodrammatiche rosse*, that staged hundreds of plays. Carrying their anarchist Ideal beyond the confines of the workplace, they organized dances, recitals, and outdoor recreations that attracted hundreds of immigrants and raised much-needed funds for organizational activities. Anarchists also produced dozens of pamphlets, poems, social dramas, and cartoons as well as newspapers.[45]

Between the appearance of *L'Anarchico* in 1888 and the last issue of *L'Adunata* in 1971, Italians published at least eighty-three U.S. newspapers, including thirty-four in the New York metropolitan area. Representing every imaginable current of anarchism, these papers, like other radical papers, led a precarious existence, and many were short-lived. Others, however, continued to publish weekly or semimonthly for many years, distinguishing themselves for the high caliber of their political coverage and literary material.[46]

The principal newspapers that antedated World War I—*Il Grido degli Oppressi* (The Cry of the Oppressed, 1892–94), *La Questione Sociale* (The Social Question, 1895–1908), and *L'Era Nuova* (1908–17)—had circulations of at least three thousand, while Tresca's *L'Avvenire* had four thousand subscribers by 1917. The major postwar publications had larger circulations, with *Il Martello* averaging between six thousand and eight thousand copies of each issue (and a peak of more than ten thousand in 1924) and *L'Adunata dei Refrattari* reaching four thousand readers by 1928.[47]

The press was pivotal to the movement's functioning and constituted its "real institutional base"—the central axis linking thousands of comrades and readers nationally and internationally.[48] Newspapers not only were sold at local newsstands but also were distributed across the nation, in Europe, and in Latin America. Conversely, reflecting close ties with the Italian movement, anarchists in New York regularly read and supported the anarchist press from Italy and elsewhere.[49] In addition to providing the primary medium of communication and information, the press also constituted a central forum of propaganda and education. Every newspaper featured extensive theoretical articles on anarchy and critical accounts of major national and international labor events, such as workers' strikes, government repression, and police brutality. They also regularly covered more general issues such as religion, free love, the "woman question," medicine, and science. Finally, these publications always included literature and art in their pages, serializing novels by literary giants such as Tolstoy, Ibsen, and Zola and printing poems of social protest and one-act dramas.

Anarchist papers served not only as a weapon of class struggle but also as a platform to expose the conditions of life of Italian immigrants and attack the exploitative powerful men of the Little Italies—the *prominenti*. The publications campaigned against colonial bosses and priests, exposing their hypocrisy, corruption, and intellectual mediocrity, a warfare that often led to libel charges against the newspapers' editors and suppression of mailing privileges.

Despite the newspapers' importance to the movement, anarchist editors refused to carry advertisements for ideological reasons and thus operated in a state of constant crisis. Picnics, plays, and dances regularly raised money for the press, but the main support came from individual contributions, which were scrupulously recorded on the last page of each edition under the heading "Sottoscrizioni" (Subscriptions). The collected offerings—a quarter, half dollar, and even a few dollars—testified to the personal sacrifices Italian workers made for their beloved ideal but were hardly enough to ensure economic stability or to survive government repression.[50]

World War I and the Red Scare

The Great War inflicted a double blow on the Italian American Left, causing strong internal dissent over Italian intervention on the one hand and open conflict with the American government on the other. Italian anarchists were notoriously antimilitarist, boasting a long history of antiwar resistance that was amply reflected in both their writings and their actions—most notably, their opposition to Italy's imperialistic campaigns in Eritrea and Abyssinia during the 1890s and in Libya in 1911. But Italy's May 1915 declaration of war on Austria-Hungary called into open question anarchists' *italianità* (Italianness), compelling some to support the war. Following the example of eminent Italian revolutionaries such as Arturo Labriola and Benito Mussolini, former anarchists Domenico Trombetta and Libero Tancredi became vociferous American advocates of Italian intervention.[51]

For the most part, however, Italian anarchists in New York remained firmly opposed to the war. Upholding their antimilitarist, antinationalist, and anti-imperialist principles, they launched a massive journalistic campaign to counter the patriotic fervor and jingoistic propaganda that compelled three hundred thousand Italian Americans to join the U.S. Army and sixty-five thousand to return to Italy to fight. New anarchist papers with distinctively antimilitarist tones—*Il Grido della Folla* (The Cry of the Mob, 1916), *La Riscossa* (The Revolt, 1916–17), and *L'Anarchia* (Anarchy, 1918–19)—were launched during this period in New York to reaffirm anarchist commitment "contro la guerra, contro la pace, per la rivoluzione [against war, against peace, for the revolution]."[52]

Through writings and speeches, anarchist leaders urged Italian immigrants not to comply with the government's order requiring the registration of all aliens of military age. In 1917, Galleani published "Matricolati!," in which he indirectly advised his followers to avoid registering for the draft. Following his counsel, scores of Italian anarchists assumed false identities, changed residences, or went into hiding. Among others, the printer of *Cronaca Sovversiva*, Joseph Moro, left Stoneham, Massachusetts, where he had originally settled, and relocated to Taunton, taking a new job in a factory making kitchen stoves. He recalled Galleani had moved to a barn in the woods nearby, and "a lot of comrades, refusing to register and out of work, lived there with him and killed time by fixing up the barn."[53] Around sixty other galleanisti fled to Mexico. Alberico Pirani, for example, traveled to Laredo, Texas, where a Mexican comrade helped him and "eighteen comrades," including Sacco and Vanzetti, cross the border and go to Monterrey. Two others were less fortunate: Paterson's Alberto Guabello and William Gallo were picked up by Texas Rangers, arrested, and jailed for six months in Del Rio, Texas.[54]

As the United States entered the war in April 1917, Italian anarchists became primary targets of the Red Scare, the antiradical hysteria that culminated with the Palmer Raids and "deportations delirium" of 1919–20.[55] *Cronaca Sovversiva*, *L'Era Nuova* (which had succeeded *La Questione Sociale* in 1908), *Il Martello*, and other radical newspapers were quickly suppressed. Raids by federal agents uncovered names and addresses of thousands of anarchist militants and supporters, providing crucial information to authorities. The records confiscated during one raid included "bulky membership rosters and ledgers showing financial transactions all over the Eastern half of the country."[56]

The movement was deprived of its main leaders. Galleani, Schiavina (manager of *Cronaca*), and seven other trusted companions were indicted and deported in 1919. Charged with conspiracy to obstruct the war, Tresca was arrested on September 30, 1918. Although he was never prosecuted, authorities initiated deportation proceedings against him, efforts that continued unabated but without success until 1925, forcing Tresca to exercise "hitherto unparalleled caution."[57] Ludovico Caminita, the editor of *L'Era Nuova* and the short-lived *Jacquerie*, was arrested along with twenty-eight other comrades on February 14, 1920, and interned at Ellis Island. Threatened with deportation, he eventually cooperated with authorities, distancing himself from the radical world.[58]

Determined to combat their enemy by any means necessary, hard-core followers of Galleani (including Carlo Valdinoci, Mario Buda, Mary Nardini, and Ella Antolini) began to retaliate with terrorist actions. Members of the Bresci group in East Harlem, who were staunch supporters of Galleani, had long been suspected of terrorism. In 1914, they and Jewish anarchists from the Ferrer Center allegedly plotted the assassination of John D. Rockefeller in retaliation for the Ludlow Massacre, in which eleven women and two children died. Amedeo Polignani, an Italian American agent provocateur working for the New York Police Department's antiradical unit, consequently infiltrated the Bresci group, and in 1915, two of its members, Frank Abarno and Carmine Carbone, were framed and convicted of a plot to bomb St. Patrick's Cathedral.[59]

But for the most part, "propaganda of the deed" had remained a state of mind, not a program of action. The violent attacks launched by the *galleanisti* between 1917 and 1920, including the September 16, 1920, Wall Street bombing, represented the exception rather than the rule. Unlike the assassinations of the 1890s, which were devoid of strategic purpose and perpetrated by solitary figures, this mini-war represented a true conspiracy involving perhaps as many as sixty militants, mostly from New England and New York. Pernicone has described the effort as "probably the most extensive, best organized, and carefully planned operation of its type ever undertaken by Italian anarchists anywhere, and in terms of theoretical conception and practical execution, it came closest to modern definitions of terrorism."[60]

Between May 1 and June 2, 1919, package bombs were mailed to prominent symbols of American capitalism and state officials who participated in the persecution against radicals. Additional bombs were delivered by hand at the doors of intended recipients in several cities, causing substantial property damage. A security guard died in the bombing of Judge Charles Cooper Nott's house in New York City, and anarchist Carlo Valdinoci was blown to pieces while setting a bomb at U.S. attorney general A. Mitchell Palmer's house.

Government agents subsequently infiltrated the conspiracy, and two Italian anarchists from Brooklyn, Andrea Salsedo and Roberto Elia, were arrested. Both were affiliated with Galleani's group and at the time of their arrest were editing *Il Domani* (Tomorrow) and *L'Ordine* (The Order) to fill the vacuum left by *Cronaca*. Held incommunicado by the Federal Bureau of Investigation, they were denied the right to an attorney and visits from family and friends. Salsedo was beaten repeatedly by agents until he provided information about the bombings. Overwhelmed by remorse, he allegedly committed suicide by jumping out of his fourteenth-floor cell window. Elia was deported to his native Calabria, where he resumed his anarchist activities until he died in 1924.[61]

In this climate of terror, Sacco and Vanzetti, two more rank-and-file *galleanisti*, were tried for robbing a shoe company and murdering two of its employees. They were quickly convicted and sentenced to death despite the absence of solid evidence against them. Italian anarchists poured all their energy into saving their comrades, denouncing the deep anti-Italian and antiradical sentiments that pervaded the case. When legal efforts failed, a new spate of bombings occurred, to no avail. In spite of worldwide protests and appeals, Sacco and Vanzetti were executed on August 23, 1927.[62]

The Anarchist Movement in the 1920s and 1930s

By the end of the 1920s, the Italian anarchist movement had fallen into disarray. The futile campaign to save Sacco and Vanzetti demoralized the activists, so that part of the movement died with them. Yet Italian anarchists did not vanish from New York despite the harsh blow.[63] As Sicilian native Valerio Isca recalled, "there were still many Italian anarchists in New York," though the movement changed after 1917. Isca and others were radicalized by the "search for justice for these two innocent men." As he later explained, they "were firmly convinced—and remain so today—that it was a frame-up."[64]

Born in 1900, Isca came to the United States in 1922. Initially a socialist, he was increasingly drawn into anarchism and eventually joined the Circolo Volontà on Central Avenue in Bushwick, not far from his home. Most of its members, like him, were Sicilians who read *L'Adunata dei Refrattari*, but unlike them, Isca believed in the need to organize and opposed the use of violence or terrorism. In addition to the campaign to free Sacco and Vanzetti, he became very active in the deportation cases of Italian anarchists who had been arrested as part of the Red Scare, particularly the case of Dominick Sallitto, who came from Isca's hometown. In 1925 Isca also began attending the meetings of the Road to Freedom Group and helped organize New York City's Libertarian Book Club, where he befriended Rudolf Rocker, helping to translate and publish in Italian two of his most important books, *Nationalism and Culture* and *Pioneers of American Freedom*. Isca and his wife, Ida, also participated in the creation of "libertarian" communities in Stelton, New Jersey, and in Mohegan, New York. He died in 1996, the last of Gotham's Italian anarchists.[65]

Like Isca, many of the anarchists active in New York City in the 1920s and 1930s were newcomers who left Italy after the dismal failure of the Biennio Rosso (Two Red Years), 1919–20, when revolution seemed to be coming. But despite the unprecedented growth of anarchism, socialism, and unionism, the revolutionary period ended with the violent reaction of the fascist Blackshirts and Mussolini's consolidation of power. Anarchists and other radicals were quickly driven into exile, confined to penal islands, or placed under house arrest.[66]

Fascism, however, helped revitalize the anarchist movement both materially and spiritually, launching a new transnational struggle that became the new raison d'être of the Italian immigrant Left. A new wave of political exiles began to arrive in America, providing new lifeline to anarchism. This group included Armando Borghi and his companion, poet Virgilia D'Andrea, who became central figures in the American Italian anarchist movement. Borghi arrived in New York in the late 1926 after a South Brooklyn anarchist group paid for his trip and expenses, and he remained in the city until 1945. With the same group's assistance, D'Andrea joined him in the spring of 1928. According to Borghi, he and D'Andrea were deeply immersed in the anarchist and antifascist struggle, and she toured the entire United States, giving lectures "that will not be forgotten." "She was very loved by all comrades," and when she died of cancer in 1933, Italian workers in Italy, the United States, and beyond grieved her loss.[67]

Many lesser-known anarchist exiles—Oreste Fabrizi, Sebastiano and Michele Magliocca, John Vattuone, Virgilio Gozzoli, and Albina Delfino—also made their way to New York in the early 1920s. Although labor unions provided the real institutional base for antifascism in the Little Italies, anarchists stood at the forefront of the struggle, harassing pro-Mussolini speakers, disrupting parades, and confronting fascists in the streets, in a few cases with serious legal repercussions. In the most famous of such cases, two anarchist tailors from Brooklyn, Donato Carillo, a follower of Tresca, and Calogero Greco, a member of *Circolo Volontà*, were arrested and indicted for the murders of two fascists in the Bronx during the 1927 Memorial Day Parade. Fearing a second

Sacco-Vanzetti case, Tresca moved quickly to organize a broad defense committee and secure the best criminal lawyer available, Clarence Darrow. Darrow demonstrated that the Bronx police had conspired with the Fascist League to frame the defendants and thus won their acquittal.[68]

Anarchists also helped raise thousands of dollars to aid victims of fascist persecution through the Comitato Italiano pro Vittime Politiche (Italian Committee for Political Victims), headed by Luigi Quintiliano, which subsidized antifascist newspapers and activities (including the 1931 attempt by Michele Schirru, a member of L'Adunata, to assassinate Mussolini).[69] Perhaps more important, anarchists played a central role in disseminating antifascist propaganda through their newspapers, exposing the true nature of fascism and the collusion between Mussolini, American capitalism, and Italian American *prominenti*.

Postwar Activities and Demise

The Spanish Civil War represented the last rallying cry of Italian anarchists. Spain, where anarchism had reached massive proportions, embodied the concrete possibility of the anarchist dream, the first triumph of a social revolution that anarchists believed would spread to other parts of the world, as expressed by Carlo Rosselli's famous slogan, "Oggi in Spagna, domani in Italia" (Today in Spain, tomorrow in Italy). Fraser Ottanelli has estimated that about three hundred Italian Americans volunteered to fight for the Spanish Republic and that about 60 percent were communists, 20 percent were anarchists, 13 percent were generic antifascists, and handful were socialists and social-democrats. According to Ottanelli, "The significant percentage of anarchists indicates the continued influence of the libertarian movement on Italians both in Italy and the United States."[70] But the communists' 1937 defeat of the anarchists and the murder of Camillo Berneri again shattered the anarchists' dreams and threw the movement in a state of deep despair from which it never recovered.[71]

True to their antimilitarist credos, Italian anarchists went on to oppose World War II, denouncing it as yet another imperialistic struggle for power and profit. In 1945 they helped found the Libertarian Book Club, and during the 1950s and 1960s, they continued to organize anarchist picnics, dramatic performances, and lectures and to publish newspapers that perpetuated the anarchist ideal. But as Pernicone has noted, anarchists had by this point given up the revolution. After decades of struggling for social justice, equality, and freedom, they had concluded that their noble ideals were aspirations that the rest of the Italian American and American community did not share. Their primary commitment and allegiance became the movement itself, which "became their spiritual home, their chief source of culture and friendship, their entire *raison d'être*." When the last issue of *L'Adunata* appeared on April 15, 1971, the editors refused to write their own epitaph or that of the movement, confident "that there will always be refractories to sound the call for justice and liberty."[72]

But Italian anarchism indeed died with *L'Adunata*. Despite Italian anarchists' admirable efforts, the movement remained essentially a first- and second-generation phenomenon. Several factors contributed to its demise. The immigration quota laws of 1924 prevented the infusion of new blood from Italy, and as Italian anarchists leaders died off, they were not replaced. Younger generations remained largely estranged from their radical world. According to Dominick Sallitto, "Children of anarchists shied away from the movement because the parents themselves often failed to practice what they preached. The women seldom participated and the Italian anarchist father was often an authoritarian at home." In contrast, Guy Liberti, an anarchist coal miner, argued that "the children were drawn away because the influence of the school and the street is more powerful than any other."[73] Indeed, American repression and nativism, exemplified in Sacco and Vanzetti's martyrdom, dealt a "debilitating blow to Italian radicalism," instituting "a reign of terror" and teaching immigrants that acceptance into white America was contingent on their rejection of radical ideas. As Rudolph Vecoli has noted, "Not surprisingly, later in life children of radicals often professed not to know about their parents' politics—or refused to discuss them."[74] Financial instability also prevented the movement from establishing solid and long-standing institutions. Perhaps more seriously, its inability to overcome persistent internal divisions prevented anarchists from establishing a visible and effective organization capable of attracting new sympathizers.

But if the days of anarchist action are long gone, their ideas, as Schiavina pointed out in 1981, can still be "of great help today, tomorrow and forever, until the total emancipation of mankind from the scourges of oppression, exploitation, and ignorance are erased from the face of the earth."[75]

Notes

I thank Carol Quirke, Evelyn Burg, Dan Wishnoff, and Kenyon Zimmer for their insightful suggestions and comments. I am especially grateful to the late Nunzio Pernicone, who was originally chosen to write this chapter and who taught me everything I know about Italian anarchism.

1. See Paul Avrich, *Sacco and Vanzetti: The Anarchist Background* (Princeton: Princeton University Press, 1991), 205–7; Nunzio Pernicone, "Luigi Galleani and Italian Anarchist Terrorism in the United States," *Studi Emigrazione/Études Migrations* 30:111 (1993): 2;

Beverly Gage, *The Day Wall Street Exploded: A Story of America in Its First Age of Terror* (Oxford: Oxford University Press, 2009).

2. Paul Avrich, *Anarchist Voices: An Oral History of Anarchism in America* (1995; Edinburgh: AK, 2005), 132–33.

3. Maurizio Antonioli et al., *Dizionario biografico degli anarchici italiani* (Pisa: Biblioteca Franco Serantini, 2003), 2:268–70; Avrich, *Sacco and Vanzetti*, 62–63, 204–7, 217.

4. Nunzio Pernicone, "The Case of Pietro Acciarito: Accomplices, Psychological Torture and Raison d'État," *Journal for the Study of Radicalism* 5:1 (2011): 67–104; Pier Carlo Masini, *Storia degli anarchici italiani nell'epoca degli attentati* (Milan: Rizzoli, 1981); Carl Levy, "The Anarchist Assassin and Italian History, 1870s to 1930s," in *Assassinations and Murder in Modern Italy: Transformations in Society and Culture*, ed. Stephen Gundle and Lucia Rinaldi (New York: Palgrave, 2007), 207–21.

5. "Anarchist Meeting Quiet," *New York Times*, August 3, 1900. See also "Searching among Paterson Anarchists," *New York Times*, August 1, 1900.

6. New evidence suggests, however, that these assassinations may have been part of a larger terrorist conspiracy. See, for example, Alex Butterworth, *The World That Never Was: A True Story of Dreamers, Schemers, Anarchists, and Secret Agents* (New York: Vintage, 2011); Enrico Tuccinardi and Salvatore Mazzariello, *Architettura di una chimera: Rivoluzioni e complotti in una lettera dell'anarchico Malatesta reinterpretata alla luce di inediti documenti d'archivio* (Mantua: Universitas Studiorum, 2014).

7. "Anarchy and Assassins," *New York Times Magazine Supplement*, September 15, 1901; *Evening Journal* quoted in Pernicone, "Luigi Galleani," 472.

8. Nunzio Pernicone, *Italian Anarchism, 1864–1892* (Princeton: Princeton University Press, 1993), 3.

9. Davide Turcato, "Italian Anarchism as a Transnational Movement, 1885–1915," *International Review of Social History* 52 (2007): 407–44; Giuseppe Ciancabilla, *Fired by the Ideal: Italian American Anarchist Responses to Czolgosz's Killing of McKinley*, trans. Paul Sharkey (London: Sharpley, 2002).

10. Avrich, *Anarchist Voices*, 316; "Manet Immota Fides," "Italian Anarchism in the United States," unpublished manuscript, International Institute of Social History, Amsterdam.

11. Gianfausto Rosoli, ed., *Un secolo di emigrazione italiana: 1876–1976* (Rome: Centro Studi Emigrazione, 1978); Piero Bevilacqua, Andreina De Clementi, and Emilio Franzina, eds., *Storia dell'emigrazione italiana* (Rome: Donzelli, 2001), vol. 1.

12. Thomas Kessner, *The Golden Door: Italian and Jewish Immigrant Mobility in New York City, 1880–1915* (New York: Oxford University Press, 1977), 14–17.

13. Pernicone, "Case of Pietro Acciarito," 68.

14. Gino Cerrito, "Sull'emigrazione anarchica negli Stati Uniti," *Volontà* 22 (July–August 1969): 269–76.

15. Carl Levy, "Italian Anarchism, 1870–1926," in *For Anarchism: History Theory and Practice*, ed. David Goodway (London: Routledge, 1989), 43.

16. See Philip Cannistraro and Gerald Meyer, introduction to *The Lost World of Italian-American Radicalism*, ed. Cannistraro and Meyer (Westport, Conn.: Praeger, 2003), 8; Nunzio Pernicone, "Anarchism in Italy, 1872–1900," in *Italian American Radicalism: Old*

World Origins and New World Developments, ed. Rudolph Vecoli (Staten Island, N.Y.: American Italian Historical Association, 1971); Marcella Bencivenni, *Italian Immigrant Radical Culture: The Idealism of the Sovversivi, 1890–1940* (New York: New York University Press, 2011); Kenyon Zimmer, *Immigrants against the State: Yiddish and Italian Anarchism in America* (Urbana: University of Illinois Press, 2015).

17. Avrich, *Anarchist Voices*, 164, 166.

18. Bartolomeo Vanzetti, *The Story of a Proletarian Life*, trans. Eugene Lyons (Boston: Sacco-Vanzetti Defense Committee, 1923), 18–20.

19. Aldino Felicani, "The Reminiscences of Aldino Felicani" (1954), 26, Oral History Collection, Columbia University.

20. Avrich, *Anarchist Voices*, 316.

21. Nunzio Pernicone, "Italian Immigrant Radicalism in New York," in *The Italians of New York*, ed. Philip V. Cannistraro (New York: New-York Historical Society, 2000), 77.

22. "Sottoscrizione permanente," *L'Anarchico*, February 1, 1888.

23. See Ciancabilla, *Fired by the Ideal*, appendix, 27–28.

24. Donna Gabaccia, *Militants and Migrants: Rural Sicilians Become American Workers* (New Brunswick, N.J.: Rutgers University Press), 139–41; Avrich, *Anarchist Voices*, 137.

25. Pernicone, "Italian Immigrant Radicalism," 85–86; Vanni Buscemi Montana, *Amarostico: Testimonianze euro-americane* (Livorno: U. Bastogi Editore, 1975), 96–108.

26. John's was regularly advertised in Italian radical papers. See also Avrich, *Sacco and Vanzetti*, 99.

27. Thomas J. Tunney, *Throttled! The Detection of the German and Anarchist Bomb Plotters* (Boston: Small, Maynard, 1919), 40, 41.

28. Jennifer Guglielmo, *Living the Revolution: Italian Women's Resistance and Radicalism in New York City, 1880–1945* (Chapel Hill: University of North Carolina Press, 2010), 150–60.

29. Bencivenni, *Italian Immigrant Radical Culture*, 85–94.

30. Guglielmo, *Living the Revolution*, 151, 173.

31. Nunzio Pernicone, "Carlo Tresca's *Il Martello*," *Italian American Review* 8:1 (2001): 12.

32. "Bomb Sleuth Lived with Anarchists," *New York Times*, March 3, 1915.

33. "Searching among Paterson Anarchists," *New York Times*, August 1, 1900.

34. "Terrorists Caught in Paterson Raids," *New York Times*, February 16, 1920; Avrich, *Anarchist Voices*, 154.

35. Pernicone, *Italian Anarchism*, 111–13; Avrich, *Sacco and Vanzetti*, 52–53.

36. Pernicone, "Luigi Galleani," 472–75. For an overview of Galleani's anarchist ideas, see Luigi Galleani, *The End of Anarchism?*, trans. Max Sartin and Robert D'Attilio (1925; Sanday, U.K.: Cienfuegos, 1982).

37. Nunzio Pernicone, *Carlo Tresca: Portrait of a Rebel* (New York: Palgrave Macmillan, 2005).

38. See Nunzio Pernicone, "War among the Italian Anarchists: The Galleanisti's Campaign against Carlo Tresca," in *Lost World*, ed. Cannistraro and Meyer, 77–97.

39. Avrich, *Anarchist Voices*, 169–75; Antonioli et al., *Dizionario biografico*, 2:52.

40. Bencivenni, *Italian Immigrant Radical Culture*, 21–22. See also Pernicone, *Carlo Tresca*, 251.

41. Galleani, *End of Anarchism?*, 69, 72.

42. Augusta Molinari, "I giornali delle comunità anarchiche italo-americane," *Movimento Operaio e Socialista* 1–2 (1981): 118; Mario Mapelli, "Giuseppe Ciancabilla: A Look at Italian-American Anarchism at the Beginning of the 20th Century," in Ciancabilla, *Fired by the Ideal*, 3.

43. Mapelli, "Giuseppe Ciancabilla," 3; Pernicone, "Italian Immigrant Radicalism," 77.

44. Kenyon Zimmer, "The Whole World Is Our Country: Immigration and Anarchism in the United States, 1885–1940" (Ph.D. diss., University of Pittsburgh, 2010), 8.

45. For a discussion of these cultural aspects, see Bencivenni, *Italian Immigrant Radical Culture*.

46. See Leonardo Bettini, *Bibliografia dell'anarchismo* (Florence: CP, 1976), vol. 1, no. 2, 169–230.

47. Nunzio Pernicone, introduction to "A Special Issue on the Italian American Radical Press," *Italian American Review* 8:1 (2001): 2–3. See also Zimmer, *Immigrants against the State*, 4–5.

48. Pernicone, "Italian Immigrant Radicalism," 86.

49. Turcato, "Italian Anarchism," 427.

50. Pernicone, introduction.

51. Michael Topp, *Those without a Country: The Political Culture of Italian American Syndicalists* (Minneapolis: University of Minnesota Press, 2001), 135–73.

52. Avrich, *Sacco and Vanzetti*, 58.

53. Avrich, *Anarchist Voices*, 113.

54. Ibid., 142, 156.

55. Avrich, *Sacco and Vanzetti*, chapter 6.

56. "Terrorists Caught in Paterson Raids," *New York Times*, February 16, 1920.

57. Pernicone, *Carlo Tresca*, 219.

58. Bencivenni, *Italian Immigrant Radical Culture*, 122–24; Zimmer, *Immigrants against the State*, 80–83.

59. "Bomb Sleuth Lived with Anarchists," *New York Times*, March 3, 1915; Avrich, *Sacco and Vanzetti*, 100–101; Tunney, *Throttled!*, 41–68.

60. Pernicone, "Luigi Galleani," 471, 472.

61. Avrich, *Sacco and Vanzetti*, 181–95.

62. The voluminous literature on Sacco and Vanzetti includes Avrich, *Sacco and Vanzetti*; John Davis, *Sacco and Vanzetti* (Melbourne: Ocean, 2004); Bruce Watson, *Sacco and Vanzetti: The Men, the Murders and the Judgment of Mankind* (New York: Viking, 2007); Michael Topp, *The Sacco and Vanzetti Case: A Brief History with Documents* (New York: Bedford/St.Martin's, 2004).

63. Pernicone, "Italian Immigrant Radicalism"; Zimmer, *Immigrants against the State*, 5, chapter 6.

64. Avrich, *Anarchist Voices*, 143, 146.

65. See ibid, 143–50; Paul Berman, "The Last of the Anarchists: A Working-Class Hero Passes Away," *Slate*, September 25, 1996. http://www.slate.com/articles/news_and_politics/subcultures/1996/09/the_last_of_the_anarchists.html.

66. Levy, "Italian Anarchism," 61–75.

67. Armando Borghi, *Mezzo secolo di anarchia* (Naples: Scientifiche Italiane, 1954), 333–63; Bencivenni, *Italian Immigrant Radical Culture*, 146–49; Francesca Piccioli, *Virgilia D'Andrea: Storia di un'anarchica* (Chieti: Di Sciullo, 2002); Robert Ventresca and Franca Iacovetta, "Virgilia D'Andrea: The Politics of Protest and the Poetry of Exile," in *Women, Gender, and Transnational Lives*, edited by Donna Gabaccia and Franca Iacovetta (Toronto: University of Toronto Press, 2002).

68. Nunzio Pernicone, "Murder under the 'El': The Greco-Carillo Case," *Italian American Review* 6:2 (1997–98): 20–44.

69. Antonioli et al., *Dizionario biografico*, 2:528–29.

70. Fraser Ottanelli, "Internationalism and the Shaping of National and Ethnic Identity: Italian American Anti-Fascist Volunteers in the Spanish Civil War," *Journal of American Ethnic History* 27:1 (2007): 9–31; Zimmer, *Immigrants against the State*, 196–205.

71. Pernicone, "Anarchism in Italy," 3. See also Zimmer, *Immigrants against the State*, 195–205.

72. Pernicone, "Anarchism in Italy," 4.

73. Avrich, *Anarchist Voices*, 157, 166.

74. Rudolph Vecoli, "The Making and Un-making of the Italian Working Class in the United States, 1915–1945" in *Lost World*, ed. Cannistraro and Meyer, 52–53, 64.

75. Raffaele Schiavina, introduction to Galleani, *End of Anarchism?*, vi.

Times of Propaganda and Struggle

El Despertar *and Brooklyn's Spanish Anarchists, 1890–1905*

CHRISTOPHER J. CASTAÑEDA

> Comrade F. Netlau: I send you a copy of the "Despertar" with all the numbers we have in the house.
> —Pedro Esteve to Max Nettlau, July 13, 1894

Pedro Esteve, a Spanish anarchist and printer, was corresponding with Max Nettlau, a German historian living in London, who had asked Esteve to send copies of *El Despertar* (The Awakening), the most important Spanish-language anarchist periodical in the United States. Esteve, recently relocated from Barcelona to Brooklyn, was the lead editor of *El Despertar*, a paper organized in 1890 by a small group of Spanish and Cuban cigar makers and printers. Nettlau eventually collected and archived a nearly complete run of *El Despertar*, which he sold, along with the rest of his extensive collection of anarchist periodicals, pamphlets, and documents, to the International Institute for Social History in Amsterdam in 1935.[1] This newspaper provides a rare view into the world of Spanish-speaking immigrant anarchists who lived in Brooklyn, New York City, and the United States during the late nineteenth and early twentieth centuries.

During the 1890s, *El Despertar* was one of many Spanish-language anarchist periodicals that comprised a transnational print network extending from Europe across North and South America.[2] *El Despertar* printed essays by Peter

Kropotkin, Mikhail Bakunin, Eliseo Reclus, Ricardo Mella, Jean Grave, José Prat, and Teresa Claramunt, among other writers and intellectuals. The paper addressed a wide range of topics, including the ideology of anarchism, labor action in Spain and throughout Europe, strikes and conflicts at cigar factories, acts of violence by and against anarchists, donations for striking workers and for families of political prisoners in Spain, Cuba Libre (the movement for a "Free Cuba"), and the Haymarket martyrs. It also published letters from subscribers in the United States and Europe as well as a multiyear series, "Entre Tabaqueros" (Among Cigarmakers), that featured often lively conversations between two representative characters, Sulfuroso and Calzazas.

During *El Despertar*'s remarkable eleven-year run, printing was temporarily suspended on several occasions, typically as a consequence of lack of funds or illnesses, although the longest hiatus occurred in 1898 during the Spanish-American War. The abrupt closing of *El Despertar* in 1902, after a total of 227 issues, marked the end of a remarkably vibrant epoch in the Spanish-immigrant anarchosyndicalist movement in the United States. *El Despertar*'s demise also foreshadowed a new era in radical unionism that began with the formation of the Industrial Workers of the World in 1905. This chapter examines Brooklyn's Spanish-language anarchist community through *El Despertar*, which sought to defend and promote workers' rights in a burgeoning capitalist economy.

The Awakening: A Newspaper and an Immigrant Enclave

By the mid-1880s, a relatively small but energetic community of Spanish-speaking immigrants resided in Brooklyn, which was a separate city until 1898, when it became a borough of New York City. Census data suggest that by 1890, Brooklyn had about fifteen hundred Spanish-born (*peninsular*) and thirty-four hundred Cuban-born residents, with roughly similar numbers in Manhattan. Many of the men were cigar rollers, packers, strippers, or peddlers. Some owned shops, while others worked in barbershops, on the docks, or aboard ships. The Spanish-speaking enclave in Brooklyn Heights, adjacent to the East River and Brooklyn Bridge, and in the area around Manhattan's 14th Street included social clubs, newspapers, and events.[3]

José Cayetano Campos, a Cuban printer, was instrumental in establishing Brooklyn's Spanish-speaking anarchist community.[4] He arrived in the United States in 1877 and soon thereafter married Isabel Durio, another Cuban émigré. By 1887, Campos was a leader of the local Unión de Torcedores (Cigar Rollers Union) and facilitated the formation of "an anarcho-collectivist group of Spanish-speaking people."[5] In the same year, Campos became the New York

Brooklyn's Spanish Colony and Anarchist Enclave

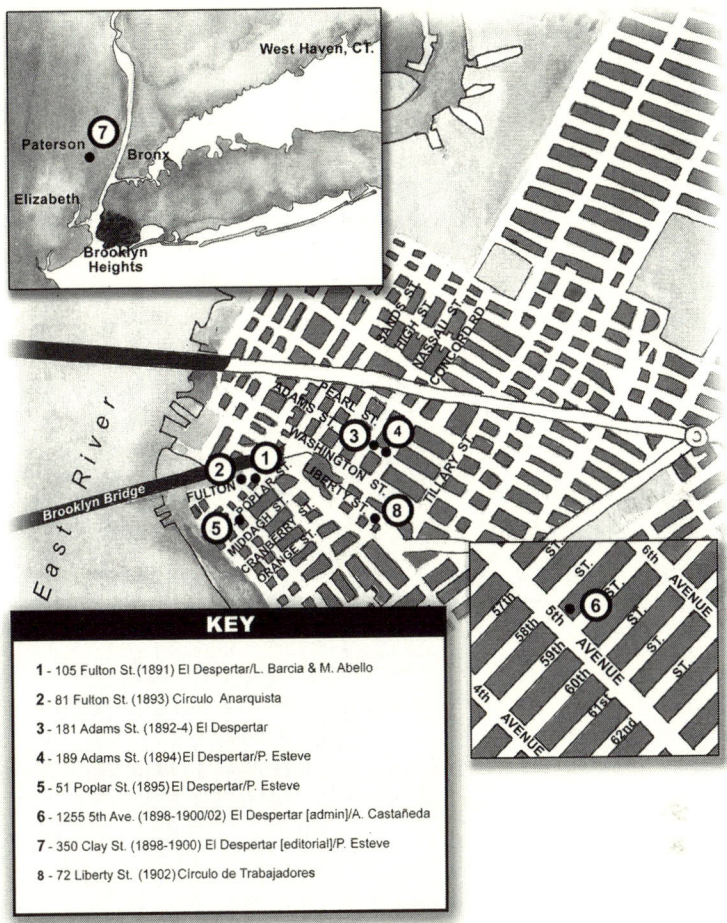

Brooklyn's Spanish Colony and Anarchist Enclave, ca. 1892–1901.
Map by Nancy Wylie.

correspondent for *El Productor*, a new Barcelona-based anarchist periodical; a Havana journal also named *El Productor* commenced publication in 1887. Campos's connection to both papers, along with his vibrant support for labor, which took precedence over the Cuban separatist cause, was critical to the emergence of Brooklyn's Hispanic anarchist community.[6]

Another Spanish émigré, Luis Barcia Quilabert, arrived in Brooklyn during 1890 and soon became active in the local anarchist community. Originally from the small Spanish seaport town of Mundaca, near Bilbao, Barcia had learned cigar making and printing in Cuba and Tampa before moving north. Although he did not speak English, friends greeted him at the dock in New York and took him to their Brooklyn home to rest from his journey, and he "felt happy because now I felt I was among my own, again." Barcia found employment in a Brooklyn cigar factory. As in Tampa, and Havana, he noted, "Spaniards and Cubans worked together. Sometimes even anglo workers were employed but this was rare because they were not able to work with the material the way it was done in Cuba." Barcia soon met other *peninsulares* and Cuban-born cigar makers and felt "the spirit of organization and self-defense among them."[7]

In Brooklyn, a group of these cigar makers deeply committed to workers' rights openly joined the international labor movement, with nine forming the Grupo Parsons (Parsons Group), which took its name to honor Albert Parsons, an anarchist printer who had been executed in 1887 for his alleged complicity in the May 4, 1886, Haymarket Square bombing. Group members then established *El Despertar* to "defend our common interest." Barcia later remembered the newspaper as "not only the voice of the cigar workers, but, also, the voice of all those who cherished freedom and economic redemption. We struggled without rest and without decline with no regard for any sacrifice. That was our *direction* and our *flag*. Freedom and well being is not achieved without sacrifice."[8]

In Barcelona, *El Productor* reported on January 1, 1891, that it had received a prospectus for *El Despertar*, which declared, "We want for the worker, for the disinherited in the social banquet, for the modern pariah, economic equality and absolute liberty." It listed *El Despertar*'s contact as Enrique Roig y Ramos, 1223 Fulton Street, Brooklyn, although his name did not appear again as an editor of *El Despertar*. *El Productor* then wished *El Despertar* "welcome and a long life."[9] From the outset, therefore, Brooklyn's Spanish-language anarchist paper was an integral part of the transnational anarchist print network.

Barcia and Campos served as *El Despertar*'s inaugural editors. Cuban émigré Manuel Martínez Abello also played a significant editorial role until family problems forced him to leave Brooklyn in late 1891. An editorial and administrative group continued to operate the paper, with some issues identifying lead editors by name, though most issues printed only addresses. Each Grupo Parsons member contributed $2.50 toward the paper's initial printing costs. During its first year of operation, the back page featured advertisements for Spanish restaurants and hotels in Brooklyn, presumably to subsidize printing expenses. After November 1, 1891, however, the paper printed no commercial advertisements.

El Despertar developed a significant subscription base (although circulation numbers are not known) in part by utilizing agents in Tampa, Key West,

Havana, Barcelona, and many other cities in the United States and abroad. Cigar factories, shops, restaurants, and barbershops also sold the paper, which consistently included four pages and usually appeared twice every month (on the first and fifteenth) or during some periods every ten days. For the first three and a half years of *El Despertar*'s existence, a subscription cost twenty-five cents for three months or five cents per issue. In June 1894, the rate increased to twenty-five cents for a two-month subscription, but the single-issue cost remained the same. These prices did not change over the next eight years. The paper also regularly printed a column, "Entre Nos" (Among Us), that listed donors to the paper. An 1897 accounting indicated that each issue cost $26.50 to publish.[10]

El Despertar generally refrained from printing stories of purely personal interest but regularly reported on local labor issues, especially at cigar factories. Nonetheless, it offered an important window into the social organization of Brooklyn's Spanish-speaking anarchist community. In July 1891, one essay congratulated newly married José Casteleiro and Merced Pereira, who had "rejected the religious ceremony as useless and harmful." The paper continued, "Free love, for consenting parties, is the best marriage and best ceremony one can desire." Several weeks later, the secular marriage of Modesto Fernández and Anita received a brief mention.[11] Deaths of family members also appeared on occasion. When Abelardo Petit's young daughter died in 1891, the paper offered its heartfelt condolences.[12]

Anarchism in this Spanish-speaking immigrant community provided a model for daily life, and the anarchist press provided a means to respond to authoritarianism and capitalism. The promise of opportunity and American ideals had certainly attracted immigrants to the United States, but those same features invoked charges of hypocrisy and disillusionment. Manuel Martínez Abello's "Por Que Soy Anarquista" (Why I Am an Anarchist) explained that in seeking to understand the social order, he examined the words *justice*, *morality*, *equality*, and *liberty* and found instead "injustice, immorality, inequality and tyranny." Abello described many of the principal tenets of anarchism, including an egalitarian society without government, private property, and religion.[13]

The apparently contradictory if not seemingly empty promise of American ideals was a regular target for immigrant anarchists. The author of one essay reflected on the Statue of Liberty in New York Harbor, observing with irony that it had "7 large caliber guns in front, and a half company of soldiers, some of them with fixed bayonets, [and] is also crowned with thorns." Concluded the article, "We know that liberty exists only in name."[14] This essay resonated in Barcelona, where *El Productor* reprinted it later that month.[15]

José Campos also wrote a series of essays, "Soy Anarquista" (I Am an Anarchist) in which he explained his beliefs. Yet even the prodigious Campos sometimes found that the living conditions in Brooklyn, particularly during the summer, severely challenged his ability to work. In mid-August 1891, rather than his regular article to *El Despertar*, he contributed a short note explaining that he was "en huelga [on strike]": " With the heat at 94 degrees in the shadow of a coal oil lamp, I cannot *be* an anarchist." The editors responded by expressing their hope "that the thermometer lowers."[16]

Spanish-speaking anarchists formed a distinct community defined not only by language but also by culture and the cigar industry. However, they were not socially isolated, and they interacted with anarchists in other ethnic communities. During the summer of 1891, *El Despertar* reported on a meeting about German anarchist Johann Most, the "tireless anarchist agitator," who had recently been sentenced to prison. August Delabar and Henry Weissmann, editor of *Bäcker-Zeitung* (Bakers' Journal), spoke glowingly of Most and his dedication to freedom and social change. Weissmann claimed that Most had been the victim of a conspiracy engineered by the chief of police.[17] The following summer, *El Despertar* reported again about Most during a special session at which New York socialists had expelled a number of members, including W. C. Owen, August Delabar, and Ernst Kurzenknabe, who had specifically been accused of sympathizing with Most. To offer support, a local craft union sponsored a concert at Clarendon Hall with proceeds to be directed to Most, and *El Despertar* encouraged readers to attend.[18]

An "Anarchist Newspaper"

El Despertar was similar in format to both *El Productor* of Barcelona and *El Productor* of Havana as well as to many other Spanish-language anarchist papers of the period. These papers expressed an anarchosyndicalist orientation, meaning generally that they espoused social organization based on egalitarian trade union principles as opposed to authoritarian governmental hierarchy and capitalism. From its first issue through March 1892, *El Despertar*'s subtitle reflected its dedication to labor rights: *Periódico Quincenal Dedicado á la Defensa de los Trabajadores* (Biweekly Periodical Dedicated to the Defense of the Workers). However, this subtitle became entirely insufficient for articulating the enclave's dedication to anarchism.

The Grupo Parsons sought to make a strong statement that would definitively situate the periodical in the transnational anarchist network. To unequivocally clarify this position, the Grupo Parsons changed *El Despertar*'s subtitle to *Periódico Anarquista* (Anarchist Newspaper), and it retained that title for the rest of its existence. *El Despertar*'s editors wanted to ensure that "there is no doubt in anyone's mind that we are anarchists and that we are ready to suffer all of the consequences [of our ideas]."[19]

In addition to supporting and maintaining *El Despertar*, the Grupo Parsons formed other Spanish-language anarchist groups. In February 1892, *El Despertar* introduced the Círculo de Anarquista (Anarchist Circle) to "serve as an effective means of propaganda, as the meeting point for the study and discussion of our ideals" and to build stronger connections among "colleagues who fight for the same ideals."[20] After an inaugural meeting on April 1, the new group held a large celebration on the evening of April 22 at the same Washington Street hall where Brooklyn's larger Spanish social club, La Nacional, held its regular meetings. The celebration featured "the honest words of our companion explaining our aims and purposes, now harmonious notes that delight, plucked mandolin, guitar or piano, and the human voice, acclaimed with enthusiastic bravos and applause [a demonstration] for the anarchist ideals felt among the emigrants to this country who speak Castilian."[21]

The members of *El Despertar*'s editorial group understood that despite their newspaper's increasing popularity and its active social groups, they needed to find new ways to distribute their ideas and educate the public about social revolution. Barcia consequently left *El Despertar* and "together with some other friends, formed another group which we called *El Ideal* (The Ideal)."[22] On January 1, 1893, *El Despertar* announced that El Ideal was dedicated to the tired and hungry workers who typically suffered from a lack of education.[23] El Ideal solicited donations to print and distribute free pamphlets and reprints of anarchist tracts in both English and Spanish, and during the following June and July, the group received $19.20.[24] The Barcelona-based *El Productor* applauded El Ideal's efforts.[25]

One of El Ideal's largest distributions of literature occurred in 1893 after the governor of Illinois, John P. Altgeld, pardoned Samuel Fielden, Oscar Neebe, and Michael Schwab, the remaining jailed Haymarket martyrs. *El Despertar*'s editors not only celebrated the release but also lambasted the criminal justice system that had wrongly kept the men in prison, for laying "bare the arbitrariness and injustice of the judges, juries and police."[26] Underscoring Haymarket's importance to the anarchist movement, El Ideal printed five thousand copies of Altgeld's message for distribution to Spanish-speaking workers in New York City and internationally.

Pedro Esteve and a Change of Direction

Pedro Esteve's arrival in Brooklyn further solidified *El Despertar*'s fundamental importance in the transnational anarchist network.[27] He disembarked from the French steamer *La Bourgogne* in New York on August 8, 1892, and immediately became one of the most influential members of Brooklyn's anarchist community. Born in Barcelona in 1865, Esteve learned the trade of typesetter and printer, and in his youth he became acquainted with a wide variety of political literature. In the process, he befriended other printers and typographers who became "very important in spreading anarchism in Spain, Cuba, Mexico, Argentina and the U.S."[28] In Barcelona, Esteve had worked as an apprentice at *La Academia* as well as at *El Productor*, and he undertook speaking tours of Europe. After Spanish officials shut down *La Academia* in May 1892, he made plans to leave Spain.[29]

Adrián Del Valle, one of Esteve's colleagues from Barcelona, had already arrived in Brooklyn and joined *El Despertar*.[30] In the United States, he and Esteve went on speaking tours and attended the international anarchist conference held in conjunction with the 1893 World's Columbian Exposition in Chicago. Esteve subsequently serialized his thoughts and recollections about that experience in *El Despertar* and then published them in a separate pamphlet.[31] Esteve next traveled to Cuba and to Tampa before returning to Brooklyn. He became well known as a speaker and writer.[32]

Adrián del Valle also served as an editor and contributor for *El Despertar*, often writing under the pseudonym *Palmiro de Lidia*, which he used when composing works of fiction and dramatic dialogue. Del Valle worked closely with Esteve and later recalled that his "dynamism and initiative" not only contributed to *El Despertar*'s success but also "intensif[ied] the propaganda among the Spanish-speaking community and develop[ed] a better relationship with members of other immigrant communities, particularly the Italians."[33] When Esteve returned to Brooklyn in 1895, he moved *El Despertar*'s editorial office to 51 Poplar Place, near the Brooklyn Bridge, where he resided with Maria Roda, a young Italian anarchist, and their first son, Pedro.[34]

Roda, too, wrote articles for *El Despertar*, perhaps most provocatively "A Las Madres" (To the Mothers), which she dedicated to herself as a married woman, "Maria Esteve." She began with elegant descriptions of nature before turning to a harsh indictment of marriage and husbands and condemning the educational system for indoctrinating young persons: "I hope not to teach them to worship a god that does not exist." She also disparaged nationalism: "One does not teach them to love the motherland, which is only a butchery among brothers, by the whim of some and the vanity of others; instead, one inculcates in them that the country is the entire world." Roda's attack on the institution of marriage was cogent. While she had taken Pedro Esteve's name, she remained independent: marriage "is only a pact of interests, an odious snare, as a sacred thing; in its place should be put pure love, natural, two hearts meet, free love."[35]

The Anarchosyndicalist Impulse

Jacob Coxey's Army of unemployed marchers arrived at the U.S. Capitol in Washington, D.C., on May 1, 1894, symbolizing the dire plight of the U.S. economy. In New York, anarchists and communists including Esteve and Most rallied at the Thalia Theater to support Coxey. At the meeting, according to a reporter, Esteve, "a black bearded Spaniard [who] spoke in his native tongue," "denounced capitalists, Congress and the police, and said that the time was coming when the laboring classes would right their wrongs by force."[36] Poor economic conditions and rising unemployment affected all sectors of the economy, including cigar factories, which lowered wages and fired workers.

As the severe economic depression buffeted the economy, labor tensions ran particularly high in Brooklyn. *El Despertar* reported in early 1895 that "in the short space of three months, there have been three grand strikes: Homestead, Chicago [Pullman] and Brooklyn, and in all of them the insolent and shameless partiality of the republican state favors the capitalist."[37] In Brooklyn, as many as six thousand streetcar workers from different railway companies shut down the transportation system over wage disputes. This action received much attention from *El Despertar*, but the Spanish and Cuban cigar makers' strike nevertheless was the paper's focal point.

Within this historical context, *El Despertar* confronted a serious challenge to its existence and even relevance. At its core, the periodical was the anarchosyndicalist propaganda arm of a community of anarchist groups that were primarily concerned with local, national and international labor issues. The New York cigar makers had regularly used ad hoc strike committees also associated with the Grupo Parsons to sponsor collections for supporting striking workers around the country, and *El Despertar* printed many of these accountings. Generally, the strike committees had been reasonably effective, but they did not provide the organizational structure that the cigar makers needed to better represent and promote their labor initiatives over the long term and in the face of unified action by the manufacturers.

The increasing labor tensions during 1894 in New York City cigar firms consequently prompted local workers to establish a more robust labor organization for their business. The Organización de los Torcedores de Tabaco Habano de las Ciudades de New York y Brooklyn (Organization of Havana Tobacco Cigar Rollers in New York and Brooklyn, popularly known as La Defensa) sought to defend the interests of the Spanish-speaking cigar workers and to establish standards for cigar workers' wages as well workshop conditions.

La Defensa implemented anarchist organizational principles. Its administrative committee included a treasurer, an accountant, and a secretary. A presiding officer could be appointed only for the duration of a single meeting. If the funds collected or distributed by La Defensa were significant, "revisors" would double-check accounts, which would also be printed in *El Despertar*. Each member of La Defensa paid an initial membership fee of ten cents, with additional dues assessed as needed after a vote by the membership.[38] With a stronger labor collective behind them, the cigar workers were ready to press their case for better wages and working conditions.

By late 1894, many of New York City's Spanish-speaking cigar workers declared a work stoppage at factories that produced Havana cigars, including workshops operated by both Spaniards and Cubans, among them Garcia y Pando, Guerra, Árgüelles y López, Ortiz, Samá y García y Vega. This strike took place during a period of increasing financial distress and unemployment, and Luis Barcia later recalled that "many [unemployed] marchers reached New York . . . where they could be seen on the streets stopping pedestrians to beg for some money with which to have breakfast. . . . In the midst of this crisis, many spanish and cuban cigarmakers left for Cuba, and I was among them."[39]

The Hispanic cigar workers who remained in New York leveled serious charges against the manufacturers, focusing on the poor quality of material provided and continuing efforts to lower the wage rate per *vitola* (a cigar's size and shape). Perhaps the most troubling issue for cigar makers was the manufacturers' attempts to rename existing *vitolas* so that they could pay cigar rollers (*torcedores*) less per thousand for production. Although the cigar rollers were the center of the cigar making operation and carried the most weight in negotiations, the *escogedores* (those who classify cigars by color) and the *rezagadores* (those who select tobacco leaves) were often marginalized within cigar factories. In solidarity, all of these cigar workers joined together and stated that "the conduct of those manufacturers could not be more arbitrary and despicable."[40]

The striking New York cigar makers also looked to their colleagues in Tampa for assistance. Barcia had earlier left New York for Cuba but stayed there only briefly before relocating back to Tampa, where he and other anarchists formed a new paper, *El Esclavo* (The Slave), in June 1894. Maintaining a very close relationship with New York *tabaqueros* and *El Despertar*, *El Esclavo* regularly reported on the New York strike and facilitated financial contributions to support the workers. Strike committees collected funds and typically transferred them via money order to those in need. Although this process is not well documented, *El Esclavo* printed one letter that provides some insight into the operation of these financial networks. On January 27, 1895, Agustín Castañeda, a Brooklyn-based *peninsular* cigar maker and member of La Defensa, wrote to the Comité de Auxilios de Tampa (Tampa Aid Committee), "We have received the money sent by money order. I did not have difficulty collecting it even though it was not addressed correctly.... I am able to receive the money in that name, since that is how they know me at the post office."[41]

The New York cigar workers' strike lasted for nearly four months; despite financial support from Tampa's cigar makers, it did not end well. Essentially, too many cigar makers had capitulated, and the anarchist press castigated those who had failed to support the strike and particularly the strikebreakers. *El Despertar* and *El Esclavo* heaped intense vitriol on the "traitors" and *escabeches* (scabs), declaring "When a worker betrays his companions he is serving the interests of the bourgeoisie."[42]

In addition to the intense labor conflict, the Cuban separatist movement brought more challenges to New York's Spanish-speaking anarchist community.[43] Despite the many essays printed in *El Despertar* about Cuba Libre, conflict between Cubans and *peninsulares* remained evident. José Campos wrote a series of essays, "El Anarquismo: Entre Los Obreros Cubanos" (Anarchism: Among Cuban Workers), that dealt with an array of issues related to Cuba, Cubans, and their relationship to Spain and Spaniards. Campos was clearly a unifying force in Brooklyn, and despite his Cuban background and sympathies, he understood the importance of maintaining at least a modicum of mutual respect between the two groups, which, in the English-speaking public's mind, were not distinct. Campos reported hearing some Cubans discussing how American workers got along with English workers but then heard a group of Cubans remark that "today the Spanish workers are our eternal enemies.... [W]ar and death to all those born in Spain!" Campos retorted, "Fatal error, Cuban workers."[44] In this context, many Cubans continued to perceive some Spaniards as colonizers, and their perceived privileging of anarchism over Cuban separatism did not help alleviate those deep-rooted concerns.

El Despertar's lack of attention to the 1895 Cuban uprising that ultimately led to the Spanish-American War exacerbated the rift between Cubans and *peninsulares*. On February 24, Cuban rebels organized by José Martí launched a long-awaited revolt against Spanish control of the island. Martí was summarily killed in battle at Dos Rios on May 19. Unlike *Patria*, the New York–based separatist paper Martí had edited, *El Despertar* essentially ignored the Cuban uprising and Martí's death, a stance that marked *El Despertar* as the voice of anarchism rather than separatism. The paper remained focused on the fallout of the failed cigar makers' strike and continued to print essays by Jean Grave on "La Sociedad Agonizante y la Anarquia" (Dying Society and Anarchy) along with tracts by Kropotkin and other anarchists. While many Cuban and Spanish anarchists supported the Cuban separatist movement, others did not. Esteve, for one, believed that simply replacing one regime with another would not solve Cuba's problems, and this perspective was clearly evident in the paper's lack of reporting on Martí's death. Del Valle later wrote that *El Despertar* displayed indifference to the Cuban Revolution, whereas *El Esclavo* actively supported separatism.[45]

By the spring of 1895, ongoing tensions among *peninsular* and Cuban anarchists combined with the debilitating and failed cigar workers' strike contributed to the decline of New York's Spanish-speaking anarchist community. *El Despertar* reported that many erstwhile local subscribers had left the city, presumably to look for work in Tampa, and asked them "to please inform us of your new address if you want to continue receiving the periodical." The editor then continued,

> The group that supports El Despertar has been making efforts to sustain this periodical, which, due to the positive reception it has gained by anarchists in both hemispheres, could be a biweekly or daily publication if everyone contributed what they should or at least something. Let it be noted, however, that we cannot complain about some agents and subscribers, who, by the way, have always done their share. What we desire is that if some have the goodwill to read it, they may also have the goodwill to contribute to the indispensable costs of its publication. The writers and the administrators work for free, gladly dedicating the hours that they have for rest for the good of this propaganda, but we must attend to other expenditures that cost us money. Our object is to create the most propaganda possible in benefit of the majority; for that there will be no shortage of effort, but it is well known that this goal would not go far if we did not count on the help of all. This you already know, comrades.[46]

Propaganda by the Deed

El Despertar focused intently on the Spanish government's brutal suppression of labor and political uprisings as well as the increasingly predictable acts of violence and retribution committed by anarchists. In this era of "propaganda by the deed," anarchists committed to direct action and martyrdom found ample opportunities. On September 24, 1893, for example, Paulino Pallás Latorre attempted to assassinate Spanish general Arsenio Martínez-Campos in retaliation for his brutal suppression of the 1892 Jerez Uprising. Pallás killed Campos's horse and two bystanders and wounded Campos as well as twelve soldiers and spectators.[47] *El Despertar* reported on Pallás's actions and subsequent execution and then initiated a campaign to raise funds for Pallás's widow and children. To initiate the collection in October 1893, Esteve, del Valle, José Campos and his wife, Isabel; and Angel Rodriguez each contributed a dollar, and by April 1894, the campaign had sent 1,025.25 pesetas to Pallás's family.[48]

More violent acts of revolt and repression occurred in Spain during 1896–97, and *El Despertar* reported on them all. On June 7, 1896, French anarchist Jean Girault threw a bomb at a procession during the festival of Corpus Christi, killing six and wounding forty-five. The Spanish government immediately arrested the suspected ringleaders of the plot and within days detained about three hundred anarchists. Many were well-known and influential lawyers and intellectuals, and those who subsequently wrote about their experiences and treatment included Anselmo Lorenzo, Tarrida del Mármol, Federico Urales, Cayetano Oller, and Teresa Claramunt. On December 11, a military tribunal at Barcelona's Montjuïc Prison began proceedings against eighty-seven detainees, many of whom were tortured. These *procesos de Montjuïc* ended with eight death sentences (five carried out), twelve acquittals, and varying terms of incarceration for the remaining prisoners. According to historian George Esenwein, "The Spanish government had 'shut its eyes to reason' and . . . the Montjuich trials had been a monumental miscarriage of justice."[49]

This colossal overreaction by the Spanish government only invited more propaganda by the deed. Michele Angiolillo, a young Italian anarchist, fulfilled that expectation when he assassinated Spanish prime minister Antonio Cánovas del Castillo on August 8, 1897. Brooklyn's Spanish-speaking anarchist community subsequently attracted increased scrutiny from the English-language press and local authorities. A reporter visited a meeting of the Círculo Estudio Sociales held in "a barber shop in Brooklyn, under the very shadow of the Brooklyn Bridge." The reporter spoke with cigar maker Gerardo Quintana, who celebrated Cánovas's assassination and drew an important connection between the Cuba Libre movement and social revolution in Spain: "We all hope that Cuba will win her independence, because this means revolution in Spain and a step towards anarchy."[50]

After the United States formally declared war against Spain on April 25, 1898, however, the local anarchist community became further factionalized, and *El*

Despertar lost more subscribers. Esteve complained to *El Despertar*'s readers about the lack of community support and interest in the newspaper's condition.[51] If the paper were to remain in business, more contributors and subscribers would have to be found. Between late February and mid-September 1898, only three issues were published. Even Esteve's commitment to Brooklyn's Spanish-speaking anarchist community appeared to waver.

Enacting Anarchism from Within

In mid-June 1898, as the U.S. military began to engage Spanish forces in Cuba, Esteve warned *El Despertar*'s readership that "our humble publication" might not survive. "Are there not even a dozen comrades scattered across the country willing to part with a peso per month?" Esteve then announced the relocation of *El Despertar* from its editorial office at 124 Fulton Street in Brooklyn to his own home at 350 Clay Street in Paterson, New Jersey. *El Despertar*, however, retained a presence in Brooklyn by establishing an administrative office at 1255 5th Avenue, the tenement of *peninsular* cigar maker Agustín Castañeda.[52] For Esteve, the move was logical: he was already affiliated with *La Questione Sociale*, the popular Italian-language anarchist paper based in Paterson, where many members of the active Italian labor community were employed in local silk factories. Roda likely also desired the change, especially with the decline of Brooklyn's Spanish community. In Paterson, Esteve edited both *La Questione Sociale* and *El Despertar* for several years, and both papers reportedly were printed on the same press.[53]

In Brooklyn, La Defensa had dissolved after the failed 1894–95 strike.[54] Cigar makers' efforts to replace it finally succeeded in late 1898, when the Sociedad de Torcedores Habano (Society of Havana Cigar Rollers) was created.[55] Modeling the Sociedad after organizations by the same name in Havana and Tampa, the cigar makers sought to join a larger federation of Spanish-speaking tobacco unions as well as provide an organizational response to Samuel Gompers's much larger and more powerful Cigar Makers' International Union (CMIU). The CMIU often called on Spanish-speaking cigar workers to honor its strike calls but did not always reciprocate, a situation that angered the Spanish-speaking cigar rollers.

The 250 members of the Sociedad de Torcedores Habano reflected a variety of ideological perspectives. They initially elected Castañeda as treasurer, but some members subsequently insisted on electing a president. Proponents of this view argued that doing so would enable the Sociedad to avoid appearing to be an anarchist group. Castañeda was also serving as *El Despertar*'s administrator, so it is entirely plausible that some members were concerned about his anarchist connections. When supporters of a presidency threatened to leave the Sociedad if the position was not created, members voted to do so. Castañeda responded by resigning as treasurer on the grounds that it was "impossible for me to continue under the direct tutelage of a president."[56] His anarchist sensibility and perspective exposed him to criticism, but he retained his general membership in the Sociedad. He then learned that some proponents of the creation of the presidency had accused him of financial dishonesty by pulling pages from the account books used during the strike of 1894–5. Furious, he responded to the charges in a letter printed in *El Despertar*:

> This infamous slander, I can't even understand why it was listened to because the accounts of that strike were published in great detail after they had been checked by our comrades J. Granda, Antonio Fernández, Sandalio Peña, Manuel Palmeiro and Juan García, in the report on the above-mentioned strike in a special issue of EL DESPERTAR. This, however, had become notorious, for which reason, in the middle of a general meeting, I demanded of these despicable slanderers that they repeat the accusations they were making in private. Nothing happened; they said nothing. I had brought the books, which luckily I still have, but no one wanted to examine them. There were some who proposed, conversely, that I be given a vote of confidence, which I emphatically rejected.[57]

Castañeda declared that the account books were open to anyone who wanted to see them and emphasized the damage such false accusations made for political purposes caused to the Spanish community. He labeled his opponents "despicable slanderers," an "accursed race of *rodents* [that] is responsible, to a great extent, for the anemic period our institutions are going through."[58]

El Despertar printed several articles that addressed the dispute. In the same issue that printed Castañeda's letter, an essay, "Hombres, No Pecoras" (Men, Not Sheep), emphasized the need for individualism and strength of character rather than for applause or titles. "Poor are those who hope for a president or steering committee to direct the good progress of an association."[59] The newspaper's next issue included a front-page story, "Ratificamos" (Let's Ratify), that disputed the notion that a majority vote in favor of a presidency should permanently settle the disagreement because "reason must never be subordinated to the law of numbers and against a real or fictitious majority."[60] Two weeks later another unattributed essay, "¿División?" (Division?), again addressed the controversy: "Our history and our ideas are well known and preach that the workers' organization must combat every vestige of authority." The stability of the cigar workers' organization and the larger community faced threats not from anarchists but from those who threatened to leave the Sociedad de Torcedores if a presidency were not established.[61] The office of the president apparently was short-lived: only the first accounting statement published after the incident listed a president; all others identified only a treasurer. This episode exemplified the severe organizational dilemma faced by anarchists and the increasing tension and rifts within the Spanish-speaking cigar-making community.

The dispute over the Sociedad de Torcedores's organizational structure was only one of several emerging fractures in the enclave. Divisions between Spanish anarchosyndicalists and Cuban separatists led the Cubans and their supporters, including José Campos, del Valle, Gerardo Quintana, and Barcia (who had returned from Tampa), to form a new Brooklyn-based anarchist newspaper, *El Rebelde*, that began publishing in September 1898 and was dedicated to the complete emancipation of Cuba from foreign domination. At the same time, *El Despertar* resumed publication after a hiatus during the Spanish-American War: suggesting a spirit of collegiality, *El Despertar* wished the new paper "good success and a long life."[62] Although *El Rebelde*'s editors sought to reinvigorate the spirit of Cuba Libre, they failed, ceasing publication after only five issues. Both Barcia and del Valle soon left Brooklyn permanently, moving to Tampa and Havana, respectively. In Havana, del Valle established *El Nuevo Ideal*, a literary anarchist paper that remained in print for several years. Campos, the Cuban émigré perhaps most responsible for establishing *El Despertar*, remained in Brooklyn.

While the divisions among Spanish-speaking anarchists, Cuban separatists, and others were palpable, efforts to unify also took place. In January 1899, community members formed the Círculo de Trabajadores (Workers' Circle) in the heart of Brooklyn's Spanish colony, taking as their model an organization by the same name that had been established in Havana in 1885.[63] The Brooklyn Círculo met first at 154 Fulton Street and then at 72 Liberty Street before moving to 102 Pineapple Street, near the Brooklyn Bridge. The Círculo, which lasted through the second decade of the twentieth century, brought together Spanish-speaking cigar workers and anarchists as well as laborers and political activists of all stripes. During the spring of 1900, it hosted a high-profile talk by the Italian anarchist Errico Malatesta.[64]

The Spanish-speaking cigar makers also encountered opposition, distrust, and at times manipulation from forces outside their community, including the powerful CMIU. In December 1900, *El Despertar* decided to confront the CMIU directly and in English, with a front-page statement, "To the Cigarmakers of the International Union." The paper's editors offered a defense of an independent Spanish-speaking cigar makers' union, recognition of members' high-quality work, and an appeal for mutual respect among the Spanish-speaking cigar makers and those of the CMIU.

> COMRADES: Being convinced that the struggle which you sustain against the Havana Cigarmakers' Unions, has become very bitter, owing principally to a prejudice inculcated and nutrified in your minds.... [W]e address our friendly voice.... Without doubt, because you do not know us [and] taking advantage of our diversity of language, [someone] has fooled you, telling you lies and falsehoods in regard to our purposes, our acts, our ideals ... our organizations of resistance, constituted in New York, Tampa, Key West, etc., give a good example, and which will shortly form a larger one with the other manufacturing centres ... which will include at least all the Havana cigar industry extended into this country, Canada and the Antilles.... We have neither presidents nor committees of directors who live at our expense and besides treat us as slaves.... The solution is very simple. It is sufficient to be just. That one union should not wish or desire to absorb the other.... This is the opinion of the cigarmakers of clear Havana who form part of the group which sustains "L Despertar."[65]

Living the Anarchist Life

Anarchism is often incorrectly defined as an ideology that simply promotes extreme acts of violence. But violent acts—particularly those committed by anarchists against government figureheads and prominent capitalists—have certainly shaped the public's opinion about the meaning and goals of anarchism. As propaganda by the deed, these acts were as much attempts to galvanize public opinion against political and economic oppression and tyranny as they were tangible anarchist statements against authoritarianism. Through the 1890s, *El Despertar* reported on these acts but was never directly connected with any of them. That began to change in 1900.

While serving as editor for both *El Despertar* and *La Questione Sociale*, Esteve was under increasing scrutiny by the Paterson police. During the summer of 1900, Gaetano Bresci, an Italian weaver and anarchist who had cofounded *La Questione Sociale*, traveled to Italy and assassinated King Umberto I. Convicted to life in prison (Italy did not have capital punishment), Bresci died the next year in jail, reportedly under suspicious circumstances. Esteve's public defense of his colleague's regicide resulted in questioning by authorities. Then, avowed anarchist Leon Czolgosz's 1901 assassination of U.S. president William McKinley brought the police back to Esteve's door. In both instances, he was cleared of any involvement.[66]

Bresci's regicide represented a particularly important victory for anarchists, who celebrated Bresci and raised funds to support his widow and two daughters. A group of Spanish and Italian anarchists organized a festive fund-raiser at New York's Germania Assembly Room on November 11, 1900, the anniversary of the execution of the Haymarket martyrs. On November 10, however, New York police "prohibited the going on of the entertainment, first with a written order, then with threats." The event's cancellation infuriated its sponsors, who took the opportunity to assail not only the police but the American system: "They will tell you that we are revolutionists; we are Anarchists; that out of our ranks came Bresci, the man who killed the King of Italy; but we shall answer that we have learned from your Declaration of Independence: 'That when a long train of abuses and usurpations, pursuing invariably the same object, evinces a design to reduce them under absolute despotism, it is THEIR RIGHT, IT IS THEIR DUTY, to throw off such government.'" This essay, written by the editors of *La Questione Sociale*, presumably including Esteve, was printed in English in both *El Despertar* and *La Questione Sociale*.[67]

Bresci quickly became a martyr for anarchists generally, especially those who had worked with and known him in New York and New Jersey. A group of Paterson's Italian anarchists formed the G. Bresci Group and joined with the Spanish members of the Grupo Parsons to host a Brooklyn benefit for both *El Despertar* and *La Questione Sociale* on February 9, 1901. As the event was about to start, a Brooklyn police inspector arrived and addressed the crowd: "What right have you people to come over to this country? and they let you in, why don't you become as good a citizen as I am, and spend your money where you earn it? People non-complying with this are not wanted on this side and if you aren't satisfied you can go to ——."[68]

In the face of intense surveillance and opposition, Brooklyn's Spanish-speaking anarchist community continued to decline, and it could no longer serve as a means to unify Brooklyn's Hispanic cigar workers. Cuba was free from Spanish rule, and McKinley's assassination brought intense scrutiny of and pressure on U.S. anarchist groups, resulting in the departure of some key members of the anarchist community. These political and financial strains translated into significantly less local, national, and even transnational support for anarchist groups and institutions.

Personal tragedy also played a role in degrading New York's anarchist community. While *El Despertar* rarely published articles about personal matters, it reported on a series of deaths that affected Esteve. Illness among members of his family caused the newspaper to temporarily cease printing on more than one occasion, including in late March 1901, when two of Esteve's children were stricken.[69] Several months later, Esteve's mother and young son, Sirio, died.

Soon thereafter, Giovanni Rolle, a weaver and administrator of *La Questione Sociale*, also passed away.[70]

The death of José Campos on November 25, 1901, dealt another major blow to the Spanish-speaking anarchist community and to *El Despertar*. In an obituary published in the paper, Gerardo Quintana described his fallen comrade as an "intelligent, ... tenacious propagandist who for twenty years stuck to his noble task of striking well-aimed blows at the old walls of the bourgeois prison in which we live."[71] Campos also had helped to bridge the divide between *peninsular* anarchists and Cuban separatists, but his death symbolized the end of that era and the beginning of one marked with increased division.

In addition, the shifting social and economic conditions of the early Progressive Era presented the increasingly difficult challenge of implementing anarchist beliefs in daily life. This dilemma was perhaps no better exemplified than in five questions that Montreal resident Pablo Sanchez posed to *El Despertar* in the spring of 1902. His queries address some of the fundamental tensions facing anarchists:

- 1st Should an anarchist in our society, saving funds, keep some of those funds for some of the contingencies of life?
- 2nd Can an anarchist deposit savings in a bank or any company or firm, and have the deposits subject to losses and gains?
- 3rd Can one be an anarchist and do little or nothing for the cause?
- 4th Can one be considered a good worker having declared a strike and stay in bed sleeping in the morning, while other colleagues lose their jobs for going to the house in question, as in the workshop of Tabaquerón?
- 5th Can one be considered a good fellow if they are afraid to distribute a worker's periodical for fear of losing their meal?

El Despertar's editors responded carefully, but the tensions between ideology and practice were palpable. After acknowledging the human struggle of daily life—"First of all we must not forget that in today's society no one, absolutely no one, can fully live according to the anarchist principle"—the paper declared, "The anarchist should have no other aim than the ideal."[72]

The pressure on *El Despertar* further increased in 1902 after a fire burned down the Paterson office at which both *El Despertar* and *La Questione Sociale* were printed. Continued fallout from the assassinations of Umberto and McKinley led to new anti-anarchist laws in New York, New Jersey, and Wisconsin.[73] And anti-anarchist sentiment led to a summer 1902 police raid at Paterson's anarchist printing house, causing another suspension of *El Despertar*. The paper reported that police were guarding the buildings as if they were castles or factories and had put the city in a state of war. *El Despertar* printed several more issues but continued to suffer from a lack of funds, and the last issue appeared in December 1902.[74] Barcia later offered a pragmatic perspective on *El Despertar*'s closing: "Our paper had a long life and did a great amount of good work until its demise due to a change in the environment among cigar workers."[75]

Esteve continued to seek ways to reinvigorate Brooklyn's anarchist community, traveling to Brooklyn in early 1905 to meet with his Spanish anarchist colleagues. They agreed to create a new periodical, and the first issue of *Doctrina Anarquista-Socialista*, edited by Esteve, appeared on February 15, 1905. More of a serial pamphlet than a periodical in the style of *El Despertar*, it ceased publication by the following summer.[76]

As the Spanish community's anarchist impulse waned, many members sought new venues for labor activism. The work of radical American labor organizers bolstered by the anarchosyndicalism of immigrant workers and the activism of internationalists led to the formation of the Industrial Workers of the World. But the increasing automation of cigar and cigarette making, along with consolidation of tobacco firms, also contributed to the failure of the Spanish-speaking cigar makers' nineteenth-century anarchist institutions. Perhaps ironically, the prized and often expensive Cuban cigar came to symbolize one legacy of these artisanal craftsmen, but their anarchist periodicals, groups, and activism exerted a more important and powerful, if largely unrecognized, influence on the U.S. labor movement.

Notes

I thank Kirwin R. Shaffer for his support and encouragement and Tom Goyens for his insightful comments. Any mistakes are mine alone. The title of this chapter is derived from the statement "Those were times of propaganda and struggle" in Luis Barcia Quilabert, "Autobiography of Luis Barcia Quilabert," 27, unpublished manuscript, Special Collections, University of South Florida, Tampa.

1. The International Institute for Social History has the most complete collection of editions of *El Despertar*, though the first nine issues have not been located.

2. For an excellent examination of another Spanish-language labor periodical, *¡Tierra!*, see Kirwin R. Shaffer, "Havana Hub: Cuban Anarchism, Radical Media and the Trans-Caribbean Anarchist Network, 1902–1915," *Caribbean Studies* 37:2 (2009): 45–81.

3. See Christopher J. Castañeda, "'Yours for the Revolution': Cigar Makers, Anarchists, and Brooklyn's Spanish Colony, 1878–1925," in *Hidden Out in the Open: Spanish Migration to the United States (1875–1930)*, ed. Phylis Cancilla Martinelli and Ana Varela-Lago (Boulder: University Press of Colorado, forthcoming).

4. See Susana Sueiro Seoane, "Prensa y redes anarquistas transnacionales: El olvidado papel de J.C. Campos y sus crónicas sobre los mártires de Chicago en el anarquismo de lengua hispana," *Cuadernos de Historia Contemporánea* 36 (2014): 259–95.

5. Joan Casanovas, *Bread, or Bullets! Urban Labor and Spanish Colonialism in Cuba, 1850–1898* (Pittsburgh: University of Pittsburgh Press, 1998), 168–69.

6. Joan Casanovas I Codina, "Pedro Esteve (Barcelona 1865–Weehawken, N.J. 1925): A Catalan Anarchist in the United States," *Catalan Review* 5:1 (1991): 68.

7. Barcia Quilabert, "Autobiography," 26.

8. Ibid., 27.

9. *El Productor* (Barcelona), January 1, 1891. Unless otherwise noted, all translations by the author.

10. *El Despertar*, October 20, 1897.

11. *El Despertar*, July 1, 1891.

12. "Sensible Desgracia," *El Despertar*, May 15, 1891.

13. Manuel Martínez Abello, "Por que soy anarquista," *El Despertar*, June 1, 1891.

14. *El Despertar*, March 1, 1892.

15. *El Productor* (Barcelona), March 31, 1892.

16. *El Despertar*, August 15, 1891.

17. "Meeting Anarquista," *El Despertar*, July 1, 1891.

18. "Actualidades," *El Despertar*, February 1, 1892. The essay identifies Union 1 as the sponsor. On Johann Most and the German anarchist community, see Tom Goyens, *Beer and Revolution: The German Anarchist Movement in New York City, 1880–1914* (Urbana: University of Illinois Press, 2007). For other anarchist communities, see Kenyon Zimmer, *Immigrants against the State: Yiddish and Italian Anarchism in America* (Urbana: University of Illinois Press, 2015).

19. "Una Aclaración," *El Despertar*, April 1, 1892.

20. "Círculo Anarquista en Brooklyn," *El Despertar*, February 15, 1893. Other groups formed during the 1890s included Derecho á la Vida (Right to Life); Todo para Todos (All for All); the Círculo de Estudios Sociales (Social Studies Circle), which met at 124 Fulton Street, Brooklyn; and the Jovenes Anarquistas (Young Anarchists), which met at 43 Sand Street, Brooklyn.

21. "Nuestra Velada," *El Despertar*, May 1, 1893.

22. Barcia Quilabert, "Autobiography," 28.

23. "Otro grupo," *El Despertar*, January 1, 1893.

24. "Suscripción voluntaria: Para la publicación de Folletos Anarquistas," *El Despertar*, June 15, July 1, 1893.

25. *El Productor* (Barcelona), July 20, 1893.

26. "Bibliografia: El mensaje," *El Despertar*, August 1, 1893.

27. See Casanovas I Codina, "Pedro Esteve"; Susana Sueiro Seoane, "Un anarquista en penumbra: Pedro Esteve y la velada red del anarquismo transnacional," *Alcores* 15 (2013): 43–66.

28. Casanovas I Codina, "Pedro Esteve," 61.

29. Ibid., 66–67.

30. Kirwin R. Shaffer, *Anarchism and Countercultural Politics in Early Twentieth-Century Cuba* (Gainesville: University Press of Florida, 2005), 15–18. See also Shane L. Thomson, "Recovering Adrián Del Valle's *Por El Camino* and Building Transnational Multitudinous Communities" (Ph.D. diss., Ball State University, 2013).

31. Pedro Esteve, *A Los Anarquistas de España y Cuba: Memoria de la Conferencia Anarquista Internacional celebrada en Chicago en Septiembre de 1893* (Paterson, N.J.: El Despertar, 1900).

32. Casanovas I Codina, "Pedro Esteve," 67–68.

33. "Pedro Esteve: 1892–1898," *Cultura Proletaria*, September 10, 1927.

34. See Jennifer Guglielmo, *Living the Revolution: Italian Women's Resistance and Radicalism in New York City, 1880–1945* (Chapel Hill: University of North Carolina Press, 2010).

35. Maria Roda, "A Las Madres," *El Despertar*, February 30, 1896.

36. "Praise for Coxey from Anarchists," *New York Herald*, May 7, 1894.

37. *El Despertar*, January 30, 1895.

38. "La Defensa," *El Despertar*, October 10, 1894.

39. Barcia Quilabert, "Autobiography," 29.

40. "La Huelga," *El Despertar*, December 30, 1894.

41. *El Esclavo*, February 6, 1895.

42. "¡Traidores!," *El Despertar*, May 20, 1895.

43. See Gerald E. Poyo, *"With All, and for the Good of All": The Emergence of Popular Nationalism in the Cuban Communities of the United States, 1848–1898* (Durham, N.C.: Duke University Press, 1989).

44. "El anarquismo: Entre los obreros Cubanos," *El Despertar*, December 20, 1894.

45. "Pedro Esteve: 1892–1898," *Cultura Proletaria*, September 10, 1927.

46. "Importante," *El Despertar*, May 20, 1895.

47. George R. Esenwein, *Anarchist Ideology and the Working-Class Movement in Spain, 1868–1898* (Berkeley: University of California Press, 1989), 185.

48. "Importante," *El Despertar*, April 1, 1894.

49. Esenwein, *Anarchist Ideology*, 197.

50. "Anarchists from Spain: Thriving Clubs in New York Whose Members Uphold Assassination," *Los Angeles Herald*, September 19, 1897.

51. Pedro Esteve, *El Despertar*, June 20, 1898.

52. Ibid. See also Casanovas I Codina, "Pedro Esteve," 70–71.

53. George W. Carey, "The Vessel, the Deed, and the Idea: Anarchists in Paterson, 1895–1908," *Antipode* 10–11:3-1 (1978): 51; Casanovas I Codina, "Pedro Esteve," 71.

54. "A cuantos se a la elaboración del tabaco Habano," *El Despertar*, June 15, 1895.

55. There also had been an earlier attempt in 1895 to establish the Sociedad. See "Mezclilla: Charla Charlando," *El Despertar*, October 10, 1895.

56. A. Castañeda, "Comunicado," *El Despertar*, April 15, 1899.

57. Ibid., trans. Dr. Hector Urrutibeheity. For a brief discussion of issues related to "organizational anarchists," see Carey, "The Vessel, the Deed, and the Idea," 51.

58. A. Castañeda, "Comunicado," *El Despertar*, April 15, 1899.

59. "Hombres, No Pecoras," *El Despertar*, April 15, 1899.

60. "Ratificamos," *El Despertar*, May 15, 1899.

61. "¿Division?," *El Despertar*, May 30, 1899.

62. "Mezclilla," *El Despertar*, September 30, 1898.

63. See Frank Fernández, *Cuban Anarchism: The History of a Movement* (Tucson, Ariz.: Sharp, 2001), 22.

64. *El Despertar*, May 1, 1900.

65. "To the Cigarmakers of the International Union," *El Despertar*, December 10, 1900.

66. "After Paterson Anarchists," *New York Times*, September 11, 1901. See also George Carey, "'La Questione Sociale,' an Anarchist Newspaper in Paterson, N.J. (1895–1908)," in Lydio F. Tomasi, *Italian Americans: New Perspectives in Italian Immigration and Ethnicity* (New York: Center for Migration Studies of New York, 1985), 289–97.

67. "To the American People," *El Despertar*, November 15, 1900; "To the American People," *La Questione Sociale*, November 17, 1900.

68. "To the American People," *El Despertar*, January 28, 1901.

69. *El Despertar*, March 30, 1901.

70. "Mezclilla," *El Despertar*, June 20, 1901.

71. Gerardo Quintana, "J. C. Campos," *El Despertar*, January 23, 1902. Castañeda resumed working as *El Despertar*'s administrator after Campos's death.

72. "Preguntas y respuestas," *El Despertar*, March 13, 1902.

73. Richard Bach Jensen, *The Battle against Anarchist Terrorism: An International History, 1878–1934* (New York: Cambridge University Press, 2014), 255. Carey, "The Vessel, the Deed, and the Idea," 54. For background on anti-anarchist activity in Paterson, see also "To Prevent Anarchist Meetings," *Daily People*, July 31, 1901.

74. "Mezclilla," *El Despertar*, June 26, 1902. See also "Rise and Fall of Anarchy in World-Famed Paterson," *Washington Post*, December 9, 1906; Casanovas I Codina, "Pedro Esteve," 72–73.

75. Barcia Quilabert, "Autobiography," 27.

76. See *Doctrina Anarquista-Socialista*, February 15, 1905.

From Union Square to Heaven

Dorothy Day and the Origin of Catholic Worker Anarchism

ANNE KLEJMENT

"I was rather surprised," Emma Goldman wrote to an anarchist comrade in 1939, "to find you have among your co-workers, members of the Radical Catholic group.... I have never known of Catholics being radical."[1] Dorothy Day likewise knew the church's reputation as an enemy of the Left. Still, the radical journalist became Catholic in solidarity with immigrants and the poor.[2] Eventually identifying as both Catholic and anarchist, Day promoted Jesus's inclusive love of neighbor at the Catholic Worker (CW) movement, which she and Peter Maurin founded on the Lower East Side in 1933. Their movement fused Catholicism, Gospel radicalism, and communitarian anarchism to create "a new society within the shell of the old" by inciting "a revolution of the heart."[3] News of the Catholic Workers amazed and perplexed Goldman.

Constructing a Radical Life

Born in Brooklyn, New York, in 1897, Dorothy Day, the middle child of five, grew up in the San Francisco Bay area and Chicago. Survivors of the 1906 San Francisco earthquake, the Days found a temporary relief community whose spontaneous generosity made a lasting impression on Dorothy. The family's fortunes swung back and forth from bourgeois comfort to well-scrubbed poverty. Inquisitive and sensitive, Dorothy was ever conscious of economic and social inequality and the need to eradicate it, sparking her lifelong radicalism.[4]

As adolescents, Dorothy and her older brothers were baptized in the Episcopal Church. She alone, however, cultivated a profound religious sensibility. From the Bible she absorbed Jesus's core teaching: love of God and neighbor. To her, "love" meant unconditional acts of generosity at personal sacrifice. "Neighbor" meant all persons, a radical inclusivity.[5] During an era when class, race, ethnicity, sex, and religious affiliation divided American society, Day discerned that following the example of Christ could heal those divisions.

She furthered her self-education by sampling the forbidden works of socialists Jack London and Upton Sinclair, whose social realism challenged polite progressivism. Unbeholden to corporations, Chicago's advertisement-free paper, *Day Book*, which employed Dorothy's eldest brother, also impressed her. However, Peter Kropotkin's anarchism "appealed to my heart." The Russian advocated cooperatives and attacked "written law" as the enemy of conscience. Day agreed, as she pondered why "so much was done in remedying [social] evil instead of avoiding it."[6]

At age sixteen, Day received an undergraduate scholarship to attend the University of Illinois at Urbana. There she abandoned religious belief in favor of socialism, since Christians were failing to create a just society. Yet, "religious fervor," she confided to her diary, "underlay my radicalism."[7] The campus Scribblers Club prepared her for life as a writer. Providing filler for a local newspaper, among other jobs, she supported her extravagant taste for books at the expense of decent food, clothing, and shelter. Fortunately, Rayna Simons, a wealthy and generous Jewish student, befriended Day and shared her room, food, clothing, and interests. When Day's family returned to New York in 1916, Dorothy dropped out of the university and joined them.

Portfolio in hand, the nineteen-year-old cajoled her way into a job at the *New York Call*, a socialist daily, located on Pearl Street, her introduction to the Lower East Side. Rooming with a Jewish immigrant family on Cherry Street, she declared her independence from her conservative father. An eclectic radical, Day confessed, "When I read Tolstoi, I was an Anarchist," yet she dismissed anarchism as a marginal movement, strongest in ethnic communities. In addition, she identified as a left-wing socialist in loyalty to the *Call*, although the direct action of the Industrial Workers of the World (the Wobblies) interested her most.[8]

An advocacy journalist, Day joined in protests while researching such issues as poverty, working women, prisoner rights, and peace. As Day and other pacifists made their way through Baltimore on a peace pilgrimage to Washington just prior to the April 6, 1917, U.S. entry into World War I, a militarist mob attacked the protesters. In the ensuing melee Day suffered two cracked ribs, a painful contribution to reporting citizen antiwar activism. A dance hall brawl with an unbalanced admirer ended her employment at the paper. Day's editor objected to her breach of radical solidarity when she repelled the man, an anarchist war resister.[9]

Friendship with student peace activists from Columbia University during the peace tour led to Day's employment at the Columbia chapter of the Collegiate Anti-Militarism League (CAML), and she joined her comrades in antiwar propagandizing after the U.S. declaration of war.[10] In May, Congress enacted a military draft, requiring men to register and serve if called up in the lottery. Three of the student CAML activists composed a leaflet decrying conscription and urging potential draftees to refuse to comply. Snitched on by a socialist printer, Day and the two men were arrested for conspiring to encourage others to resist the draft before the tract saw print. The men were tried and found guilty, although Day went free after the men testified that she had completed her work before the law went into effect. Day escaped legally unscathed, but local newspapers headlined the arrests and trial.[11]

Socialists, anarchists, and Wobblies opposed the war and conscription on humanitarian and political grounds.[12] Radicals believed that the war pitted farmers and laborers against their brothers and sisters overseas. Belief in class conflict and worker solidarity grounded the Left's internationalism. Day engaged in cautious activism that evaded the gaze of officials and vigilantes eager to round up dissenters. Defending freedom of expression over wartime postal censorship, she published an editorial in the summer 1917 issue of *War?*, the CAML magazine.[13] She also supported friends who agonized over cooperating with the draft. Anarchist writer Irwin Granich and socialist cartoonist Maurice Becker eventually fled to Mexico to avoid military service and jail. Their experiences further exposed for her the government's suppression of freedom of expression and promotion of personal insecurity for suspected opponents of the war. These experiences contributed to her lifelong opposition to war and the surveillance state.[14]

That summer, Day became an assistant at *The Masses*, a brilliant, avant-garde socialist monthly dedicated to social, cultural, and political rebellion. She moved to an apartment on MacDougal Street, near Union Square, and expanded her circle of literary and artist acquaintances in Greenwich Village's bohemian Left. Within weeks, enforcement of the Espionage Act, enacted in June, further restricted actions and speech by dissenters. By November the magazine was shuttered and its senior staff members were indicted for conspiracy to violate the law. Coached by socialist attorney Morris Hillquit, Day testified on behalf of the *Masses* staffers, helping to win their acquittal. Her cautious opposition to war enhanced her professional credentials and persona as a radical journalist.[15]

Again unemployed, Day and a friend, Peggy Baird, traveled in November to Washington, D.C., where militant suffragists, facing arrest and imprisonment, were picketing at the White House gates to pressure President Woodrow Wilson to support a federal amendment granting voting rights to women. Picketing, arrest, and incarceration in the company of respectable women would enable Day to fatten her freelance portfolio, support political prisoners, and indirectly protest the war. Anarchist editor Hippolyte Havel, himself a veteran of European jails, had explained to her the rights of political prisoners. Kropotkin's influence had convinced her of the uselessness of voting. Ballots, she insisted, could never magically compel politicians to legislate a just society into existence. Only direct action would lead to revolution.[16]

Day and Baird protested with the National Woman's Party (NWP), the militant wing of the woman suffrage movement, headed by Alice Paul and Lucy Burns. Throughout 1917 the NWP regularly sent small delegations of women to picket at the White House. The picketers' presence and their sometimes provocative banners challenged Wilson's stated war goal of "making the world safe for democracy," since American women as well as many Americans of color lacked full citizenship rights. By June, the small but influential group of politically savvy women faced jail sentences and brutal treatment. Their militancy and ambiguous if not oppositional stance on the war contrasted with that of other suffragists, who hoped to trade unquestioning loyalty for the vote.[17]

While picketing, Day fought off drunken servicemen who attacked the "unpatriotic" demonstrators, was arrested three times, and served time for blocking pedestrian traffic, the charge lodged against the NWP picketers. Conditions at the District of Columbia jail and the notorious Occoquan Workhouse appalled the mostly white middle-class women. Not only were they served infested food and denied mail delivery and other rights that were supposed to be accorded to political prisoners, but corrections officials regularly meted out brutal treatment, including beatings, forced feedings, solitary confinement, and other forms of intimidation. To support all political prisoners, Day resisted her jailers by joining the hunger strike and refusing to work or wear prison garb. The NWP thus introduced her to nonviolent resistance, which eventually shaped her way of life and influenced the lives of many of her companions among the Catholic Workers.[18]

After serving sixteen days of her thirty-day sentence, Day was released from jail the Wilson administration granted her a reprieve. She immediately joined seven suffragists who filed affidavits against the brutish Occoquan superintendent and planned a four-hundred-thousand-dollar lawsuit charging that they had been denied their rights as political prisoners during their incarceration. Their threats of legal action faded after the jailer's resigned and the president declared his support for the suffrage amendment. The women thus ultimately won crucial gains in their campaign for the recognition of their citizenship rights. Day, however, disparaged her role as inconsequential.[19]

Determined to be useful, she entered nurse training at Brooklyn's Kings County Hospital in 1918 and wrote on the side. Before completing her course, she became involved in a doomed romantic relationship. After a brief rebound marriage and European sojourn, she unsuccessfully attempted to rekindle the affair with her abusive lover in Chicago. There, during the postwar Red Scare, she was arrested in a Wobbly rooming house with a troubled female friend. Jailed on a trumped-up prostitution charge.[20] As she searched for domestic bliss, Day had not entirely neglected radical politics. In Chicago, she worked briefly for Robert Minor, editor of *The Liberator*, whom she had known at *The Masses*, and contributed a few reviews to the journal, which had become an organ of the Communist Party.

With royalties from her 1924 autobiographical novel, *The Eleventh Virgin*, Day purchased a beach cottage on Staten Island. Ensconced in a warm community of communists and anarchists, she met Forster Batterham and in 1926 gave birth to their daughter, Tamar. The couple shared a passion for nature and a strong distaste for government oppression. They and their circle were deeply troubled by the 1927 execution of anarchists Nicola Sacco and Bartolomeo Vanzetti.[21]

As Day marveled at the gifts of sea, soil, and flesh, her religious inclinations deepened, while the agnostic Batterham fiercely opposed allowing the tentacles of church or state to diminish his freedom. With the encouragement of an elderly nun, Day had Tamar baptized a Catholic but postponed converting for a year and a half in hopes that Batterham would agree to marriage. Stubbornly clinging to their respective principles, the couple separated when she joined the Catholic Church in December 1927. Day nevertheless continued to hope that she and her soul mate would marry, and not until 1933 did she finally accept that the painful separation would be permanent.[22]

To support herself and Tamar, Day worked briefly in the office of the communist-affiliated All-America Anti-Imperialist League, writing publicity and conducting interviews. Financial need and her continuing opposition to the domination and exploitation of poor countries by powerful ones created the unusual situation in which a Catholic was working for a communist organization. Day had known her boss at the League, Manuel Gomez, when he was a student war resister named Charles Phillips. Granich, another longtime friend of Day's who had changed his name to Mike Gold, had switched his allegiance from anarchism to communism and had become editor of the *New Masses*, and she contributed a few articles to the communist literary magazine. Day never joined the Communist Party, instead embracing a heterogeneous radicalism based on long-standing friendships and ideas to which she was attracted. Especially after her conversion, the compelling example of Jesus's love for the poor and marginalized permeated her radicalism.[23]

Catholic and Radical

In December 1932, at the peak of the Great Depression, Day boarded a bus in New York City bound for Washington, D.C. She and labor journalist Mary Heaton Vorse planned to write about the Hunger March organized by communist-influenced Unemployment Councils. The magazine assignments for *Commonweal* and *America* marked a new chapter in Day's life as she struggled to reconcile her religious faith with radical activism.[24] She could not march under the communist banner because the Catholic Church had condemned communism, but she could report to Catholic readers the situation of the unemployed marchers. Having deliberately chosen to join the church of immigrants and the poor, she sought a way to work for social revolution for and with the common people whom Jesus loved.[25]

Day presented a nuanced perspective on communism, one unfamiliar to most Americans and Catholics, who absorbed the Red Scare message then trumpeted by the government, the media, and the churches. Her article for the Jesuits' *America* magazine lambasted the sensationalist coverage of the Hunger March by the "capitalist press," whose biased journalism tainted public opinion by demonizing legitimate protest. Although organized by Communist Party cadres, the march attracted mostly union folks "demonstrating . . . the power of the proletariat." Frightened officials used "machine guns, gas guns, tear and nauseous gas bombs" to greet the peaceful protesters until authorities lifted the ban on the parade to the Capitol.[26] Poverty and inequality caused the unrest, she suggested, not communist agitation.

Day understood that atheistic communists provided an essential service to Christians by demonstrating a concern for workers that highlighted Christians' failure to imitate Jesus's love for the poor. By addressing social needs ignored by the government, the churches, and complacent Christians, communists practiced a "dangerous goodness" that Day expected would encourage workers to give their allegiance to its godless "heresy."[27] If Christians generously practiced works of mercy that fed, clothed, and sheltered all to the point of creating a new social order, she believed, exploitative capitalism would be checked, a new social order would be established, and communist activism would evaporate. By scrimping on accommodations and meals, Day and Vorse gave their savings to the workers' food fund. The women shared the misery of the protesters and provided immediate relief but avoided subsidizing the Communist Party.[28]

Day's assignment marked another personal turning point. In a rare display of an ecumenical spirit during this era, she praised the Fellowship of Reconciliation and the Quakers, Protestants committed to nonviolence, who protested the government's "ludicrous and uncalled-for show of force."[29] Within months, Day was proclaiming and living these beliefs through the Catholic Worker movement, where volunteers crossed class, gender, racial, and ability barriers while advocating cooperation over coercion and nonviolence over force.

Catholic Worker Anarchism

After the December 1932 Hunger March, the thirty-five-year-old Day returned to the tenement apartment on East 15th Street that she and Tamar shared with her brother, John, and his wife, Tessa. Awaiting her return was a stranger, an unkempt fifty-five-year-old undocumented immigrant. The soapbox orators of Union Square would have recognized Peter Maurin as one of their own. Born in 1877 into a large peasant family in southern France, Maurin had been a Christian Brother, a farmer in western Canada, and a French teacher in Chicago. When he met Day, he was working as a day laborer to support his simple needs. Having experienced a profound spiritual rebirth, Maurin took to the streets, proclaiming his "green revolution" program to "rebuild society in the shell of the old." He sought out Day to serve as his publicist, explaining his Christian revolution to the masses.[30] Possessing one suit of clothes and eating and sleeping in Bowery flophouses, Maurin favorably impressed Day as "the most completely detached person it has ever been my privilege to meet."[31]

With his encouragement, Day began editing, publishing, and distributing a paper, affordably priced at a penny and aimed at workers and intellectuals. The *Catholic Worker* publicized a message of radical Christian love and nonviolent strategies for reconfiguring the social structure, which seemed to be collapsing under the weight of the Great Depression. To finance the printing of the first edition, she delayed payment of her utility bills and scraped together writing fees and small donations. Future issues would be financed in a similar fashion, with authors donating their work. In the spirit of anarchism and the "little way" spirituality of St. Therese of Lisieux, Day preferred small donations over large ones or the support of foundations. This strategy not only prevented moneyed interests from dictating conditions that could undermine Catholic Worker principles but gave ordinary people a stake in the movement.

First sold on May Day 1933 to a largely communist mob at Union Square, the *Catholic Worker* proposed a Christian anarchist alternative to the Communist Party and its paper, the *Daily Worker*. Cheers and jeers greeted the first edition of the paper. Catholic Worker activists typically hawked the paper in public spaces where working folks congregated, including Columbus Circle, Madison

Reading the *Catholic Worker*, Union Square, 1940.
Courtesy of the Department of Special Collections and University Archives, Marquette University Libraries, Milwaukee, Wisconsin.

Square Garden, outside St. Patrick's Cathedral, and on the subway. Catholic Workers and communists occasionally encountered each other when selling their papers on the same corner. One of the volunteers playfully taunted the communists by calling out, "Read *The Catholic Worker* daily."[32] Circulation multiplied with subscriptions by mail, including parish bulk orders, spreading the CW program throughout the United States and to remote parts of the world.[33]

Written from a socially engaged Catholic viewpoint unfamiliar even to many Catholics, the paper opposed communism and atheism as well as capitalism and materialism by advocating systemic change that addressed the root causes of injustice.[34] Articles on racial inequality, strikes, and boycotts filled the publication's pages, along with excerpts from papal statements in support of economic justice and criticism of certain communist tactics. Maurin's "Easy Essays," free verse reflections illuminating his program of houses of hospitality for the homeless, farming communes for sustenance, and discussion for the "clarification of thought," presented the movement's platform in everyday terms. By exposing social, economic, and political abuses and providing a revolutionary communitarian program to eliminate them, the paper advocated a Christian anarchist social order.

During the paper's first decade of publication, Day typically referred to the Catholic Workers generically as a radical Catholic movement. Alert readers discerned the influence of anarchist thought. Following the lead of Kropotkin and Tolstoy, Day and Maurin inspired a Christian anarchist spirit that empowered individuals to create small communities with minimal rules to advance nonviolent revolution through love of neighbor and direct action. "The Catholic Worker professed itself pacifist and anarchist in principle," she later noted, "and those who did not like those terms, Maurin among them, used 'personalist and communitarian.'"[35]

The *Catholic Worker* announced scheduled discussions at the house of hospitality, which had been opened on East 15th Street and provided space for Maurin, who relished face-to-face indoctrination, and invited speakers to interact with whoever showed up. In 1934 he took his message of Christian revolution to an annex on 7th Avenue in Harlem. The rental agreement soon collapsed because his pacifist ideas irritated the landlord. Next, he proposed a daily workers' school for ten months, causing Day to grumble about already working fifteen-hour days.[36] Even at Tamar's 1944 wedding, the indefatigable Maurin could not resist lecturing against a "pigs for profit" scheme advanced by some at the farming commune near Easton, Pennsylvania.[37]

Priest advisers had proposed that Day begin the Catholic Worker movement without asking permission of church authorities. She followed their advice, claiming, with humor, that the archbishop would not wish to incur the debts of an unproven movement. In 1936, church officials asked Day to name a spiritual adviser, an approved priest who was qualified to guide the paper on doctrinal issues only.[38] Day readily agreed, since social and political issues constituted "matters on which [the laity] are free to express our opinion."[39]

Day regularly exercised her "absolute liberty" on these issues. Although she found much to admire in Catholic social teaching, she sometimes openly disagreed with church officials on nondoctrinal matters. She criticized Pope Pius XI's position on the Spanish Civil War, commenting that the Falangists' program to provide food for children "does not prove they are not fascist in tendency."[40] Closer to home, she supported a 1949 strike by cemetery workers employed by the archdiocese and petitioned Cardinal Francis Spellman to meet the laborers' demands.[41] In stark contrast to the cardinal's "America right or wrong" approach to Cold War policies, Day advocated an activist pacifism that refused to engage in war manufacturing, to take cover during a compulsory air raid drill, or to submit to military induction. To his credit, Spellman and successive New York prelates recognized the soundness of Day's spirituality and tolerated her movement.

Houses of Hospitality

Day's apartment and office, where visitors could "enter the kitchen to make... a pot of coffee," initially served as precursor to a full-fledged house of hospitality where guests and volunteers could find food, shelter, clothing, and community. By the winter of 1933, following Wobbly tradition, Day planned to have a pot of stew "to which everyone contributes a potato or carrot" bubbling on the stove for all to share.[42] Poor folks, she claimed, would see a storefront "so humble that no one passing by... is afraid to come in."[43] For homeless men, she soon rented an eight-dollar-per-month apartment "abandoned even by slum dwellers."[44] Day modeled CW houses on the familiar hospitality of the Left, whereas Maurin sought to replicate the hospitality of medieval monasticism. From this modest start, the movement grew to include a succession of tenements and apartments scattered throughout the Lower East Side in which Day and volunteers would live in community with the poor as well as affiliated houses and farms throughout the country.

At the height of the depression in 1932–33, the poor of the Lower East Side at best could find housing in neglected, old tenements lacking modern amenities, such as steam heat and appliances. Unemployment in New York City topped 30 percent. Although cold water flats were available, many poor people could not pay the minimal rent. Such folks moved into more crowded quarters, lodged with friends or extended family, moved every few months when evicted, or found themselves out on the streets. Overcrowded and unpleasant, the Municipal Lodging House sheltered others. Rent strikes and demonstrations, many organized by communists, helped to draw attention to the housing crisis and provided the poor with a measure of relief, but many still needed assistance.[45]

By 1936, a larger CW house of hospitality was operating on Mott Street, where neighbors from Eastern Europe mingled with Chinese and Italian immigrants and the down and out. Scrubbing and painting brightened the twenty-room rear tenement and storefront, but Day admitted that even after improvements, the old building failed city code requirements. Not only did it "conflict with fire laws," but its kitchen attracted unwanted attention from the Health Department. Day responded to officials with a lesson in Catholic anarchism by arguing that St. Joseph's House was a private home and that all of the residents were family—brothers and sisters in Christ.[46] Consequently, laws that applied to an organized charity, where professional staff served clients, should not apply to the Mott Street house. To support her claim, Day demonstrated that the New York CW had not registered as a tax-exempt nonprofit institution.

Even those for whom St. Joseph's House could not provide a bed could receive a meal in the house's breadline, which at times of high unemployment stretched nearly a full block along Mott Street between Hester and Canal.[47] Neighbors, too, could depend on the CW for emergency assistance, including help during evictions, and generously reciprocated when able.

Guests and volunteers—sometimes difficult to distinguish one from another—created a community of shared poverty. Whereas unemployment or disability caused the poverty of guests, many volunteers freely chose poverty. Guests and volunteers shared rooms and meals. Volunteers received no wages. Those with earnings from other jobs contributed to the common pot. Small donations of money and essentials from supporters met most of the community's needs. When debts mounted and donations declined, Day prayerfully "picketed" St. Joseph by slipping unpaid bills under his statue and wrote appeals in the paper.[48]

Unlike settlement houses and skid row missions, the Catholic Workers welcomed the needy without attempting to conform dysfunctional behaviors to bourgeois respectability or force participation in religious services, viewing the poor as "the ambassadors of God" with a birthright of human dignity and a respect for their ability to make their own decisions. Unlike the situation at the Municipal Lodging House, the Catholic Workers' guests were community members to their chosen extent, free to remain in the building during the day, and not clients to be quizzed and processed. "Ours is not a turnstile charity," Day insisted.[49] The sterile and impersonal approach all too common in public welfare and professional social work had no place in houses of hospitality. Women and men volunteers crossed white middle-class gender boundaries to care for guests, write for the paper, and engage in nonviolent revolution.

Catholic Worker houses typically operated with a minimum of rules imposed on residents. When overzealous volunteers occasionally posted rules for community members, guests appealed to Day, who ordered the rules removed.[50] As a guide for the movement, Christ's law of love required all to recognize the needs of others and take personal initiative in meeting those needs as much as possible. The operation of the houses reflected the values of Christian anarchism, the catechism teaching of human dignity for all, and French philosopher Emmanuel Mounier's idea of personalism. A contemporary of Day and Maurin, Mounier emphasized the Christian ideals of individual responsibility, loving service, and community. Personalists encouraged selflessness, cooperation, and patience through example. Day performed disagreeable tasks, among them cleaning toilets and battling vermin infestations, in addition to publishing the paper and speaking throughout the country to raise funds. Ideals such as individual initiative, responsibility for oneself and others, rejection of coercion, and disdain for hierarchy grounded the anarchist Catholic Worker community.

In addition to meeting the immediate needs of the poor with dignity, Catholic Workers labored for a social revolution. Traditional Catholic teaching advocated the practice of the works of mercy, including feeding the hungry, housing the homeless, and forgiving all injuries. For centuries, people of faith had practiced these charitable acts, but observing them had failed to accomplish justice on earth. By embracing nonviolent direct action as well as acts of charity, Catholic Workers rejected the notion that ordinary people must endure injustice on earth and await their pie-in-the-sky reward after death. Small communities provided an alternative to the oppressiveness of rugged individualism and the nation-state and prepared for social transformation.

Farming Communes and Industrial Unions

A man of the soil, Maurin developed a revolutionary theory of labor that challenged dysfunctional industrial capitalism. Day agreed with much of his message. For Maurin, the displacement of farming as the foundation of society by industrialization initiated a seismic shift that produced economic depression, unemployment, and attendant social ills. Referencing Mohandas Gandhi's insight that "industrialism is evil," Maurin observed that it "brings idleness both to the capitalist class and the working class." Thus, Maurin proposed the establishment of "farming communes" or "agronomic universities" that would teach families how to feed themselves and create small cooperative communities. Handicrafts would meet simple needs. Commune members could produce and share all that was required to meet basic standards of decency. As an alternative to wage labor, he favored persons "offering their services as a gift."[51] Farming and handicraft labor, he believed, also served a spiritual purpose by contributing to greater happiness and meaning in life. Influenced by the example of St. Francis of Assisi and by Kropotkin's writings, Maurin decried the "superfluous goods" produced by industrial capitalism. A Christian communitarian anarchist society, he suggested, could function without corporations, money, banks, or lending. Prosperity and growth did not matter.[52]

The first attempt to go to the land began in 1935 with the purchase of a one-acre garden plot on Staten Island, a most inadequate farming commune. The following year, the Catholic Worker purchased Maryfarm, near Easton, Pennsylvania. For approximately a decade, the CW facility there combined farming with religious retreats, summer camp for urban children, and a healing escape from urban life. The poor level of capitalization and a spiritual preference for manual labor made work arduous, and not all volunteers performed physical tasks effectively. Catholic Workers steadfastly tried to find ways to make the farming commune work, but friction developed between those who worked and those who philosophized about it. The attempt of a few Catholic Worker families to privatize their parcels at Easton and to isolate themselves from the sometimes unruly guests from the city increased the pressure on Day to resolve the dispute. She eventually ceded the plots claimed by the families, sold off the rest, and purchased property near Newburgh, New York. Responding to changing needs, the Catholic Worker subsequently relocated its farm to Staten Island and later north of the city on the Hudson River in Tivoli.[53]

To complement farm labor, Day enthusiastically supported industrial unions as an essential path toward social revolution. Long a supporter of labor, she discovered the social encyclicals of Popes Leo XIII and Pius XI, "Rerum Novarum" (1891) and "Quadragesimo Anno" (1931), which clarified the rights and duties of workers and employers and approved of organizing unions. Not all Catholics, however, accepted these nondogmatic teachings.[54]

In the pages of her paper, Day blasted dangerous working conditions and valorized labor organizers while defending the movement's efforts to support industrial unions. Taking a position at odds with the U.S. Catholic bishops, most of whom defended child labor as the right of families, she endorsed its prohibition.[55]

When Borden Milk delivery workers and the company disagreed over the drivers' membership in the Teamsters Union in 1936, Day sided with the workers and asked CW supporters throughout the United States to boycott Borden products. Her position alienated readers who approved of feeding, sheltering, and clothing the poor without addressing the underlying causes of injustice. Whereas Day criticized the individualistic and elitist values of the American Federation of Labor, she provided generous support to striking seamen in 1936 who favored the National Maritime Union, an affiliate of the Congress of Industrial Organizations. Catholic Worker dedication to the seamen's cause led to the opening of a temporary house of hospitality on 10th Avenue, near the Chelsea docks, despite opposition from those who feared communist influence in the National Maritime Union. In 1937, Day traveled to Flint, Michigan, and hoisted herself through a window to interview sit-down strikers at the Fisher Body Company. This radical nonviolent strategy recognized that workers had a right to own the means of production, a position that Day passionately supported, since it sought to build a new society. In 1973, at age seventy-five, she was imprisoned for the final time when she traveled to California to support peaceful picketing as part of Cesar Chavez's attempt to unionize migrant farm laborers into the United Farm Workers.[56]

Politics and Pacifism

Initially opposed only to imperialist wars, Day rejected the use of violence after her conversion. She championed Christian anarchopacifism in the pages of the *Catholic Worker*. The essential Christian beliefs that supported CW hospitality, labor justice, and social revolution likewise sustained its pacifism. These included the brotherhood and sisterhood of all persons as children of God, the biblical command to love one's neighbor, and Mystical Body of Christ theology, which respected human uniqueness and the contributions of each individual to society while eliminating divisive distinctions.

Day repudiated the concept of a just war. Adhering to a stricter standard than that required by the Catholic Church, she based her position on Jesus's acceptance of death and on the destructive nature of modern warfare.[57] Christian pacifism required bold action; it was not synonymous with inaction or cowardice, as critics suggested. She favored preparing an arsenal for peace—"spiritual weapons" that included prayer, fasting, penance, and picketing. Spiritual weapons released the grace of God and in combination with human agency could alleviate suffering and end conflict. Furthermore, they strengthened pacifists' resolve to engage in noncooperation with the war effort, even in defiance of the law.[58]

Catholic Worker pacifism privileged respect for individual conscience, a right guaranteed by the Catholic Church but not always honored in practice. Like other Christian anarchists, Day taught that neither government nor human authority had the right to compel persons to violate their religious or ethical beliefs. When Jesus said to "render unto Caesar the things that are Caesar's, and to God the things that are God's," Day understood him to mean that God's law always superseded human laws. The right of conscience, she believed, guaranteed individuals their right to resist cooperation with any aspect of war making. She thus saw imprisoned war resisters as political prisoners.[59]

As a Catholic anarchist, Day opposed divisive ideologies such as nationalism. Criticizing state power, respecting individual conscience, resisting oppression nonviolently, and working toward the common good and the unity of all people constituted key values of the CW's anarchopacifism.[60]

Catholic Worker pacifism challenged the beliefs of conventional Catholics and Left and Right radicalism. In 1927, strong public revulsion in the wake of World War I inspired a few prominent Catholics to organize the first American Catholic peace group, the Catholic Association for International Peace. The organization rejected pacifism outright, instead adhering to just war teaching, which required Christians to apply criteria to determine whether the reasons for war and the means of fighting it met certain standards. In practice, the group regularly concluded that U.S. wars met just war requirements, whereas the CW remained pacifist in wartime.[61] In 1936, during the Spanish Civil War, Day proposed a neutrality of thought, much to the irritation of Catholics who believed that Francisco Franco's forces were defending the rights of the church against communism. Despite Day's frequent criticism of the growing threat of fascism in Europe, the Left accused the CW of fascist sympathies for failing to aid the Loyalists and the Lincoln Brigade against Franco. The Right branded Day and the CW communists. Day did not back down.[62]

Reflecting the unsettling rise of fascism and Stalinist totalitarianism, by early 1937 the New York CW initiated a peace group, Pax, to educate Catholics about the impossibility of a just war in the modern era. Insisting that honoring one's conscience supplanted "misguided loyalty to specious ideals," Pax pioneered support for Catholic conscientious objection at a time when the law recognized this status only for members of the historic peace churches.[63] In 1940 Day and volunteer Joseph Zarrella traveled to Washington, D.C., to testify against the proposed peacetime draft. But the Burke Wadsworth bill became law.

The practice of pacifism in wartime came at a high cost. The Japanese attack on Pearl Harbor and Nazi aggression as well as such lofty war aims as the Four Freedoms sparked public support for World War II. A majority of ordinary

Catholics and the U.S. church hierarchy considered the war against Japanese militarism and Nazism just. Concerned about preventing Nazi atrocities, some Catholic Workers openly criticized pacifism as an ineffective response, a few members joined the war effort. Day did not condemn them, but she demanded that CW houses distribute the pacifist *Catholic Worker*, whether or not they agreed with it. Those who refused to do so, she declared, did not belong to the movement. She also urged workers to avoid taking jobs in war industries. Despite complaints to the Archdiocese of New York about Catholic Worker pacifism, it did not violate church doctrine, and church authorities took no action against Day or the paper. Director J. Edgar Hoover of the Federal Bureau of Investigation secretly recommended her internment if deemed in the national interest, but she was not interned, and the government did not censor the *Catholic Worker*.[64] Low wartime unemployment and strong public support for the war led to the closure of several CW houses, and the paper's circulation declined drastically.[65]

Undaunted, Day broadened the CW's pacifist activism during the war. Despite limited resources, the Catholic Worker furnished modest financial aid to Catholic conscientious objectors in Civilian Public Service camps. In response to a 1942 proposal for total mobilization, Day joined other women pacifists in signing a statement refusing to cooperate with any draft of women. Day criticized the internment of Japanese Americans and condemned the use of atomic bombs against Japan as intrinsically immoral for their indiscriminate slaughter of tens of thousands.[66]

Rejecting the anticommunist militancy of the government and American church leadership at the height of the Cold War, Day and other Catholic Workers joined radical pacifists in resisting compulsory civil defense air raid drills. For several years in the 1950s and early 1960s, Day and her companions refused to take cover, were arrested, and served jail sentences. Radical pacifists, including the CW and the War Resisters League and Judith Malina of the Living Theatre, disagreed with the government's stand that citizens could survive nuclear war. Pacifist noncooperation with the compulsory drills helped to end them.[67]

One of the earliest critics of U.S. policy in Vietnam, Day in 1954 prophetically repudiated a war for the protection of the American standard of living.[68] As military involvement in Southeast Asia increased during the 1960s, she supported conscientious objectors and war resisters. She welcomed the creation of a new Pax group and the Catholic Peace Fellowship, part of the interdenominational Fellowship of Reconciliation, and signed complicity statements that put her at risk for prosecution. The Catholic Worker's compelling case for peace, its well-established nonviolent activism, denunciations of war by Popes John XXIII and Paul VI, and teachings on war and conscience approved during the Second Vatican Council (1962–65) drew young volunteers to the CW movement during the Vietnam War era. Picketing, draft card burning, support for conscientious objectors and resisters, thoughtful engagement with changes in Catholic thinking on war, as well as prayer and fasting inspired Catholics and others to question and challenge war as a means of settling scores within and among nations.[69]

Although Day had influenced many participants in draft board raids, in which activists seized and destroyed draft files, these actions generated heated debate about the nature of CW nonviolence. Could innocent bystanders be harmed while opposing war? Was it moral to seize and destroy what did not belong to the protesters? Did surreptitious actions or escape underground violate the openness advocated by Gandhi? Day ultimately responded with loving support for the imprisoned activists and a disclaimer: their acts did not define the Catholic Worker approach.[70]

Conclusion

In the aftermath of World War II, the Catholic Worker frequently identified itself as an anarchist movement, a rhetorical shift that likely stemmed from postwar developments. Whereas Cold War–era government repression further demonized and diminished the domestic communist movement, Day courageously maintained the integrity of CW radicalism by continuing to criticize the inherent faults of capitalism and the national security state and by defending human rights for all, even communists. Volunteers such as Robert Ludlow, a Catholic anarchist theorist, and Ammon Hennacy, the self-proclaimed "one man revolution," boldly articulated and creatively practiced Catholic Worker anarchism as befitting a movement that, against the odds, had survived the depression, war, and antiradical repression. Simultaneously, an emerging postwar American anarchism, bold and vibrant beyond ethnic enclaves, espoused a "practical" way "to prefigure the world anarchists hoped to live in."[71] Empowered by nonviolent spiritual weapons, the Catholic Worker pioneered communities of Christian "practical anarchism."

New to the Catholic Worker in 1975, volunteer Robert Ellsberg asked how Day reconciled anarchist thought with Catholicism. "It's never been a problem with me," she replied.[72] Day had managed to synthesize a critique of economic, social, and political power grounded in insights from Jesus, Catholic social teaching, and diverse radical thinkers such as Marx and Kropotkin. Thanks to her efforts and those of volunteers and supporters, the experiment of a Catholic paper addressed to workers, urban houses that housed and nourished body and soul, farming communes that taught self-sufficiency and sharing, and pacifism that underscored the common humanity of all persons, Catholic Worker anarchism suggested ways to challenge capitalist, communist, fascist, nationalist, and racist systems of human oppression.

Until her death in November 1980, at the heart of Day's belief was Jesus's law of love. It had informed her youthful radicalism and beckoned her into the church of the immigrant and the poor. Eventually, it guided her founding of a movement dedicated to serving the poor, nonviolently advancing social revolution, and renewing faith by refocusing Christian spirituality on a "revolution of the heart"—the potential of love to make a difference in people's lives and in society. For Catholics and other religious believers, the CW challenged the notion of privatized faith as the fulfillment of spiritual practice. For anarchists and other radicals, the movement demonstrated care for the poor combined with revolutionary acts to challenge the political, social, and economic status quo. Dorothy Day labored to bring the Bowery, Union Square, and other Catholic Worker spaces a little closer to heaven.

Notes

I thank Theresa Ahern, MSBT, Faith Bonitz, Wendy Chmielewski, and Phillip Runkel for providing me with access to obscure sources. Sarah Elbert, Kaitlyn Hennessy, Christine Igielski, Andrew Leet, and David O'Brien generously commented on earlier drafts. The University of St. Thomas Center for Faculty Development provided essential support. I accept responsibility for the content.

1. Emma Goldman to Ammon Hennacy, July 24, 1939, Catholic Worker Papers, Series 11.2, Box 1, Marquette University, Milwaukee, Wisconsin.

2. Dorothy Day, *From Union Square to Rome* (Silver Spring, Md.: Preservation of the Faith Press, 1938), 138–39.

3. Peter Maurin, *Easy Essays* (London: Sheed and Ward, 1938), 99; Dorothy Day, *The Long Loneliness* (New York: Harper and Row, 1952), 196; Dorothy Day, *Loaves and Fishes* (New York: Harper and Row, 1963), 210.

4. Sources documenting Day's early life are limited. She wrote three memoirs: the thinly fictionalized *Eleventh Virgin* (New York: Boni, 1924); *From Union Square to Rome*, the story of her conversion; and *Long Loneliness*, which also covers the Catholic Worker. Although similar, the three volumes differ somewhat in details and perspective.

5. In *The Eleventh Virgin*, written prior to her conversion, Day described her childhood religiosity; see 16–19, 41, 48–53.

6. Day, *From Union Square to Rome*, 45–47.

7. Dorothy Day, *The Duty of Delight: The Diaries of Dorothy Day*, ed. Robert Ellsberg (Milwaukee, Wis.: Marquette University Press, 2008), 37.

8. Day, *From Union Square to Rome*, 68; Day, *Long Loneliness*, 62.

9. Day, *From Union Square to Rome*, 71–78; Day, *Long Loneliness*, 58–61.

10. Day, *From Union Square to Rome*, 76–79. Day erroneously referred to the CAML as the "Anti-Conscription League," perhaps confusing it with Emma Goldman's No Conscription League, whose members included Day's friend, Irwin Granich.

11. "Columbia Men Found Guilty," *New York Sun*, June 22, 1917. For a more complete account of Day's opposition to World War I and her friends' difficulties, see Anne Klejment, "The Radical Origins of Catholic Pacifism: Dorothy Day and the Lyrical Left during World War I," in *American Catholic Pacifism: The Influence of Dorothy Day and the Catholic Worker Movement*, ed. Anne Klejment and Nancy L. Roberts (Westport, Conn.: Praeger, 1996), especially 16–22.

12. For a thoughtful analysis of wartime coercion, see Christopher Capozzola, *Uncle Sam Wants You: World War I and the Making of the Modern American Citizen* (New York: Oxford University Press, 2008). The *New York Call*, among other New York dailies, provided detailed accounts of radical protest and arrest.

13. Dorothy Day, "The Right to Criticize," *War?*, Summer 1917, 5–6.

14. Day, *Long Loneliness*, 71; Dorothy Day, *On Pilgrimage: The Sixties* (New York: Curtis, 1972), 304; Klejment, "Radical Origins," 20.

15. Day, *Long Loneliness*, 68–69, 87.

16. Day, *From Union Square to Rome*, 81–87; Day, *Long Loneliness*, 72–83. Day wrote a thinly fictionalized but detailed account of the suffrage protests in *Eleventh Virgin*, 180–218.

17. J. D. Zahniser and Amelia R. Fry, *Alice Paul: Claiming Power* (New York: Oxford University Press, 2014), 254–97.

18. For the "silent sentinel" campaign, see ibid. For a more complete account of Day's suffrage activism based in part on the NWP's records, see Anne Klejment, "Dorothy Day: Political Prisoner," paper presented at the Spring Meeting of the American Catholic Historical Association, 2014.

19. Doris Stevens, *Jailed for Freedom: The Story of the Militant American Suffragist Movement* (1920; New York: Schocken, 1976), 241; "Last of Women Pickets Set Free," *New York Herald*, November 29, 1917; "Pickets Sue for $400,000.00," *Suffragist*, December 15, 1917; Klejment, "Dorothy Day: Political Prisoner."

20. Charles Shipman, *It Had to Be Revolution: Memoirs of an American Radical* (Ithaca: Cornell University Press, 1993), 143–44. Shipman (who also went by the names Gomez and Phillips) helped Day during this episode, but her accounts and his differ in details.

21. Day, *Long Loneliness*, 109–47.

22. For Day's life during the 1920s, see Day, *Long Loneliness*, 93–151. For supplemental information, see Jim Forest, *All Is Grace: A Biography of Dorothy Day* (Maryknoll, N.Y.: Orbis, 2011), 56–95.

23. Day, *Long Loneliness*, 152, 137; Klejment, "Radical Origins," 23.

24. Dorothy Day, "Hunger Marchers in Washington," *America*, December 2, 1932, 277–79; Dorothy Day, "Real Revolutionists," *Commonweal*, January 11, 1933, 293–94. Both magazines were highly regarded.

25. Day wrote several accounts of the march that differ slightly in details and perspective. See Dorothy Day, "Human Document," *The Sign* 12 (November 1932): 223–24; Dorothy Day, *House of Hospitality* (New York: Sheed and Ward, 1939), v–xiii; Day, *Long Loneliness*, 162–66.

26. Day, "Hunger Marchers," 277.

27. Dorothy Day, "The Diabolic Plot," *America*, April 29, 1933, 82.

28. Day, *Long Loneliness*, 165.

29. Day, "Hunger Marchers," 278.

30. Key interpretations of Maurin's life include Arthur Sheehan, *Peter Maurin: Gay Believer* (Garden City, N.Y.: Hanover House, 1959); Mary Segers, "Equality and Christian Anarchism," *Review of Politics* 40 (1978): especially 196–220; Marc Ellis, *Peter Maurin: Prophet in the Twentieth Century* (New York: Paulist, 1981); Dorothy Day with Francis Sicius, *Peter Maurin: Apostle to the World* (Maryknoll, N.Y.: Orbis, 2004); Anthony Novitsky, "Peter Maurin's Green Revolution," *Review of Politics* 37 (1975): 83–103.

31. Day, *House of Hospitality*, xix.

32. Stanley Vishnewski, *Wings of the Dawn* (New York: Catholic Worker, 1984), 46.

33. For circulation statistics, see Nancy L. Roberts, *Dorothy Day and the Catholic Worker* (Albany: State University of New York Press, 1984), 179–82.

34. Dorothy Day, "The Catholic Worker," *The Rosary*, November 1933, 11.

35. Day, *On Pilgrimage*, 13.

36. Day, *House of Hospitality*, 68.

37. Day, *Long Loneliness*, 242.

38. Dorothy Day, *All the Way to Heaven: The Selected Letters of Dorothy Day*, ed. Robert Ellsberg (Milwaukee: Marquette University Press, 2010), 85.

39. Day, *House of Hospitality*, 78.

40. Day, *Duty of Delight*, 35.

41. Day, *All the Way to Heaven*, 170–71.

42. Dorothy Day, "Start of 'Catholic Worker' Described by Its Founder," *Queen's Work*, April 1934, 3; Day, "Catholic Worker," 11, 30.

43. Day, *All the Way to Heaven*, 57.

44. Day, *House of Hospitality*, xxxi.

45. Jared Day, *Urban Castles: Tenement Housing and Landlord Activism in New York City, 1890–1943* (New York: Columbia University Press, 1999), 169–80.

46. Day, *House of Hospitality*, 212, 240.

47. Ibid., 200.

48. Forest, *All Is Grace*, 130–33; Day, *House of Hospitality*, 118.

49. Day, *House of Hospitality*, 189.

50. Rosalie Riegle, *Dorothy Day: Portraits by Those Who Knew Her* (Maryknoll, N.Y.: Orbis, 2003), 3.

51. Maurin, *Easy Essays* (1938), 76–84.

52. Ibid., 82–83, 76; Marc H. Ellis, *Peter Maurin*, 43; Peter Maurin, *Easy Essays* (Chicago: Franciscan Herald, 1977), 122–23.

53. For more on the farming communes, see Mel Piehl, *Breaking Bread: The Catholic Worker and the Origin of Catholic Radicalism in America* (Philadelphia: Temple University Press, 1982), 63–64, 128–33, 242.

54. Dorothy Day, *By Little and by Little: The Selected Writings of Dorothy Day*, ed. Robert Ellsberg (New York: Knopf, 1983), 235–51. The paper occasionally used quotations from the encyclicals as filler. See, for example, *Catholic Worker*, October 1936. During the 1930s, Day frequently referenced the social teachings of these popes.

55. Virtually every issue of the *Catholic Worker* during the 1930s contained major articles on working conditions and strikes. One of Day's most notable (unsigned) statements on labor was "C.W. States Stand on Strikes," *Catholic Worker*, July 1936. For additional writings on labor in the *Catholic Worker*, see Anne Klejment and Alice Klejment, *Dorothy Day and The Catholic Worker: A Bibliography and Index* (New York: Garland, 1986), 43–111. For a brief account of the child labor issue, see William D. Miller, *A Harsh and Dreadful Love: Dorothy Day and the Catholic Worker Movement* (New York: Liveright, 1973), 85–87.

56. For CW support for labor, see Neil Betten, *Catholic Activism and the Industrial Worker* (Gainesville: University Presses of Florida, 1976), 48–72.

57. Dorothy Day, "The Use of Force," *Catholic Worker*, November 1936.

58. Day may have borrowed the concept of spiritual weapons from John J. Hugo, a priest whose teachings she favored. See, for example, John J. Hugo, "Weapons of the Spirit. IV," *Catholic Worker*, February 1943. From the 1940s onward, Day advocated the use of "spiritual weapons" against war. See, for example, Dorothy Day, "Poverty and Pacifism," *Catholic Worker*, December 1944; Anne Klejment, "The Spirituality of Dorothy Day's Pacifism," *U.S. Catholic Historian* 27:2 (2009): 18–23; "Lay Apostolate," *Catholic Worker*, November 1939.

59. Patrick G. Coy, "Conscription and the Catholic Conscience in World War II," in *American Catholic Pacifism*, ed. Klejment and Roberts, 47–63; Dorothy Day, "If Conscription Comes for Women," *Catholic Worker*, January 1943.

60. Fred Boehrer, "Diversity, Plurality, and Ambiguity . . ." in *Dorothy Day and the Catholic Worker Movement: Centenary Essays*, ed. William Thorn, Phillip M. Runkel, and Susan Mountin (Milwaukee: Marquette University Press, 2001), 95.

61. Patricia McNeal, *Harder Than War: Catholic Peacemaking in Twentieth-Century America* (New Brunswick, N.J.: Rutgers University Press, 1992), especially 19, 155–56.

62. John Leo LeBrun, "The Role of the Catholic Worker Movement in American Pacifism, 1933–1972" (Ph.D. diss., Case Western Reserve University 1973), 65–74; J. David Valaik, "American Catholic Dissenters and the Spanish Civil War," *Catholic Historical Review* 53:4 (1968): 542–44.

63. Dorothy Day, "C.W. to Organize Catholic Group to Protest War," *Catholic Worker*, October 1936.

64. J. E. Hoover, "Memorandum for Mr. L. M. C. Smith," April 3, 1941, Dorothy Day—The Catholic Worker—FBI-FOIA 62-61208, vol. 1; Francis J. Sicius, "Prophecy Faces Tradition: The Pacifist Debate during World War II," in *American Catholic Pacifism*, ed. Klejment and Roberts, 65–76.

"To the Workers: An Appeal to Workers to Sacrifice for Peace," *Catholic Worker*, October 1939.

65. Roberts, *Dorothy Day*, 132, 180.

66. Gordon C. Zahn, *Another Part of the War: The Camp Simon Story* (Amherst: University of Massachusetts Press, 1979), 36; McNeal, *Harder Than War*, 57. "Forty-Eight Women Will Not Register," *Catholic Worker*, December 1942; Dorothy Day, "If Conscription Comes for Women," *Catholic Worker*, January 1943; Dorothy Day, "Grave Injustice Done Japanese on West Coast," *Catholic Worker*, June 1942; Dorothy Day, "We Go On Record—," *Catholic Worker*, September 1945.

67. Day, *Loaves and Fishes*, 160–78.

68. Dorothy Day, "Theophane Venard and Ho Chi Minh," *Catholic Worker*, May 1954.

69. Eileen Egan, "The Struggle of the Small Vehicle, Pax," in *American Catholic Pacifism*, ed. Klejment and Roberts, especially 126; McNeal, *Harder Than War*, 280 n. 24; Anne Klejment and Nancy L. Roberts, "The Catholic Worker and the Vietnam War," in *American Catholic Pacifism*, ed. Klejment and Roberts, 156–58, 160, 162–63, 165–66.

70. Anne Klejment, "War Resistance and Property Destruction: The Catonsville Nine Draft Board Raid and Catholic Worker Pacifism," in *A Revolution of the Heart: Essays on the Catholic Worker*, ed. Patrick G. Coy (Philadelphia: Temple University Press, 1988), 284–300.

71. Andrew Cornell, "A New Anarchism Emerges, 1940–1954," *Journal for the Study of Radicalism* 5:1 (2011): 106.

72. Quoted in Riegle, *Dorothy Day*, 169.

New Wind

The Why?/Resistance Group and the Roots of Contemporary Anarchism, 1942–1954

ANDREW CORNELL

In 1920, Audrey Goodfriend was born into a Jewish anarchist family residing in the Bronx. She remained an anarchist until the day she died in 2012, regularly attending a weekly anti-authoritarian discussion group in Berkeley, California, well into her eighties despite being decades older than the other participants. Goodfriend did not simply witness the periods of growth and decline that anarchism experienced during the twentieth and early twenty-first centuries. She played an active role in reformulating and reshaping the movement, especially as a founding member and secretary of the New York City–based Why? Group. Established in 1942 to publish the monthly journal *Why?*, the group renamed itself and its publication *Resistance* in 1947 and remained active until 1954.

Though barely remembered by scholars or activists today, the Why?/Resistance Group played an essential role in keeping the anarchist movement alive in the United States during the inhospitable middle years of the twentieth century. Goodfriend and other members served as connective tissue between the prewar American anarchist movement rooted in working-class immigrant communities and the circles of younger artists, writers, and intellectuals that carried anarchist ideas and practices into the New Left of the 1960s. In their writings, activities, and ways of living, members of the Why?/Resistance Group pushed anarchism in new directions that reverberate up to the present.

Members embraced pacifist ideas and tactics, abandoned attempts to organize workers at their places of employment, placed new emphasis on the politics of sexuality and family, devoted considerable attention to the arts, and decided strategically to focus on "living an anarchist life" in prefigurative communities of like-minded individuals. This chapter briefly examines the origins of this coterie of New York anarchists, the ideas that shaped their practice, their relations with other important individuals and organizations, and the group's eventual dissolution.

Origins

The roots of the Why? Group lie in a multipurpose room at the Shalom Aleichem cooperative housing complex, just south of Van Cortland Park in the Bronx. The Shalom Aleichem Houses were one of four cooperative apartment complexes built in the area by Jewish unionists and radicals in the late 1920s.[1] Audrey Goodfriend's family, which had immigrated from Poland before she was born, took an apartment there, joining many other Jewish anarchists, socialists, and communists who wanted more space, fresh air, and communal resources than the tenements of the Lower East Side offered.

Goodfriend's father, a bookbinder, was active in a network of overlapping organizations that comprised New York City's Jewish anarchist movement during its declining years. He served as secretary of the Ferrer Center Branch of the Workman's Circle; was a member of the Jewish Anarchist Federation, which published a Yiddish-language weekly, *Fraye Arbeter Shtime* (Free Voice of Labor); and participated in the Modern School Association. Goodfriend's parents also joined the Am-Shal Group, a loose affiliation of anarchists living in the Shalom Aleichem buildings and the nearby co-ops built by Amalgamated Clothing Workers union. Goodfriend remembered attending an annual *Fraye Arbeter Shtime* fund-raising bazaar at Irving Place Hall, near Union Square, as well as Memorial Day picnics at the Stelton anarchist colony near New Brunswick, New Jersey.[2]

Despite this infrastructure, the movement was struggling in the early 1930s, as many former Jewish anarchists joined the Communist Party. Yet when Goodfriend read Alexander Berkman's *Now and After: The ABC of Communist Anarchism* as a young girl, it resonated deeply. "I read the *ABC* when I was eleven," she recalled, "and I discovered what the word *anarchism* was, and I knew I was an anarchist-communist. I knew that."[3] With her friend Sally Genn, Goodfriend launched a youth group, the Young Eagles, and found a mentor in Abe

Bluestein, a City College student who had grown up in the Stelton colony and had cofounded an anarchosyndicalist journal, *Vanguard*, in 1932.

The Vanguard Group, which produced the journal, sought to rebuild an anarchist presence in New York labor unions, but the group became preoccupied with promoting anarchist perspectives on the New Deal and the rise of fascism in Europe and in marshaling support for Spain's anarchists when war and revolution broke out there in 1936. However, members of the Vanguard Group worked to cultivate the politics of high-school-age anarchists, drawing the Young Eagles and a similar group in Brownsville, Brooklyn, into their fold as Vanguard Juniors. According to Goodfriend, "On Saturday morning, [Bluestein] would come out and have a study group with us.... We would read an article from *Vanguard* and discuss. And we read some Kropotkin, or talked about Kropotkin."[4] Vanguard Juniors also attended public lectures and debates in a building at 94 5th Avenue, near Union Square, that *Vanguard* shared with the Industrial Workers of the World and Carlo Tresca's newspaper, *Il Martello* (The Hammer). The Vanguard Group dissolved in 1939 as a consequence of romantic conflicts and arguments about how to relate to the labor movement, the Communist Party, and the war in Europe.[5] However, a number of Vanguard Juniors went on to play key roles in the Why? Group during the 1940s on the basis of relationships and political perspective they had developed during the preceding decade.

The first issue of *Why?* hit newsstands in April 1942, four months after the United States had officially entered World War II. The founding group consisted of *Vanguard* stalwarts Sam and Esther Dolgoff; Franz Fleigler, a member of the merchant marine and of the Industrial Workers of the World, along with his wife, Bessie; Audrey Goodfriend and her partner, David Koven, who had been a member of the Brooklyn Vanguard Juniors; and an older woman, Dorothy Rogers. Rogers had befriended Goodfriend when she and another female Vanguard Group member hitchhiked to Toronto in 1939 to meet Emma Goldman. At the time, Rogers lived in Toronto with intrepid Italian anarchist Artillio Bortolloti and served as Goldman's personal assistant. After Goldman's death in 1940, Rogers relocated to New York and took an apartment with Goodfriend, who was working as a bookkeeper after attending Hunter College on a full scholarship and earning a degree in mathematics.

This small group launched *Why?* at a moment of great change and historical uncertainty. Years later, Franz Fleigler recounted, "I was the one who suggested the name. I looked back on the rise of fascism, on workers sitting on their ass, on the war, on Soviet Russia, where I had just been, and asked, 'Why? Why did all this happen?'"[6] Though the group wanted to grapple with the big issues, the journal was a modest affair: it ran to a mere eight pages, published monthly in a nine-by-seven-inch magazine format.

The first issues retraced much of the terrain covered by *Vanguard*, reprinting essays by Mikhail Bakunin and considerations of the nature of Soviet power and the state of the U.S. labor movement. The contributors, all of whom wrote under pen names or initials during the war, argued that the American Federation of Labor's and Congress of Industrial Organization's use of the 1935 National Labor Relations Act, in which the federal government legally recognized and regulated labor unions, amounted to a "great surrender" in which the labor movement became a tool of a sophisticated form of "state capitalism" that could more effectively manage working-class demands. The pages of *Why?* depicted the growing corporatist welfare state as a form of fascism growing within the United States. Still, the group saw a revitalized, militant, and independent labor movement as the best hope for achieving social justice.[7]

Why? almost immediately began to suffer from long-standing schisms within the American anarchist movement—most notably, how anarchists should relate to the crises of World War II. Rudolf Rocker, a highly respected German anarchosyndicalist, had recently fled to the United States and urged support for the Allied war effort as the only realistic means of defeating the fascist regimes, which had gutted the Left in Europe.[8] Aware of the fascists' ethnic cleansing of Jews across Europe, the majority of Jewish anarchists supported this position. Many activists involved with the Spanish-language newspaper *Cultura Proletaria* (Proletarian Culture) and the Italian-language *L'Adunata dei Refrattari* (Summoning of the Unruly), however, held fast to the traditional anarchist opposition to statist wars, declaring the war at base another conflict between imperialist rivals. The Dolgoffs and Fleiglers supported Rocker's position and decided to break with *Why?* when the remainder of the group insisted on taking an antiwar position.[9]

Underlying the debate over the war was the conflict over political vision, strategy, and methods of organization that had for decades divided anarchists. As a result of her friendship with Bortolloti in Toronto, Rogers was embraced by the "antiorganizational" Italian anarchists who published *L'Adunata dei Refrattari* in New York City. The Vanguard Group and the Italian American syndicalists grouped around Tresca had clashed repeatedly with this group over the previous decade. Whereas *Vanguard* argued for worker-owned industrial production, *L'Adunata* called for a return to village-level self-sufficiency. While *Vanguard* believed that organizing radical labor unions was the key to revolution, *L'Adunata* insisted that unions merely re-created power hierarchies and remained committed to "propaganda of the deed." While *Vanguard* labored (albeit fruitlessly) to establish a nationwide anarchist federation, *L'Adunata* disparaged any attempt at organization beyond small, temporary action groups.[10] Although significant issues were at stake, the anarchist movement as a whole was so miniscule in the 1940s that some younger anarchists perceived this theoretical conflict as an absurd sectarianism, and Rogers served as something of a bridge between the camps.

Why? editorial board members grew even closer to *L'Adunata* after Diva Agostinelli joined the group. Agostinelli was born into a family of Italian immigrant anarchists who worked as coal miners in central Pennsylvania. Agostinelli's uncle, a militant follower of the *L'Adunata* school, had died when a bomb he was manufacturing for use against Italian American fascists accidentally detonated.[11] She earned a degree from Philadelphia's Temple University, with her tuition paid by her parents' comrades, and then relocated to New York City. The trust born of Agostinelli's name and facility with the Italian language translated into crucial support for the English-language *Why?*. When the socialists who had printed the first issue balked at the journal's growing criticism of the war, the Italians agreed to produce it in their own shop and to donate money toward other expenses. Beginning with the fourth issue, translations of articles originally published in *L'Adunata* appeared in *Why?* An advertisement for a fundraising "Dance and Entertainment" at the Galileo Club, L'Adunata Group's social center at 118 Cook Street in the Bushwick section of Brooklyn, appeared in the November–December 1942 issue.[12]

In 1944, members of the English-language group translated and published a pamphlet, *War or Revolution?* penned by *L'Adunata* editor Max Sartin.[13] Sartin was the pseudonym of Raffaele Schiavina, who was living in the United States illegally after being deported alongside his mentor, Luigi Galleani, in 1919. The pamphlet presented a position similar to that of the editorial committee of the British anarchist newspaper *Freedom*, which at that time appeared under the title *War Commentary*. *Why?* had quickly established a genial correspondence with the Freedom Group and adopted and reprinted the Londoners' position statement.[14] This editorial, like Sartin's pamphlet, called for independent resistance to fascism, much like the Resistance in Europe, and for radical workers to use the chaos generated by war to carry out a social revolution, as the Bolsheviks had done during World War I and the Paris Communards did during the Franco-Prussian War in 1871. Though the likelihood of this course of action coming to pass was near zero, the Why? Group's principled antiwar position directly led to the establishment of a series of personal and organizational relationships that fundamentally altered the course of the postwar anarchist movement in the United States.

New Connections

In the midst of one of the most popular wars in history, one to which nearly the entire political Left lent support, opponents of the war and resisters of the draft found one another and found grounds for collaboration across geographic and ideological divides. During its first year, the Why? Group made contact with Holley Cantine, a Columbia University dropout who had begun editing and hand printing *Retort*, a journal of literature and politics, from a cabin just outside Woodstock, New York. *Retort* took a clear antiwar position, praised the anarchopacifist ideas of Leo Tolstoy, and editorialized against mass production. Alongside astute editorials in which Cantine drew on Freud and Boasian anthropology, *Retort* featured poetry and prose by an array of authors who went on to leave their mark on American letters, including Saul Bellow, Norman Mailer, and Kenneth Rexroth.

Why? and *Retort* were soon cross-promoting each other. They also encouraged readers to subscribe to the journal *politics*, launched by Dwight and Nancy MacDonald in 1944. Dwight, a former editor of the highbrow Trotskyist-leaning *Partisan Review*, had been forced out for his antiwar commitments. He and Nancy launched *politics* with a donation from Margaret de Silver, Tresca's widow, shortly after the respected anarchosyndicalist was gunned down in the street in 1943. *politics* went on to publish a remarkable array of European and American social thinkers, including Albert Camus, Bruno Bettelheim, Simone de Beauvoir, and C. Wright Mills.[15] As Dwight MacDonald worked to carve out a contemporary libertarian socialist and pacifist politics in his contributions to the journal, Nancy MacDonald embarked on a practical effort that the anarchists responsible for *Why?* and *Retort* could enthusiastically endorse: the creation of the Spanish Refugee Aid Committee, an organization that provided material support and immigration assistance to exiled partisans of the civil war living precariously throughout war-torn Europe.

These shared intellectual commitments developed into friendships. Goodfriend later recalled that she and Koven "went up to Woodstock and we walked over ... to meet Holley." The Why? Group later bought a small hand printing press in case the government sought to repress antiwar voices as it had done in 1917. Goodfriend and Koven lived at 635 E. 9th Street, just east of Manhattan's Tompkins Square Park, and according to Goodfriend, "Across the street in the basement we had the printing press. So Holley actually taught us how to print, and he lived there for a while too when he came down and lived in New York."[16]

In November 1944, recognizing that others beyond their small circle were taking interest in their ideas, the Why? Group began hosting weekly discussions.

The meetings were held on Saturday afternoons at the hall of Solidaridad Internacional Antifascista, an anarchist center that aging Spanish-speaking anarchists maintained on the second floor of a building at 813 Broadway, two blocks south of Union Square. Speakers ranged from German émigré council communist Paul Mattick to novelist James Baldwin. Dwight MacDonald spoke, as did A. J. Muste, chair of a Christian pacifist organization, the Fellowship of Reconciliation.[17]

Through these meetings and other activities, *Why?* attracted additional recruits, including poet Jackson Mac Low; an African American student at Brooklyn College, Dan DeWeiss; and a young journalist, Michael Grieg, and his wife, Sally. Perhaps the most influential person to join the group in the mid-1940s was Paul Goodman, a poet and essayist who had returned to New York after earning a doctorate at the University of Chicago. Like MacDonald, Goodman had burned his bridges to the city's Marxist literary community through his staunch criticism of the war and efforts to craft an anti-authoritarian politics relevant to current conditions. Goodman brought an interest in sexual politics to *Why?* through his promotion of the theories of Austrian psychoanalyst Wilhelm Reich and through a personal life as a husband and father who also openly pursued sexual relationships with younger men. In the 1960s, Goodman published *Growing Up Absurd*, which became a best seller, and subsequently became a mentor to campus radicals.[18]

By 1945, *Why?* had extended its influence beyond New York. In addition to aging Italian-, Spanish-, and Russian-speaking subscribers, the group mailed bundles of each issue to distributors in Phoenix and San Francisco. Ammon Hennacy, a self-described "Christian Anarchist" and member of the Catholic Worker movement, sold the paper in Arizona, and radical poet Kenneth Rexroth distributed *Why?* and *Retort* among a circle of writers, artists, and war resisters in California's Bay Area. Curious about the New York milieu, poets Phillip Lamantia and Robert Duncan, both of whom were associated with Rexroth, attended Why? Group meetings while visiting New York City.[19]

Radical Pacifism

Anarchists built alliances in the 1940s not only through their writings but also, and more powerfully, through action. Refusing to participate in the mass slaughter of World War II was more than an intellectual exercise for the draft-age men of the *Why?* milieu. Each had to decide how he would relate to the Selective Service Board and the alternative service programs offered to religiously motivated conscientious objectors (COs). Koven, who worked on a New Jersey railroad in the early 1940s, decided to join the merchant marine to avoid direct military service. Nevertheless, he was briefly jailed for insubordination to a military official during a required accreditation process.[20] *Why?* contributor Clif Bennett went underground to avoid the draft, evading authorities until the war was nearly over. Female members of the group also risked arrest by helping draft resisters flee the country, just as Vietnam-era activists did on a larger scale twenty years later.[21] Perhaps of greatest consequence to the broader movement were the actions taken by David Thoreau Wieck.

Wieck was born in the small mining community of Belleville, Illinois, to parents active in the Progressive Miners of America. Forced out of Illinois, they relocated to the Bronx when Wieck's father landed a research job with the Russell Sage Foundation. In high school Wieck dabbled with the Young Communist League before attending Vanguard Junior meetings at the nearby Shalom Aleichem Houses, where he met Goodfriend and Bluestein. Though Wieck contributed a few articles to the first issues of *Why?*, he "stayed on the sideline" of the group in 1942, focusing on his studies at Columbia University.[22] However, Wieck refused to register for the draft, arguing, like contributors to *Why?*, that the effort to defeat fascism by war was leading the United States to become totalitarian. Denied CO status, Wieck received a three-year sentence at Connecticut's Danbury Federal Penitentiary after being apprehended during a poorly planned attempt to flee to Mexico in the spring of 1943.[23] Wieck accepted that he would have to serve time for his refusal to kill but did not anticipate that his sentence would open new intellectual vistas and provide opportunities to engage in defining acts of political resistance.

Danbury's medium-security facility was designated to house draft resisters from across the eastern United States. According to Wieck, "Of the prison population of six hundred or so, Jehovah's Witnesses, who kept to themselves, were the largest single group. The COs were of many varieties but most were pacifists who belonged to the wrong church or none; a few were 'absolutists' who refused to cooperate with the draft in any fashion."[24] Among the first war resisters incarcerated at Danbury were the Union 8, a group of seminary students from privileged backgrounds who, inspired by Mahatma Gandhi, had launched "ashrams" in African American ghetto neighborhoods in Harlem and Newark, New Jersey. Though most of this group had been released by 1943, they had established a pattern of coordinated, nonviolent protest against aspects of prison life that they could not abide.

Shortly after Wieck arrived, approximately two dozen Danbury war resisters launched a successful strike against the prison's racial segregation, a practice standard in all federal penitentiaries at the time. Many of the strike organizers were pacifist members of the Fellowship of Reconciliation, which had begun to address race and class inequality under Muste's leadership and had studied Gandhi's methods of nonviolent civil disobedience in India's national liberation struggle. Others belonged to the War Resisters League, a secular organization similar to the Fellowship that attracted many Jews. Danbury seemed an ideal location to test the applicability of Gandhian tactics in the United States. Wieck took part in the four-month strike, refusing to work, to take his allotted time in the yard, or to eat meals in the segregated cafeteria. Hoping to prevent the protest from spreading, the warden at Danbury did the young nonviolent militants an unintentional favor by housing them together in a secluded section of the prison and allowing them to interact in a common space.[25]

A sense of community quickly developed among strike participants. Wieck wrote to his mother, "I have been having a swell time up here in my new quarters. We have very interesting discussions, debates and arguments on a variety of subjects, currently, primarily 'the beard,' the label one of the infidels here plastered on God. But [also] the labor movement ... and racial segregation."[26] In this way, Wieck befriended Lowell Naeve, an anarchist painter from Iowa. Together they wrote a manuscript about their experiences and smuggled it out of the prison inside a hollowed out papier-mâché picture frame. Wieck also established enduring friendships with individuals such as Ralph DiGia, who dedicated his life to the War Resisters League after his release, and Jim Peck, who became a stalwart of the Congress of Racial Equality despite nearly being beaten to death during the first freedom rides in 1947.

With the aid of outside supporters, including African American politicians such as Adam Clayton Powell, the Danbury strike gained national media attention and resulted in the full desegregation of the mess hall beginning in February 1944. The Danbury strike inspired collective acts of civil disobedience in other penitentiaries holding war resisters, including in Lewisburg, Pennsylvania, where Union 8 member David Dellinger was now housed, and the prison in Ashland, Kentucky, where a young Bayard Rustin was incarcerated.[27]

News of these acts of resistance circulated among COs and draft resisters through Fellowship of Reconciliation and War Resisters League newsletters as well as through the anarchist press. Cantine kept up a lively correspondence with Dellinger during his second incarceration for war resistance and published Dellinger's statement to the draft board in *Retort*. The May 1945 issue of *Why?* saluted COs who objected to performing "forced labor" at Civilian Public Service (CPS) camps. The article quoted Roy Kepler, a pacifist CO at the Germansk camp in Michigan, as claiming that "more and more CPS men are beginning to oppose the State and its power to make war."[28] With the

Communist and Socialist Parties supporting the war, anarchism gained a new appeal to many war resisters seeking ideological grounding for their actions.

The connections forged between anarchists and pacifists in prison and CPS camps also led the Why? Group to establish friendly relationships with the War Resisters League and the Catholic Worker, organizations Why? might previously have snubbed as insufficiently radical or too religious. Goodfriend remembered that the Why? Group "would do street corner meetings, stuff like that. There was one time we were scared shitless that we would be hurt because we were near Hell's Kitchen and a bunch of Catholics were coming out. But the Catholic Worker was antiwar and we were having meetings with all groups of people like that—War Resisters League, Catholic Worker—and so we were safe! These kids came out and saw a Catholic paper and they backed off!" This small coalition also picketed Danbury prison in February 1946 alongside parents of COs who remained incarcerated after the armistice (including Wieck's father). Although the warden met briefly with a small delegation that included Goodman and Agostinelli, the picketers were not well received. According to Goodfriend, "It was scary! We were practically run off the road by Danbury residents!"[29]

These interactions profoundly affected all involved. Members of the Why? Group shifted from an opposition to interimperialist war to an embrace of pacifism per se. Wieck later wrote, "I did not go to prison as a pacifist but rather as an objector to war and conscription. (I take words seriously.) It was in prison that I learned the methods of nonviolence. If I didn't dislike hyphenations I would characterize myself as an anarchist-pacifist."[30] Beyond the prison strikes, the group was affected by reading *The Conquest of Violence*, a 1937 book by Dutch anarchist Bart de Ligt, a correspondent of Gandhi's who chaired War Resisters International. De Ligt argued that pacifism must run much deeper than denunciation of war, since "war, capitalism and imperialism form a veritable trinity" fused together through nationalism. Sincere pacifists, then, should be anarchists and should work to transform the culture as a whole. Interpreting the histories of the recent Russian and Spanish Revolutions, de Ligt insisted on means-ends congruence, positing the maxim, "The more violence, the less revolution."[31]

The influence of prisoners such as Wieck and Naeve helped move other COs and pacifists such as Dellinger, DiGia, and Peck in the direction of anarchism. The wave of nonviolent direct action in prison and CPS camps united the radical pacifists and prompted them to discuss the potential for a broad postwar movement of "revolutionary nonviolence" against war, racism, and economic inequality in the United States. They expected—wrongly—that the war's end and especially the use of nuclear bombs in Japan would lead to a mass upsurge in pacifist sentiment that could be channeled to broader social purposes. After their release, many former COs threw themselves into a flurry of activities. Dellinger; his wife, Elizabeth Peterson; and others established an intentional community at Glen Gardner, New Jersey. They published a journal, *Direct Action*, and helped organize the Committee for Nonviolent Revolution. On the West Coast, former COs, including Roy Kepler, established radical bookstores and the Pacifica radio network, which went on to serve as important vectors for disseminating anarchist ideas in the 1950s.[32]

New Emphases, New Strategies

Wieck was released from prison in May 1946 and quickly gravitated back to the Why? Group. There he met and began a romance with Diva Agostinelli that would persist for the rest of their lives. In 1947, the Why? Group decided to change the paper's (as well as the group's) name to *Resistance*, indicating the greater clarity they now felt about the social order and how to respond. Brimming with postprison energy, Wieck took on increasing responsibilities for the production of the paper. He expanded the size and page count and drew on new printing technology to add photographs and original artwork. Beginning with the first issue, *Resistance* devoted considerable space to chronicling and promoting the activities of radical pacifists, especially their expanding efforts to subvert Jim Crow segregation in the U.S. South. The group also handed printing responsibilities over to Libertarian Press, which Dellinger and another anarchist war resister, Igal Roodenko, had established at Glen Gardner. Libertarian Press also issued Wieck's and Naeve's prison memoirs, a novel by Paul Goodman, and Ammon Hennacy's autobiography.

With the war over and the paper functioning smoothly, Goodfriend and Koven embarked on a bus trip across the United States to meet with subscribers and answer the question, "What do anarchists do these days?" In Cleveland, Detroit, Chicago, Phoenix, and Los Angeles, they found immigrant anarchists of their parents' generation but little activity among younger people for whom English was their first language. The situation only added to their excitement when they encountered the vibrant community of poets, artists, and former COs that made up the Libertarian Circle, founded in 1946 by Rexroth and Duncan in San Francisco. Goodfriend recalled, "We loved San Francisco. We stayed for the year of 1947. Then we went back to New York, tried to get all our friends, tell them about how wonderful it is, and how we should all move out to San Francisco, buy land, and start a community."[33]

The following summer Dan DeWeiss, the Griegs, and Wieck and Agostinelli made the journey. Wieck and Agostinelli, too, visited subscribers while traveling west. The couple noted with surprise the apparent complacency of working people and youth. Accustomed to the radical hothouses of New York City and of prison, they found themselves baffled by the quiescence they experienced elsewhere during these years of postwar affluence and entered a period of introspection on the nature of social change.[34] Mel and Sally Grieg established a communal house with Goodfriend and Koven, predating by two decades the urban collectives of the Haight-Ashbury period. Despite their excitement at meeting Rexroth's circle and older Italian militants, Wieck and Agostinelli disliked the Bay Area, and DeWeiss experienced significant racism, leading all three to return to New York within a few months.[35]

Wieck and Agostinelli remained in San Francisco until the spring of 1948, when they returned to New York and resumed publishing *Resistance*. Despite the anarchists' long-standing antipathy to the Communist Party, the editors spoke out early and vehemently against the rising tide of McCarthyism and the suppression of speech rights for Communists. While regularly reporting on the small protest actions organized by the editors' friends active in pacifist and antiracist work, *Resistance* took on a more philosophical tone. Wieck addressed the confusion he harbored about what anarchism might mean in the postwar era, exploring the psychosexual aspects of oppression, the value of decentralization, and a renewed focus on living according to one's values as a political strategy, among other topics.[36]

Anarchists in New York and San Francisco, like many other intellectuals of the 1940s and 1950s, expressed considerable interest in the theories of Austrian psychoanalyst Wilhelm Reich. Agostinelli remembered that the first time she met Goodman, he was on the floor demonstrating a "Reichian orgasm."[37] Reich had been a student of Freud but had broken with him on matters both political and therapeutic. Reich attempted to combine the insights of psychoanalysis with those of Marxism, arguing that the "neurotic" behaviors therapists treated were responses to economic exploitation (poverty), sexual repression, and other aspects of the social order. He organized the Society for Proletarian Sexual Politics, which worked in Germany's working-class neighborhoods to promote sexual expression among teens, contraception, abortion, and divorce. Physical and psychic health, he argued, depended on patients' ability to achieve the emotional release that came with powerful orgasms.[38]

Members of the Why? Group found that Reich's *The Sexual Revolution* and *The Mass Psychology of Fascism* accorded with and enriched their anarchist politics.[39] The first book argued that the male-dominated nuclear family was central to reproduction of capitalist states. Reich pointed to the ways that not only churches but also governments of all sorts promoted monogamous heterosexual marriage in a manner verging on compulsion, punished homosexuality, and suppressed adolescent sexuality through public schools and other channels. The second book contended that average working people had acceded to Stalinism and Nazism because they had first been acclimated to "authoritarian order" and taught not to rebel when their sexual impulses were suppressed by their parents.[40]

The Resistance Group's exploration of these topics marked the first substantial engagement with the politics of family and sexuality by anarchists in the United States since Emma Goldman's 1919 deportation. This engagement led to experimentation with open relationships and communal living within the group; although the experiments sometimes ended painfully, they also helped make the anarchist and pacifist Left a supportive environment for gay, lesbian, and bisexual individuals. Beyond an attention to sex and gender roles, the group's reading of Reich and Freud led to an acknowledgment of the psychological aspects of power—the way it could structure the internal life and behavior of individuals—that pointed beyond classical anarchist notions, which saw power mainly as the ability of the boss to fire and starve backed by the police's ability to bludgeon. Reich's ideas also ran against the grain of economic determinism that many classical anarchists, including Why? Group members in the early 1940s, shared with Marxists. Reich's explanation for working-class support of fascism seems to have contributed to growing doubts that the proletariat was, by nature, fated to become a collective agency of revolution. Still, most members of the Resistance Group were quite skeptical that shame-free, full-bodied orgasms provided a panacea for the world's ills, as Reich seemed to suggest.[41]

Ralph Borsodi, Mildred Loomis, and others associated with the School for Living constituted another set of relatively unknown thinkers on which the Resistance Group drew. In 1921, Borsodi, a successful business consultant, and his family established a "homestead" in Rockland County, New York, in a bid to escape what he saw as dehumanizing aspects of modern life. In line with sociologists of the era, such as Thorstein Veblen and Louis Wirth, Borsodi diagnosed the key feature of American life as the centralization of production, ownership, decision-making power, and education. His longtime collaborator, Loomis, defined centralization as "the operating of activities, of any kind, in which control is held by fewer and fewer hands."[42] While most sociologists saw this trend as inevitable, Borsodi declared the United States "an ugly civilization" and looked for ways to encourage change without resorting to centralization in the form of mass politics.[43] Borsodi and Loomis taught that decentralization—"the organizing of activities in smaller units, both efficient and voluntary, in which all participants involved develop initiative and responsibility"—led to an array of personal and social benefits, among them the development of a range of skills, a sense of worth and fulfillment, and consideration of how one's actions affect others.[44] The School of Living promoted these ideas in publications, seminars, and live-in instruction at a handful of intentional communities developed in New York, Pennsylvania, and the Midwest. The Why? Group began trading publications with the School of Living beginning in 1943 and according to Goodfriend "would go out there frequently to talk to them. None of them called themselves anarchists, but their ideas were definitely ideas that all of us could subscribe to."[45]

The School of Living's focus on elective, small-scale community was consistent with ideas put forth by other thinkers of the period. Cantine had dropped out of Columbia to live a "Thoreauvian life" away from industrial society. Goodman's most enduring contribution to anarchist theory was his "May Pamphlet," first published in sections in the May and June 1945 issues of *Why?*, *Retort*, and *politics*. In those essays he argued, "A free society cannot be the substitution of a 'new order' for the old order; it is the extension of spheres of free action until they make up most of the social life.... Free action is to live in the present society as though it were a natural society."[46] Goodman's definition of natural society was complex, but the strategic implications of his theory were clear: rather than focus on organizing protest movements, anarchists should break repressive social conventions among themselves and promulgate new ways of living, starting with their own communities. In 1947, Paul Goodman and his brother, Percival, an architect, coauthored *Communitas*, in which they reviewed the history of community planning and suggested ways of organizing life based on principles other than profit maximization, such as a focus on making each person's work spiritually rewarding.[47] Two years later, Martin Buber published his influential *Paths in Utopia*, which defended the utopian tradition within socialist thought, placed anarchism squarely within that tradition, and celebrated Israeli kibbutzim as a flourishing modern example of experimentation with *living* socialist values.[48]

Contributors to *Resistance* regularly explored psychological conditioning, the politics of the family, communal living, and individual acts of resistance, but Wieck perhaps most powerfully synthesized those ideas. At the end of 1948, Wieck penned an essay, "Anarchism," that the *Resistance* editorial committee adopted as a statement of its position. The group declared itself "in complete agreement" with the goals and values of the anarchist tradition and announced its belief that "freedom is the core of a society of healthy, happy human beings; that State and Government—that is, law; institutionalized violence; war; individual, group and class domination—are the antithesis of freedom and must be destroyed."[49] Nevertheless, the group expressed grave doubts about the traditional methods anarchists had employed to reach their goals.

The group rejected an economistic view of humanity's oppression and a teleological view of history—that is, the old faith that the majority of people were becoming increasingly immiserated and therefore radical. "The mass of the people is increasingly indifferent to radical ideas—indifferent even to thinking," Wieck tartly asserted. Anarchists, therefore, needed to recognize that

> the revolution is not imminent, and it is senseless to expend our lives in patient waiting or faithful dreams: senseless because the revolution of the future requires active preparation: not the preparation of conspiracy and storing of arms, but the preparation of undermining the institutions and habits of thought and action that inhibit release of the natural powers of men and women....
>
> The revolution as a "final conflict" exploding out of the condition of man is an illusion; revolutionary growth is necessarily the hard-won learning and practice of freedom.[50]

"Anarchism" went beyond similar statements of the 1940s to suggest a number of practical steps for the movement. First, the essay recognized the importance of winning "concrete victories" and "improving existing conditions"—that is, reform struggles. To this end, the statement suggested that direct action campaigns should be prioritized in the workplace and against militarism and racism. Second, the anarchist movement should serve as a sphere of freedom. Wieck suggested, "Perhaps our strongest achievement and our strongest propaganda is a movement where ... people can find a refuge of sanity and health, where they can learn in practice what anarchism and an anarchist society are. To put it another way: It is much more important to be an anarchist, and live anarchistically, than to merely have anarchist ideas."[51]

Finally, the statement suggested that anarchists should refocus on education. However, rather than emphasizing newspapers and forums, anarchists needed to stress relationships within the family: "We believe the present state of 'human nature' is largely responsible for the present state of human society, and that this 'human nature' is formed in the early part of life when the family and morality and discipline (and not economic or political institutions) are the dominant facts in the life of the individual."[52] When the magazine ceased publication in 1954, group members turned overwhelmingly to education.

Disintegration and Linkages

When Wieck and Agostinelli returned from San Francisco, the Resistance Group resumed holding weekly discussions at the Solidaridad Internacional Antifascista Hall on Broadway, attracting a few new noteworthy participants. Most significantly, Judith Malina and Julian Beck, a young couple who had launched the experimental Living Theatre, attended frequently. Beck and Malina carried the anarchist ideas they learned there—through association with the Catholic Worker—into the 1950s and 1960s.[53] Greenwich Village habitué Stuart Perkoff also attended meetings for a time before becoming a fixture of the Venice Beach, Los Angeles, Beat community. The early 1950s proved difficult, however. Instead of a mass revolt against war, the United States settled into the anxieties and hostilities of the Cold War, with many former radicals retreating in the face of a growing Red Scare mentality.[54] With the former core of the Resistance Group split between the coasts, energy ebbed. Years later, according to Wieck, the Solidaridad Internacional Antifascista "meetings had become depressing. We were going there every Saturday as an obligation.... My feeling was that the only people we were attracting were the crazies."[55] In the early 1950s, the group held public events less frequently and eventually ceased organizing them altogether. Unaware that the civil rights movement would explode onto the national scene in less than a year, the group decided to cease publishing *Resistance* in 1954.

Two years later, Wieck returned to Columbia University to earn a doctorate in philosophy. In 1960 he and Agostinelli moved to Troy, New York, where he took a faculty position at Rensselaer Polytechnic Institute and she worked as a school librarian.[56] Wieck gave an anarchist cast to Rensselaer's programs in philosophy and science and technology that remains evident today. Throughout the late 1950s and early 1960s, he regularly contributed articles to *Liberation*, the monthly magazine founded by Dellinger, Muste, Rustin, and Roy Finch in 1955.

The communal home established by Goodfriend, Koven, and the Griegs in San Francisco lasted only for a year. The two couples' experiments with non-monogamy proved more painful than they had anticipated. And though they had hoped to raise children as a large group, when Sally Grieg found herself pregnant, she and Michael decided to raise the baby separately, as a traditional family, while Michael pursued a career in mainstream journalism. Goodfriend returned to school to be certified as a teacher. In 1958, she and Koven launched Berkeley's Walden School, which drew heavily on the pedagogical theories of British educator A. S. Neill, a disciple of Reich. They also helped to establish

Pacifica Radio with a handful of anarchist and pacifist former COs. For a short time, Koven edited a literary journal, *The Needle*, that featured the writings of Allen Ginsburg, Gary Snyder, and other poets in his social orbit who soon became known collectively as the Beat Generation.[57]

Histories of anarchism often depict the 1940s and 1950s as "dead years" when anarchism seemed to have been defeated as an ideology and mass social movement. Historians and political scientists in the late 1960s consequently were caught off guard when youth and student movements in the United States, France, and elsewhere again began to wave black flags and declare themselves anarchists, just as many commentators were baffled by the visibly anarchist aspects of the more recent Global Justice and Occupy movements. It is true that the traditional anarchist movement declined rapidly in the United States after the Spanish Civil War (a process that began during the Red Scare during and after World War I). However, at its height, the Why?/Resistance Group distributed about four thousand copies of each issue of its journal to subscribers throughout the United States (as well as a few abroad).[58] This generation of New York and Bay Area anarchists, along with their radical pacifist friends, established an institutional and ideological seedbed in which the Beat Generation and later the 1960s counterculture were able to germinate. These cultural movements, in turn, fundamentally shaped post-1960s anarchism.[59]

It is not an exaggeration, then, to describe the Why?/Resistance Group as a missing link that elucidates the long, complex evolution of the anarchist movement from its early twentieth-century manifestations to its contemporary forms. Group members began to articulate a more complex understanding of power and oppression that anticipated the insights of both radical feminists and philosopher Michel Foucault. The group launched a critique of mass culture, just as the Situationists and anarchopunks did in later decades. The group insisted that anarchism could find adherents beyond the industrial working class and promoted forms of collective living, polyamory, and artistic expression that are characteristic of anarchist culture today. While anarchists have always considered the need for congruence in their means and ends, the Why?/Resistance Group's prioritization of living anarchist lives and building anarchist institutions—over and above practicing propaganda of the deed and organizing mass movements and unions—is one of the clearest and earliest statements of the strategy of "prefigurative politics" emphasized by contemporary anarchists such as Cindy Milstein and David Graeber.[60] Finally, the members of the Why?/Resistance Group embodied the midcentury demographic shift that occurred in anarchism: it was the first American anarchist group to be composed primarily of members with a college education, even though many of them had been born into working-class families. In retrospect, then, the new directions in which Goodfriend, Wieck, and the other members of their cohort took anarchism reflect both the social mobility and the isolation they experienced as radical anticapitalists during the golden age of American capitalism.

Although a variety of individuals shaped the face of the anarchist movement in the 1940s and 1950s, the Why?/Resistance Group is particularly notable because of the personal and familial roots its members shared with self-identified anarchists who had been active in earlier phases of the movement. While other groups had ideas that were anarchistic, the Why? Group possessed some amount of authority to redefine and refocus anarchism as a result of the trust and respect they received from anarchist old-timers and of the relations and dialogues they maintained with European anarchist groups involved in reconsidering anarchist orthodoxies. The ability of group members to interact with such a variety of mentors—from the *Vanguard* and *L'Adunata* anarchists to sympathizers such as Muste and Borsodi—owed much to their base in New York City, the center of American anarchism for more than sixty years at the time they began publishing.

Notes

1. See *At Home in Utopia* (DVD), produced by Michal Goldman with Ellen Brodsky (Harriman, N.Y.: New Day Films, 2008).

2. Audrey Goodfriend, interview by author, November 10, 2008, Berkeley, Calif.

3. Ibid. See also Audrey Goodfriend, interview, in Paul Avrich, *Anarchist Voices: An Oral History of Anarchism in America* (Oakland, Calif.: AK, 2005), 460–61.

4. Goodfriend, interview by author.

5. See Andrew Cornell, "'For a World without Oppressors': U.S. Anarchism from the Palmer Raids to the Sixties" (Ph.D. diss., New York University, 2011), 278–302.

6. Franz Fleigler, interview, in Avrich, *Anarchist Voices*, 455–56.

7. Bill Young, "The Great Surrender," *Why?*, April 1942, 2–3.

8. Mina Graur, *An Anarchist "Rabbi": The Life and Teachings of Rudolf Rocker* (New York: Magnes and St. Martin's, 1997), 224–28.

9. Fleigler, interview, 456; David Koven, interview, in Avrich, *Anarchist Voices*, 462.

10. See Michael Schmidt and Lucien van der Walt, *Black Flame: The Revolutionary Class Politics of Anarchism and Syndicalism* (Oakland, Calif.: AK, 2009), 123–47.

11. Diva Agostinelli, "A 79 Year Old Woman Who Bowls: An Interview with Diva Agostinelli, Anarchist," *Perspectives on Anarchist Theory* 5:1 (2001), http://flag.blackened.net/ias/9diva.htm.

12. Sam Dolgoff, *Fragments: A Memoir* (London: Refract, 1986), 33.

13. *War or Revolution: An Anarchist Statement* (New York: Why? Publications Committee, 1944). No author is given in the pamphlet, but Goodfriend attributed it to Sartin in her interview with the author.

14. "Our Position in Brief," *Why?*, November–December, 1942, 6.

15. Gregory D. Sumner, *Dwight MacDonald and the Politics Circle* (Ithaca: Cornell University Press, 1996).

16. Goodfriend, interview by author. The group never printed the journal on the hand press but did use it to print occasional leaflets and pamphlets.

17. Taylor Stoehr, introduction to *Drawing the Line: The Political Essays of Paul Goodman*, ed. Stoehr (New York: Dutton, 1979), xvii.

18. See Taylor Stoehr, preface to Paul Goodman, *Drawing the Line Once Again: Paul Goodman's Anarchist Writings* (Oakland, Calif.: PM, 2010).

19. Louis Cabri, "'Rebus Effort Remove Government': Jackson Mac Low, Why?/Resistance, Anarcho-Pacifism," *Crayon* 1 (1997): 44–68; Ekbert Faas, *Young Robert Duncan: Portrait of the Poet as a Homosexual in Society* (Santa Barbara, Calif.: Black Sparrow, 1983), 190–91; Franklin Rosemont, "Surrealist, Anarchist, Afrocentrist: Phillip Lamantia before and after the 'Beat Generation,'" in *Are Italians White? How Race Is Made in America*, ed. Jennifer Guglielmo and Salvatore Salerno (New York: Routledge, 2003), 124–43.

20. David Koven, "Live an Anarchist Life!," *Social Anarchism* 42 (2008–9): 72–77.

21. Agostinelli, "79 Year Old Woman Who Bowls."

22. David Thoreau Wieck, *Woman from Spillertown: A Memoir of Agnes Burns Wieck* (Carbondale: Southern Illinois University Press, 1992), 199.

23. Ibid., 202–3.

24. Ibid., 203.

25. See James Tracy, *Direct Action: Radical Pacifism from the Union Eight to the Chicago Seven* (Chicago: University of Chicago Press, 1996), 35–39; Scott Bennett, *Radical Pacifism: The War Resisters League and Gandhian Nonviolence in America, 1915–1963* (Syracuse: Syracuse University Press, 2003), 98–133.

26. David Wieck to Agnes Wieck, October 18, 1943, David Wieck Papers, Swarthmore College Peace Collection, Swarthmore, Penn.

27. Tracy, *Direct Action*, 35–39; Bennett, *Radical Pacifism*, 98–133.

28. G. A. [Audrey Goodfriend], "C.P.S. and the State," *Why?*, May 1945, 9.

29. Goodfriend, interview by author; Wieck, *Woman from Spillertown*, 215.

30. David Thoreau Wieck, "Peace-Related Activities, Post World War II," Wieck Papers, Swarthmore College Peace Collection.

31. Goodfriend, interview by author; Bart de Ligt, *The Conquest of Violence: An Essay on War and Revolution* (1937; London: Pluto, 1989).

32. Tracy, *Direct Action*, 47–75.

33. Goodfriend, interview by author.

34. Diva Agostinelli to Agnes and Edward Wieck, October 24, November 2, 1947, David Thoreau Wieck Papers, Tamiment Library, New York University, New York.

35. Goodfriend, interview by author.

36. Goodfriend, interview by author; David Wieck, "Anarchism," *Resistance*, November–December 1948; David Wieck, "Anarchism, Anarchy, Anarchists," in *The World Scene from the Libertarian Point of View*, ed. Free Society Group (Chicago: Free Society Group, 1951), 51.

37. Agostinelli, "79 Year Old Woman Who Bowls."

38. See Chris Turner, *Adventures in the Orgasmatron: How the Sexual Revolution Came to America* (New York: Farrar, Straus, and Giroux, 2011).

39. Goodfriend, interview by author; Wieck to Taylor Stoehr, July 1, 1983, Wieck Papers, Tamiment Library.

40. Wilhelm Reich, *The Sexual Revolution: Toward a Self-Governing Character Structure* (1936; New York: Farrar, Straus, and Giroux, 1963); Wilhelm Reich, *The Mass Psychology of Fascism* (1933; New York: Farrar, Straus, and Giroux, 1980).

41. Goodfriend, interview by the author; Martin Duberman, *A Saving Remnant: The Radical Lives of Barbara Deming and David McReynolds* (New York: New Press, 2011).

42. Mildred Loomis, "The Life and Work of Ralph Borsodi," *Green Revolution* 34:10 (1977): 10.

43. Ralph Borsodi, *The Ugly Civilization* (New York: Simon and Schuster, 1929).

44. Mildred Loomis, "Decentralized Human Well-Being," *Green Revolution* 35:5 (1978): 12.

45. Goodfriend, interview by author.

46. Paul Goodman, "The May Pamphlet," in *Drawing the Line Once Again*, 25–26.

47. Paul Goodman and Percival Goodman, *Communitas: Means of Livelihood and Ways of Life* (Chicago: University of Chicago Press, 1947).

48. Martin Buber, *Paths in Utopia* (New York: Macmillan, 1950).

49. David Wieck, "Anarchism," *Resistance*, November–December 1948, 4.

50. Ibid., 5.

51. Ibid., 14.

52. Ibid., 15.

53. See Alan Antliff's chapter in this volume.

54. See Stephen J. Whitfield, *The Culture of the Cold War* (Baltimore: Johns Hopkins University Press, 1996).

55. Wieck to Taylor Stoehr, October 14, 1978, Wieck Papers, Tamiment Library.

56. Wieck, *Woman from Spillertown*, 233.

57. Goodfriend, interview by author; Koven, interview, 462–63.

58. David Wieck, untitled manuscript, Wieck Papers, Box 4, Folder 2, Tamiment Library. Wieck noted that Why?/Resistance "never printed more than 4,000 copies" but does not further specify dates or circulation figures.

59. See Chris Dixon, "Building 'Another Politics': The Contemporary Anti-Authoritarian Current in the U.S. and Canada," *Anarchist Studies* 20:1 (2012): 32–59; Andrew Cornell, *Oppose and Propose! Lessons from Movement for a New Society* (Oakland, Calif.: Institute for Anarchist Studies and AK, 2011); Andrew Cornell, "'For a World without Oppressors.'"

60. See Cindy Milstein, *Anarchism and Its Aspirations* (Oakland, Calif.: Institute for Anarchist Studies and AK, 2010); David Graeber, *The Democracy Project: A History, a Crisis, a Movement* (New York: Spiegel and Grau, 2013); Chris Crass, *Toward Collective Liberation: Anti-Racist Organizing, Feminist Praxis, and Movement Building Strategy* (Oakland, Calif.: PM, 2013).

Poetic Tension

The Aesthetic Politics of the Living Theatre

ALLAN ANTLIFF

In 1947, Judith Malina and Julian Beck founded the Living Theatre, which went on to become an outstanding example of political engagement in experimental performance.[1] During their first period of activity in New York (late 1940s–1964), Malina and Beck developed their conception of a "poetic" theater and grounded it in anarchist theory and practice. This chapter explores that development and the context in which it took place.

Just before World War II, New York's anarchists were in a state of disarray. In 1938, a group of fifty leading activists had formed the Libertarian Socialist League and stopped using the term *anarchism*. The next year, New York's only English-language anarchist journals, *Vanguard* and *Challenge*, folded, in part as a consequence of financial issues and in part as a result of interpersonal conflicts and the advent of war in Europe.[2] A time of crisis, however, can also be productive. Andrew Cornell points to the 1942 founding of the New York–based journal *Why?* as the beginning of renewal. Edited primarily by cofounders Audrey Goodfriend and Dorothy Rogers with Sally Grieg and Diva Agostinelli, *Why?* brought together activists promoting nonviolent tactics (general strikes to end capitalism, for example) and insurrectionists seeking to overthrow state power through mass armed uprisings.[3] In May 1947, after the war had ended and anarchist revolutions had failed to materialize across liberated Europe, *Why?* changed its name to *Resistance*, and plans for mass mobilization gave way to a more concise goal: the collective would deepen its critique of the existing social order to inspire individuals to start living according to anarchist principles.[4] Other currents promoted similar politics. In June 1947, the executive committee of the pacifist War Resisters League (WRL), founded in 1923, which had hitherto restricted its activities to single-issue anti-war work, was taken over by former conscientious objector David Dellinger and other anarchists. They rededicated the WRL to "the promotion of political, economic, and social revolution by non-violent means."[5] In April 1948, 250 "militant pacifists" formed the Peacemakers. Advocating "the development of pacifist cells to promote communal life and personal 'inner-transformation,'" the group "extolled absolutism, moral responsibility, commitment, and civil disobedience."[6] During the 1950s and 1960s, Peacemaker/WRL activists initiated a series of direct action campaigns, many of which are discussed in the WRL's monthly magazine, *Liberation* (1956–77). A third anarchist organization advocating nonviolent social revolution through individual initiative was the Catholic Worker movement. Founded by Dorothy Day in the 1930s, the movement's New York chapter published a newspaper, *Catholic Worker*, and ran a series of "houses of hospitality" on Manhattan's Lower East Side during the 1940s and 1950s. The houses addressed the needs of the destitute, with activists serving "a coffee line in the morning and a soup line at noon, and supper for those [homeless] living in the house."[7] Civil disobedience was their weapon of choice in the political arena, where Christian imperatives were deemed above secular authority.[8] In short, individualist-oriented activism was on the ascendance among New York's anarchists, and the founders of the Living Theatre found their place in this community.

Malina and Beck had been in a relationship for five years before marrying in October 1948, and they initially were reluctant to commit themselves to the movement. Although Malina was a longtime reader of *Why?* and its successor, *Resistance*, she wrote in her diary on July 1, 1948, that she "hardly paid attention to the magazine ... because I distrust militant politics. And though Kropotkin writes splendidly on the future society, I don't know how to share his faith."[9] According to Malina and Beck's biographer, John Tytell, anarchist social theorist Paul Goodman (who wrote for *Resistance*) was the key influence guiding them toward anarchism. Malina preferred him to other anarchists because he had an "ordered" home life with a wife and children. At the same time, he openly engaged in homosexual relationships, in keeping not only with his personal inclinations but also with his belief that anarchists should pursue their inclinations. Since Beck, too, was bisexual and he and Malina had an open marriage, Goodman's lifestyle likely also played a role in swaying them toward his position.[10] Most important, Goodman's anarchism was grounded in an individualist ethos—"drawing the line" on moral grounds and refusing to submit to the demands of any oppressive or destructive authority—that applied to the idea of violent all-encompassing revolution as well as to everything else.[11] To this end, he was a pacifist who believed that anarchism "must" be established gradually by the spread of self-sufficient "fraternal" collectives that would "progressively incorporate more and more ... social functions" into the emerging "free society."[12]

Malina and Beck shared Goodman's position. Following a meeting at the Solidaridad Internacional Antifascista Hall, where the Resistance Group organized talks and discussions, Malina observed in her April 24, 1950, diary entry, "The concept of nonviolence is not clear to these people. They regard pacifism only as a form of resistance to the state and its wars; they seem to have no fundamental objection to killing."[13] She and Beck clearly drew the line at nonviolence with regard to political activism. However, Goodman did not necessarily object to all violence. In *Art and Social Nature* (1946), which Malina and Beck read in 1948, Goodman distinguished between violence in a "natural society" founded in freedom and "unnatural society's" marshaling of violence to enforce hierarchical systems of power over others.[14] "Natural violence" had a psychological function—"the destruction of habits or second natures in the interests of rediscovering the primary experiences of birth, infantile anxiety, grief and mourning of death, simple sexuality, etc." "Unnatural violence," conversely, served authoritarian social and political ends. Its primary tool was subtle and not-so-subtle coercion (legal, economic, and social) to perpetuate conditions of inequality and exploitation. Humanity's deepest psychological needs (the realm of the natural), however, could also be co-opted to serve the ends of unnatural violence. Goodman speculated that the psychological appeal of wars, for example, lay in the false promise that the violence might "liberate natural associations and release social inventiveness." However, because war's violence was "unnatural," it resulted in nothing of the sort.[15] This qualification was important. On February 8, 1950, Malina recorded a discussion she had with Beck and Goodman about "How to stop the wars?" Malina found Goodman's answer, "remove burdens," reminiscent of a "saint" and impractical: "Paul says people need violence, but he really means passionate expression. The tenets of life annul petty concerns and express ardent rebellion against confining circumstances. Paul doesn't make the distinction between ardor and violence."[16] At this juncture, Malina (and presumably Beck) endorsed Goodman's idea that a natural way of being might, from time to time, entail fundamental social (and psychological) reordering, but the engine of this process, they believed, was "ardor"—passion, love, desire without violence.

In *Art and Social Nature*, Goodman argued that "love and fraternity" were the natural forces binding humans into social groups and that within "the creative unanimity and rivalry" of a "revolutionary fraternity," individuals could catch "fire from each other," achieving "what none of them had it in him to do alone."[17] How, then, should anarchists "fired" by such passions proceed politically, as activists? In the "mixed society of coercion and nature" in which we live, Goodman argued, the most effective tactic was to "act so as to avoid the isolation of a particular issue and the freezing of the coercive structure." Prefiguring the values of a natural society founded on freedom, anarchists would "submit the [contested] issue to the dynamism of the common natural powers that nobody disputes" by appealing to principles humanity holds in common ("freedom, justice, and nature"). For example, "exercising civil rights within the framework of the State" "trapped" activists within the existing system, but the trap could be escaped by asserting that the court was "our court," as were the "civil powers that were liberated by our own great men"—that is, America's revolutionary founders. Operating in this way, anarchists could demonstrate to the general populace that "we are not alienated from society [but] on the contrary, Society is alienated from itself."[18]

Writing on contemporary activism, Leela Gandhi has observed that anarchists build movements out of "communities of trust" that respect difference within shared affinities and that in so doing, these activists undermine "the compartmentalization of causes and specializations of interests so characteristic of the anti-relational style of global or corporate governance, a style determined by the culture of 'branding' and its devastating mediative modality."[19] Malina and Beck engaged in just such an endeavor during the 1950s and early 1960s, as they sought (in accord with Goodman and their pacifist convictions) to disrupt the fictive consensus cloaking institutionalized oppression. Disobeying the strictures of governance, they enacted a politics of "ardor" intent on triggering affective responses among the general populace, awakening individuals to the oppressive unnaturalness of the entire social system and their own alienation from its values.

"Last night Julian read to me from the *Times* about the hydrogen bomb. H-bomb, Hell bomb, and all night I dream of war," Malina wrote poignantly in her diary on January 30, 1950, encapsulating the desperation that propelled the couple's politics.[20] Convinced of the need to stop a "planetary forest fire," they pondered strategies. "Julian suggests a peace pledge to rouse everyone's conscience," Malina noted, but nothing came of the idea. In July, after the outbreak of the Korean War the preceding month, Malina and Beck signed an international petition calling for peace and produced (with the assistance of

Dachine Rainer and Holley Cantine, editors of *Retort*) thousands of stickers bearing such slogans as "Answer War Gandhi's Way," "Don't Let Politics Lead You to War," "War Is Hell. Resist It," and "All Politicians Make War. Don't Vote" to be placed "on lampposts, houses, mailboxes, subways." In August, searching "for some kind of action," they organized a letter-writing campaign. Throughout this period, Malina and Beck attended Resistance meetings and mulled over the efficacy of their efforts. On January 24, 1951, they also participated in a Peacemakers meeting at a communal house in Harlem. "The hope of the world," Malina wrote, "is in such handfuls of good people—a 'cell,' they call themselves."[21]

After January 1951, the couple became increasingly absorbed with preparing for the Living Theatre's public debut at the Cherry Lane Playhouse at 38 Commerce Street in Greenwich Village. Its first manifestation was short-lived (August 1951–August 1952), as a fire department inspector closed the venue after declaring that the company's costumes and sets posed a fire hazard.[22] Beck had sunk a six-thousand-dollar inheritance into the project, but the enterprise still bled money.[23] From March 1954 to November 1955, the Living Theatre made its home in a loft on 100th Street, sustaining the operation with funds donated at the door until the building department shut it down. The theater's third incarnation, which lasted from January 1959 to October 1964, was in a refurbished building at 530 6th Avenue, at the corner of 14th Street.[24]

According to Beck, the plays produced at Cherry Lane "stressed the sacredness of life," which was pacifism's core ethic.[25] Goodman's play *Faustina* (staged January 13–27, 1952), is particularly relevant in this regard. *Faustina* concerned the bloody intrigues of a sadistic gladiator during the reign of Emperor Marcus Aurelius.[26] The performance culminated with the ritual sacrifice of the gladiator, after which the "formal walled architecture" symbolizing Roman civilization disappeared, leaving an empty stage set. "Faustina, Empress of Rome" (played by Malina) then turned to the audience, stated her real name, and challenged them about their inaction (although Goodman left the wording of this challenge up to the actor). Malina declaimed, "We have enacted a brutal scene, the ritual murder of a young and handsome man. I have bathed in his blood, and if you were a worthy audience, you'd have leaped on the stage and stopped the action."[27] The program for the Living Theatre's inaugural play at Cherry Lane, *Doctor Faustus Turns Out the Lights* (December 2–16, 1951), includes a short essay by Goodman, "Vanguard and Theatre," that throws light on Malina's call to action. "Vanguard" playwrights and performers play a radicalizing role by turning "away from the usual language and usual assumptions" to "affect a character-change in the audience, more than all the manifestos can accomplish."

This vanguard is "alienated" from present-day society, but audiences are also alienated. They simply "don't recognize it" until they encounter the work of the theatrical vanguard. "We stubbornly belong to your community," Goodman insisted, "tho you often seem not to like that. But now, in the theatre, we suddenly find that we have a community indeed.... And in our days, when people seem so very 'alienated' from one another, so lacking in 'community' (tho there is the devil's plenty of uniformity), my chief aim as an artist is—that we suddenly meet—in this theatre—to our mutual surprise." A vanguard performance thus had the potential to break this multitiered alienation.[28] However *Faustina* failed to induce the public to identify with Malina's heartfelt anarchopacifist point of view.[29] "The audience," according to Beck, "was insulted and went away annoyed, riled."[30]

The Living Theatre's next incarnation was resolutely noncommercial. "We wanted to be free of money," explained Beck, "so we decided on the loft, where we would not advertise, would not invite critics, would not charge admission."[31] The concept of an economy not dependent on monetary exchange had been one of the factors that convinced Malina of anarchism's practicality and figures in an essay by anarchist Harold Norse included in the program for Kenneth Rexroth's *Beyond the Mountains*, first produced at Cherry Lane.[32] On October 20, 1949, Malina recorded in her diary snippets of a discussion with Norse and others about how to realize "a cooperative, moneyless, self-determining society."[33] Norse's essay, "The Poetic Theatre," expanded on this idea, presenting the Living Theatre as an anticapitalist force within existing society by virtue of its "poetic" commitment. Poetry's concern was the "life of the imagination," which is "no less real than the world in which people make business deals."[34] The Living Theatre may have gone bust for lack of money on Cherry Lane, but moneymaking was not the point of the Living Theatre, and on 100th Street, "the life of the imagination" reigned supreme. That said, those involved in the theater had to hold down day jobs to make ends meet, and the performers' ability to devote themselves wholly to their artistry suffered.[35] Nonetheless, decoupling the theater from commercialism represented a small step toward nurturing cultural anarchism within the existing social system.[36]

Beck judged Goodman's *The Young Disciple*, presented in 1955, as the loft theater's high point. Directed by Beck and performed "half in verse, half in prose," the play pitted natural impulses against the dictates of an inflexible society.[37] The pseudobiblical plot revolves around a "miraculous event" that is never directly addressed. Instead, the "community ... strives to interpret it, to blot it out, to mythologize it, so that life can go on as ordinary." The resulting stress becomes the index of blocked creativity, as people's natural impetus to adjust to a new reality comes into conflict with existing social beliefs. In fact, this "martyr-play" (Goodman's term) encapsulates the anarchist approach to psychoanalysis codified in his coauthored study, *Gestalt Therapy* (1951).[38] As Michael Fisher summarizes, Goodman's "approach to psychoanalysis centered on what he called the principle of organismic-self-regulation[which] happened best in small-S society, where relationships based on autonomous individual initiative were the main shaping force in people's lives."[39] *The Young Disciple* depicts the strife of blocked psychological development, but freedom nonetheless manifests itself, although not as scripted narrative but as a reality-based encounter involving playwright, actors, and audience. Performers' emotional outbursts, heavy breathing, dancing, trembling, and so forth represented Goodman's means of enabling their personhood to break free from obedience to "some preconceived notion or formula" (the scripted dictates of the playwright). Goodman saw himself as working "to free the slaves" from an alienating situation he likened to "a factory or army where one person has fallen under another's influence."[40] Those in attendance were also liberated from the role of disinterested spectator: according to Beck, audience members "were disgusted, affronted, annoyed, terrified, awed, and excited" as actors vomited or crept about "on all fours in total darkness making night noises, strange husky grating and chirping sounds."[41]

Aesthetic politics aside, content seems to have been the New York Police Department's main concern. On October 10, 1955, Malina recorded that the police had been "interviewing cast members" while *The Young Disciple* was in rehearsal, intimating that it was obscene. By October 14, the harassment was intensifying: "they stop actors on the street and ask 'you doing a dirty play up there?'" Alarmed and exasperated, Malina and Beck took Goodman's script to the local precinct so that officers could determine what might be illegal under the obscenity statutes. The desk sergeant was uncooperative, declaring, "If we raid you we raid you."[42] The play opened without further incident on October 16.

Activism likely piqued the authorities' sudden interest in the Living Theatre. In 1955, the federal government was ramping up its domestic Cold War campaign against the Soviet Union by instituting "civil defense" drills. On June 15, 1955, New York State staged its first "Operation Alert," a drill staged annually thereafter until 1962. The 1955 drill involved fifty-five cities (thirteen of which had no advance knowledge): after sirens began to wail, civilians were herded into bomb shelters to wait for the all-clear.[43] New York's WRL and Peacemakers chapters, working with the Quakers' Fellowship of Reconciliation, disobeyed the drill on the grounds that it conditioned the public "to accept and expect war, instead of demanding peace and working for it." Malina and others converged at City Hall Park to deliver a letter of protest to the mayor's office, and when the drill began, they were arrested.⁴⁴ In court a hostile judge, annoyed by Malina's attitude, committed her to the Criminal Psychiatric Observation Ward of Bellevue Hospital.⁴⁵ Goodman put Beck in touch with a staff doctor, who declared her sane, and Malina was released on bail the morning of July 17.⁴⁶ The experience galvanized the couple, and on August 9, 1955, they marked the tenth anniversary of the bombing of Hiroshima by joining WRL and Catholic Worker activists handing out protest leaflets in front of New York's Japanese consulate. Malina also took part in a fast "for the sin of the A-bomb" and picketed the Internal Revenue Agency while holding a sign declaring "Love & Life Not Death & Taxes." On September 28, she and six other arrestees pled guilty to violating the New York Emergency Act, under which participation in the drills was mandatory, and police harassment of the Living Theatre commenced a week later. Ironically, the theater was closed in November by a WRL activist working as a licensing inspector for New York City's Building Department.⁴⁷

After the loft was shut down, Malina and Beck determined that they needed a building they could renovate to code. Anarchist composer John Cage and his partner, dancer and choreographer Merce Cunningham, agreed to establish a dance studio at the future location, and Paul Williams (anarchist, architect, and husband of *Resistance* contributing artist Vera Williams) offered to refurbish it.⁴⁸ On June 21, 1957, Cage and Cunningham drove Malina, Beck, and Williams to an abandoned department store at 530 6th Avenue, and Williams declared it workable.⁴⁹ Four weeks later, on July 21, Malina and Beck were arrested and sentenced to thirty days in prison for defying another air raid drill. They presented their political analysis of the experience in "All the World's a Prison," published in the *Village Voice* the following September. Malina and Beck contrasted a social system "without forgiveness" with the spirit of those it incarcerated: "Realizing that they are all suffering" behind bars, prisoners embrace the "freedom to love" and "share in communal life." In the face of intense persecution by the state, the prisoners forge a natural community fired by ardor within the unnatural social order that oppresses them, a community analogous to that of a Peacekeepers cell or a Catholic Worker house of hospitality, albeit without the political consciousness. Trapped in a place of suffering, the prisoner begins breaking down the interpersonal alienations that permeate society. However, once freed from jail, he "walks into a world in which prisons exist as a threat to [everyone's] freedom." Bereft of "the neighborly love that made prison bearable" in a "hostile and competitive community bound by innumerable laws," the prisoner remains "tied forever to the prison he has left," just like those who, having adapted to the capitalist state's norms and values, shackle themselves to their own self-alienation. Echoing Goodman's analysis in "Vanguard and

Theatre" and *Art and Social Nature*, Malina and Beck conclude, "The whole world is a prison. Having been to prison you know this and are never again free; and even if you have not been to prison, and even if you have obeyed the laws and have hidden in fear when the sirens sounded, are you free?"[50]

On January 13, 1959, the Living Theatre opened its new location with "Many Loves," by American poet William Carlos Williams. The play showcases three love stories directed by a young idealist who wants to stage performances whose "poetry" resides in "the audience itself." Its crowning moment occurs when the seasoned financier who has backed the director dismisses his vision on the grounds that theater audiences are composed exclusively of bored middle-class entertainment seekers who can afford to buy tickets.[51] Harkening back to Norse's argument in "The Poetic Theatre," the Living Theatre's dedication to awakening the "poetic" in its audiences was again pitted against the deadening forces of cultural commercialism.[52] The program included a statement, "Drama and Theatre," reprinted from a 1957 collection published by cultural theorist Martin Buber, who was deeply influenced by anarchism.[53] Poetic drama, according to Buber, intensifies the creative "tension" of communication—"namely that two men will never mean the same thing by the words that they use; that therefore there is no pure reply; that at each point of the conversation, therefore, understanding and misunderstanding are interwoven; from which comes then the interplay of openness and closedness, expression and reserve." This quality marks poetic drama as a "natural" form of communication that originates "in the elemental impulse to leap through transformation over the abyss between I and Thou that is bridged through speech." Galvanized by "the *word*... that convulses through the whole body of the speaker," poetic drama is more than mere "entertainment": emulating the gravitas of ancient mystery plays, it constitutes a "sacred reality" that addresses vital social and psychological aspects of our being, "penetrating [the spectator's] life" as well as the lives of the performers.[54]

By 1959, Malina and Beck had realized their project in noncommercial terms and had radicalized theater on the level of affect, but they had yet to introduce substantive political issues directly pertinent to the lives of their audiences. This changed with *The Connection*, written by a hitherto unknown playwright, Jack Gelber.[55] Before arriving in New York and introducing himself to Malina and Beck, Gelber had lived in San Francisco, where he and his wife, Carol Westenberg, moved in anarchist circles that mixed poetry, jazz, and drugs. He befriended Kenneth Rexroth (who gave poetry readings accompanied by jazz musicians) as well as poet and heroin user Philip Lamantia, who served as coeditor, with Saunders Russell, of a San Francisco–based anarchist journal, *The Ark*.[56] Gelber showed a draft of his play to Malina and Beck around

March 1958, and they subsequently worked together to craft the final version, with Gelber and Westenberg assisting with the selection of the cast.[57] Directed by Malina, *The Connection* premiered in July 1959 and was a sensation through 1961, attracting praise, condemnation and packed houses.[58]

The plot concerns a producer, Jim, and writer, Jaybird, who are presenting a play about a quartet of jazz musicians and other heroin junkies waiting in a slum apartment for another junkie, Cowboy, to return with heroin so they can shoot up. Reality and performance commingle from the start as Jim and Jaybird introduce themselves between banter with various members of the cast who will appear in their play. Jaybird attempts to coax the junkies through a loose rendition of his script while two documentary cameramen film everything. The addicts interact with each other, the writer, the producer, and the cameramen while waiting for their next fix. The musicians improvise jazz tunes and occasionally slip into a state of semiconsciousness as a consequence of their heroin usage.

However, the "actors" on the stage were not acting. The Living Theatre hired performers who had lost their licenses to work at the musicians' union rate as a consequence of heroin-related convictions, and during the play many were actually high.[59] In fact, *The Connection* continuously blurs the line between reality and performance. As Bradford Martin notes, the play unfolds in real time and is punctuated by tediously long passages during which nothing much happens.[60] Theater's "fourth wall" that separates the performer from the audience is also nonexistent. For example, just before the end of Act 1, Jaybird cautions the audience about actors panhandling during intermission: no matter what the junkies may say to con money, they are getting paid for their work with a "scientifically accurate amount of heroin," which will be administered during the play.[61] Theatrically framed as artifice, hard-bitten capitalism sutures the producer/writer–junkie/actor–audience relationship by corrupting the only available anticapitalist gesture of goodwill (charity), which turns out to be an offstage scam by junkies to exploit their exploiters.[62] Real-life hypocrisy is targeted. When one junkie argues that all sorts of addictions permeate society, another addict replies, "You happen to have a vice that's illegal." They discuss when heroin became illegal and who benefits from the situation. Pointing out that the authorities justify the atomic bomb on the grounds that it is needed to "protect us from themselves" (though the Japanese "disagree"), Cowboy concludes, "Everything that's illegal is illegal because it makes more money for more people that way."[63]

During Act 2, the junkies anxiously take turns retreating into a bathroom with Cowboy to shoot up. Matters come to a head when an older junkie, Leach, who has been using so long that he needs more than one shot to get high, insists that he needs more. After warning him of the danger, Cowboy relents and gives him another hit, which Leach prepares and injects in full view of the audience. He overdoses, and most of the other junkies drift off, wanting to avoid becoming caught up in a situation that could involve the police. Cowboy and another junkie care about Leach and remain behind with Jaybird (who is panicking) and Jim to revive the addict. While the audience confronts this traumatizing spectacle, conversation meanders through such other present-day horrors as the hydrogen bomb and prefrontal lobotomies and electroshock therapy. Jaybird concludes that reality and theater "all fits together": "We wouldn't all be on stage if it didn't fit. That's what I had in mind in the first place. I didn't learn anything [from the play]. I knew it. Find a horror. Then you try to tell people it isn't a horror. And then I have the gall to be horrified. Well, if it wasn't junk, I would have been involved with something else."[64] *The Connection* ends with a knock on the door. An old man carrying a portable record player enters the room, plugs it in, plays a jazz record, packs up, and leaves.

Reviews repeatedly commented on the addicts' suffering and audiences' (and reviewers') discomfort. In response to a question one of the junkies angrily asks the audience—"Why are you here? You stupid—you want to watch people suffer?"—*New York Post* theater critic Francis Herridge wondered, "Man, which one of us is suffering?"[65] *Village Voice* journalist Jerry Tallmer referred to the "crackling skin of anyone who watches, and cares" as "electrical ripples of tension and latent violence" course through the cast "waiting in agony" for a fix.[66] Lee Pomex, writing for *Show Business*, characterized the play as "depressing," "incisive," "shocking," and filled with "unspoken tensions."[67] *Nation* reviewer Harold Clurman remarked that "spectators eager for 'art' or 'entertainment'" will find neither in an "unpleasant" performance charged with "genuine pathos" that verged on a "wretched sort of heroism."[68] And the *New Republic*'s Robert Brustein, writing in *Theater*, vividly described how, in the absence of theater's "imaginary fourth wall," the audience discovered its presence heightening the "distress" of the junkies on stage in "a performance of frightening integrity" whose only "false note" was "your own conventional expectation, conditioned by years of phony drama and sociological indoctrination."[69]

The agitating power of anarchist poetics had finally found its activist touchstone: the grotesqueness of Goodman's unnatural, capitalist society. While Malina and Beck were rehearsing Gelber's play, *Resistance* contributor Mary Catherine Richards introduced them to French theorist Antonin Artaud's collected essays, *The Theatre and Its Double* (1938).[70] Artaud's analysis enthralled them, and they reprinted his preface, "The Theatre and Culture," in the program for *The Connection*.⁷¹ Artaud discusses his desire for a "savage" theater that makes use "of everything—gestures, sounds, words, screams, light, darkness" to "compel us to return to nature, i.e. to rediscover life." In so doing, theater would become "culture-in-action," communicating with the intensity of "victims burnt at the stake, signaling through the flames." *The Theatre and Its Double* includes a series of manifestos and statements conceptualizing a "theatre of cruelty" that could become "believable reality." Such theater would pulverize the separation of stage and auditorium to "attack the spectator's sensibility on all sides." Man's "interior" life, his "taste for crime, his erotic obsessions, his savagery, his chimeras, his utopian sense of life and matter, even his cannibalism" are all fodder for Artaud's extravagant vision of a theater of "perpetual conflict, a spasm in which life is continually lacerated, in which everything in creation rises up and exerts itself." Qualifying his use of the term *cruelty*, Artaud redefines it "from the point of view of the mind" as signifying "rigor, implacable intention and decision, irreversible and absolute determination, a kind of higher determinism to which the executioner-tormentor himself is subjected and to which he must be determined to endure when the time comes. Cruelty is above all lucid, a kind of rigid control and submission to necessity." Marshaling these forces, Artaud predicts that "a bleeding spurt of images in the poet's head and the spectator's as well" will cleanse us of our will to violence: "I defy that spectator to give himself up, once outside the theatre, to ideas of war, riot, and blatant murder."⁷²

Malina and Beck found common cause with Artaud's concept of "culture-in-action," his call for a theater synonymous with life and the poetic value of a "theatre of cruelty" that could bring us face-to-face with our deep-seated destructive impulses. They did not, however, agree with his belief that "each stronger life tramples down the others, consuming them in a massacre which is a transfiguration and a bliss. In the manifested world, metaphysically speaking, evil is the permanent law and what is good is an effort and already one more cruelty added to the other."⁷³ The Living Theatre's adaptation of the "theatre of cruelty" was a means of drawing audiences into a critical frame of mind amenable to Beck and Malina's pacifist-anarchist outlook rather than to Artaud's darkly truncated worldview.

The audience's reaction to the spectacle of self-inflicted cruelty when Leach jabs his arm with a hypodermic needle and then spasms in an overdose-induced coma certainly testifies to the power of Artaud's concept: some audience members fainted.⁷⁴ Similarly, the audience's discomfort (a kind of suffering) with their "theatrical" role as cruelty's consumers goes some way toward an Artaudian effect. At the same time, the play advances anarchist politics. Faced with the criminalization of their desire for drug-induced euphoria (not the acquisition of property or power over others), the addicts repeatedly critique their condition, pointing out that the user is on the bottom rung of an exploitative series of power relationships structured by the law. Furthermore, compassion and mutual aid exist among the addicts, who team up to buy drugs (increasing affordability), share a space where they can get high, feed each other, and even prevent a death. Much like Malina and Beck's community of the incarcerated, *The Connection*'s junkies are subordinated by an unnatural community whose state-sanctioned horrors (most notably, the bomb) far outstrip their own criminality, and their humanity endures as the "natural" complement to an awakening critical consciousness. In this way, theatrical politics merged with politics in the street, and when Malina dedicated *The Connection* to Thelma Jackson, a former cellmate of Malina's who had died of an overdose, "and to all other junkies, dead or alive, in the Women's House of Detention," she served notice of that fact.[75]

The Connection brought recognition, but the Living Theatre remained mired in debt, had not paid its rent, and was facing legal action for tax evasion.[76] At the same time, the world situation was worsening. In 1961 the Soviet Union announced it was ending a self-imposed moratorium on atomic bomb testing, a development that led the U.S. government to consider additional atmospheric tests. Malina and Beck responded by organizing the General Strike for Peace to unite war resisters around the globe. During 1962–63 the couple threw themselves into the mobilization effort, which included three New York–based "general strikes" involving hundreds of people who picketed, marched, paraded, engaged in sit-down demonstrations, and were repeatedly arrested.[77] In January 1963, Malina and Beck also began work on *The Brig*, which would prove to be the Living Theatre's last performance at 530 6th Avenue. The playwright was a former U.S. Marine, Kenneth Brown, who had been held in a military brig for thirty days while stationed in Japan.[78] In the brig, prisoners followed a strict sequence of routines, day in and day out, for the length of their incarceration. The goal was to strip them of their identity and instill unquestioning obedience. Each inmate was given a number and forced to answer to it. Prisoners were forced to study the *Guide for Marines* to the letter while obeying rigid protocols of behavior within a tightly confined space sectioned off by lines that could not be crossed without permission or an order to do so. Guards screamed at, punched, and constantly humiliated prisoners and enforced a strict code of silence between inmates. Brown's play presents a day in this brig, with all its attendant brutality.[79]

The Living Theatre regarded its performance of *The Brig* as a political statement and an audience-activating experience keyed to Artaud's "theatre of cruelty." In her director's notes, published in 1964, Malina interprets the play as a transformative critique of society's authoritarian structures: "Whether that structure calls itself a prison or a school or a factory or a family or a government, that structure asks each man what he can do for it, not what it can do for him, and for those who do not do for it, there is the pain of death or imprisonment, or social degradation, or the loss of animal rights." Outlining her techniques for staging the marine brig's "structure" of psychological and physical cruelty, she cites Artaud's challenge to his audience—"I defy that spectator to give himself up, once outside the theatre, to ideas of war, riot, and blatant murder"—to underline her ambition to radicalize people.[80] She also interprets the play's message as anarchist, referencing Goodman's *Drawing the Line*. *The Brig's* brutalized marines and their guard-persecutors are united by the choice, at some juncture, to submit. Each soldier has decided to "draw the line at that line," providing "the symbolic key of his repressed powers" and his suffering.[81] In a free society, no such line need ever be drawn by any individual.[82] What inner force could free us to usher in such a society? "Love, the saving grace in everything human," was the Living Theatre's answer. In *The Brig*, Malina reveals, the Living Theatre "called on pity last, on basic human kinship first" so that the audience may "know violence in the clear light of the kinship of our physical empathy." When humanity grasps the truth of violence, she predicted, we will "confront the dimensions of the Structure, find its keystone, learn on what foundations it stands, and locate its doors. Then we will penetrate its locks and open the doors of all the jails."[83]

The Brig opened on May 15, 1963, shortly after the final "general strike" action. By that time, Malina and Beck's activism and rehearsals of Brown's highly charged play had politicized the entire troupe. Opening reviews were hostile, but the play attracted an audience and began to prove financially successful. However, on October 17, the Living Theatre was served with a notice of eviction for unpaid rent, and the next day, Internal Revenue Service agents declared the contents of the theater "government property in lieu of $28,435 in back taxes."[84] Malina, Beck, and members of the cast refused to leave, and protesters rallied to their cause while police set up barricades. On the evening of Saturday, October 19, supporters entered the building through a rooftop fire door and watched the performance of *The Brig*. After it ended, twenty-five members of the cast and audience were arrested and charged with a range of offenses. Malina and Beck turned their trial into a protest event, asserting their right to defend "beleaguered beauty and art" against "the anonymous instruments of oppression of the military-industrial complex."[85] The couple were found guilty on seven counts, ordered to pay back taxes and penalties, and fined. Malina was sentenced to thirty days in jail for contempt of court, while Beck received sixty days; both were placed on probation for five years. Malina and Beck were released on bail in July, pending an appeal (which was never pursued), and they then traveled to Europe, where the Living Theatre had engagement. The couple returned to the United States in late 1964, stayed long enough to serve their sentences, and rejoined their troupe in Europe immediately thereafter.[86]

To paraphrase Goodman, the Living Theatre was dedicated to "unfreezing" the psychological and social "coercive structures" that alienate us from ourselves and perpetuate authoritarian cultural, economic, and political institutions. To this end, Artaud's "theatre of cruelty" offered a means of galvanizing poetic affect to radicalize the audience's political outlook in the deepest, most heartfelt sense. For Malina and Beck, the efficacy of such poetics arose from their pacifist conviction that an anarchist society had to be based on love, not violence: if people could come to understand the true nature of violence as the root of self-alienation (Artaud's promise), they would perforce renounce it. But what if aestheticizing "cruelty" fell short of this goal? By what criteria would the worth of their aesthetics be assessed? On July 19, 1963, Shortly after *The Brig* opened, Jackson Mac Low, a poet, pacifist-anarchist, and frequent collaborator of Malina and Beck, wrote a letter raising this issue:

> I'm still puzzled as to the "aesthetics" of "The Brig." As a work of production & direction & acting, it seem well-nigh perfect . . . from a craftsman's point of view. But whether something that produces only nausea, disgust, revulsion & other painful feelings (as it is *meant* to) but which in no way brings these feelings to a Katharsis—even one of the hope of a possible change—is an aesthetic in any sense except that of craft (the only possible *pleasure* [except for perversities] is one's admiration at its being "done" so well—at the fact that such horror is portrayed so perfectly), is a question I still *cannot* resolve. Maybe it is not important. Then, however, the work *must* have real social effects—it must be an effective work of *rhetoric* & cause not only temporary changes in its viewers/auditors, but a real change in the Marine Corps' imprisonment system (at the very least) &, if possible, in the whole system of violence—of military establishments and prisons. Have you had any *evidence* that it has begun to bring about any definite changes (at least in the "defense" depart.)? Please let me know if you hear of any.[87]

Mac Low's desire for an aesthetic in the anarchist sense as opposed to "craft" is challenging, but it can be resolved by taking into account the radicalization of the actors who performed in *The Brig*. Many of those actors followed Malina and Beck to Europe, where the troupe became a nomadic anarchist collective (a "horde," in Malina's words).[88] And the willingness of protesters to rally to Malina and Beck's defense when their theater was shut down suggests that *The Brig* indeed had a "real social effect," however modest, on the individual audience members involved. The Living Theatre's aesthetic was anarchist and as such was antithetical to the social institutions of violence. In July 1964, Beck commented on *The Brig*, "Artaud's mistake was that he imagined you could create a horror out of the fantastic. Brown's gleaming discovery is that horror is not in what we imagine but is in what is real."[89] The Living Theatre formulated an aesthetic of tension within the "real" that was as self-actualizing and transformative as direct action in the streets. This was Malina and Beck's gift to the postwar renewal of anarchism in New York.

Notes

1. Arnold Aronson, *American Avant-Garde Theatre: A History* (London: Routledge, 2000), 48, 53.

2. Andrew Cornell, "'For a World without Oppressors': U.S. Anarchism from the Palmer Raids to the Sixties" (Ph.D. diss., New York University, 2011), 306–17. See also Andrew Cornell's chapter in this volume.

3. Cornell, "'For a World without Oppressors,'" 337.

4. "Our Resistance," *Resistance*, May 1947, 2–3, 15–16.

5. James Tracy, *Direct Action: Radical Pacifism from the Union Eight to the Chicago Seven* (Chicago: University of Chicago Press, 1996), 56–58.

6. Scott H. Bennett, *Radical Pacifism: The War Resisters League in America, 1915–1963* (Syracuse: Syracuse University Press, 2003), 148–49.

7. Ammon Hennacy, *The Book of Ammon* (Salt Lake City: Hennacy, 1970), 318. See also Anne Klejment's chapter in this volume.

8. Patrick G. Coy, "The One-Person Revolution of Ammon Hennacy," in *A Revolution of the Heart: Essays on the Catholic Worker*, ed. Patrick G. Coy (Philadelphia: Temple University Press, 1988), 143.

9. Judith Malina, *The Diaries of Judith Malina, 1947–1957* (New York: Grove, 1984), 42.

10. John Tytell, *The Living Theatre: Art, Exile, and Outrage* (New York: Grove, 1995), 55, 46.

11. Michael C. Fisher, introduction to Paul Goodman, *New Reformation: Notes of a Neolithic Conservative* (San Francisco: PM, 2010), 11.

12. Paul Goodman, "Revolution, Sociolatry, and War," in *Drawing the Line: Political Essays*, ed. Taylor Stoehr (New York: Free Life, 1972), 31.

13. Malina, *Diaries*, 107.

14. Tytell, *Living Theatre*, 47. *Art and Social Nature* (1946)'s contents include "Reflections on Drawing the Line," "A Touchstone for the Libertarian Program," "Natural Violence," and "Unanimity."

15. Paul Goodman, "Natural Violence," in *Drawing the Line*, 23–25.

16. Malina, *Diaries*, 98.

17. Paul Goodman, "Reflections on Drawing the Line," in *Drawing the Line*, 8.

18. Paul Goodman, "Unanimity," in ibid., 36, 37.

19. Leela Gandhi, *Affective Communities: Anticolonial Thought, Fin-De-Siècle Radicalism, and the Politics of Friendship* (Durham, N.C.: Duke University Press, 2006), 20, 188.

20. Malina, *Diaries*, 97.

21. Malina, *Diaries*, 97, 117, 119, 145.

22. Julian Beck, "Storming the Barricades" (1964), in Kenneth Brown, *The Brig: A Concept for Theatre and Film* (New York: Hill and Wang, 1965), 17, 19.

23. Tytell, *Living Theatre*, 85–86.

24. Beck, "Storming the Barricades," 20. Beck gives incorrect dates.

25. Ibid., 18.

26. The script is reprinted in Paul Goodman, *The Young Disciple, Faustina, Joseph: Three Plays by Paul Goodman* (New York: Random House, 1965), 63–130.

27. Quoted in Beck, "Storming the Barricades," 13.

28. Paul Goodman, "Vanguard and Theatre," in *The Living Theatre: Doctor Faustus Lights the Lights by Gertrude Stein* (New York: Living Theatre, 1951), 1. "Vanguard and Theatre" is reprinted in the program for anarchist poet Kenneth Rexroth's *Beyond the Mountains* (performed December 2, 1951–January 6, 1952). Both programs may be found in Living Theatre Records, Box 109, Uncat MSS 1006, Beinecke Rare Book and Manuscript Library, Yale University, New Haven, Conn.

29. Erika Munk, "Only Connect: The Living Theater and Its Audiences," in *Restaging the Sixties: Radical Theaters and Their Legacies*, ed. James Martin Harding and Cindy Rosenthal (Ann Arbor: University of Michigan Press, 2009), 37.

30. Beck, "Storming the Barricades," 13.

31. Ibid., 20.

32. Tytell, *Living Theatre*, 55; Harold Norse, "The Poetic Theatre," in *The Living Theatre: Beyond the Mountains by Kenneth Rexroth* (New York: Living Theatre, 1951), 1, 7.

33. Malina, *Diaries*, 88.

34. Norse, "Poetic Theatre," 1.

35. Beck, "Storming the Barricades," 20.

36. See Jackson Mac Low, "The Human Condition: Hunger-Art & the Hungry Artists," *Resistance* 9:1 (1950): 8.

37. Beck, "Storming the Barricades," 23.

38. Paul Goodman, "Comment on the Young Disciple" (October 1954), in *Young Disciple, Faustina, Joseph*, 61; Paul Goodman, Frederick Perls, and Ralph F. Hefferline, *Gestalt Therapy* (New York: Delta, 1951).

39. Fisher, introduction, 13.

40. Paul Goodman, "Art of the Theatre" (1964), in *Young Disciple, Faustina, Joseph*, xii.

41. Beck, "Storming the Barricades," 24.

42. Malina, *Diaries*, 385.

43. "Federal Highway Administration: Infrastructure, 1955," http://www.fhwa.dot.gov/infrastructure/civildef.cfm.

44. Bennett, *Radical Pacifism*, 208; Malina, *Diaries*, 368.

45. Malina, *Diaries*, 369–70.

46. Tytell, *Living Theatre*, 116.

47. Malina, *Diaries*, 377–78, 284, 389, 387; Bennett, *Radical Pacifism*, 149–53, 209.

48. See Allan Antliff, "Donald Judd's First Element," in *The Writings of Donald Judd*, ed. Marianne Stockebrand and Richard Shiff (Marfa, Tex.: Chinati, 2009), 191 n. 42.

49. Tytell, *Living Theatre*, 197; Renfreu Neff, *The Living Theatre/USA* (Indianapolis: Bobbs-Merrill, 1972), 7.

50. Julian Beck and Judith Malina, "All the World's a Prison," *Village Voice*, September 7, 1957 (clipping), Living Theatre Records, Box 287.

51. Tytell, *Living Theatre*, 151.

52. The troupe also kept ticket prices low or allowed people to donate what they chose. See Neff, *Living Theatre/USA*, 8.

53. Martin Buber, "Drama and Theatre (A Fragment, 1925)," in *Pointing the Way: Collected Essays* (London: Routledge, 1957), 63–66; Peter Marshall, *Demanding the Impossible: A History of Anarchism* (London: Harper Perennial, 2008), 573–75.

54. Buber, *Pointing the Way*, 63–66.

55. Jack Gelber, *The Connection* (New York: Grove, 1960).

56. Jerry Tallmar, "Jack Gelber of 'The Connection': The Boy Who Broke the Circle & UnSquared It," *Village Voice*, November 4, 1959 (clipping), Living Theatre Records, Box 179. On Lamantia, Saunders, Rexroth, and *The Ark*, see Linda Hamilian, *A Life of Kenneth Rexroth* (New York: Norton, 1991), 152–53.

57. Tallmar, "Jack Gelber of 'The Connection.'"

58. Beck, "Storming the Barricades," 25–26.

59. Tytell, *Living Theatre*, 156–57.

60. Bradford Martin, *The Theater Is in the Street: Politics and Performance in Sixties America* (Amherst: University of Massachusetts Press, 2004), 58.

61. Gelber, *Connection*, 53–54.

62. See Nathan Cohen, "Nathan Cohen's Corner: The Drug Addict, as a Symbol," *Toronto Daily Star*, September 8, 1959 (clipping), Living Theatre Records, Box 179.

63. Gelber, *Connection*, 31, 90, 91.

64. Ibid., 95.

65. Francis Herridge, "Six Hipsters in Search of a Play," *New York Post*, July 16, 1959 (clipping), Living Theatre Records, Box 179.

66. Jerry Tallmar, "Theatre: The Connection," *Village Voice*, July 22, 1959 (clipping), in ibid.

67. Lee Pomex, "Off-Broadway Reviews," *Show Business*, July 27, 1959 (clipping), in ibid.

68. Harold Clurman, *The Nation*, August 15, 1959 (clipping), in ibid.

69. Robert Brustein, "Junkies and Jazz," *Theater*, September 29, 1959 (clipping), in ibid.

70. Tytell, *Living Theatre*, 146.

71. Mike Sell, *Avant-Garde Performance and the Limits of Criticism* (Ann Arbor: University of Michigan Press, 2008), 119.

72. Antonin Artaud, *The Theatre and Its Double*, trans. M. C. Richards (New York: Grove, 1958), 8, 10–13, 85, 86, 92, 102, 82.

73. Ibid., 103.

74. Beck, "Storming the Barricades," 27.

75. Martin, *Theater Is in the Street*, 59–60.

76. Tytell, *Living Theatre*, 161.

77. Ibid., 170–84. Extensive documentation of the "General Strike for Peace" is preserved in a black binder and a blue binder held in the Living Theatre Records, Box 179.

78. Tytell, *Living Theatre*, 179, 180.

79. Brown, *Brig*.

80. Judith Malina, "Directing *The Brig*" (1964), in ibid., 83, 82.

81. Goodman cited in ibid., 103. See also Goodman, "Reflections on Drawing the Line," 9.

82. Malina, "Directing *The Brig*," 103. She cites and sequentially inverts the order of two passages from "Reflections on Drawing the Line." See Goodman, "Reflections on Drawing the Line," 10, 9.

83. Malina, "Directing *The Brig*," 103, 106–7.

84. Tytell, *Living Theatre*, 183, 186.

85. Martin, *Theater Is in the Street*, 63.

86. Tytell, *Living Theatre*, 194, 202–4; Neff, *Living Theatre/USA*, 10–13.

87. Jackson Mac Low to Julian Beck and Judith Malina, July 19, 1963, Living Theatre Records, Box 113.

88. Malina quoted in Tytell, *Living Theatre*, 204.

89. Beck, "Storming the Barricades," 35.

Up against the Wall Motherfucker

Ideology and Action in a "Street Gang with an Analysis"

CAITLIN CASEY

By the late 1960s, America's rebellious youth had adopted a multitude of forms—political activists, cultural activists, antiactivism dropouts, and everything in between. Yet, even in this multifaceted subculture, one group stood out, according to activist Susan Stern, as "the downright dirtiest, skuzziest, and loudest group of people I'd ever laid eyes on"—the Motherfuckers, short for Up against the Wall Motherfucker (UAW/MF).[1] Stern's background as a radical politico, drug user, and member of the Weather Underground makes her characterization even more evocative.[2] According to Osha Neumann, one of the original Motherfuckers, as a "long haired, dirty, bearded Motherfucker, I could look in the mirror and see . . . my mother's nightmare."[3] They were "Hell's Angels with manifestoes," flipping switchblades on St. Marks Place; they were "a street gang with an analysis," shadowing the police to ensure fair treatment of the hippies; they were "flower children with thorns," writing angry political poetry.[4]

The Motherfuckers were a militant Lower East Side–based activist group rooted in the anarchist tradition. They were equally devoted to political and cultural activism, to performing and being recognized on a national and local scale. Although the Motherfuckers never had more than twenty members, they inspired a substantial following among the denizens of the Lower East Side from late 1967 to mid-1969. They called themselves an "affinity group" and thought of themselves as a "family" or "tribe," a new social organization brought together through shared ideals, intense devotion to the realization of a new society, and the belief that America was rotten through and through. They organized crash pads for runaway youths, published poetry and drawings in leaflets and underground papers, and staged theatrical and confrontational demonstrations.[5] They were violent and aggressive, frequently spouting revolutionary rhetoric that alienated not just mainstream society but even their putative allies in the youth culture. They did not survive long, but they loom large in the personal narratives of many activists, and even at the time, they generated a certain lore.[6] They are remarkable for their near total reliance on poetry and visual arts, published on broadsheets and in the underground press, to spread their revolutionary message and to explain and promote both their national and local actions.[7] They rejected the mainstream press, choosing an unprintable name and refusing to speak with reporters. Most important, the Motherfuckers created an ad hoc strategy that blended action, art, and politics to an unprecedented level in the name of total revolution.

One reason that historians have overlooked the Motherfuckers is that they challenged the common analytical categories—the "New Left" and "the counterculture"—that traditional 1960s scholarship used to define the youth rebellion. Insofar as the Motherfuckers were a white group that protested the Vietnam War, complained about the structure of the universities, and admired the Black Power movement, the group shares some of the qualities associated with the New Left. However, the New Left was closely linked with Students for a Democratic Society (SDS), an organization that the Motherfuckers rhetorically rejected for its limited vision, preoccupation with strategic efficacy, and assertion that students were the principal force for change. Moreover, the Motherfuckers argued on behalf of a total restructuring of society, declaring, "Regime change isn't Revolution."[8] The Motherfuckers also had much in common with the counterculture—that is, the wing of the youth movement that emphasized personal and sexual freedom, authenticity, community, and love. But whereas the counterculture was often apolitical or even convinced that the political structure was irrelevant to a revolutionary lifestyle, the Motherfuckers were keenly political. Indeed, they advocated a total restructuring of both the cultural and political spheres of American society and believed that the hippies' cultural vision was a fantasy without political revolution.[9]

More recent histories suggest, however, that cultural politics in the movement may have been more fluid than the traditional dichotomy between the New Left and counterculture implies.[10] These were predominantly young people who lived, worked, and struggled for freedom together. Their politics could often not be separated from their lifestyles, and most were seeking a restructuring of both. The Motherfuckers saw themselves as part of this struggle for a new world; they were an independent collective formed with the goals of individual freedom and authenticity as well as a national cultural and political revolution. This rhetoric of revolution, though commonly used in the late 1960s, was for many "less a form of political agency than a moral and existential stance—a way of announcing one's opposition to the established order and desire for something radically better," according to historian Jeremy Varon.[11] While the Motherfuckers certainly used the language of revolution to express their "opposition to the established order," they also had an exaggerated sense of their political agency. In spite of their small numbers, many believed that through laying the foundations for a national radical community in their own neighborhood, they could engender a global social, political, and cultural shift.

The Motherfuckers came out of a Lower East Side that was a mix of artists, the first influx of counterculturalists, and traditional immigrant communities. They embodied both the artistic sensibilities and the hardscrabble realities of the community they called home. They also relied on the underground press that had flourished in the area. The neighborhood was home to both the *Rat* and the *East Village Other*, two of the nation's most influential alternative papers. In New York and elsewhere, underground reporters were often activists, giving them unfettered access to various groups such as the Motherfuckers. These papers provided the publicity that created a national name for the Motherfuckers as well as helped ground them in the activist community of the Lower East Side.[12]

Most of the Motherfuckers were college graduates or dropouts, and, according to SDS activist Jeff Jones, who knew them well, many were "very well read, especially in the philosophies of anarchism."[13] Anarchism, according to philosopher and writer Murray Bookchin, one of the Motherfuckers' mentors, "developed in the tension between two basically contradictory tendencies: a personalistic commitment to individual autonomy and a collectivist commitment to social freedom."[14] It should scarcely come as a surprise, then, that those involved in the political counterculture—individuals striving for a sense of authenticity and meaning and a collective framework for their actions—found the tenets of anarchism appealing. Anarchists advocated self-directed social communities that "involved people in face-to-face relations based on direct democracy, self-management, active citizenship, and personal participation."[15] The Motherfuckers' desire for action as well as discourse was well suited to the tenets of anarchism. Ben Morea, the charismatic de facto leader of the Motherfuckers, remembered that he understood anarchism not as "an ideological 'confine'" but as something to be lived through deeds. Though they educated themselves about anarchism, for Morea and many other members of the Motherfuckers, Bookchin's conception of the term skewed too "scholastic"; ideology, the activists believed, was "less spoken and more acted." To further his understanding of anarchism, Morea sought out veterans of the anarchist brigades of the Spanish Civil War. Whereas Bookchin's version of anarchism was nonconfrontational, these veterans resonated with Morea; they, too, understood the necessity of conflict and even violence in the name of the revolution.[16]

Although Bookchin and other thinkers provided the Motherfuckers with an intellectual grounding, their radicalism was equally colored by the cultural and political milieu of the era. Their beliefs and attitudes were shaped by the same phenomena that radicalized young whites from coast to coast—the tremendous moral power of the civil rights movement, the student movement, the antiwar movement, and the burgeoning youth culture, with its emphasis on personal and sexual freedom and community. The Motherfuckers' roots in New York placed them at the heart of many of these movements. Morea credits the Living Theatre, an iconic New York experimental theater troupe, with first introducing him to the term *anarchism*.[17] The city's experimental art scene demonstrated that artists—as the Motherfuckers identified themselves—could be and perhaps ought to be politically engaged. Though the Motherfuckers were highly critical of SDS's moderate stance and bureaucracy, the student organization helped solidify the idea that young people were a central political force. The Motherfuckers' amorphous program seemed to be in harmony with sections of SDS's 1962 Port Huron Statement, which advocated participatory democracy—the notion that "decision-making of basic social consequence [should] be carried on by public groupings." The authors of the Port Huron Statement believed that personal involvement allowed people to create relationships that would help give "meaning [to one's] personal life."[18] Though the Motherfuckers eventually rejected the term *participatory democracy* as too narrowly political, one SDS national officer who knew them noted that "local and personal involvement was very much a part of the Motherfuckers' challenge of existing cultural norms and its goal of [a] decentralized, non-hierarchical organization."[19] That SDS and the Motherfuckers had a stormy relationship should not obscure the fact that the groups' theoretical foundations overlapped.

The Motherfuckers gleaned ideas from the counterculture as well. The Diggers, a flamboyant group of San Francisco–based hippies that also came into being in the late 1960s, served as a particularly influential model for UAW/MF. The Diggers were "community anarchists"; they performed guerrilla theater in the streets, opened a "free store," and served free meals to the community (often by pressuring local merchants to "donate" food). The Diggers believed that creating a new and free society required acting act as if such a society already existed, a principle that the Motherfuckers shared. At the same time, important differences existed between the two groups. The West Coast counterculture was more playful and mellow than the edgier version that emerged in New York City. Stew Albert, a well-known Yippie who lived in both places, explained the difference: "In the West Coast, there were flower children. In the East Coast, there were weed children. They just grew up out of the sidewalk."[20] The Motherfuckers admired the Diggers but believed that New York's environment demanded a tougher counterculture. While the hippies talked of love and dropping out, the Motherfuckers spoke of anger—not only their own anger with America but just as important, "the dangerous rage of society against [them]."[21]

Before the group's formation in 1967, individual Motherfuckers had found few arenas in which to express their frustration with America. Neumann was painting in a crash pad, trying to fulfill "art's promise of liberation."[22] Creek, another member of the group, was in the army's brig for defying orders.[23] Travis came to the Lower East Side from Texas, where he found few people who shared his radical ideology and style. In October 1966, Ben Morea, who had spent his formative years in and out of trouble with the New York police, began publishing an anarchist magazine, *Black Mask*. Its name referenced both Frantz Fanon's canonical anticolonial book, *Black Skin, White Masks*, and the anarchist identification with the color black. The magazine espoused the necessity of a cultural front in the struggle for total revolution, a tenet that came to undergird UAW/MF. Those who trivialized the cultural aspects of the revolution, Morea said, were mistakenly equating culture with "western-bourgeois culture"—the type of culture trapped in museums and art books.[24] In fact, he claimed, everyone was fighting for their own culture: in the face of American occupation, the Vietnamese were "fighting against the destruction of their culture"; the Africans struggling against colonialism "have always been concerned with culture's preservation"; the Black Power movement was urging African Americans to become "more aware of [their] culture."[25] Morea saw these as struggles for "living culture" and as having nothing to do with the establishment's definition of art. Morea saw the Vietnamese', Africans', and black Americans' successful integration of political and cultural goals as the model for white American radicals to follow.

Two local events—Angry Arts Week and the 1967 Newark riots—catalyzed the formation of Up against the Wall Motherfucker and firmly rooted it within New York. These moments contributed to the facets of UAW/MF that make it so remarkable—its anger, its simultaneous national and local scope, and its emphasis on action. Angry Arts Week was a series of protests that ran from January 29 to February 5, 1967, involving approximately 250 artists, mostly from the Lower East Side. It featured protest art, street theater, and demonstrations revolving around opposition to the Vietnam War. Neumann was among a group that disrupted High Mass at St. Patrick's Cathedral to protest Cardinal Francis Spellman's support of the war. The demonstrators carried posters "of napalmed children into the church. Each picture had above it the Fifth Commandment, 'Thou Shalt Not Kill,' and below it the word 'Vietnam'—very tasteful." Though the protesters barely had time to reveal their posters before police hustled them away, the demonstration illustrated the abrasive nature of many of the week's protests. According to Neumann, UAW/MF naturally emerged from the organizing around Angry Arts Week: "We just kept meeting when the week ended."[26]

Newark had one of the worst standards of living for African Americans in the United States and, like many cities that summer, tensions exploded into racial conflict. Between July 12 and July 17, 1967, twenty-six people were killed, twenty-four of them black, including a ten-year-old boy.[27] The police were accused of shooting into the windows of apartments, beating innocent people, and breaking the windows of black-owned stores.[28] The uprising spurred Morea to move beyond the rhetoric within his magazine to action in the streets. Initially, he looked to SDS to help him transition to action-based work: SDS was the highest-profile organization in the city, and he was looking for allies. The result was a rally on the Lower East Side, organized by SDS members and Lower East Side radicals, in support of the Newark protesters' demands. By all accounts, the mood at the rally was tense and angry.[29] It was just the type of action that Morea was seeking. From 1967 to 1968, *Black Mask* was published only sporadically as Morea devoted more time to the development of the Motherfuckers. In its last issue, published in April 1968, *Black Mask*'s founders declared that they would channel all their energy toward creating revolution—"the movement must be *real* or it will not be. Now the call is INTO THE STREETS."[30] In their local nature, the national attention that they received, and their tangible sense of anger and urgency, Angry Arts Week and the Newark riots reflected many of the elements that would become fundamental to the Motherfuckers.

A group that evolved out of such spontaneous protests and found its intellectual footing in anarchism logically would eschew traditional hierarchies. Unlike SDS or the Student Nonviolent Coordinating Committee, UAW/MF was not a formal organization. It had no membership rolls, no dues, and no leaders, although Morea was often identified as the Motherfuckers' spokesperson. It referred to itself as an "affinity group"—an unstructured, voluntary merging of individual energies and ideas to produce action and change. At the same time, the group prefigured the revolutionary society members were trying to create. Their size allowed them to function effectively without structure and avoid the factionalism that undermined more established organizations. The Motherfuckers could join with other groups in a "federation" for specific projects without sacrificing their individuality or their personal connections. The Motherfuckers condemned the "poverty of present forms of organization" in which "men work, study and sometimes love and die together—but they do not any longer know how to LIVE together—share the wholeness of their lives."[31] They wanted their group to resemble a family or tribe, coming together "out of love and trust . . . a merging of individual energies becoming one strength."[32] The Motherfuckers saw the nuclear family as a hopelessly outdated concept but their new family as presaging the postrevolutionary society.[33]

Art lay at the core of the Motherfuckers' revolution. Their writing was poetic and was accompanied by drawings by Neumann. They were proud to avoid the manifestos that seemed ubiquitous among their peers. They saw their writing as having multiple purposes. The literal act of putting pen to paper in protest not only constituted an act of rebellion but also served functional purposes: the words and images were meant to inspire readers to action. When read today, Motherfucker poetry seems heavy-handed: aggressive toward those with whom they disagreed and glorifying the freedom and love of the hip community. At the time, however, it was an effective organizing tool. The Motherfuckers' broadsheets published in the underground paper the *Rat* and the leaflets distributed on the street allowed them to reach nearly everyone living on the Lower East Side. While the ubiquity of their images—nearly every *Rat* issue in 1968 published a drawing by the Motherfuckers—certainly strengthened their base, Morea and his group also saw poetry and images as a way to reach out to those who considered themselves apolitical, or even antipolitical. People who were unwilling to read a treatise or attend a rally might still look at an image or read a poem. Roz Payne, a member of Newsreel, a political filmmaking collective, claimed that the "image *was* the words. People were going to remember that."[34] The Motherfuckers' work took on themes ranging from the local to the national but primarily focused on the Lower East Side community's need for space, the role of white radicals, and their complicated relationship to violence and revolution.

The call for space resonated among those living on the Lower East Side community. The call was symbolic—community members needed free space to "survive, grow freaky, breathe, expand, love, struggle, and turn on" as well as logistical.[35] The lack of space on the Lower East Side made the accessibility of free places central to the Motherfuckers' platform. Crash pads and communal offices were temporary solutions. Rather, group members imagined their neighborhood becoming a "liberated territory in which fantasy moves"—the fantasy of a society based on love and community but also physical access.[36]

The Motherfuckers' skin color was a complex issue for their politics. They were an all-white group working within a primarily white community. Although the militant Black Power movement served as a potent source of inspiration, the group believed that white activists needed to secure their own survival before they could address the issues of other oppressed people. Moreover, the Motherfuckers concluded that most whites did not recognize their own oppression and that the majority of white people had "yet to see the possibility of being human."[37] Only then would "revolutionary power replace Black Power, revolution replace nationalism."[38] However, though the Motherfuckers defended the possibility of white radicalism, they rejected white society—precisely the structure against which they revolted. According to Morea, they never imagined themselves as white, which they saw as "a state of mind, and privilege."[39] Instead, they sometimes called themselves *lights*, as in "light-skinned brothers."[40] To further disavow their whiteness, the Motherfuckers often deployed the symbolic markers of Native Americans. Native American warriors, totem poles, and tribal-inspired designs are by far the most common images in the Motherfuckers' leaflets and broadsheets. Native Americans' supposed authenticity and willingness to fight for their culture attracted the Motherfuckers, but the Motherfuckers' understanding of actual Native Americans was simplistic and even cartoonish. In a 1968 interview, Morea asserted that American Indians had "a nonviolent community. . . . There was little fighting between themselves." When contradicted by the reporter—"But they had extensive tribal wars. American history verifies that"—Morea immediately changed the subject.[41]

The Motherfuckers defended the use of violence and insisted on the necessity of revolution. Though many individuals who turned to violence in the later 1960s had attempted to use nonviolence or work through the system, the Motherfuckers believed in the need for violence from the outset. They argued that violence was a necessity when combating a society rooted in violence. "Chattel slavery is violence, wage slavery is violence, strengthening the police force is violence, crushing discontent is violence so why," they demanded to know, are "the protesters always the only people to be associated with it?"[42] Furthermore, violent language was a protest action in itself—a rejection of polite society and the older generation of activists. They chose the group's name so that it could never be printed in any respectable paper. They tried to emphasize what middle-class America most feared—they "defied law and order with [their] bricks bottles garbage long hairy filth obscenity drugs games guns bikes fire fun and fucking," they said.[43] Their aggressive language, laced with references to rape, death, and destruction, was justified as a logical response to an oppressive system.

The Motherfuckers' violent rhetoric and imagery were often awkwardly fused with the counterculture's emphasis on peace and love. They called the summer of 1968 a "hot house / what grows is flower cong, violent flowers."[44] The use of the flower motif recalled the 1967 Summer of Love and the emergence of Flower Power, but it also reflected the Motherfuckers' beliefs that the counterculture was impotent. The flower alone was not enough; rather, flowers (and all they represented) had to be linked to Vietnamese freedom fighters and guerrilla warfare. The Motherfuckers took as their motto "Armed Love." *Love* was the core; *Armed* was a modifier. By meshing violent imagery with the flowery language of the hippies, the Motherfuckers attempted to bring militancy to the counterculture.

More than violence, the main theme in the Motherfuckers' writing (and indeed, a central part of post-1968 New Left rhetoric) was revolution. The Motherfuckers advocated a complete overhaul of American political, social, and cultural life. This call for "total revolution" reflected the increasingly commonplace New Left argument that all injustices were linked. However outlandish this talk of revolution may seem today, in the exhilarating atmosphere of the late 1960s as colonial nations were rebelling, Vietnam was winning a war against the United States, and an insurgent youth culture had taken hold from coast to coast, many radical activists grew convinced that they were living on the edge of a revolutionary moment. Morea remembered that revolution was not only possible but imminent. Agreed activist Robin Palmer, "Revolution was a heady wine," and particularly on the Lower East Side, "everyone was drunk."[45]

Though the Motherfuckers saw art as their primary form of revolutionary action, certain national events attracted everyone in the movement. These moments offered opportunities to illustrate to America the sheer number of the disenchanted and an occasion for the hip community to come together in joyous and dramatic fashion.

The October 1967 Pentagon action was the first big demonstration that drew the Motherfuckers out of New York. As some thirty thousand hippies, Yippies, and New Left activists faced off against National Guardsmen and military police (MPs) guarding the Pentagon, members of the Motherfuckers carried Vietnamese National Liberation Front flags and urged the crowd to storm the building. Wisely, the vast majority of protesters rejected this idea. Greg Calvert, an SDS national officer who helped plan the Pentagon protest, recalled that attacking the U.S. military headquarters seemed like an "absurd idea. If you wanted to get a lot of people killed, you might have stormed the Pentagon."[46] But at some point in the standoff, a few militants, among them Morea, spotted a service ramp guarded by only a few MPs. The group rushed the door, overpowered the guards, and penetrated the seat of American military power. Though MPs forcibly evicted the intruders after only a few moments (leaving "patches of blood behind," according to the *New York Times*), radicals claimed an important symbolic victory.[47] This action was typical of UAW/MF behavior at national demonstrations. The Motherfuckers participated in the mainstream action but tried to inject a degree of confrontation into already tense situations. In the moment, they might be seen as the aggressor, but aggression was necessary "to defend the values that we pose as an alternative to amerika."[48]

In the Chicago 7 trial, in which the organizers of the protests at the August 1968 Democratic National Convention were charged with crossing state lines to incite and organize a riot, Neumann was named as an unindicted coconspirator. After a particularly grotesque example of police brutality in Chicago's Lincoln Park during the convention, Neumann had taken the stage and announced to the audience members, who were literally penned in by the police, "We have decided, some of us, to move out of the park in any way we can, to move into their space in any way that we can and to defend ourselves in any way that we can."[49] Neumann also publicly denounced several pacifist options that had just been presented, declaring them to be "bullshit." He warned people, already frightened and aware of the potential for police violence, that they were "going to listen to speech after speech and follow [pacifist leader] Dave Dellinger like sheep to a slaughter."[50] Nonviolence had resulted in nothing but injuries and arrests for the protesters, Neumann pointed out.[51]

The last big communal event of the 1960s that the Motherfuckers attended was the Woodstock festival on August 15–17, 1969, although they scarcely regarded it as three days of peace and love and music. Instead, they complained that it was an egregious example of the commodification of the countercultural lifestyle. Organizers had originally planned to charge eighteen dollars for the event, but the first wave of concertgoers quickly overwhelmed the paltry fences surrounding the campground.[52] The Motherfuckers, having independently decided that the fences were coming down, arrived at Woodstock armed with pliers and dismantled a large section of the fence to create a "ticket optional" entrance. Once inside, the Motherfuckers "liberated" the concessions by strong-arming vendors. It was a truly Motherfucker kind of action; they used legitimate complaints about the politics of space and communal living to justify fundamentally illegal actions.[53]

The Motherfuckers also frequently traveled to national SDS meetings, where they amused a few of the attendees and infuriated the rest. The Motherfuckers had joined SDS in part so that they could go to these meetings and point out the insignificance of endless plenary sessions to the revolution. On one occasion, they proposed and even passed an amendment (ostensibly in support of the California grape strikers) suggesting that SDS members should talk less and drink more wine.[54] In response to one SDS faction's advocacy of a "worker-student alliance" at the 1968 SDS convention, the Motherfuckers dressed one person as "Student" and another as "Worker" and performed an elaborate mock wedding.[55] As SDS member Jim O'Brien recalled, UAW/MF also nominated a "wastebasket for national secretary of SDS during the election of officers. Only one human candidate ran, and the wastebasket did pretty well."[56] Though this action appeared silly, it had a serious point: despite SDS's emphasis on "participatory democracy," the election of unopposed candidates was problematic.[57] The Motherfuckers' actions at SDS conventions were also intended to "disrupt and chastise suitably impressed students for their lack of daring." To underscore this point, Neumann once "dropped my pants, and with my penis flapping in the wind, condemned intellectual masturbation."[58] Such tactics did not win the Motherfuckers widespread support within SDS but did extend their visible influence within the movement and forced the student organization to confront the growth of the angrier, more militant factions.

Despite these attention-grabbing national actions, the group focused primarily on the Lower East Side. One of UAW/MF's first community protests was the February 1968 Garbage Action. The group had started to coalesce the previous summer, but this action cemented the jump from *Black Mask* affiliates to Up against the Wall Motherfucker. New York City's sanitation workers had gone on strike that winter for higher wages and better working conditions. Some neighborhoods hired private sanitation firms, but those that could not afford to do so faced chest-high piles of garbage and an explosion in the already sizable rat population. The Motherfuckers believed that because wealthier New Yorkers were not directly affected by the strike, city officials were in no great hurry to settle it. In retribution, the Motherfuckers staged a "culture exchange: garbage for garbage."[59] A Newsreel recording of the event shows the Motherfuckers, dressed in black leather, beating drums and singing as they carried bags of garbage from the Lower East Side through the subways and onto the pristine steps of Lincoln Center for a "garbage planting ceremony." They danced and shouted as patrons of the city's finest cultural space looked on, visibly disturbed by the activists' appearance. Though the film never shows them actually dumping garbage onto the steps (and Todd Gitlin claims that only "one rambunctious fellow had the nerve to dump the garbage into the fountain"), it does capture the moment when the protesters were hustled away from Lincoln Center by police and followed back into their neighborhood by plainclothes policemen.[60] Only Neumann was arrested: he was detained after shouting out a poem that drew explicit connections between the garbage on New York's streets and America's destructiveness at home and abroad: America had turned "the world into garbage / its ghettoes into garbage / Vietnam into garbage."[61] The Lincoln Center protest illustrates the marriage of culture and politics that was so central to the Motherfuckers' ideology from the group's beginning but lacks the edge of its later actions.

The conflict between the Motherfuckers and legendary rock promoter Bill Graham displayed an unambiguously confrontational tone. In March 1968, Graham, a leading figure on the West Coast music scene and an early champion of the Grateful Dead, Janis Joplin, and Jefferson Airplane, opened a club, the Fillmore East, at 2nd Avenue and East 6th Street. It soon became New York's premiere countercultural venue. However, its high ticket prices irritated the community, and many annoyed activists maligned Graham as a "'vampire-like' capitalist eating the culture."[62] The Motherfuckers decided late in the year that the Fillmore East should serve as a community space "for people to come together and ask each other about the shape of a new freedom."[63] They called their bid to gain control of the Fillmore the Reclaiming Project and vowed to take back what "belonged" to the community.[64]

After weeks of tense community meetings, Graham agreed to allow the activists to offer free concerts at the club on Wednesday nights but soon changed his mind in the wake of flagrant drug use, physical altercations, and damage to the building. Graham blamed patrons' disregard for his rules: had the activists behaved civilly and abided by the basic guidelines of the agreement, he chastised, he would have allowed the gatherings to continue.[65]

On December 26, 1968, the MC5, Detroit-based band whose members touted themselves as "revolutionary rockers," appeared at the club. Graham and the Motherfuckers disagreed over the distribution of free tickets to the concert, and a confrontation between the Fillmore staff and people who wanted to get into the venue ended with someone hitting Graham in the face with a chain, shattering his nose. After the concert, some members of the crowd refused to leave the club and swarmed the stage, breaking some of the band's equipment. After a Motherfucker told the crowd that the members of the MC5 were heading to a high-profile nightclub, Max's Kansas City, the mob surged outside the building, pulled the musicians out of their limousine, "messed them up a bit," and denounced them as "phonies." Morea denied responsibility for the damage or the violence, placing the blame squarely on Graham for causing the tension.

Graham, however, called the Motherfuckers "filthy, low-life scum" and accused them of instigating a riot in his building.[66]

The Fillmore debacle split the Lower East Side into pro- and anti-Motherfucker factions. Though many locals sided with the Motherfuckers and appreciated the free nights, another, quite vocal, faction disavowed any connections with the group, the violence associated with it, and its Reclaiming Project. Allen Katzman, editor of the *East Village Other*, became the most prominent spokesperson for the anti-Motherfucker faction and maintained that the Motherfuckers offered only aggression.[67]

Nevertheless, the Motherfuckers maintained pockets of support within the Lower East Side community, largely because they made real efforts to improve the lives of local youth and immigrants. They briefly operated a store where customers paid whatever they could for goods. The Motherfuckers were also one of the forces behind the Common Ground, a cheap coffee shop located next to the Yippies' Liberty House, near Tompkins Square Park. The Common Ground was characterized as a "brief inlet in the sea of the street, where the swift currents of street people are briefly quiescent for meeting and planning before they rush back out into the turmoil": it was "liberated space."[68] The shop was open to everyone—activists, troubled runaways, local residents, or anyone else who wanted something to eat or drink and although many people became fed up with the "street bums, alcoholics, [and] crazies" who made up a significant portion of the clientele, the Motherfuckers never barred anyone.[69]

Though Common Ground was short-lived, it served an important function as a gathering place for the Motherfuckers. The Lower East Side had its own police division, the "oppressive" and "openly antagonistic" Tactical Police Force, which was especially tough on the runaways and homeless who congregated near St. Marks Place. In one instance, according to Creek, policemen broke into the SDS office in the West Village and destroyed documents, supplies, and furniture.[70] The Motherfuckers felt that they had a responsibility to defend their community and used Common Ground to launch the Lower East Side Patrol, also known as ACID (the Action Committee for Immediate Defense) or the AntiPig Militia. Following the style of the Black Panthers, the patrol shadowed the police during their rounds, ensuring that they were held accountable for their actions and arrests. The patrols had multiple physical confrontations with the police, which the Motherfuckers always justified as self-defense, though the officers, not surprisingly, often took a different view.[71]

The Motherfuckers also ran karate classes, maintained bail and defense funds, served communal meals, and operated crash pads. They held soup dinners at St. Marks Church, followed by poetry readings, speeches, and political films by Newsreel.[72] Many of those who attended these gatherings were runaways. The only "program" the Motherfuckers ever publicly announced was to "feed [runaways] well, lick them into loving . . . and then send them bopping down the subways of existence."[73] Most runaways did not remain on the Lower East Side for long, but the Motherfuckers hoped that when these transient youths moved on, they would spread the Motherfucker message and create a national community. Many runaways lived in Motherfucker apartments. Though UAW/MF certainly never had a reputation as a clean-living group, drugs were discouraged in these spaces to ensure that the police did not shut them down.[74] The group also regularly printed a "Hip Survival Bulletin" in *Rat*, the *East Village Other*, and occasionally other underground papers across the country. These guides informed readers what was going on in the community—where drug busts were being made locally and nationally, how many people were in jail, where the next protest was, who was an undercover federal agent, and where to send bail money. The product of the "East Side Service Organization," the bulletins were directed at the national community, and each announced that "communication between hip communities is essential to building a tribal network."[75]

The Motherfuckers also integrated their penchant for theatricality into their local activities. For example, they outfitted a wooden flatbed with wheels and placed a desk, chair, and typewriter on it. Motherfuckers would push this portable office around the Lower East Side, with Neumann sitting at the desk and frantically typing everything he saw as well as announcements requested by neighborhood residents. When three or four pages had accumulated, someone would take them to a mimeograph machine and run off a hundred copies of the spontaneous street newspaper. These "publications" usually consisted primarily of Neumann's haphazard observations and musings, but they spread some useful news and demonstrated that the Motherfuckers were in tune with the goings-on in their neighborhood.

The end of the Motherfuckers, like that of many other 1960s groups, did not result from any single incident or any pronounced ideological split. In Palmer's words, they "just ran out of gas."[76] Reflected Morea, "The fading is never as glorious as the moment," and the LSD and marijuana of the Lower East Side hip culture was replaced by amphetamines and heroin.[77] According to Neumann, ever-increasing numbers of young runaways brought a "nervous, jagged edge" to the neighborhood.[78] Fed up with the group's hypermasculinity, many women abandoned the Motherfuckers for the women's movement. More important, the Motherfuckers, too, had begun to change. Though their revolutionary fervor was always tinged with an edge, optimism ultimately began to give way "to a tight lipped struggle for survival."⁷⁹ Many activists began to see New York as a constant battleground and chose to live someplace less intense and more communal. New York was becoming too inhospitable for radicals, the Vietnam War was not ending, and the Motherfuckers' lack of a clear direction eventually took a toll. By the end of 1969, the Motherfuckers were building adobe houses in New Mexico, forming communes in San Francisco, and disappearing underground. By the next year, they were gone, having left New York and their lives as Motherfuckers behind them. All in all, UAW/MF existed as an affinity group for little more than a year. Then, as Neumann put it, the "season of love and rage and extravagant expectations" ended "before we knew it."⁸⁰

The members of Up against the Wall Motherfucker were unique in their desire to merge the cultural and the political, the local and the national, the theatrical and the militant. They took their ideology into the streets and the national scene to foster a movement that moved. They attacked the dominant social and cultural mores through their poetry and art, forcing even the most apolitical hippies to know who the Motherfuckers were and what their revolution was about. Their theatrical flair and its underlying edginess made them attractive to those tired of SDS's interminable meetings or unsatisfied with the aimlessness of the dropout culture. However, their increasing militancy alienated much of the movement. The free nights at the Fillmore and the establishment of ACID hint at the influence that the Motherfuckers might have had if they had sustained their efforts. But as activist Paul Johnson remembered, "organizing on the Lower East Side was like writing on water. As soon as you stop, it's gone."⁸¹

Notes

1. Susan Stern, *With the Weathermen: The Personal Journey of a Revolutionary Woman* (New York: Doubleday, 1975), 22.

2. The Weather Underground (also known as Weathermen or the Weatherpeople) was an ultramilitant faction of SDS that committed at least two dozen political bombings in the early 1970s.

3. Osha Neumann, "Motherfuckers Then and Now: My Sixties Problem," in *Cultural Politics and Social Movements*, ed. Marcy Darnovsky, Barbara Epstein, and Richard Flacks (Philadelphia: Temple University Press, 1995), 58.

4. Todd Gitlin, *The Sixties: Years of Hope, Days of Rage* (New York: Bantam, 1987), 241; Neumann, "Motherfuckers Then and Now," 56, 57.

5. A crash pad was essentially an apartment that served as a communal living space in which transient street youths could stay for a few days or weeks without paying rent.

6. As early as 1969, the Jefferson Airplane used a Motherfucker broadsheet as the basis for the lyrics to its youth culture anthem, "We Can Be Together." The song announces that

they are "obscene, lawless, hideous, dangerous, dirty, violent and young / but we should be together / come on all you people standing around" and ends with the refrain, "Up against the wall, Motherfucker!" Jefferson Airplane, "We Can Be Together," *Volunteers* (RCA, 1969). For the Motherfucker broadsheet that contains the same phrase, see *Rat*, September 6–19, 1968, 7.

7. There were other groups during the sixties that also attempted to blend the cultural and the political in their activism—the San Francisco Mime Troupe and the Diggers most notably.

8. Ben Morea, email to author, September 12, 2015.

9. David Farber, "The Counterculture and the Antiwar Movement," in *Give Peace a Chance: Exploring the Vietnam Antiwar Movement*, ed. Martin Small and William D. Hoover (Syracuse: Syracuse University Press, 1992), 8.

10. For examples of SDS-centric histories of the 1960s, see Gitlin, *Sixties*; James Miller, *"Democracy Is in the Streets": From Port Huron to the Siege of Chicago* (Cambridge: Harvard University Press, 1994); Kirkpatrick Sale, *SDS* (New York: Random House, 1973); Maurice Isserman, *If I Had a Hammer . . . : The Death of the Old Left and the Birth of the New Left* (New York: Basic Books, 1987). The scholarship that has come to critique this mode includes Wini Breines, "Whose New Left?," *Journal of American History* 75:2 (1988): 528–45; Doug Rossinow, "The New Left and the Counterculture: Hypotheses and Evidence," *Radical History Review* 67 (1997): 79–120; Doug Rossinow, "The Revolution Is about Our Lives: The New Left's Counterculture," in *Imagine Nation: The American Counterculture of the 1960s and '70s*, ed. Peter Braunstein and Michael William Doyle (New York: Routledge, 2002), 99–124; Maurice Isserman, "You Don't Need a Weatherman but a Postman Can Be Helpful," in *Give Peace a Chance*, ed. Small and Hoover, 22–34; John McMillian and Paul Buhle, eds., *The New Left Revisited* (Philadelphia: Temple University Press, 2003); Alice Echols, "We Gotta Get out of This Place: Notes Toward a Remapping of the 1960s," *Socialist Review* 22 (April–June 1992): 9–33; Barbara Tischler, "'It Was Twenty Years Ago Today'; or, Why We Need More Sixties Scholarship," in *Sights on the Sixties*, ed. Barbara Tischler (New Brunswick, N.J.: Rutgers University Press, 1992), 1–12.

11. Jeremy Varon, "Between Revolution 9 and Thesis 11; or, Will We Learn (Again) to Start Worrying and Change the World," in *New Left Revisited*, ed. McMillian and Buhle, 226.

12. The underground papers often shared stories through the Underground Press Syndicate, an organization founded by the editors of *EVO* that functioned similarly to the Associated Press wire services. During the late 1960s, the syndicate often distributed Motherfucker broadsheets or articles on the Motherfuckers to a national audience. See Abe Peck, *Uncovering the Sixties: The Life and Times of the Underground Press* (New York: Pantheon, 1985), 71.

13. Jeff Jones, interview by author, November 18, 2002.

14. Murray Bookchin, "Anarchism Past and Present," May 1980, http://dwardmac.pitzer.edu/Anarchist_Archives/bookchin/pastandpresent.html; Roz Payne, interview by author, November 20, 2002.

15. Bookchin, "Anarchism Past and Present."
16. Ben Morea, email to author, September 15, 2015.
17. Ibid.
18. "The Port Huron Statement," in Miller, *"Democracy Is in the Streets,"* 333.
19. Robert Pardun, email to author, November 24, 2002.
20. Stew Albert, interview by author, December 6, 2002.
21. Neumann, "Motherfuckers Then and Now," 57.
22. Ibid., 56.
23. Creek and Travis both changed their names during their time with the Motherfuckers and asked to be referred to by only first names in this article.
24. Ben Morea, "Letter to Louise Crowley," in *Black Mask and Up against the Wall Motherfucker: The Incomplete Works of Ron Hahne, Ben Morea, and the Black Mask Group*, ed. Ron Hahne (London: Unpopular and Sabotage, 1993), 8.
25. "War Street Is Wall Street," *Black Mask*, January 1967, in ibid., 21.
26. Neumann, "Motherfuckers Then and Now," 56.
27. "Victims Identified in Newark Rioting," *New York Times*, July 16, 1967.
28. "Racial Violence Erupts in Newark," *New York Times*, July 13, 1967.
29. Though a rally does not seem especially militant in light of many of the other actions of the later 1960s, Jeff Jones recalled that another SDS activist, Bill Epson, had recently organized a similar type of rally and been jailed for sedition as a result (interview by author, November 18, 2002).
30. "Brothers, Sisters, Comrades, Friends," in *Black Mask and Up against the Wall*, ed. Hahne, 79.
31. "Affinity Groups," in ibid., 103, 102.
32. Motherfucker Broadsheet, *Rat*, March 14–20, 1969, 20.
33. Some group members even chose to use *Motherfucker* as their surname (for example, Travis Motherfucker).
34. Payne, interview.
35. "Fillmore Free Theater Leaflets," in *BAMN (By Any Means Necessary): Outlaw Manifestos and Ephemera, 1965–1970*, ed. Peter Stansill and David Zane Mairowitz (Harmondsworth: Penguin, 1971), 162.
36. Motherfucker Broadsheet, *Rat*, July 18–28, 1968, 6.
37. "From Revolt to Revolution: Nigger as Class," *Black Mask*, April–May 1968, in *Black Mask and Up against the Wall*, ed. Hahne, 68.
38. "The New Proletariat," *Black Mask*, October–November 1967, in ibid., 49.
39. Ben Morea, email to author, September 12, 2015.
40. "The Theory of Synthesis and the Synthesis of Theory," *Black Mask*, April–May 1968, in *Black Mask and Up against the Wall*, ed. Hahne, 72.
41. "Up against the Wall Motherfucker: Press Conference Report in the Free Press," in ibid., 81.
42. "Harlem Six," *Black Mask*, May–June 1967, in ibid., 42.
43. Motherfucker Broadsheet, *Rat*, September 6–19, 1968, 7.

44. Ibid., June 15–29, 1968, 6.

45. Robin Palmer, interview by author, February 19, 2003. According to SDS chronicler Kirkpatrick Sale, one 1970 study found that 1,170,000 U.S. college students labeled themselves revolutionaries, and "given the character of the left at the time, there must have been something like twice that many again who thought of themselves as revolutionaries and were to be found . . . in the Movement organizations, high schools and the streets" (*SDS*, 547).

46. Greg Calvert, interview, 249, Student Movement of the 60's Collection, Columbia University Oral History Office, New York.

47. Joseph Loftus, "Guards Repulse War Protesters at the Pentagon," *New York Times*, October 22, 1967.

48. "Up against the Wall Motherfucker: Press Conference Report in the Free Press," 83; Motherfucker Broadsheet, *Rat*, August 9–22, 1968, 10.

49. David Farber, *Chicago '68* (Chicago: University of Chicago Press, 1988), 197.

50. Payne, interview.

51. Ibid. In many ways, Neumann was right. Events in Chicago deteriorated into what the Walker Commission later described as "a police riot," with hundreds of arrests and beatings. Many people, including some Democratic delegates, denounced Mayor Richard Daly for encouraging police aggression. The officers behaved as "avenging thugs," making arrests for even the most minor infractions and, on occasion, clubbing protesters indiscriminately. The Chicago protests marked a turning point for many activists, convincing them that pacifism was inadequate and that they needed to be willing to defend themselves when faced with an aggressive opponent (Milton Voist, *Fire in the Streets: America in the 1960s* [New York: Simon and Schuster], 327).

52. Joel Makower, *Woodstock: The Oral History* (Albany: State University of New York Press, 2009), 177, 180.

53. Travis Motherfucker, interview by author, December 11, 2002. According to Travis, sleeping bags were selling for twenty dollars apiece, an outrageous price considering that monthly rents in the Lower East Side could be close to that.

54. Sale, *SDS*, 417.

55. Creek, interview by author, January 25, 2003.

56. Jim O'Brien, "Memories of the Student Movement and the New Left in the United States, 1960–1969" (unpublished manuscript), 49.

57. Sale, *SDS*, 462–68.

58. Neumann, "Motherfuckers Then and Now," 62.

59. Motherfucker Leaflet, reprinted in *East Village Other*, February 9–15, 1968, 12.

60. Garbage newsreel, 1968, https://www.youtube.com/watch?v=KtX8IEWabTY; Gitlin, *Sixties*, 239.

61. Motherfucker Leaflet, reprinted in *East Village Other*, February 9–15, 1968, 12.

62. Albert, interview.

63. "Fillmore East Round 2," *Rat*, November 1–14, 1968, 22.

64. Motherfucker Broadsheet, *Rat*, January 3–16, 1969, 4.

65. Paul Nelson, "Fillmore East vs. the East Village," *Rolling Stone*, February 15, 1969, 10.
66. Ibid.; Palmer, interview.
67. Allen Katzman, "Fillmore East vs. the Motherfuckers," *East Village Other*, January 3, 1969, 2.
68. Wolfe Lowenthal, "Common Ground," *Rat*, December 13, 1968–January 2, 1969, 7.
69. Payne, interview.
70. Creek, interview.
71. "Self Defense," *Rat*, August 9–22, 1968, 10–11.
72. Payne, interview.
73. Motherfucker Broadsheet, *Rat*, June 15–28, 1968, 8.
74. Creek, interview.
75. "Hip Survival Bulletin," *Rat*, April 25-May 1, 1968. *Rat* regularly printed these "bulletins."
76. Palmer, interview.
77. Ben Morea, email to author, September 12, 2015.
78. Neumann, "Motherfuckers Then and Now," 62.
79. Ibid., 63.
80. Ibid., 62.
81. Paul Johnson, interview by author, January 15, 2003.

Gordon Matta-Clark's *Anarchitecture*

ERIN WALLACE

> If needed, we work to disprove the common belief that all starts with the plan. There are forms without plans—dynamic orders and disorders.
>
> —*Anarchitecture*

Gordon Matta-Clark was an urban artist, activist, and a key participant in the alternative arts community of SoHo in the 1970s. Though his art and politics were based in and primarily concerned with his native city of New York, his family roots were transnational. His parents, Chilean painter Roberto Matta and American designer Anne Clark, met in the vibrant cultural milieu of Paris between World War I and World War II and participated in the 1938 Exposition Internationale du Surréalisme, held at the Galerie des Beaux-Arts. At the outbreak of World War II, the couple joined a wave of artist émigrés to New York, where twin sons Gordon and Sebastian were born in 1943. The boys' lives were steeped in art from the outset: Gordon was named for surrealist painter Gordon Onslow-Ford, and Dada kingpin Marcel Duchamp and his wife stood as godparents. Although the twins inherited their father's art-world connections, his artistic influence was at best remote. He abandoned the twins when they were months old, leaving the United States permanently by 1948. Matta-Clark later recalled, "I never saw him for more than an hour of my life." Roberto had his greatest impact on Gordon by insisting that he study architecture.[1] Matta-Clark eventually complied with his father's wishes, earning a bachelor's degree in architecture from Cornell University in 1968, though later regarded the experience with contempt. By the time of his graduation, he had abandoned the discipline to follow in the footsteps of his artist parents, albeit in a way that resisted comparison. While his father worked in traditional media, Matta-Clark wielded a saw, taking disused buildings, garbage, and organic matter as his *prima materia*. Architecture remained in his purview as an object of critique, and his insider knowledge allowed him to confront the failings and limitations of both art and architecture. He emphatically stated, "Why hang things on the wall when the wall itself is so much more a challenging medium? I am offended by the closed minds of people who think that only architects can create walls and artists decorate them."[2] This challenge was encapsulated by his "building cuts," a subtractive technique that radically reconfigured buildings by subverting the conventions of architectural design. The works were striking and disorienting and constituted an attack on architecture as an exclusionary and hierarchical operation. In accord with these values, Matta-Clark aptly termed his approach *anarchitecture*, a portmanteau of the words *anarchy* and *architecture*. Matta-Clark's anarchitectural works directly—and often illegally—confronted the institution of private property while prefiguring alternative modes of participatory architecture. He addressed problems of urban waste and homelessness by building shelters that utilized available refuse material (*Garbage Wall, Jacks, Open House*) and reclaimed structures that were abandoned or slated for demolition. Community projects such as FOOD and La Plaza Cultural Garden realized his ideal of participatory DIY (Do It Yourself) architecture, wherein inhabitants reclaimed urban space through their own efforts and initiatives.

Matta-Clark adamantly resisted the tendency to reduce his building cuts, however spectacular, to an aesthetic that would neutralize the violence they entailed. He conceptualized his use of violence as "discreet violations," an initial shock that undermined conventions of architecture and property while awakening the spectator to myriad possibilities for spatial intervention and agency: "The first thing one notices is that violence has been done. Then the violence turns to visual order and hopefully, then to a sense of heightened awareness.... My hope is that the dynamism of the action can be seen as an alternative vocabulary with which to question the static inert building environment."[3]

Unfortunately, since his death from cancer in 1978, Matta-Clark's violence has been aestheticized by way of familiar academic categories (such as "the Sublime") or oversimplified as purely destructive.[4] Architecture critic Antony Vidler dubs Matta-Clark "the enraged James Dean of the art scene" and a "violent anti-architect," while cultural historian Maud Lavin insists that his work is "paradigmatic of a modernist macho-individualism" and argues that his cuts merely restate the destruction of the architectural programs they critique.[5] The irony in labeling his cuts as "destructive" and "against architecture" is that Matta-Clark was working with buildings already doomed to the wrecking ball. Despite his efforts to transform abandoned spaces into sites of artistic and social value, none of his building cuts has been preserved in situ. While widely referred to as a tragedy, the complete destruction of Matta-Clark's architectural works highlights the indifference of the real estate market as well as the art market's failure to support artwork outside of the gallery context.

More charitable readings of Matta-Clark's work fall short of addressing the complexity, context, and implications of his use of violence. *Window Blowout*, his most explicitly violent protest—he shot out the windows of an architecture school—resists the aestheticizing, individualistic, and politically void interpretations that have proliferated since his death and thus has been largely ignored. This chapter addresses the oversight through an in-depth study of *Window Blowout*, Matta-Clark's most direct and explicit protest against architecture as an apparatus of social control. Establishing the context of New York in the era of "master builder" Robert Moses's notorious "slum clearance" projects is essential to understanding *Window Blowout*. I discuss Matta-Clark's ongoing engagement with the South Bronx and the devastation wrought on that community by Moses's projects to argue that *Window Blowout* is a statement of solidarity with South Bronx residents.

I also situate *Window Blowout* within the range of art and activism in New York City in the late 1960s and 1970s, including a brief genealogy of symbolically violent actions influenced by French anarchist dramatist Antonin Artaud's artistic and political manifesto, "theatre of cruelty." Artaud's activated spectator, symbolic violence ("cruelty"), and rejection of conventional theater space sheds new light on Matta-Clark's frequent references to theater and the nature of symbolic violence in *Window Blowout*. Alternative perspectives on the social significance of acts of vandalism in the anarchist writings of Uri Gordon and Colin Ward help reframe and provide a better understanding of the power relations highlighted by Matta-Clark's symbolically violent gesture.

• • •

In 1976, the Institute for Architecture and Urban Studies, an architecture school and think tank under the directorship of architect Peter Eisenman, hosted an exhibition, *Idea as Model*, that sought to demonstrate that "models, like architectural drawings, could well have an artistic or conceptual existence ... independent of the project that they represented."[6] This assertion of artistic autonomy rested on the treatment of architectural designs as objects of aesthetic or philosophical value that exist in platonic isolation.

Gordon Matta-Clark's Anarchitecture

Gordon Matta-Clark was invited to contribute to the exhibition, most likely in an attempt to appropriate the emerging artist for the validation of a new, art-centered architectural discourse. A polemical essay in the exhibition catalog devotes several pages to demonstrating that land art, minimalism, and site-specific sculpture have "stolen much of the ground from architects," suggesting that Matta-Clark's inclusion was part of a layered campaign to reabsorb these art movements back into the "host body."[7] The Institute's repositioning of architecture as a purely aesthetic art reflected, in part, a desire to distance the profession from recent high-profile failures. By the 1970s, the ideology of infinite progress underlying architectural modernism had been tarnished by catastrophes such as the Pruitt-Igoe public housing project in St. Louis. There, thirty-three high-density apartment towers had been built in 1956 and demolished just sixteen years later, an event that architecture critic Charles Jencks swiftly canonized as "the death of modern architecture."[8] What Matta-Clark termed the "monolithic idealist problem solving of the international style" was irrevocably discredited; as a consequence, emerging architects faced a growing backlash of criticism and a crisis of purpose.[9] The *Idea as Model* catalog reflects popular disillusionment with the model of social improvement through architecture: these architects' "ideas have not been utopian or expressionistic or futuristic in the manner of the 1920s or again of the 1960s. These architects have been too little confident of an alternative reality for any of that; their proposals and their buildings recall us to mind or art, not to a vision or hope."[10]

Matta-Clark accepted the invitation to exhibit at *Idea as Model* with the intention of disassembling a classroom at the Institute, but his proposal was rejected. He settled instead on a display of photographs, but the proposed installation went severely awry. According to Institute fellow Andrew MacNair, Matta-Clark arrived the night before the opening with an air rifle and shot out the windows of the exhibition hall. In the emptied window casements he placed photos of apartments in the Bronx where vandals had shattered floor after floor of windows. MacNair was horrified, and Eisenman vehemently condemned the event, likening it to Kristallnacht, or Night of Broken Glass, the 1938 Nazi pogrom against Jews and their buildings.[11] Matta-Clark's violent injection of reality proved too much for the Institute, and his installation was swiftly expunged from the exhibit before the opening.

Eisenman's slanderous equation of Matta-Clark's work with Kristallnacht was unquestioningly accepted as justification for the installation's hurried erasure. MacNair mawkishly lamented his failure to intervene: "The institute was a sacred space. How could someone blow out the windows? I remember it was December, it was Christmas and Chanukah, the high emotional climate of the time, the religious holidays. . . . If I had any inkling that Kristallnacht would have been one of the readings of the piece, I would have stopped the action immediately."[12]

The response to *Window Blowout* was not uniformly negative. Artist Dennis Oppenheim, who loaned Matta-Clark the air rifle, openly supported the action: Matta-Clark "borrowed my air gun to do a piece at the Institute for Architecture and Urban Studies. I was extremely excited about that. It was such a radical gesture. Such a definitive statement—a metaphor about architecture."[13]

In 1981, well after Matta-Clark's death, the Institute retroactively tempered its response in a belated catalog commemorating the exhibit: "The late Gordon Matta-Clark wanted to show photographs of vandalized New York windows against panes broken for the occasion at the Institute, but at the last minute, with the cold air coming in, his exhibit was pulled. A pity, whatever the reasons: it would have called attention to the rival conceptions of younger artists, who often seem less afraid of social statements than these architects do."[14]

In spite of its censorship, the work represents a pivotal moment in Matta-Clark's oeuvre, clarifying his position and foreshadowing a more explicitly political approach. *Window Blowout* culminates Matta-Clark's long-standing engagement with the South Bronx. His interest in the blighted area's residents and culture is present in several earlier works and is well documented by a wealth of unpublished photographs in his archive. The images record 1970s Puerto Rican Day parades, including demonstrations by Puerto Rican Independentistas, with signs bearing slogans such as "Down with the Colony." Matta-Clark pointedly documented the large and unfriendly police presence at such events. By way of contrast, he photographed portraits of the Ghetto Brothers, a peacekeeping "gang" from the South Bronx who were involved in Puerto Rican nationalism and community advocacy through their music performances and recordings.[15]

Matta-Clark's most direct artistic engagement with the Bronx began four years prior to *Window Blowout* with *Bronx Floors* (1972–73). He trespassed into abandoned residences and extracted large angular portions of the floors with a handsaw. Each piece had patterned linoleum on one side and ceiling planks on the other, evoking the once interconnected lives of former residents. Exhibited upended, the pieces resembled walls positioned in gritty opposition to the sterile white backdrop of the gallery. While potent in their evocation of decay and dispossession, *Bronx Floors* did not disclose the full extent of the conditions and immediate dangers presented to the artist during his work. Gaining access to the buildings meant avoiding patrolling police, packs of feral dogs, and roving gangs. The vacant interiors were an obstacle course of hazards, typically littered with broken glass, used needles, garbage, and excrement.[16]

Matta-Clark was bearing witness to the planned destruction of a once-vital neighborhood that he recognized as similar to the Greenwich Village in which he had grown up.[17] The decline of the Bronx began with the passage of the Housing Act of 1949, which granted federal subsidies and powers of eminent domain to municipalities so that they could "revitalize" cities under the rubric of "slum clearance." By 1974, more than two thousand urban renewal projects had been completed, "modernizing" cities with expressways to new suburbs for the middle and upper classes and high-rise ghettos for the poor.[18]

The destruction of the Bronx originated in the development of Robert Moses's Cross Bronx Expressway (constructed between 1948 and 1972). From the 1930s to the 1960s, Moses helmed New York's urban renewal efforts, manipulating the bureaucracy by simultaneously serving as chair of the Mayor's Committee on Slum Clearance, city planning commissioner, and commissioner of parks, among other titles. The $128 million Cross Bronx Expressway project satisfied two of Moses's foremost concerns: the "modernization" of the city through increased motorization and the clearance of "slums," an arbitrary malediction used to the advantage of developers.[19]

Prior to the expressway, the Bronx was an ethnically diverse, lower-middle-income borough, with rents affordable to the southern blacks and recent Puerto Rican immigrants who continued to pour into the city after World War II. While many residents treasured their large prewar residences, Moses condemned the walk-ups as slums lacking in modern conveniences. The highway might have easily taken a less invasive route, but Moses insisted on clearing a seven-mile strip through the heart of the borough. Journalist and Moses biographer Robert Caro estimates that nearly half a million people were evicted from their homes due to Moses's projects, and a disproportionate number of those affected were poor, black, or Puerto Rican. Excluded from many areas by racism and poverty, the refugees from slum clearance projects had nowhere to go except into already overflowing ghettos. When new housing was created to accommodate the displaced, it was "bleak, sterile, cheap" and "expressive of patronizing condescension in every line."[20] Those fortunate enough to gain new housing often found themselves in poorly constructed, cramped, and sometimes unventilated units in locations devoid of basic amenities, public transit, and opportunities for employment.

Bronx residents not directly displaced by the expressway were scarcely better off. The decades of demolition caused property values to plunge so quickly that the remaining buildings could be neither rented nor sold. Empty and abandoned buildings were left to the ravages of rot, vandalism, and fire. As a consequence of the city's lack of low-income housing, those least able to pay higher rents were forced to stay in the disaster zone. The same disadvantaged residents were unfairly accused of accelerating decay, which, in turn, spurred an epidemic of fires. As New York City teetered on the verge of bankruptcy in the 1970s, officials made cuts to fire departments in the poorest areas, where there would be the least protest. More than 80 percent of South Bronx housing was destroyed by fire within a decade. By 1980 seven census tracts reported that 97 percent of housing had been lost to fires and associated demolition.[21]

The photographs Matta-Clark prepared for *Window Blowout* document this cycle of dispossession and decay, highlighting the rows of broken windows in both new housing projects and heritage buildings in the South Bronx. The identical windows of modernist buildings are punctuated by the resentment of the alienated and displaced, who, in an act of defiance, lashed out at the immediate object of their misery. Recognizing the ease with which viewers might assume that the buildings were abandoned, Matta-Clark deliberately includes the image of a visibly occupied flat in the ruins of the old neighborhood. In the photograph, a white dog peers out through the jagged edges of a broken window, and a birdhouse sits on an adjacent ledge. In the context of such appalling conditions, the presence of life and symbols of home in *Window Blowout* most pointedly critiques the role of architects and urban planners in the epic failures of urban renewal.

• • •

Urbanist Richard Sennett, who grew up in a Chicago housing project, once observed that "of all the world's cities, New York has the most destroyed itself in order to grow; in a hundred years people will have more tangible evidence about Hadrian's Rome than about fibre-optic New York."[22] Matta-Clark lived through this dramatic restructuring, recalling that "the city evolved in the Fifties and Sixties into a completely International Style steel and glass megalopolis; by contrast great areas of what had been residential were being abandoned."[23] As New York shifted from an industrial hub to a commercial center, federal funds were devoted to relocating people through suburb and highway development. Increasing distances between home and work necessitated the automobile and drastically altered the experience of city space, which became, in Sennett's words, a "means to the end of pure motion."[24]

New York City had the most extensive mass transit system in the world when Moses began his development projects in the 1930s, but he halted further expansion and channeled funds into "modernizing" the system of roads.[25] Growing up in Greenwich Village, Matta-Clark was first affected by Moses's plans in 1952, when the neighborhood was threatened by a proposed highway that would gouge through historic Washington Square Park. A young Matta-Clark and his mother participated in a seminal grassroots protest movement against this development, attending demonstrations and sit-ins spearheaded by celebrated urbanist Jane Jacobs.[26] These events not only formed Matta-Clark's views on urban space but also served as the catalyst for a sea change in urban studies.

When Washington Square Park was closed to traffic in 1959, Greenwich Village residents—including Jacobs and Eleanor Roosevelt—celebrated by burning a car in effigy. But the related slum-clearance project went ahead without the residents' consent. Washington Square Village, a mammoth "superblock" of high-rise housing, was completed in 1960, just one block from the Judson Memorial Church at 55 Washington Square South. Another three-block area south of Washington Square Park was sold to New York University for a token sum. Matta-Clark's family lived on La Guardia Place and was one of many households displaced for the subsequent expansion of the university campus.[27]

In 1969, the twenty-five-year-old Matta-Clark assumed a significant role in the SoHo arts community as that neighborhood fought against plans for another expressway through downtown Manhattan. This time, Moses proposed linking the east and west sides of the island with a ten-lane elevated highway by razing fourteen blocks of Broome Street in SoHo and Little Italy. Because these areas were highly populated with artists' studios, Julie Judd, the wife of artist Donald Judd, founded a lobbying group, Artists against the Expressway, whose members included such art-world heavyweights as Robert Rauschenberg and Leo Castelli.[28] In June 1969, hundreds of artists and allies met at the Whitney Museum of American Art to rally against the plan. Barnett Newman, whose studio was directly in the path of the proposed road, delivered an affecting polemic against art patron David Rockefeller, calling him "the most vocal advocate for the expressway" and accusing him of selling out the artists he professed to support.[29] This was no exaggeration, as Rockefeller's primary interest lay in plans to redevelop the old industrial "slum" into a corporate and financial district centered on Rockefeller's Chase Manhattan Bank. To establish a neighborhood identity and help to defend the area, attendees at this meeting dubbed the neighborhood *SoHo*.

The collective spirit that ultimately preserved SoHo continued to thrive well after the proposal was blocked. Matta-Clark's widow, Jane Crawford recalled, "None of us had money so our support system was our peer group.... [A]ll the lofts had been renovated by the artists, they were the people that made SoHo ultimately livable."[30] By the early 1970s Matta-Clark was applying his knowledge of architecture in a hands-on manner, helping retrofit existing buildings for live-work studios, performance spaces, and galleries. He helped organize the cooperative gallery 112 Green Street and cofounded FOOD, an artist-run restaurant on the corner of Prince and Wooster Streets. Matta-Clark later described how the resourcefulness required in these undertakings enriched his practice: "Artists were confronted with their own housing needs. [It] was an atmosphere in which many were compelled to transform their real and illusory environment as well as the nature of their works.... I imagine this is one of the ways that I became used to approaching space on an aggressive level."[31] Matta-Clark's efforts were by no means limited to SoHo. Together with Green Guerillas founder Liz Christy, he founded and led the construction of La Plaza Cultural Garden, a pioneering community garden in Alphabet City on the Lower East Side.[32] Residents, artists, and urban activists collaborated to create a green space out of a series of garbage-strewn lots. Architect and futurist Buckminster Fuller participated with the members of CHARAS, an urban reclamation group, in the construction of an on-site geodesic dome.[33]

The following year, Matta-Clark received a grant for a project that would teach construction skills to youth from impoverished neighborhoods. The proposal specified the creation of an urban scrap yard and recycling depot for reusing salvaged materials from demolished buildings in these areas. Matta-Clark's death in 1978 prevented the realization of this innovative project. Nevertheless, his final writings and interviews reflect his plans for participatory architecture projects that would be "responsive to the express will of occupants."[34]

• • •

Life in New York shaped Matta-Clark's work and politics: the critique of architecture, private property, and urban planning's encroachment on the commons is consistent across his oeuvre. *Fresh Air Cart* (1972) addressed increasing air pollution caused by the onslaught of car traffic through the city. Equipped with a mobile oxygen tank, Matta-Clark and painter Ed Baynard offered "souvenirs of what used to be" in the form of "pure air" to passersby. Focused on the Wall Street district, the work had a decidedly anticapitalist dimension, although the ironic offering of "free" air was apparently lost on most people. According to Baynard, "Nobody could believe it was just a nice thing, that it wasn't a rip off. What they didn't seem to realize is that we've all been ripped off already."[35]

Matta-Clark was an early supporter of the graffiti that proliferated in New York in the 1970s. Perceived by most people as vandalism, graffiti excited Matta-Clark, who interpreted it as a creative response to an increasing state of urban alienation. In 1973, he set about documenting spray-painted subway trains and then—knowing well that he would be met with antipathy—submitted the photographs to the popular (and conservative) Washington Square Outdoor Art Exhibit. When the proposal was unanimously rejected, he launched his own exhibition, *Alternatives to the Washington Square Art Fair*. The focal point was *Graffiti Truck*, a collaborative work with residents of the South Bronx. Matta-Clark invited passersby to spray-paint his old delivery truck any way they pleased. When the work was completed, he parked the truck outside the entrance to the Art Fair and, as a joke on the surfeit of canvases produced for sale in the style of abstract expressionism, cut square "paintings" from the graffiti-decorated truck with an acetylene torch.[36]

Fake Estates (1973–74) was another pointed critique of capitalism and development that entailed buying up the unwanted miscalculations of surveyors. These awkward slivers of land were inaccessible and unbuildable and as a result were auctioned off for a pittance as "gutter-space." Matta-Clark meticulously collected official deeds and maps for fifteen such "estates." Contrasting photos of the actual sites with their imperious official documents ridiculed the property system, exposing it as an abstract construct. Highlighting such accidents of planning also questioned the supremacy of New York's famous grid layout, which since the Commissioners' Plan of 1811 had served primarily to line the pockets of real estate speculators. Sennett explains that the grid's identical plots meant that "land could be treated just like money; each piece worth the same amount.... [T]he supply of land could be increased by extending this turf, so that more city came into being when speculators felt the need to speculate."[37] Matta-Clark harshly criticized the grid's systematic exploitation. Augmenting the absurdity of *Fake Estates*, Matta-Clark created *Hair* (1972), an action in which his unruly shoulder-length locks were sectioned, labeled, and mapped according to a grid before being cut off. In effect, his body was configured as a for-profit real estate product.

That Matta-Clark's "building cuts" originated as a personal protest against the inequities of the private property system is a little-known but essential part of understanding both his artistic approach and his politics. His former partner, Carol Gooden, recalled that in 1971, she and Matta-Clark were unfairly evicted from their loft when ownership changed hands: "I had built a sauna, a shower, and a toilet compartment out of three public toilet areas in an old loft. We were unjustly forced out when the landlord changed. Gordon was angry and thought he would take a part of what I had built, which he loved, with him. So he made a horizontal slice through the walls of the sauna/shower."[38] The resulting piece, *Sauna Cut*, is now in Vaduz, Liechtenstein, in the permanent collection of the Kunstmuseum Liechtenstein, where it is egregiously referred to as "modern architecture in small format" with an "autonomous sculptural shape."[39] No mention is made of the significant circumstances that spawned both the work's creation and the artist's signature approach.

• • •

Matta-Clark's confrontational artistic practice emerged in the upsurge of creative dissent concentrated in New York in the 1960s and 1970s. In 1967, Artists and Writers Protest, based in New York, organized one of the largest antiwar arts festivals in history: Angry Arts Week brought together more than six hundred artists, musicians, dancers, filmmakers, poets, and photographers. It is very likely that a young Matta-Clark attended the event, as his father, Roberto Matta, contributed to the festival's centerpiece, *The Collage of Indignation*. This enormous interactive mural was filled with violent imagery expressing outrage at the U.S. government's war atrocities in Vietnam.[40]

As the war continued, protests in New York became more urgent and symbolically violent. In 1969, the Guerrilla Art Action Group deployed *Bloodbath*, a performance that simulated the murder of civilians in Vietnam. Unannounced, the group entered the Museum of Modern Art and enacted a massacre, screaming and bursting concealed bags of blood strapped to their bodies before dropping to the ground. Pamphlets demanding the immediate resignation of David Rockefeller from the board of trustees as a consequence of his interest in arms manufacturing were spread among the carnage. One year later, the Vietnam War returned to the museum when the Art Workers Coalition protested in front of the most famous artistic tribute to civilian casualties, Pablo Picasso's *Guernica*. Displaying photographs of the slaughtered women and children of the My Lai Massacre, the coalition solicited a direct comparison between fascist war crimes and the actions of the U.S. military while exposing the Museum of Modern Art as a depoliticizing diversion. A more aggressive follow-up action occurred in 1974 when coalition member Tony Shafrazi responded to Richard Nixon's pardoning of My Lai war criminal Lieutenant William Calley, by spray-painting the words "Kill Lies All" across *Guernica*.[41]

Like *Window Blowout*, these actions directed symbolic violence at cultural institutions to radicalize them, insisting on art's potential as a revolutionary force. Viewing *Window Blowout* in the context of similar protest actions also calls attention to the element of performance in Matta-Clark's projects, validating his conception of his work as "intimately linked with the process of a form of theater."[42] The proliferation of symbolically violent actions in New York art activism was a tactic directly informed by theater—specifically, the writings of French anarchist playwright Antonin Artaud.[43]

A visionary actor, writer, and theorist, Artaud is known for his radical reenvisioning of the theater, which he asserted had powerful liberatory potential.

In his 1938 treatise, *The Theatre and Its Double*, he imagines an active spectator who, more than being intellectually engaged (as in Berthold Brecht) is "physically affected" and made palpably aware that "our present social state is iniquitous and should be destroyed." Artaud elicited this response using "cruelty," in which catharsis and social awakening would be achieved through modes of symbolic violence: "A violent and concentrated action is a kind of lyricism: it summons up supernatural images, a bloodstream of images, a bleeding spurt of images in the poet's head and in the spectator's as well. . . . I defy that spectator to give himself up, once outside of the theatre to ideas of war, riot, and blatant murder."[44]

While Artaud's influence on American art and activism remains largely unacknowledged, it was anything but marginal. The Artaudian ethos that permeates such actions as *Blood Bath* arrived in New York by way of Black Mountain College near Asheville, North Carolina, a cultural conduit for the midcentury American avant-garde. In the early 1950s, Artaud's writings on the theater became the subject of intense interest among anarchist-oriented faculty members John Cage, David Tudor, Pierre Boulez, and M. C. Richards.[45] Richards produced the first English translation of Artaud's *The Theatre and Its Double*, which then inspired Cage to create *Theatre Piece #1*, otherwise known as the first "happening."[46] Richards later introduced Artaud's concepts to the founders of the Living Theatre, Julian Beck and Judith Malina, who adopted *The Theatre and Its Double* as a key text.

Resistance to the programmatic "text" underpins *The Theater and Its Double*, which is intended to function as a generative model. Artaud's theater "is born out of a kind of organized anarchy . . . that spirit of profound anarchy which is at the root of all poetry." Artaud's ideas necessitate creative spontaneity: "The composition, the creation, instead of being made in the brain of an author, will be made in nature itself, in real space."[47] Matta-Clark's writings display a striking affinity with Artaud's particularly in the search for a participatory, spatially engaged art. Matta-Clark asserts, "You have to deal with a specific situation and the character of your dealing with that specific situation is the piece, the work."[48] He contrasted engaged and organic creativity with the prescriptive and removed designs of architects: "If. . .you unquestioningly admit the notion that things can be asserted with finality, that the human condition can be dictated . . . then you unquestioningly also assume that things can be solved. This is one of the attitudes that the politics of architecture intentionally promulgates, one which is inherent in the machine tradition. . . . Where you have people solving, eventually you get the total solution."[49]

Matta-Clark describes his anarchitectural approach as "intimately linked with the process of a form of theater in which both the working activity and the structural changes to and within the building are the performance."[50] Much of Matta-Clark's work utilized performance as an antidote to the domestic isolationism of twentieth-century American life. While works such as *Splitting* (1974) and *Bingo/Ninths* (1974) infringed on the hermetic privacy of domestic space, *Clock Shower* (1974), which entailed the artist climbing to the face of the Manhattan Clock Tower to perform toiletries, turned private quotidian activities into a gripping and humorous public display.

Matta-Clark's interest in theater is a chronically underacknowledged facet of his oeuvre. Though much is made of his art-world pedigree, his upbringing in New York was equally involved with theater. His mother, Anne Clark Alpert, was a costume designer, and his stepfather, Hollis Alpert, was a Broadway theater critic and historian. Matta-Clark volunteered as an actor and experienced Artaud's theories in practice through his involvement in the early projects of director and playwright Robert Wilson. Matta-Clark attended Wilson's movement workshops and in 1969 performed as "the man with the snake" in Wilson's *The Life and Times of Sigmund Freud* (1969).[51] Wilson's method incorporated "theatre of cruelty" features: for example, in *The Life and Times of Sigmund Freud*, a large glass panel was smashed on the floor to signify the end of the performance. Like Matta-Clark, Wilson's university background in architecture contributed to his adventurous approach to set design. According to Wilson, Matta-Clark "told me once that an image of mine had meant a lot to him. In *The King of Spain*, I had as a setting a dark interior of a room, and to one side of the room was a vertical slit about three feet wide that went from the floor to the [rigging]; through this slit one could see a sunny landscape outside. Gordon thanked me for that image, which came out later in his work."[52]

But while Wilson's image of architectural space pried open was illusionary, Matta-Clark's was real: "By undoing a building there are many aspects of the social condition against which I am gesturing: first, to open a state of enclosure which had been preconditioned not only by physical necessity but by the industry that profligates suburban and urban boxes as a context for insuring a passive, isolated consumer—a virtually captive audience. [It is] a reaction to an ever less viable state of privacy, private property, and isolation."[53]

Out of the ruins of formerly private spaces, Matta-Clark created functional stages for the public. In 1976 he constructed an amphitheater out of reclaimed building materials for the La Plaza Cultural Garden on the Lower East Side.[54] While it receives no mention in the extensive scholarship on Matta-Clark, the amphitheater remains in operation today.

In an allusion to the Roman amphitheater in Orange, France, *Circus: Caribbean Orange* (1978) created a complex open-air stage from a Chicago brownstone that was slated for demolition. For this publicly accessible work, Matta-Clark produced a series of multistory spiraling cuts through the interior, opening the building to air, light, and snow. Curiously, the writing on *Circus* neglects to mention the play that inaugurated the work. Anarchitecture colleague and frequent collaborator Tina Girouard contributed to the project by staging *Spread*, in which a cast of twenty-one people were "spread" throughout the space. Not confined to a central stage, the performers activated the entirety of the dynamic structure, creating multiple viewpoints and experiences. *Circus*'s structure eerily resembles a design mapped out by Artaud in his first manifesto for the "theatre of cruelty," calling for the replacement of theater architecture with a "vertiginous, layered structure eliminating the centrality of the stage within the auditorium."[55] Like Matta-Clark, Artaud planned to construct his theater out of existing architecture such as a "hangar or barn."[56]

The circular design of *Circus* refers to the *choros*, the original circular stage of the classical amphitheater. Rather than an aesthetic design, the form was preconditioned by the circular dances of the chorus, after which it was named. In classical theater, the chorus represented the citizenry, who played a central role in the dramatic action, mediating "between the actors and the spectators in a form of direct participation."[57] Matta-Clark described *Circus* in terms of an association between the words *circle* and *circulate*. The reconfigured structure would function as a "place of activity, a circle for action" where "people were given a kind of circular stage to look at or circulate through." A circle suggests constant movement in a symbolically egalitarian formation, as there is no hierarchy of positions or fixed points. The spatial politics of conventional theater space are therefore eliminated, since the divisions between stage and audience, object and subject, are no longer spatially enforced but instead are a matter of individual agency—an anarchist ideal. As Matta-Clark explained, the work "sets a stage for people, sets a kind of stage from the ground up."[58]

Both Matta-Clark and Artaud sought to remove the aesthetic distance naturalized by conventional theater architecture and gallery etiquette. The pursuit of an embodied spectatorship led Artaud to his "theatre of cruelty" and Matta-Clark to an analogous concept, "discreet violation," which undermined the visitor's "sense of value, sense of orientation" by subtly reconfiguring familiar architectural elements.[59] The technique unmasked architecture's ostensible immutability while suggesting possibilities for direct participation in the built environment.

Shock and disorientation are vital components of "discreet violation," and in *Window Blowout*, these qualities are distilled into a direct social statement against conditions in the South Bronx. As in Artaud's "cruelty," the action effected a profound physical and emotional response that the viewer could not easily rationalize.

• • •

Window Blowout cannot be adequately understood without addressing the blanket term of *violence* often used to discredit Matta-Clark. Uri Gordon's anarchist study of violence emphasizes how commonly the word is misused and manipulated to support the values and interests of the status quo. To clarify the issue, Gordon defines violence as that which "generates an embodied sense of attack or deliberate endangerment *in its recipient*."[60] Distinguishing between violence toward people and the destruction of property is necessary to refute criticisms that attempt to bury Matta-Clark's critique by conflating it with actions that cause personal harm. Maud Lavin's oft-cited critique equates Matta-Clark's building cuts to rape, completely ignoring the role suburban planning plays in perpetuating real violence against women by isolating them from the public sphere. Similarly, Eisenman's comparison of *Window Blowout* to Kristallnacht exploits historical guilt by equating Matta-Clark's attack on institutional property with a Nazi pogrom. Both of these critics use their subject positions (as female and Jewish, respectively) in falsely accusing Matta-Clark of violence that threatens them personally.

In his investigation of vandalism, Gordon isolates the strategy of "look who's talking," which contrasts institutional violence with the relative insignificance of minor property damage. *Window Blowout* utilizes this tactic to destabilize normative definitions of violence, juxtaposing the vandal with his rock against the immensely destructive machine of urban planning. Describing the urban renewal methods used to destroy the South Bronx as "violent" is no exaggeration—the harm to individuals is multifaceted and ongoing. If the area called to mind a war zone, it was no coincidence: the conditions Matta-Clark highlighted originated in the "raze and rise" development strategies of postwar London. As British anarchist urbanist Colin Ward explains, "When the poor of the working-class districts of our cities were devastated by bombing in the Second World War it was said that Hitler had provided the opportunity for massive slum clearance and reconstruction which could never have been achieved in peace-time. Comprehensive redevelopment of the bombed areas was undertaken. But so wedded was the planning profession and its municipal employers to the huge, utilitarian rehousing project that they proceeded with their own blitzkrieg, with the demolition contractor taking the place of the bomber."[61]

This practice of what Ward calls "planned vandalism" was taken up with vigor in New York City, with the large majority of projects going ahead despite residents' protests. The demolition of Pennsylvania Station in 1963 was famously described as a "monumental act of vandalism," not only because it destroyed an irreplaceable architectural heritage but also because it proceeded against the wishes of an overwhelming majority of New Yorkers.[62]

As a New Yorker, Matta-Clark was critical of the disciplinary function of architecture. Architecture acts as an indirect agent of violence, communicating authority, ownership, and class; it can imprison, exclude, direct behavior, alienate, and cause harm or even death by denying access. Matta-Clark identified modern housing projects as "sad prison towers that at best are clean cells," echoing Michel Foucault's assertion that the prison is the architectonic epitome of symbolic violence.[63] The punitive and isolating power of urban planning is evidenced by the segregation and poverty that continues in the South Bronx to this day. In 2010, sixty-five years after Moses's intervention, the area remained almost exclusively black and Puerto Rican and was the poorest and most health-compromised district in the United States, with a child poverty rate of 49 percent.[64]

The rise in vandalism in New York in the 1970s constituted an act of resistance to decades of violence in the form of "urban renewal." Residents made their opposition visible, undermining the symbolic imposition of order and conformity. Vandalism contests a status quo that legally reserves creative agency in space for planners and property owners. Architectural convention maintains that housing is a scientific construct too difficult for the lay person, and this mind-set ostensibly legitimizes the hierarchical nature of the profession. Ward argues that alienation will continue to manifest as vandalism until people are permitted to participate in the creation of their living spaces: "People care about what is theirs, what they can modify, alter, adapt to changing needs and improve for themselves."[65] Architect and urban theorist N. J. Habraken shares this sentiment, advocating an active form of ownership rather than the abstract possession of property: "We may possess something that is not our property, and conversely something may be our property, which we do not possess. Property is a legal term, but the idea of possession is deeply rooted in us.... [P]ossession is inextricably connected with action. To possess something we have to *take* possession. We have to make it part of ourselves, and it is therefore necessary to reach out for it."[66]

Matta-Clark wanted to work with residents, those "who have a real vested interest in spending time working on a 'property' basically for their own occupant's sake." As he explained, "The idea would be that kind of scenario or script set up by certain amounts of money, certain kinds of financing, personality, leadership, then that leadership would become dissolved within the activity.

Instead of most architectural situations where you dictate the plan or you dictate the situation, it would be a situation constantly subverted, a dictatorship constantly subverted by the people who were investing their time and energy in making it happen."[67]

Matta-Clark's anarchist vision of meeting needs and sharing skills through direct action inverts the normative power relations of architecture. It is an anticapitalist vision of ownership; rather than holding a "property," people would truly invest in their surroundings through a process of active engagement. Matta-Clark's leadership in the situation would diminish as the residents took over, until his presence in the project became obsolete. In this way, Matta-Clark resisted the technocratic impulses of architectural modernism, opting instead for a nondeterministic approach that empowers and secures the ongoing involvement of the residents. Having seen the social potential of architecture corrupted and exhausted, Matta-Clark chose to undermine the existing system while searching for alternatives. In an explicit definition of *anarchitecture*, he stated, "If you like the law, yet at the same time recognize that the ultimate law cannot possibly exist, then wouldn't it be better to talk about the impossibility of law than run around being a lawyer practicing law? Better perhaps to discuss the impossibility of architecture than the possibility of being an architect."[68] *Window Blowout* is an attack on "the impossibility of architecture" that seeks to shatter not only windows but also the legitimacy of architecture's privileged and removed position.

• • •

In the mid-1980s, Matta-Clark's friend and fellow artist, Joseph Kosuth, reflected, "I think we've learned over time that the best political art isn't a truck carrying a message. What I liked about Gordon's work was that politically it was more a test than an illustration."[69] Matta-Clark's interventions transcended the didacticism of agitprop, but this quality also leaves what remains of the work vulnerable to co-optation and misinterpretation. Matta-Clark decried the depoliticizing effect of the gallery, where "the pieces were used simply to fill up space" and "the work was NEVER there."[70] He found galleries as limiting as any other architecturally prescribed setting: "The whole question of gallery space and the exhibition convention is a profound dilemma for me. I don't like the way most art needs to be looked at in galleries any more than the way empty halls make people look or high-rise city plazas create life-less environments."[71]

Because much of Matta-Clark's work was impossible to exhibit, undue importance has been placed on the conventional display of documentary material and building fragments. Former *Anarchitecture* colleague Laurie Anderson commented that she "felt really frustrated with Gordon's shows ... because without the talk, the background, the thing that was left was really blank."[72] The lack of context in posthumous depictions of *Window Blowout* is the primary reason the work has been ignored, misinterpreted, or treated as an isolated incident. Because *Window Blowout* is a direct statement of Matta-Clark's anti-authoritarian politics, restoring this context is vital to understanding his art.

Relating *Window Blowout* to other modes of artistic dissent is equally important. I have traced a current of symbolic violence in protest to Artaud, whose wide-ranging influence on protest art and activism in the 1960s and 1970s in New York City warrants further examination. Artaud's "theatre of cruelty" sheds new light on the liberatory aspirations of Matta-Clark's violence, challenging the marginalizing discourse around *Window Blowout*.

Artaud's framework also highlights two interrelated aspects of Matta-Clark's work that have previously been overlooked: the centrality of the theater as a metaphor for Matta-Clark's sociospatial interrogations and the anarchist dimension of his anarchitecture. Matta-Clark's prefigurative anarchism is evident in projects such as FOOD, the La Plaza Cultural Garden, and his proposal for a community-based architecture school. His work within existing conditions suggests a constructive anti-authoritarian alternative to the teleological utopianism underlying both modernist planning and the Marxist model of revolutionary change: "I am experimenting with alternative uses of space that are most familiar. I like to think of these works as bypassing questions of imaginative design by suggesting ways of rethinking what is already there. I do not want to create a totally new supportive field of vision, of cognition. I want to reuse the old one, the existing framework of thought and sight. . . . [I]t is an organic response to what has already been done."[73]

The irony of critics' accusations that Matta-Clark's work was essentially destructive is that none of what he termed his "building cuts" (the buildings as a whole) remain. He regarded fragments as mere documentation, and their value as art objects has been imposed by art dealers and galleries, against his wishes. Throughout his career, Matta-Clark accepted the transient status of his work, but when it became known that his life would be cut short by cancer, supporters sought to preserve what was left of his work. Shortly after his death, more than two hundred artists from around the world, including Christo, Robert Rauschenberg, and Sol LeWitt, donated original works for an auction to raise funds to preserve Matta-Clark's only extant building cut, *Office Baroque* (1978). Despite this outpouring of support, *Office Baroque* was hastily demolished for no better reason than to clear the property. The remaining lot sat vacant for more than a decade thereafter, a testament to the destructive logic of urban renewal.[74]

Notes

1. Roberto Matta-Echaurren to Gordon Matta-Clark, 1962, Gordon Matta-Clark Archive, Canadian Centre for Architecture, Montreal.
2. Gordon Matta-Clark, interview, September 1977, in *Gordon Matta Clark*, ed. Corinne Diserens (London: Phaidon, 2006), 188.
3. Ibid.
4. Pamela Lee, "On Matta-Clark's 'Violence'; or, 'What Is a Phenomenology of the Sublime?,'" in *Object to Be Destroyed: The Work of Gordon Matta-Clark* (Cambridge: MIT Press, 2000), 114.
5. Anthony Vidler, "Splitting the Difference: Anthony Vidler on Gordon Matta-Clark," *Artforum International* 41:10 (2003): 35; Maud Lavin, "Gordon Matta-Clark and Individualism," *Arts Magazine* 58:5 (1984):138–41.
6. Peter Eisenman, introduction to *Idea as Model* (New York: Rizzoli, 1981), 1.
7. Ibid.
8. Charles Jencks, *The Language of Post-Modern Architecture* (London: Academy, 1987), 8.
9. Wall, interview, 184.
10. Robert Pommer, "The Idea of 'Idea as Model,'" in *Idea as Model*, 3.
11. Andrew MacNair, interview, ca. 1985, in *Gordon Matta-Clark: A Retrospective*, ed. Mary Jane Jacob (Chicago: Museum of Contemporary Art, 1985), 111.
12. Ibid.
13. Dennis Oppenheimer, interview, ca. 1985, in ibid., 96.
14. Pommer, "Idea of 'Idea as Model,'" 3.
15. The Gordon Matta-Clark Archive is housed at the Canadian Centre for Architecture, Montreal.
16. Frederik Le Roy, *Tickle Your Catastrophe! Imagining Catastrophe in Art, Architecture, and Philosophy* (Ghent: Academia, 2011), 41.
17. Matta-Clark, interview, in *Gordon Matta Clark*, ed. Diserens, 187.
18. Robert Caro, *The Power Broker: Robert Moses and the Fall of New York* (New York: Knopf, 1974), 1014.
19. Ibid., 12.
20. Ibid., 20.
21. Ibid.
22. Richard Sennett, *Flesh and Stone: The Body and the City in Western Civilization* (London: Faber and Faber, 1996), 360.
23. Matta-Clark, interview, in *Gordon Matta Clark*, ed. Diserens, 187.
24. Sennett, *Flesh and Stone*, 18.
25. Caro, *Power Broker*, 933.
26. *Laurie Anderson, Trisha Brown, Gordon Matta-Clark: Pioneers of the Downtown Scene, New York 1970s* (London: Prestel, 2011), 70.
27. Gordon Matta-Clark, *Works and Collected Writings*, ed. Gloria Moure (Barcelona: Poligrafa, 2007), 177.

28. David Raskin, *Donald Judd* (New Haven: Yale University Press, 2010), 46.

29. Charles Simpson, *SoHo, the Artist in the City* (Chicago: University of Chicago Press, 1981), 150.

30. Jane Crawford, "Dancing with Gordon Matta Clark—Radio Papesse Interview," 2008, https://archive.org/details/JaneCrawford-DancingWithGordonMattaClark-RadioPapesseInterview.

31. Matta-Clark, interview, in *Gordon Matta Clark*, ed. Diserens, 187.

32. "Our History," Green Guerillas, http://www.greenguerillas.org/history.

33. "A Brief History of La Plaza," http://laplazacultural.com/?page_id=15.

34. Wall, interview, 186.

35. Jan Hodenfield, "Street Gets a Breath of Fresh Air," *New York Post*, September 9, 1972.

36. Lee, *Object to Be Destroyed*, 164.

37. Sennett, *Flesh and Stone*, 359.

38. Carol Gooden, "FOOD and the City," *Collapse* 7 (July 2011): 249.

39. "Gordon Matta-Clark, Sauna Cut, 1971," Kunstmuseum Liechtenstein, http://www.kunstmuseum.li/?page=2215&cid=52&monat=3&jahr=2010&lan=en.

40. Paul Wood, *Modernism in Dispute: Art since the Forties* (New Haven: Yale University Press, 1993), 109.

41. Julie Ault, *Alternative Art, New York, 1965–1985: A Cultural Politics Book for the Social Text Collective* (Minneapolis: University of Minnesota Press, 2002), 27; David McCarthy, *American Artists against War, 1935–2010* (Berkeley: University of California Press, 2015), 82; Gijs van Hensbergen, *Guernica: The Biography of a Twentieth-Century Icon* (London: Bloomsbury, 2013), 276.

42. Gordon Matta-Clark, interview by Donald Wall, ca. 1976, Estate of Gordon Matta-Clark, on Deposit at the Canadian Centre for Architecture, Montreal.

43. See also Allan Antliff's chapter in this volume.

44. Antonin Artaud, *The Theater and Its Double*, trans. Mary C. Richards (New York: Grove, 1958), 42, 8.

45. Allan Antliff, "Situating Freedom: Jackson Mac Low, John Cage, and Donald Judd," *Anarchist Developments in Cultural Studies* 2 (2011): 39–57.

46. Mariellen Sandford, *Happenings and Other Acts* (London: Routledge, 1995), 17.

47. Artaud, *Theater and Its Double*, 51, 111–12.

48. Gordon Matta-Clark, interview by Judith Russi Kirshner, February 13, 1978, in Matta-Clark, *Gordon Matta-Clark*, 330.

49. Matta-Clark, interview by Wall.

50. Ibid.

51. Jorn Weisbrodt, "The Brain Is a Building," in *Robert Wilson: From Within*, ed. Margery Arent Safir (Paris: Arts Arena, American University of Paris, 2011), 89–95.

52. Robert Wilson, interview, ca. 1985, in *Gordon Matta-Clark*, ed. Jacob, 100.

53. Matta-Clark, interview, in *Gordon Matta Clark*, ed. Diserens, 187.

54. Michela Pasquali, *Loisaida: NYC Community Gardens* (Milan: A & M Bookstore, 2006), 99.

55. Dorita Hannah, "Towards an 'Architecture of Cruelty': Mining the Spatial Speech of Antonin Artaud," in *Architecture and Violence*, ed. Bechir Kenzari (Barcelona: Actar, 2011), 106.

56. Artaud, *Theater and Its Double*, 74.

57. Louise Pelletier and Alberto Pérez-Gómez, eds., "Theatrical Space as a Model for Architecture: A Bibliography on Ephemeral Structures, Theatrical Urban Space, and the Architecture of the Stage in Modern Europe," http://digital.library.mcgill.ca/tspace/.

58. Matta-Clark, interview by Kirshner, 328.

59. Ibid., 327.

60. Uri Gordon, *Anarchy Alive: Anti-Authoritarian Politics from Practice to Theory* (London.: Pluto, 2007), 79.

61. Colin Ward, *Anarchy in Action* (New York: Harper and Row, 1973), 60.

62. Ada Louise Huxtable, "Farewell to Penn Station," *New York Times*, October 30, 1963.

63. Gordon Matta-Clark, "Anarchitecture 4," 1972, Estate of Gordon Matta-Clark, on Deposit at the Canadian Centre for Architecture, Montreal; Michel Foucault, *Discipline and Punish: The Birth of the Prison* (New York: Vintage, 1995).

64. Richard Sisk, "South Bronx Is Poorest District in Nation, U.S. Census Bureau Finds: 38% Live below Poverty Line," *New York Daily News*, September 29, 2010.

65. Ward, *Anarchy in Action*, 73.

66. N. J. Habraken, *Supports: An Alternative to Mass Housing*, trans B. Valkenburg (London: Architectural Press, 1972), 12.

67. Matta-Clark, interview by Kirshner, 330.

68. Matta-Clark, interview by Wall.

69. Joseph Kosuth interview, ca. 1985, in *Gordon Matta-Clark*, ed. Jacob, 111.

70. Matta-Clark, interview by Wall.

71. Wall, interview, 183

72. Laurie Anderson, interview, ca. 1985, in *Gordon Matta-Clark*, ed. Jacob, 18.

73. Matta-Clark, interview, in *Gordon Matta Clark*, ed. Diserens, 188.

74. Roberto Matta-Echaurren to Gordon Matta-Clark, 1962, Gordon Matta-Clark Archive, Canadian Centre for Architecture, Montreal.

ABC No Rio as an Anarchist Space

ALAN W. MOORE

ABC No Rio is a long-running cultural institution on the Lower East Side of Manhattan. It is a nonprofit corporation under New York State law. It was founded and run on radical democratic principles, and its current director is an erstwhile anarchist organizer. A metal plaque out front states that it is dedicated to the "culture of resistance." So is it an anarchist space? At the very least, ABC No Rio has an anarchist past. This chapter lays out some histories of the project, how it evolved through art and politics, and its present position in the midst of a major capital project to construct a new center on the site of the old.

ABC No Rio was founded after a direct action in which I participated—the occupation of a vacant city-owned building for an art exhibition, the *Real Estate Show*, on January 1, 1980.[1] The City of New York gave us another space to use at 156 Rivington Street, and a two-week show became an ongoing adventure. The space's leaders—Becky Howland, Robert Goldman (Bobby G), and me—took the name from a storefront sign visible across the street through our plate glass window. The sign had once advertised legal services, "ABOGADO NOTARIO," but most of the letters were gone. ABC's economic and political development was continuously involved with institutions. Although it was always fiercely autonomous, its funding and housing largely depended on a group of government agencies. Its history, then, is part of the history of cultural provision for art, understood as schooled artistic practice, together with provision for minoritarian cultural activities in poor communities in New

York City and across the United States. ABC evolved on its own, in its own way, as a radically democratic open and fluid organization. It has politics—radical politics even by the standards of the art world of its day—but is not committed to any political viewpoint exclusively. It began life under the wing of another organization, Colab (Collaborative Projects), a group of artists that formed as an open assembly in 1978. Colab made shows, films, magazines, projects of all kinds.[2] One of these was the *Real Estate Show*.

ABC No Rio began with basically no overhead other than electricity. We paid no rent and had no gas, and water was free at the time. We paid for incidentals—mops, buckets, soap, lightbulbs. Colab paid for the programs, allocating money for artists to make shows in the space. Because Colab was a nonprofit corporation that received state and federal cultural funds, ABC No Rio was free to develop as it wished. For the first few years, Howland, Goldman, and I ran it as a troika, with an open meeting every Monday night where proposals were presented and discussed and problems were hashed out. After we—the troika of founding artists—had done a number of shows, we left.

New York City's Department of Housing Preservation and Development, which controlled the building, had an institutional animus against ABC No Rio. Although William Emmicke, a deputy commissioner under Mayor Ed Koch, had assigned the *Real Estate Show* artists to the building at 156 Rivington Street, the department's rank and file never seemed to like this arrangement. They worked ceaselessly to clear the building of tenants, an effort that intensified after the city began to auction off "vacant" properties during the later 1980s. Though ABC had been granted the use of the storefront, we quickly expanded by breaking into the basement when it became clear that the proprietor had abandoned it. The city did not seem to notice. The department subsequently relocated all the residential tenants who occupied the floors above the ABC No Rio storefront, and ABC expanded its working areas into the rest of the building. With thousands of properties to manage, the agency never had the resources to overcome the tenacious artists and activists of ABC No Rio, who were organized and refused to leave.

This struggle with the city enabled the artists of ABC No Rio to form connections with the militant squatter movement that arose in the East Village (the northern part of the Lower East Side) in the late 1980s. Movement activists were involved in networked defense of the buildings they had occupied and were renovating, despite threats of police evictions and arson attacks in the middle of the night. After the Tompkins Square Riot of 1988, the squatters' struggle with the police became much broader and deeper, and more of the East Village community was drawn into it.

First Goldman and then his successors as the space's directors, Jack Waters and Peter Cramer, lived illegally in the basement of ABC. Waters and Cramer ran their own nonprofit corporation, Allied Productions, whose constituency was the radical queer performance community, although *queer* was not common parlance at the time. In 1990, a group of punk rock musicians asked if they could put on shows at ABC No Rio. The hard-core punk rock matinee shows at CBGB's rock club, which drew many young people from around the region, were becoming difficult for gay kids, people of color, and women, who were subjected to fights and beatings. The money brought in by the punk music events eventually became ABC's single most significant source of revenue. The punk collective that organized these shows was thoroughly politicized and became a strong force in the place as the Allied Productions people increasingly moved their activities away from ABC No Rio. At one point, the punk collective was running the space.

To protect ABC No Rio, the artists and their allies occupied the vacant apartments at 156 Rivington Street as residential squatters beginning in the early 1990s. During these years, ABC had its closest connection with militant anarchists. Steven Englander, who worked with anarchist publications, took on management tasks at ABC.[3] The Blackout Books collective organized in the basement and ran an infoshop there before renting a space in the East Village. It was one of a number of similar ventures that sprouted up around that time.[4]

The city's war on squatters heated up under Rudy Giuliani's mayoral administration. In the spring of 1995, hundreds of police and some armored vehicles were mobilized against squatters occupying a group of buildings on East 13th Street, a battle that gained world headlines—and cost the city a lot of money. The city subsequently became less confrontational and began offering the remaining squatters paths to legalization. ABC No Rio took advantage of such an offer and now occupies its space legally.

Now I will consider this history more closely, using primarily materials online at ABC No Rio's website.[5]

The "Decadent Performance Era"

In 1983, Howland, Goldman, and I retired from ABC No Rio, and it was taken over by a group of performance artists involved in the nightclub circuit in the newly vibrant, rapidly changing cultural scene in the East Village. To start off, these artists slept and performed together for *7 Days of Creation*, a weeklong performance devoted to "the theme of myths and legends of creation." The experience was formative for the participants. Performing artist Philly later recalled that "there was this sense of what is there left to celebrate, what is there left to create, everything has already been co-opted and commercialized. So people were reaching for something else. Basically, everyone was drunk, high, deranged and ambisexual, those seven days were more like one long day of creativity and madness. I couldn't tell where one day ended and the next began." Waters described "Aline Mare from Erotic Psyche pissing into a vase and then reading a ritualized poem over it, with Bradley Eros down on all fours pushing a fish across the stage and Aline following carrying the vase and chanting. There was film projected over every surface of the room. Bradley also made an enormous dome out of fabrics and cushions which was called the Sensory Tent. When one would enter the tent they would be caressed anonymously by arms covered in velvet." Carl George, newly evicted from his living space, brought his oversized futon into the gallery, and people slept on it together. Kembra Pfahler, a young artist from California, found at ABC No Rio a community that would take her seriously: "There were people there who were coming from the same place I was, of wanting to test limits. The stuff we did was about transforming yourself, daring yourself in public to see your own bravery emerge."[6]

Jorge Brandon (1902–95), known as El Coco que Habla (the Talking Coconut), was a key figure in the emergence of the New York Puerto Rican (Nuyorican) school of poetry, which expressed the Caribbean identity of New York's second-largest concentration of immigrants from the island. Brandon wandered the streets of the barrio Loisaida (Spanglish for Lower East Side), reciting poetry in the *declamador* tradition of the Island.[7] Pfahler remembered Brandon as "this remarkable, charming neighborhood poet who was just incredible, he was like this old but still very strong tropical surfer who could captivate anyone with his words and the strength of his personality."[8] His self-styled job, which he started in the 1940s in Union Square Park, was to inform the living of what had taken place in the past. Brandon worked as a sign painter and pushed his supplies around in a shopping cart. "In order that his poetry—never handed over to the press—might continue to be heard, even when he was tired, Jorge had planted a tiny tape recorder inside a hollowed-out coconut."[9] Brandon had performed at ABC No Rio years earlier with Bimbo Rivas, who worked with the theater at the CHARAS social center, and Miguel Algarín, the founder of the Nuyorican Poets Cafe. That poetry series was produced by Josh Gosciak, a writer and editor of the journal *Contact II*, who was later a member of the organizing committee of the New York Anarchist Book Fair. In the later 1980s and early 1990s, Brandon became active in the Tompkins Square Park encampment of homeless and lived for a time in a squatted building. In this role, his image appears on the cover of Seth Tobocman's graphic novel, *War in the Neighborhood* (1999/2016), declaiming from a balcony in the face of the police.[10]

Brandon's occasional presence in the midst of an extremist experimental queer scene reminded the artists of the cultural depth of the community in which they were working. Like those of us who had worked there before, the new artists at ABC felt a sense of responsibility toward the existing residents of the neighborhood. We participated in the *Not for Sale* exhibitions organized by the Political Art Documentation and Distribution group (PAD/D).[11] The new artists at ABC worked with children at the nearby school, first offering a workshop on creation myths and then developing theatrical programs. We all opened the doors of the gallery to local children, including those of a troubled family living upstairs.

At the same time, many neighbors were wary. ABC No Rio acquired a reputation as a wild place where anything might happen. Artists unable to show anywhere else came to ABC. Philly often finished her shows by projectile vomiting. At a benefit performance in a nearby nightclub, Philly threw live crabs into the audience. A Virginia group, Psychodrama, staged a show reminiscent of the notorious Viennese Actionists of the 1960s. Recalled Samoa, a musician, "One guy was reading a poem while giving himself an enema and the others started throwing buckets of horseshit," which they had brought from a farm, "at everyone in the gallery. When the shit started flying the room cleared out, everyone ran screaming down Rivington Street with these naked guys chasing them and throwing shit. A lot of people got hit with shit. The neighbors just thought that anyone who went to No Rio was insane."[12]

Money Changes Everything—Except ABC

During the 1980s, the East Village became the focus of an intense short-lived commercial art gallery scene. In 1985, Cynthia Carr, the performance critic for the *Village Voice*, wrote,

> After the galleries opened here, I waited for them to close. More quantity than quality. It can't last. But they flourished. They multiplied. Soon we had "East Village" everything all over the photo spreads [in magazines]. That meaningless term. It'll die. Instead it was heard round the world. I had made the mistake of thinking this phenom[enon] was about art. I even thought that calling the scene "commercial" was a put-down, only to see its most fervent apologists embrace commercialism as something positive. Then I began to understand. *East Village Eye* critics Carlo McCormick and Walter Robinson cheerfully described the East Village as "'a marketing concept" that "suits

the Reagan Zeitgeist." ... And the neighborhood itself, with its garbage, its junkies, my old block between C & D that lost half its buildings to arson? "An adventurous avant-garde setting of considerable cachet." Such attitudes are more shocking than any artwork can hope to be in 1985.[13]

ABC No Rio was emphatically out of sync with the commercial exuberance of the Reagan era. "Moloch soars over the city. Those ruled by Moloch do not know it, but they love the stern taste of his whip." These words begin Okra P. Dingle's zine history of these years, part of an imaginary dialogue between the gods Dionysus and Kali, who have launched the ABC "experiment" in an attempt to rebalance the world of mortals seduced by money and run by watchdogs such as Ronald Reagan, the National Endowment for the Arts, and the Museum of Modern Art. The rise of ABC's "lusty playground" is part of the gods' plan to restore the balance of power so that Moloch can be overthrown: "We have to help these mortals to recognize the Moloch that is in each of them so that they can either transform or exorcise it."[14]

By the late 1980s, the directors of ABC No Rio had become more deeply involved in their film production and exhibition project, *Naked Eye Cinema*. The artists who came to work at ABC No Rio began to reflect the more individualistic careerist nature of the East Village gallery movement. The government funding agencies tightened their requirements. The already decrepit building continued to fall apart. The city became more insistent on evicting the cultural center, and Waters and Cramer finally decided to move on from their management roles, although they remained on the board of directors.[15]

By this time, ABC No Rio had become a venue for spoken word and music performers. The downtown New York open-mic scene of performative poetry and "antifolk" music was hot, with television scouts nosing around, and the railing of poets at ABC was an important part of the tableau. Matthew Courtney's *Wide Open Cabaret* was ABC's most successful program during these years. Run by a genial, syrupy-voiced MC, the show had unusual rules: anyone reading for the first time could go first; each reading was limited to eight minutes; and the performers had to time themselves. Was this egalitarian way of structuring performance political? Lou Acierno, a videomaker with the collective Rehab who served as program director, explained, "Viewing the similarities between life, politics and art, the underlying concepts are the same. A food co-op, a squat and Rio are basically the same thing. Only the methods are different, and the approach." Agreed performance director David Shea, "If there is any interest in 'political revolution,' in creating a working context, a basis for a new culture ... No Rio is a basis for building a new alternative."[16] Winchester Chimes, a key participant in the Sunday night performances, eloquently expressed the political consciousness of the new group of spoken-word and performance artists when he voiced his resentment of the conditions of his precarious office job in "Master Business":

> I walk on you / I turn you 'round / Your emptiness
> Will make me proud:
> I AM MASTER BUSINESS! (Kneel Dog: Crawl)
> I AM MASTER BUSINESS! (Give me your pathetic all!)
>
> I am your own division! / The poseur called "success"!
> Your buying/selling structure! / I am Master Business!
>
> I have reduced all Earth to cash!
> Money is God
> And employees are trash!!!![17]

While open-mic readings and performances were in vogue in Lower Manhattan during this period, Courtney's program was marked by a rare sense of community and by a "tolerance for eccentricity and marginal points of view which were not to be found in the club scene." In addition to the artists, the *Wide Open Cabaret* attracted "the eccentrics, crackpots, ideologues and neighborhood characters which No Rio has always drawn its share of."[18] It was a fiercely anticommercial performance place, a community of outsiders.

Jennifer Blowdryer, a regular participant in these evenings, saw ABC No Rio overall during these years as "low energy," with building problems, both physical and legal, and its leaders as "older, cranky, pissed off artists bickering with each other." Unlike other open-mic venues in the district, No Rio had a "tolerance for the weird scary people who were drawn to the place, in the absence of real structure or rules these people seemed to come in droves and thrive and work out their stuff and contribute in ways that wouldn't have been possible at other places, they would have been ostracized. . . . We hated, admired, slept with, cheated, and loved each other—you know, what people do. It cost a dollar to attend, but it was pretty fucking free."[19] With such a deep engagement with the gay scene, the plague of AIDS hit the ABC No Rio community especially hard. In the 1980s and 1990s, many New York City artists, including Chimes and numerous others with ties to the ABC No Rio scene, died of AIDS, and Courtney stopped doing the open-mic.[20]

While many of the declaimers at the Sunday open-mics gave eloquent voice to the frustrations of temporary wage work, vilified the bosses, and cried out against the real estate speculation overtaking the Lower East Side, others around

ABC No Rio actively resisted the changes taking place in the neighborhood. The squatter movement in the East Village gained momentum as the City of New York began to sell off vast holdings of tax-forfeited properties. Long-abandoned tenement buildings that had fallen into ruin and the vacant lots where they had been demolished were being "flipped" (sold and resold) in the emerging speculative frenzy and construction boom that created what is now a bourgeois neighborhood. Culture—specifically, the East Village gallery movement of the 1980s—played a vital role in making the Lower East Side safer and more appealing to the new residents and the workers in FIRE (financial, insurance, and real estate) and ICE (information, communications, and entertainment) enterprises.

Activists in the housing justice field were alarmed, with academics like Neil Smith and Rosalyn Deutsche publishing influential analyses of the situation. The movement's history on the Lower East Side put anarchists in a good position to act. The gist of their analysis was that the city government was selling off common resources to speculating capitalists, and artists were being used to grease the wheels. Buildings that could be used to house the rapidly increasing homeless population and vacant land that could be used to make community gardens in a densely built urban neighborhood were being auctioned off. Frank Morales, a charismatic priest born on the Lower East Side who had worked with the squatting movement in abandoned city-owned buildings in the South Bronx, promoted a systemic activist analysis, "spatial deconcentration."[21]

With a historical commitment to direct action, many anarchists had become involved in squatting. This practice had spread in New York City during the 1970s in response to landlord abandonment and the withdrawal of capital from the neighborhood. The city initially tolerated the tactic and ultimately regulated it as "urban homesteading." Puerto Rican nationalists and other activists also took over some larger buildings that had previously housed schools and social service agencies, creating social centers such as CUANDO and CHARAS. An early inspirational occupation was undertaken by the Black Panthers, who occupied the enormous Christodora building on behalf of community groups from the mid-1960s until the city violently evicted them all in 1969.[22]

In the mid-1980s, artists connected to the Rivington School group (which showed in a row of rented art galleries and performance spaces that abutted a squatted vacant lot on which a large welded-metal sculpture garden had been erected) started a squat called Bullet. With its well-known origins in an artists' occupation and the close involvement of many artists in the squatting movement, ABC No Rio not surprisingly became an important node for squatters.

Enter the Anarchists

The Tompkins Square Park riot in the summer of 1988 galvanized resistance on the Lower East Side.[23] Police beat a small band of angry squatters, punks, and anarchists after a tense standoff and then rampaged up and down the streets near the park for hours, administering indiscriminate beatings to people on the street or stepping out of their apartment doors. After this major police riot, community support for the squatters grew as never before.

The squatters had been at the park that August night to defend a large encampment of homeless people who were protesting the city's housing policies. The riot was an important moment in a long series of struggles over the uses of this large green space, a public commons with a long radical past.[24] During these years, the Anarchist Switchboard at 384 East 9th Street, just blocks from the park, served as the unofficial headquarters for activists involved in the issue. It was a dank, cramped basement space, "a dingy one-room spot with couches, exposed lightbulbs and red concrete walls."[25]

The Anarchist Switchboard was opened in 1986 by Bob Palmer and comrades from the Libertarian Book Club, a longtime anarchist group that organized lectures and meetings. Until 2008, Palmer also led radical history walking tours through Lower Manhattan's "points of freedom and destiny," many on St. Marks Place (8th Street).[26] Both artists and activists used the space. Posters on the (old) Myspace page of Donny the Punk showed that vegans, squatters, and antiracist musicians used the space.[27] The touring punk band Mecca Normal played there in 1988 with a gig set up by Bob Z of the *Bad Newz* zine. Sean Meehan, later a volunteer and board member at ABC No Rio, performed improvisational music at the Anarchist Switchboard as part of the Improvisors Network's *A Mica Bunker* series.[28] This highly noncommercial avant-garde music practice continues at ABC No Rio, organized by the COMA group.

Steven Englander, who worked at the Anarchist Switchboard during these years, described the area as undergoing a "mini compressed '60s," with regular demonstrations in the park, eviction battles with police, and street brawls with fascist skinheads. Squatters, "freelance anarchists and radicals," and other people organizing in the neighborhood used the Anarchist Switchboard's space for presentations, workshops, and meetings. Englander was also active then with the Libertarian Book Club and with Autonomedia. "There was a sort of tangible buzz" during between 1986 and 1992, with squatters and artists, punks and skinheads, cops and yuppies circulating in the neighborhood. At the Anarchist Switchboard, Englander was "one of the responsible ones who would open it up and lock it up" and contribute money to pay the rent. He was working freelance in the film industry and "could work ten days a month and have all this free time."²⁹ Englander first came by ABC No Rio in 1986 or 1987, during Courtney's open-mic days.

By that time, Lou Acierno was serving as ABC's day-to-day manager and living upstairs in the building. The city informally recognized him as the building's superintendent (maintenance person). He and Englander got along well—both men worked in film and video, and they shared a critical analysis of commercial media. Acierno went on tour in Europe with Waters, Cramer, Max Schumann, Fly Orr, and other artists in 1990 and asked Englander to manage No Rio in his absence. Nearly three decades later, Englander remains ABC No Rio's director and administrator.

While Englander clearly has an anarchist past, he describes ABC as always "anarchistic":

> Because of the way it's been structured and run, No Rio does attract people who do call themselves anarchists, but nowhere in any of No Rio's documentation, whether it's the founders or the people in the '80s, were they ever explicitly anarchist. In the early days they'd sort of established a sense of working collectively and having a high degree of spontaneity, which, years later, attracted a certain kind of person. And then, during the late '80s and early '90s, No Rio got more closely involved with the squatters' scene on the Lower East Side, and that probably added to this veneer of its anarchistic quality. But there's no political litmus test, and it's actually pretty ecumenical in terms of people getting involved. I'm sure there are a lot of people who'd be horrified to be called an anarchist. There's all sorts here, but pretty much generally on the left.³⁰

During the late 1980s and early 1990s, however, anarchists came in the front door of ABC as a key part of the punk music scene.

The Punks Move In

Sometime in 1989, the Dwarves band was supposed to play at ABC No Rio but canceled a few hours before the gig was to start. Someone called the Lismar Lounge, a local bar that featured live music, to find a replacement band on short notice. Bugout Society showed up. They played, liked the space, and told their friend Mike Bullshit, who began programming Saturday matinees of hard-core punk music at ABC in December 1989.³¹

Only a month earlier, Hilly Kristal had pulled the plug on the Sunday hard-core matinees at his Bowery club, CBGB's, the focal point for New York's 1980s punk and hard-core scene. According to Jim Testa, "These weekly moshathons were hugely popular but plagued by violence—skinheads beating up suburban kids, straightedgers bashing drinkers, as well as the usual mayhem, fistfights, bloody lips, and black eyes that resulted as an inevitable consequence of NYC slamming."[32] The violence escalated to the point where people started showing up with guns. Kristal had intended the club to cater to his pals in the Hell's Angels, but that was just too much.

In setting up the new venue, organizers locked out the machos who had made CBGB's such a rough place. "Changing the ugly, sneering face of NY hardcore was at the forefront of ABC No Rio's mission," Testa writes, "from the beginning, the club's booking policy proclaimed, 'No racist, no sexist, no homophobic bands.' The self-destructive punk-on-punk violence that had ravaged the CBGB hardcore scene disappeared; there were never any fights at ABC No Rio." Mike Bullshit soon came out as gay. After some shows in the main space, the punks moved into the basement and set it up like a rock club. After local bands established the venue, touring bands soon followed, and ABC No Rio was on its way to becoming an internationally important punk music venue. According to Testa,

> Tim Singer (of No Escape, and more recently, Deadguy) set up a regular record and tape table where bands could sell merchandise. That developed into a long-standing policy of different vendors working the shows so that you could find cheap, DIY and indie label punk records every time you went to a show at ABC....
>
> "It wasn't just the bands either," recalls John Woods, who attended the ABC shows as a fan. "People would go to the shows and start fanzines. Record labels came out of it. You could go every week and not be in a band, and still felt like you were part of what was going on. It was pretty unparalleled just in terms of creativity. Everybody was doing something, whether sweeping the floor or a fanzine or starting a band."[33]

The "goofy, cleancut suburban kids" who started the venue were soon pushed aside, Testa wrote. Or maybe their favorite bands just broke up. Bullshit moved on, and people he never really liked—including a guy from the Squat or Rot record label—took over and "started booking some of the crustier Lower East Side bands."[34] The geeks were disillusioned. Neil Robinson of Squat or Rot was a long-haired Londoner who told the *Village Voice* in 1990, "We're trying to get some politics going." Anarchist politics, not fascist: skinheads and "boneheads" were not welcome. "We're the only non-profit, volunteer-run, cooperative all-ages venue in New York," said Peruvian Freddy Alva. "We're losers, we're faggots." Alva and Robinson "built a stage and sound booth in ABC's basement.... Records and T-shirts [were] sold upstairs, and anarchist, squatters, animal rights, and Greenpeace literature [was] handed out.... Jesus Chrust, Insurgence, Yuppiecide, the Worst, and Huasipungo play[ed] a benefit for ABC and Food Not Bombs."[35]

The combination of movements that came together in ABC No Rio during the hard-core matinees recalls the milieu of Crass, an influential anarchist-pacifist English punk band. The original anarchopunks, Crass formed in 1977 and enjoyed a spectacular subcultural success in the United Kingdom during Margaret Thatcher's neoliberal prime ministership. Crass was the counterpart to the U.S. punks who saw Ronald Reagan's "Morning in America" as "Mourning in America," as Englander put it. The movement also included art punks, who were radically expressive using Dada and Situationist ideas. "Be exactly who you want to be, do what you want to do / I am he and she is she but you're the only you," wrote Crass founder Penny Rimbaud.[36]

Whether they were throwing fast-food hamburgers at their audience or railing against capitalism, the squatters and the geeks had more in common than not. All were committed to a life lived within a resolutely noncommercial ethos, and all believed in the collective process. Political activists felt a magnetic attraction. As Greg Pason explained in *The Socialist*,

> The libertarian-socialist idea of "dual power" calls for building "a new society within the shell of the old." Every DIY [do-it-yourself] space, band-organized show, fanzine and pirate radio show follows that ethic. This applies to other music scenes but has been a big part of the DIY punk movement. The idea is not just to set up an independent space for music but a community space where issues can be addressed and skills can be learned—a space where community can practice solidarity. A DIY punk motto is "Fix Shit Up." Thousands of young people have learned about building community, addressing problems without the involvement of the state or police, and sharing resources and building relationships in punk collectives and events.

Pason joined the ABC No Rio hard-core collective in 1994, when he was also active with the anarchist magazine *Love and Rage*. In 2012, he and the ABC punk collective sought to revitalize the giant Punk Island free summer concert festival.[37]

Fractionation and Consolidation

Even as the punk collective was injecting new life into ABC No Rio and activity in the place was increasing, ABC came under pressure from the city and from internal strife. After Acierno returned from Europe, he asked Englander if he wanted to continue as ABC's director. In Englander's words, "Continuing meant being the person who was here on 24-hour call, so to speak." Acierno moved out, and Englander took over the super's tasks. The Monday night meetings had become traditional, but they had been reduced to one a month and were often poorly attended. Englander discontinued them and decided that anyone who wanted to do something at ABC should just talk to him.[38]

In 1991, tensions with the board of directors reached the point where both Acierno and Englander resigned. According to Englander, "There were differences between what Lou and I wanted to try to do and what the board was willing to let us do."[39] In Englander's view, the board, made up of people who had worked at ABC in the past, was too controlling. Young people currently working in the space lacked a voice. The organization broke into factions, and Acierno, Englander, and their artist friend, Fly, went on a Midwest tour. They wanted to get away from a physical space and to think about projects they could do without a place, because that seemed to be in the cards. In 1993, however, the entire board of directors of ABC No Rio resigned. The punk collective and Acierno were now running the place legally.[40]

The hard-core punk collective managed the building's affairs through regular meetings, a form of management also used within the squatting movement. (In Spain these would be called *asembleas*; in Germany, *plenums*.) Anyone who worked at ABC No Rio was expected to attend and to share the burdens of management. This mode of organization persists today. ABC No Rio is a group of autonomous projects whose representatives meet regularly with Englander. Thus, ABC No Rio is called a "collective of collectives."

In the summer of 1993, Blackout Books, a recently formed collective, was among those operating tables upstairs at the punk shows. The Blackout crew was considering starting an anarchist bookstore. By 1994, they had gathered a core group and funding and found a storefront at 50 Avenue B, up the street from ABC. At the grand opening, a few hundred folks turned out, celebrating the new store and *Zapatistas!*, a book published by Autonomedia. A key component of that Mexican group's revolutionary practice was the concept of "dual power"—that is, building institutions alongside those of the state.[41] Could this be the start of a New York City node in such a network in the United States? The Blackout Books store became something of a hangout and served as an activist center for the nearby squats. The store maintained a watch list of some fifty people who could be called by the volunteer on shift if a squat or community garden was in danger of eviction.

In the optimistic moment of its beginnings, Blackout planned to publish an anarchist guide to New York City in the summer of 1995 and to host "many art exhibits."[42] However, the storefront bookstore soon closed. Blackout Books was one of a number of attempts to create radical activist support centers during these years, all of which quickly failed. An essay in *Love and Rage* questioned the anarchist movement's heavy investment in infoshops—raising money to pay rent, clean up and promote spaces, and so forth.[43] Only ABC No Rio persisted. As the squatter movement grew in size and militancy, the city redoubled its efforts to evict ABC. Harassment and burglaries became more common. A construction accident next door pierced the basement wall of ABC's building and offered the city a chance to condemn the structure. The remaining tenants were relocated, and their apartments stood empty. Architect Paul Castrucci filed a structural report, and the basement was shored up, forestalling eviction.

The punks, who were managing the building as well as producing their shows, had signed a "stipulation" with the city, but officials were already violating the terms of the agreement, and the punks feared that ABC would soon be evicted. In 1994, three years after quitting, Englander was invited back to ABC No Rio. His job this time was to organize the squatting of the building to protect it from cops and vandals. City officials clearly knew that they were dealing with a vital node in the network of Lower East Side squatter resistance. According to Testa, "The question is, why would New York City be so deadset on evicting a group of people who voluntarily provide such a range of services, in a neighborhood that's been criminally neglected and badly in need of whatever help it can find?" The answer, Testa wrote, was that the city was retaliating for a near riot that occurred when the city attempted to evict a group of squatters from a row of 13th Street tenements. According to Amanda Trevens, a punk show volunteer, "Nobody from ABC was arrested or had any part in what happened at 13th Street, but we've had benefits here for the 13th Street people and I guess the city knows that the people here support them. But that's just an excuse. The city was making noises about getting us out of here years ago, before 13th Street ever happened."[44]

In 1994, ABC No Rio was a new squat. It had never been squatted before. The place had a long history of relations with city, state, and federal cultural agencies as well as ties to other art spaces, organized activist groups, and elected officials. Waters and Cramer had long since initiated a lawsuit against the city for bad management, and the case and the massive dossier of violations that accompanied it had kept the Department of Housing Preservation and Development at bay for many years. Officials did not want to litigate. Now, however, the pressure was unrelenting and the city was in court in earnest. Bizarrely, ABC No Rio's case hinged on a lightbulb. City workers had ripped out the electrical system in the hallway, but the city was legally required to provide outside lighting for commercial tenants. Because the city had failed to provide this service, a judge denied the city's request for an order of eviction.

Frustrated in court, the city devised a novel strategy. A local housing group, Asian Americans for Equality (AAFE), very badly wanted another large building, and officials agreed to give it to the group but required that it also take 156 Rivington. ABC supporters objected and staged protests on the street in front of the AAFE's offices. One person dressed in a Mao Tse-Tung costume, tricked out with dollar signs, an allusion to the organization's founding by Maoists; other ABC partisans chained themselves to the facade of the AAFE building. In response, the AAFE declared that it would not be used to evict another cultural organization and insisted that the city abrogate the deal.

In 1998, ABC partisans went to the offices of the commissioner of the city's Department of Housing Preservation and Development and prepared to stage a sit-in. They expected to be arrested, and Englander remained at ABC, preparing to do jail support. To the demonstrators' surprise, commissioner Lillian Barrios-Paoli invited them into her office and shared her memories with the young activists: she had been a student in Mexico City during the 1968 Tlatelolco Square massacre. She ultimately offered ABC No Rio a deal: if the activists could raise the money to renovate the building, it was theirs.

With that, ABC No Rio became legal. But fund-raising immediately became the primary task, and punk shows and bake sales would not be enough. ABC No Rio's volunteers have lobbied elected officials for city money, obtained foundation support, and convinced subsequent city administrations to authorize the building project. ABC No Rio has raised the funds to demolish its three-decades-old home and has begun construction on its new facility.

What Do You Do If You Win?

This, as Englander remarked, was the new problem facing activists who were more experienced at losing their fights with power.[45] His first task, in keeping with the new agreement, was to arrange to have all the squatters at ABC No Rio (including Englander himself) move out. He was not delicate about the process, and people complained about it for years. He has subsequently maintained close control over all aspects of programming at ABC, and it often seems frozen in time.[46] Englander and the board have devoted themselves to raising eight million dollars for the construction of the new facility, an incredible sum for a grassroots arts organization. Englander has steered the construction project through the city bureaucracy, and in the summer of 2016, the collective moved out of the building so that demolition could begin, the first step in ABC No Rio's rebirth. During this current "exile" phase, ABC has moved projects to other institutions and will produce exhibitions at other venues.

More recent activist projects in New York have tended to bypass ABC No Rio. In 2004, the place was an occasional convergence center for the major wave of demonstrations against the Republican National Convention, serving as a node of national and international resistance. Eric Goldhagen, board member and cyberactivist, told the Krax City Mine(d) conference in Barcelona in 2008 that "ABC is infrastructure—a resource for people who plan actions and protests" and for artists. "But as an organization we don't do those things. ... The goal of the space as a whole is to develop a dialogue and a connection between artists and political activists.... We expect them to talk to each other." The Lower East Side around ABC has changed completely and has become one of the most expensive areas of Manhattan, meaning that "what was once our community is now just where we exist." Asked Goldhagen, how can ABC No Rio "remain a community center when the community has been crushed?"[47]

Many years have passed since ABC played a key role in the Lower East Side squatter movement and spun off an anarchist infoshop from its punk music program. Nearly all of the squats have been legalized.[48] Punk has been mainstreamed. Anarchist groups of those bygone days have faded away, and New Left libertarian formations have emerged. When Occupy Wall Street arose in 2011, ABC was not involved. ABC has become a cultural center.

So is ABC No Rio an anarchist space? Formally, the place continues to share many aspects with recent anarchist-driven projects in Europe and the United States—an autonomous radical library (zines); a silkscreen printing shop; music-presenting collectives, both punk and experimental; a bicycle workshop and skill share; and more (though a number of them have fallen away). It is public and run by volunteers (although not by assembly). It has had periods of connection with explicitly anarchist projects. But according to Englander, who has directed the space for more than a quarter century and who has previously participated in explicitly anarchist projects, it is not an anarchist space. ABC No Rio has always been an embedded cultural institution, dependent for monies on state arts agencies and foundations. Because of its past, its carefully cultivated autonomy, and its cultural underpinnings in punk and squatting, ABC nevertheless has links to recent North American and European anarchism.

In recent years, the United States has shown few signs of a live squatting movement like those in Europe, either for housing or for provision of political and cultural space. The old guard of squatters on the Lower East Side has now turned to history making. In 2012, The Museum of Reclaimed Urban Space (MoRUS) opened in the storefront of C Squat, with murals and displays of the squatter movement's past. It is run by a collective that includes bicycle activist Bill Di Paolo, whose Times Up! group was housed for years in ABC's basement. Times Up! is a longtime supporter of the community gardens, a movement for urban land occupation that went hand in hand with squatting on the Lower East Side. Many of these community gardens are now facing pressure from the city and from developers.

Englander and I share a passion for ABC, but we have differing ideas about what should be going on there. I would like it to be much more active and to engage more continuously in the rapidly evolving sphere of global Left movements and activist art. But he runs the place, and in the end, I must aver that Steven and his cohorts have accomplished work I and mine never could have—steering the ABC ship through the straits of institutionalization, thereby ensuring that this, nearly the last of New York City's long-term Left-based institutions, will survive as an integral part of the landscape of the future city.

ABC No Rio is a place founded by a collective of artists seeking autonomy and social engagement. It has persevered, at times together with anarchists and anarchist-inflected movements. However it has been managed over its many years, the main job of the place has been survival—sheer persistence as an outpost of autonomy and a signal of its possibilities. As the United States faces the specter of an authoritarian future, directed, ironically, by a New York City–based real estate developer, a place like ABC is a pearl beyond price.

Notes

1. The *Real Estate Show* involved a number of other artists who did not continue with ABC, most notably Ann Messner and Peter Mönnig. Appearing on cable TV, Mönnig called the *Real Estate Show* a *Freiraum* (German for free space, meaning an occupation or squat). Alan Moore and Marc Miller, eds., *ABC No Rio Dinero: The Story of a Lower East Side Art Gallery* (New York: Collaborative Projects, 1985), has a substantial section on the *Real Estate Show*. Much of it is online at Marc Miller's http://98bowery.com/return-to-the-bowery/abcnorio-the-book.php. The author's zine, *House Magic* 6 (2014), has a special issue on the *Real Estate Show* for a series of exhibitions, *Real Estate Show Revisited*.

2. On Colab, see Alan W. Moore, *Art Gangs: Protest and Counterculture in New York City* (Brooklyn, N.Y.: Autonomedia, 2011).

3. Steven Englander told me that he worked with the Neither East nor West project and the Autonomedia editorial and publishing collective. See Bob McGlynn, "Neither East nor West: Some History...," *Anarchy* 37 (Summer 1993), spunk.org.

4. Dan Sabater, "A Brief History of NYC Anarchist Bookstores, 1988–2005," March 19, 2013, signs-of-life-nyc.blogspot.com (originally https://nyc.indymedia.org/es/2006/01/63707.html); Eugene Reznik, "The Radical Bookstores of New York," *Animal New York*, March 11, 2013, animalnewyork.com/2013/the-radical-bookstores-of-new-york.

5. Many of the texts on which this essay is based are available at abcnorio.org/about/history/history.html.

6. Okra P. Dingle, *Art Effects: Decadent Performance Era at ABC No Rio* (New York: ABC No Rio, ca. 1998) (ABC No Rio zine library).

7. Center for Puerto Rican Studies website, Loisaida barrio timeline for the 1940s (demounted).

8. Dingle, *Art Effects*.

9. Mario Maffi, *Gateway to the Promised Land: Ethnic Cultures in New York's Lower East Side* (New York: New York University Press, 1995), 136.

10. Seth Tobocman, *War in the Neighborhood: A Graphic Novel* (Brooklyn, N.Y.: Autonomedia, 1999; Toronto: Ad Astra Comix, 2016). Tobocman's book is based on his experiences as well as on extensive research and interviews.

11. Gregory Sholette, "A Collectography of PAD/D," n.d., gregorysholette.com/. Sholette has spoken often on the *Not for Sale* campaign. ABC artists also participated with PAD/D in related demonstrations.

12. Dingle, *Art Effects*.

13. C. Carr, "'Money Changes Everything': The East Village Art Mart," *Village Voice Literary Supplement*, September 1985, abcnorio.org/about/history/history.html. In the summer of 1984, Walter Robinson and Carlo McCormick had published "Slouching Toward Avenue D," *Art in America* 72:6 (1984). Robinson was a member of Colab and was among those who worked as an artist at ABC No Rio in its early days. McCormick curated shows there and has continued as a dedicated critic of street art and underground culture.

14. Okra P. Dingle, *Artifice: Matthew Courtney's Wide Open Cabaret* (New York: ABC No Rio, ca. 1999), 3 (ABC No Rio zine library).

15. Steven Englander, interview by Liza Kirwin, September 7, October 10, 2007, Archives of American Art, Smithsonian Institution, aaa.si.edu/collections/interviews/oral-history-interview-steven-englander-13660. Unless otherwise cited, all quotations from Englander and other information in this section comes from this interview. There was also less money. When the National Endowment for the Arts cut funding for ABC, Waters believes, it was an early victim of what came to be called the culture wars of the 1990s waged by right-wing legislators against federal funding for the arts. Waters wrote to me that his belief is based on research Emily Rubin of CHARAS did on numerous organizations that served communities of color or were "progressive." During Reagan's first term, many were simply suddenly defunded. In his second term, explicit ideological reasons were given (Jack Waters, email to the author, November 11, 2016).

16. Sasha Forte, "Guerrilla Space: A Few Many Things about ABC No Rio," *X-POSURE*, Summer 1989, abcnorio.org/about/history/xposure_89.html.

17. Dingle, *Artifice*.

18. Ibid.

19. Ibid.

20. Waters and Cramer became increasingly preoccupied with AIDS-related activism during these years. Courtney moved west before returning to New York, where he continues to work as a street artist.

21. Yolanda Ward, "Spatial Deconcentration," *World War III Illustrated* 6 (1985), abcnorio.org/about/history/history.html. Ward, an activist, was later murdered; her analysis was the earliest and influenced New York City activists. The academics include Rosalyn Deutsche and Cara Gendel Ryan, "The Fine Art of Gentrification," October 31, 1984,

reprinted in *Portable Lower East Side* 4:1 (1987), abcnorio.org/about/history/history.html; Neil Smith, "Tompkins Square: Riots Rents and Redskins," *Portable Lower East Side* 6 (1989): 1–36; Christopher Mele, *Selling the Lower East Side: Culture, Real Estate, and Resistance in New York City* (Minneapolis: University of Minnesota Press, 2000); Neil Smith, *The New Urban Frontier: Gentrification and the Revanchist City* (London: Routledge, 2005). For texts from the squatters' movement, see Clayton Patterson, Joe Flood, Alan Moore, and Howard Seligman, eds., *Resistance: A Social and Political History of the Lower East Side* (New York: Seven Stories, 2007).

22. See Yuri Kapralov, "Christodora: The Flight of a Sea Animal," in *Resistance*, ed. Patterson et al., 87–100; *House Magic* 6 (2014); Susan Simensky-Bietela, "The Tompkins Square Community Center," *House Magic* 6 (2014).

23. See Sarah Ferguson, "The Struggle for Space—10 Years of Turf Battling on the Lower East Side," in *Resistance*, ed. Patterson et al., 141–65. Clayton Patterson videotaped the riot for three and a half hours. When the tape was subpoenaed, he refused to hand it over and subsequently served time in jail. The case was noteworthy because it was one of the first to involve the rights of citizen-journalists. See Patterson et al., *Resistance*.

24. Bill Weinberg, *Tompkins Square Park: Legacy of Rebellion* (Ithaca, N.Y.: Autumn Leaves, 2008).

25. Mecca Normal (punk band), 1988–93, meccanormal.wordpress.com/1988–1991/.

26. "Bob Palmer, Anarchist Activist, 1924–2009," April 7, 2009, revleft.com.

27. Donny the Punk, MySpace pages: myspace.com/politicalpunknyc/ (demounted). Donny the Punk, aka Stephen Donaldson (1946–96), was a writer on the punk scene. He was a gay man who was raped in jail after an arrest for activism, which led to a lifetime of agitation against jailhouse rape. See "Stephen Donaldson (activist)," https://en.wikipedia.org/wiki/Stephen_Donaldson_(activist); Stephen Donaldson Papers, 1985–96, Manuscripts and Archives Division, New York Public Library, New York.

28. The name may derive from the remnants of a sign for the Alchemical Theatre, a spin-off of the Living Theatre, which had earlier occupied the space (Englander, interview by Kirwin). On the Living Theatre, see Allan Antliff's chapter in this volume.

29. Englander, interview by Kirwin.

30. Whitney Kimball, "The ABC No Rio Interviews: Steven Englander," December 20, 2012, at Artfcity (formerly Art Fag City), artfcity.com/2012/12/20/the-abc-no-rio-interviews-steven-englander/.

31. Jim Testa, "The Rise and Fall (and Rise Again) of NYC's Only All-Ages Non-Racist, Non-Sexist, Non-Homophobic Punk Scene," *Jersey Beat* 56 (Spring 1996), abcnorio.org/about/history/jersey_beat.html.

32. Ibid.

33. Ibid.

34. Ibid.

35. "Rockbeat: 'Boneheads Need Not Apply,'" *Village Voice*, December 1990, abcnorio.org/about/history/boneheads_no_90.html.

36. "Crass," https://en.wikipedia.org/wiki/Crass; Penny Rimbaud, "Big A Little A," Crass Records 1980; Englander, interview by Kirwin. For the influence of Crass, see Jon

Savage, *England's Dreaming: Anarchy, Sex Pistols, Punk Rock, and Beyond* (New York: St. Martin's Griffin, 2002).

37. Greg Pason, "Punk and Politics," *The Socialist* 2 (2013), socialistparty-usa.org/socialist/2013/april13/punkpolitics.pdf. The Punk Island Facebook page started in 2012. See https://www.facebook.com/PunkIslandNYC/.

38. Englander, interview by Kirwin.

39. Ibid.

40. Vikki Law, ed., *Enter the Nineties: Punks and Poets at ABC No Rio* (New York: ABC No Rio, 2005) (ABC No Rio zine library); for the tour, see Fly, *Chron!Ic!Riots!Pa!Sm!* (Brooklyn, N.Y.: Autonomedia, 1998).

41. See Roy San Filippo, ed., *A New World in Our Hearts: Eight Years of Writing from the Love and Rage Revolutionary Anarchist Federation* (Oakland, Calif.: AK, 2002).

42. Rachel Rinaldo, "Blackout Bookstore and Info-Shop," *Temp Slave*, no. 7 (1995), abcnorio.org/about/history/blackout.html.

43. San Filippo, *New World in Our Hearts*.

44. Testa, "Rise and Fall."

45. Englander, interview by Kirwin.

46. Anarchist Delfina Vannucci was expelled from ABC, and although she does not name the organization or any of the people involved, she later coauthored a book with Richard Singer, *Come Hell or High Water: A Handbook on Collective Process Gone Awry* (Oakland, Calif.: AK, 2009), that I have been told reflects her painful experiences at ABC No Rio. Englander offers a different take on the self-evictions that followed the deal with the city: "The radical elements that came out to support No Rio and put themselves on the line thru direct action were in favor of the deal. They put themselves on the line to defend ABC No Rio, not the half dozen people living upstairs." He also disagrees with my description of the place as static, declaring it "a mischaracterization" that "demonstrates a misunderstanding of how day to day operations at ABC No Rio work. It's also insulting to all the other collective members doing projects here.... I'm not aware of any other collectively run space that operates on a similar scale and scope" (email to the author, October 5, 2015).

47. Video of Eric Goldhagen and Rick Jungers, "ABC No Rio, NYC," April 26, 2008, Krax City Mine(d) Conference Proceedings, Barcelona, Spain, 2008, blip.tv/krax/abc-no-rio-nyc-889766. ABC No Rio was most likely included in the conference because of its squatting past and because the space's collective-based projects mirror those found in European social centers, which originated in the squatting movement. In addition, many of the public projects of the European squatting movement, like ABC No Rio, have been legalized and institutionalized as cultural centers (e.g., Rote Fabrik and Shedhalle in Zurich; Overtoom301, Vrankrijk, OCCII in Amsterdam, among many others). Others continue openly resistant (Rote Flora in Hamburg, Forte Prenestino in Rome). See A. W. Moore and Alan Smart, eds., *Making Room: Cultural Production in Occupied Spaces* (Chicago: Other Forms, 2015).

48. See Amy Starecheski, *Ours to Lose: When Squatters Became Homeowners in New York City* (Chicago: University of Chicago Press, 2016).

The Influence of Anarchism in Occupy Wall Street

HEATHER GAUTNEY

Occupy Wall Street (OWS) is part of a long history of protest movement activity in New York City against the detriments of capitalism, from the crowds that gathered outside the New York Stock Exchange during the Great Depression to the masses of students, housewives, beatniks, and nuns protesting the Vietnam War to Occupy Wall Street's months-long occupation of Zuccotti Park. Despite the fact that most banks and actual trading are no longer located on or even near Lower Manhattan, Occupy reinvigorated these historical fights and urban uprisings in the aftermath of the Great Recession to counter the devastating effects of unbridled greed and unregulated speculation on everyday people.

Occupy Wall Street was not explicitly "anarchist" or even anticapitalist per se, but it bore the deep imprint of anarchist praxis in its emphasis on building alternative forms of political and social engagement outside conventional politics and the hegemony of the commodity form. In fact, most occupiers would probably have rejected the moniker, since the figure of the nihilistic, bomb-toting anarchist continues to dominate the national imaginary. Some anarchists seek to literally "smash the state" as well as the corporation, the school, and other agents of social control. But most are committed to the long-term project of movement building and challenging illegitimate forms of authority without inflicting undue harm. Many anarchists believe that radical change and ultimately freedom and the good life can be discovered through nonviolent direct action and the development of cooperative projects and countercultural communities rather than through the realization of a predetermined revolutionary moment or participation in electoral processes abstracted from the conditions of everyday life.

It is no coincidence that anarchism featured so prominently in the organization and character of the Occupy movement—more prominently than any other system of political and social thought. OWS sought to accommodate the needs and aspirations of diverse segments of the population—indeed, "99 Percent" of it—from various class backgrounds and political orientations.[1] The movement attempted to deploy an anarchist organizational logic to accommodate a wide array of political actors and foster a broad-based coalition, enabling contentious yet nonviolent engagement with state and corporate forces.

In the U.S. context, anarchism signifies a politically heterogeneous set of actors who sometimes disagree about its meaning and use. As countless theorists have pointed out, it is nearly impossible to present a single theory of it. Not only are there multiple strands—anarchosyndicalism, primitivism, mysticism, communist anarchism, libertarian socialism, and so on—but anarchism itself generally eschews the idea of formulating (imposing) a general, all-encompassing theory of social change. Anarchism is thus better understood by its methods and principles rather than through a single, unified theory, political strategy, or specific group of actors.[2]

This chapter explores three key principles in anarchist thought and discusses how they were applied, both successfully and unsuccessfully, in shaping the course of the Occupy movement. In the process, it analyzes the particularity of New York City as an incubator for anticapitalist politics within what is arguably the world's most significant center of global finance.

Anarchist Principles

Anarchism involves a rejection of hierarchy and formal organization, but anarchists do tend to coalesce around organizational principles, including prefiguration, anti-authoritarianism, and anticapitalism. The first principle, prefiguration, embodies the latter two, as it combines anarchists' anticapitalist and anti-authoritarian orientations into an overarching organizational ethic that seeks to balance desires for freedom with problems of structure, coordination, and mediation. Prefiguration reflects anarchists' belief that movements and their organizations should "prefigure" the political and social relations they seek to establish. As Murray Bookchin has written, "What different anarchist organizations have in common is that they are developed organically from below, not engineered into existence from above.... They try to reflect as much as is humanly possible the liberated society they seek to achieve, not slavishly duplicate the prevailing system of hierarchy, class and authority."[3]

The term *prefiguration* also references the temporal aspects of social change. Serbian anarchist Andrej Grubacic describes anarchism's emphasis on prefiguration as "life despite capitalism," which includes constructing commons, autonomous spaces, and other forms of sociality in the present while foreshadowing what a "life after capitalism" would look like and theoretically moving toward it.[4] Rather than accepting a political and legal order imposed by state and other coercive forces or a social order dominated by market relations, anarchists want to establish their own sets of rules and community life—in the here and now—according to their own egalitarian moral sensibilities.

A second principle, anti-authoritarianism, generally refers to anarchism's antistatist character, which dates back to Mikhail Bakunin in the nineteenth century. The state was at the center of anarchism's break with Marxism, and Bakunin in particular warned of the dangers of a Marxist "red bureaucracy." Marx theorized the transition from capitalist to communist society as involving a seizure of state power by the working class, but Bakunin rejected this idea, citing "the true despotic and brutal nature of all states."[5] While Marxists viewed the state as an executive of the ruling class and asserted ruling-class control over the means of production as the ultimate relation of oppression, anarchists saw the state as an autonomous entity with its own logic of domination.[6]

Although anarchism is historically antistatist, some who identify as anarchists acknowledge that some aspects of state entities can provide important public services, though most anarchists would argue that these services would be better organized via local or regional assembly. Some, like Noam Chomsky, even assert that supporting the state sector in neoliberal societies may constitute a step toward its abolition.[7] Much of anarchist anti-authoritarianism involves placing the burden of proof on existing authority structures and limiting or dismantling the power of institutions or individuals whose authority proves illegitimate. Anarchists reject the systems of coercion that undergird state authority, which, they believe ultimately undermines its potential to serve as an agent of liberation.[8] This critique of authority extends to other media of social control, including the family, educational systems, physical and mental health care facilities, and norms regarding sexuality, religion, and artistic expression.[9]

In terms of the third principle, anticapitalism, anarchists share Marxism's concern for social inequality and alienation as well as its emphasis on labor as an important concept through which to understand human history and potential. They oppose private property and argue for a direct reappropriation of resources by people rather than through the state or any other mediations. In this regard, anarchists' anti-authoritarianism and anticapitalism are interrelated: anarchism insists on "democratic control over one's life" as well as advocates for social ownership of the means of production, a kind of "stateless socialism."[10] They use the term *mutual aid*, initially theorized by Peter Kropotkin, to refer to the voluntary exchange of goods and services for the mutual benefit of members of a given society.

Many of today's anarchists refer to mutual aid in terms of commons, a concept that has its roots in the property-sharing practices of medieval Europe but generally refers to any resource that is or should be collectively shared. Against the dominant system of private property, commons are "forms of *direct* access to social wealth, access that is not mediated by competitive market relations."[11] In keeping with the anti-authoritarian ethos of anarchist thought, *commons* also refers to coordinated, cooperative practices that are directed neither by a central point of command nor from some "spontaneous harmony." Street and subway raves; squat houses; open-source software; food and housing collectives; editorial collectives; co-op bookstores; and Internet pirating, in which people trade commodities, like music and film, instead of buying them from multinational corporations, are just a few examples of attempts to reclaim commons.

Occupy Wall Street and the Logic of Occupation

OWS was founded by anarchists within a broader climate of intense protest movement activity in Europe, the Middle East, and beyond. While most of these movements did not explicitly identify as anarchist, many of them adopted a "leaderless" structure that rejected centralized authority, in keeping with a primary tenet of anarchist praxis—the idea that communities and movements should prefigure the noncoercive societies they seek to create. In some places, leaderless organization manifested through the institution of general assemblies (GAs), which were decision-making bodies that enabled mass participation and collective decision making. Such movements were not, of course, really leaderless, but as anarchism implies, they operated "without rulers."[12] Social media, with its network structure and openness to broad participation, helped foster the necessary connections for these often large-scale assemblies, and the lack of formal leadership helped these movements strategically avoid police repression and co-optation."[13]

Influenced by this global cycle of movements, Occupy Wall Street emerged in its own national context of social inequality and political unrest. Just months earlier, "Walkerville" activists set up an encampment outside the Wisconsin State Capitol and occupied the building to protest Governor Scott Walker's

Budget Repair Bill, which aimed to strip public employees of their pensions, health insurance, and collective bargaining rights. Influenced by Walkerville, New Yorkers against Budget Cuts set up a similar camp, Bloombergville, to protest Mayor Michael Bloomberg's proposed cuts to social services and public employee layoffs, including six thousand teaching jobs.[14] Bloombergville attracted roughly one hundred protesters at first, but lost numbers early on.

Cognizant of the encampments in Wisconsin and New York and inspired by the Arab and European uprisings, a Vancouver-based magazine/activist network, *Adbusters*, organized the occupation of Wall Street for September 2011. The editors of *Adbusters* identify as anarchist, and their magazine reflects an explicitly anticapitalist agenda. Local New York City anarchists played a vital role as well, planning the occupation on the ground and undertaking much of the online legwork that brought the calls to action from *Adbusters* (and Anonymous) to large segments of the population. New Yorkers also created a general assembly for decision making, which helped to prevent more hierarchically organized groups from dominating the movement. The GA would become a primary mechanism for bringing people into the movement and connecting Occupy groups across the country and the globe.[15]

Zuccotti Park was selected as a potential site of occupation because of its unusual status as a privately held public space. Unlike city parks, which have curfews, Zuccotti, owned by Brookfield Office Properties, was zoned to be available twenty-four hours a day to the general public as part of an exchange for increased air rights for a development project. The park was situated in a hugely symbolic, high-traffic, high-price-tag area in Lower Manhattan. An encampment in Zuccotti meant that OWS was occupying both Wall Street, "the capitol of capital," and the World Trade Center, which many people continued to see as a tragic symbol of American imperialism. On September 17, a relatively small number of activists set up camp in Zuccotti Park, and for about a week, they staged street demonstrations on a daily basis. When police clashed with protesters, a video of Officer Anthony Bologna pepper-spraying screaming female college students at point-blank range aired on TV stations around the globe, drawing larger numbers to the occupation. On October 1, occupiers marched to Chase Manhattan Plaza; while crossing the Brooklyn Bridge, seven hundred of them were arrested.[16] The jailed protesters refused to broker plea deals, and the Transit Workers Union Local 100, one of the city's largest unions, filed a lawsuit against the use of city buses and workers to transport OWS protesters to jail.[17] The heavy-handed police response at both events spurred public outrage, and Occupy camps began to proliferate in major cities and rural towns across the country.

The Occupy movements' national emergence took the form of a network, much like federated structures conceptualized by anarchists. Anarchists operationalize their ethics of autonomy and anti-authoritarianism by calling for organizational forms that involve decentralized, autonomous (self-organized) units interconnected via federal arrangements.[18] They not only eschew electoral politics and juridical (rights-based) solutions to social problems but also reject the imposition of national boundaries and other spatial arrangements that deny the autonomy of local communities and fix social relations around artificial borders.

Anarchists understand such boundaries to be artificial in the sense that they do not conform to the more organic ways in which communities emerge and reproduce, especially in the context of neoliberal globalization, where freer flows of goods and services are matched by highly regulated and policed immigration systems. Instead, anarchists argue for an alternative social ecology comprised of self-organized and -managed communities and local units that allow for an unbridled flow of people around the globe in lieu of boundaries imposed by states. For anarchists, local organic units are more likely to prevent illegitimate hierarchies because they require a minimum delegation of authority; when representation is deemed necessary, there is at least a high degree of accountability between representatives and their communities.[19]

The Occupy movement as a whole was constituted by a network of autonomous units. The network was organized not to force movement toward some ideal state of affairs or support for a single project or politician but rather to link heterogeneous groups with unique histories. The majority of Occupy camps established their own GAs to meet the needs of their local communities and address the particular political conditions in which they were operating. Occupiers in New York City, for example, were uniquely positioned to take Wall Street institutions head-on, but Detroit occupiers, positioned in a zone of corporate abandonment, wanted to avoid blanket anticorporate activism out of respect for the businesses that decided to stay (and employ people). They instead opted to work with welfare rights and environmental groups to protest utility rate increases and lobby for more green jobs. A centralized movement might have imposed the hard-line anticorporate sentiment emblematic of OWS, but doing so would have been insensitive to the needs of the people of Detroit.

For anarchists, direct action plays an important part in their contesting of authority by circumventing it as well as in their refusal to cede sovereignty to illegitimate authority figures. While some political tendencies use protest to push power holders toward action, anarchists engage in direct action to achieve a particular goal, thereby circumventing existing power structures and in effect delegitimizing them. The logic of occupation operates similarly, if not the same. In *The New Imperialism*, David Harvey elucidates some of the underlying forces that OWS's strategy of occupation sought to address.[20] He points out that neoliberal capitalists rely only in part on profitable investment to accumulate capital. Their wealth also derives from processes of dispossession that involve usurping social and natural wealth from other people by way of privatization, deregulation, and financialization. These forces have helped a select few siphon lower- and middle-class wealth while steamrolling rights to resources that should be commonly held. In this light, OWS's strategy of occupation should be read as a program of repossession in which the term *occupy* means taking back institutions, places, people, ideas, and rights that neoliberalism has taken away.

OWS's encampment in Zuccotti Park followed decades of struggle by housing and public space activists to reclaim their right to the city against such revanchist-style dispossession. In the 1990s, Neil Smith theorized New York City's political transition over the preceding five decades as reminiscent of the revanchist movement in nineteenth-century Paris, where reactionaries attempted to reinstate the bourgeois order by hunting down and exacting revenge on their liberal enemies, who were believed to pose a threat to the moral order.[21] As Smith points out, the liberal social approach of the 1960s, characterized by redistributive and antipoverty policy, gave way to a neoliberal program of revenge in the 1980s and 1990s, in which New York City's poor and working-class people as well as political dissenters were positioned as public enemies by state and corporate forces. Mayor Rudolph Giuliani's program of "zero tolerance" found widespread public support in the wake of increased reactionary paranoia brought by economic recession, setting the stage for Michael Bloomberg, an exceptionally rich politician who succeeded Giuliani as mayor and made New York one of the country's most unequal and heavily policed cities. According to the *New York Times*, "No mayor in New York's history has done more to consolidate the city's identity with Wall Street. Mr. Bloomberg obviously does not bear responsibility for the creation of the indecipherable, huckster financial instruments that resulted in our economic crisis and the litany of personal miseries that followed, but he was one of the country's most impassioned and nurturing supporters of Wall Street during its most ethically unhinged hour."[22] In a context in which political and corporate holders of power had long been foreclosing on poor and middle-class citizens, Occupy offered a new political and social space in which people were neither overregulated nor required to buy a ticket or consume a product.

The camp provided mutual aid for people in need of food, shelter, and support and an open venue for political interaction and creative expression. It sponsored daily teach-ins and published a newspaper, the *Occupied Wall Street Journal*.[23] A self-organized "People's Library" lent some five thousand titles, and the "People's Kitchen" fed hundreds per day, garnering support from the New York Culinary Institute for a couple of meals. With the logic of Wall Street permeating all parts of the city, including its aesthetic, large numbers of people from New York's arts communities joined the encampment, as did workers looking to hold Wall Street accountable for double-digit unemployment and students, parents, and teachers hurt by tuition increases and mired in debt. Teams of reporters and media vans camped around the perimeter of the park and were themselves encircled by police. In addition to the multitude of occupiers in the camp, the park attracted swaths of people who did not necessarily identify with the movement but who saw Zuccotti Park as a curiosity or scene.

In addition to the camps, "Occupy" became a common theme (and euphemism) in the mainstream culture, spurring hundreds if not thousands of self-organized groups, Internet memes, websites, and actions. A few of the most notable Occupy splinter groups and actions include Occupy Harlem's all-day occupation of a boiler room in a rundown building, which forced the slumlord to replace the boiler and restore heat and hot water to poor residents; Occupy the Department of Education, which took on New York's decaying educational system and among other activities rallied a group of teachers, parents, and students to "occupy" policy meetings; "Occupy Colleges," in which students at public universities protested budget cuts and other austerity measures in a broader effort to repossess the country's increasingly privatized public education system; Occupy Our Homes, which circumvented government bureaucracy to get people back into their foreclosed homes; and Occupy Sandy, which provided mutual aid for those hard hit by Hurricane Sandy and organized protests against the private developers' posthurricane land grab.

The outward growth of Occupy also involved large- and small-scale demonstrations, including a massive Global Day of Rage that brought out hundreds of thousands of people in some nine hundred cities around the world as well as more focused actions such as the Bank Transfer Action, in which one million people moved their accounts from banks such as Chase and Bank of America into credit unions (which saw $4.5 billion in new deposits).[24] Nationwide civil disobedience actions took place at Goldman Sachs, Bank of America, Citibank, and Chase Manhattan, and massive university walkouts, zombie marches, flash mobs, and other actions occurred as well. Occupiers in New York went on "Billionaire Marches" to restaurants, theaters, luxury apartment buildings, and the private homes of such wealthy people as Jamie Dimon, Rupert Murdoch, and David Koch. Such actions did not follow traditional forms of protest as a contentious form of lobbying but rather involved direct actions aimed at reclaiming the economy, media, political institutions, and the city itself from these particularly nefarious corporate elites.

Occupy's cyberlife involved far more people. Social media, particularly Facebook and Twitter, fostered immediate communication across immeasurably extensive networks of people within and outside the movement, and the iPhone and other mobile devices helped people virtually attend meetings regardless of location and coordinate street actions in real time. In addition, Occupy the Media, Twitter and Livestream activism, Anonymous, and WikiLeaks attempted to substitute for mainstream media with DIY (direct action) reporting and analysis. Many of these technologies were not available to New York activists during the 1990s alter-globalization movement that prefigured OWS.

The Anarchist Influence in Occupy's Democracy

In addition to shaping OWS's strategy of occupation, anarchism played a major role in the development of the movement's distinct style of political organization, the GA. GAs had been used in the Spanish "15m" movement just months earlier, with varying success, as well as by the alter-globalization movement activists, many of whom went on to become early organizers of OWS. GAs also constituted a prominent means of organizing in the aftermath of Argentina's 2001 economic collapse, when workers formed assemblies to help rebuild their factories, as well as in Bolivia's "water wars," when people took control of the nation's water utility after disastrous waves of privatization.[25]

GAs are fluid and flexible organizational forms that apply in a variety of settings and can accommodate the needs and desires of diverse sets of actors.[26] Each local Occupy had a GA that responded to local conditions and communities, bringing trade unionists, third parties, students, nongovernmental organizations, celebrities, socialists, anarchists, and various others to share equally in the development of the movement—on equal footing, without sacrificing their individual or institutional autonomy. Specific issues such as media, outreach, diversity, direct action, and others were handled by working groups—also open and inclusive—that reported back to the GAs.

Because of the large number of working groups (roughly seventy) in New York, OWS formed a spokescouncil—an additional assembly of working group delegates. A spokescouncil is a horizontal, deliberative structure in which representatives from various groups gather in an inner circle and their members form spokes behind them. Meeting facilitation regularly rotates so that each person or group has an opportunity to run the meeting (that is, there are no permanent leaders). The idea is to avoid top-down organizing and allow for a diversity of ideas and theories to emerge on questions of strategy. As David Graeber put it, "Where the democratic-centralist 'party' puts its emphasis on achieving a complete and correct theoretical analysis, demands ideological uniformity and tends to juxtapose the vision of an egalitarian future with extremely authoritarian forms of organization in the present, these openly seek diversity. Debate always focuses on particular courses of action; it's taken for granted that no one will ever convert anyone else entirely to their point of view. . . . Their ideology, then, is immanent in the anti-authoritarian principles that underlie their practice."[27]

OWS spokescouncil meetings tended to operate according to "Points of Unity," commonly defined ethical standards that provided general principles—for example, equality of opportunity and mutual respect—that helped to foster affinity and understanding among those present. Points of Unity also secured participants' commitment to the decision-making process itself, which followed a consensus model. With consensus process, participants could discuss and collectively revise ideas until everyone (or at least an overwhelming majority) agreed on a given course of action. Getting everyone to listen and achieve consensus can be time-consuming and emotionally draining but is also key for building solidarity. On a broader level, consensus process mitigates the conundrum of majority versus minority rule by taking into account the needs, desires, and ideas of each person, without class or other forms of privilege.

OWS's goal of prefiguring radical democracy in its political organization also informed the movement's decision to forgo issuing formal demands, a strategy that remained a point of controversy both within and outside the movement. The word *formal* is crucial here, since Occupy raised a variety of concrete, policy-related issues, including electoral reform (overturning the *Citizens United* decision), Wall Street regulation, equitable taxation, universal education and health care, debt forgiveness, environmental and animal rights, opposition to war and intervention, and so on. Much like Students for a Democratic Society and other parts of the New Left, the movement sought to avoid working within the electoral system, in part because it did not recognize the authority (or the competency) of the U.S. government but also because it did not want to degrade the complexity of problems it was addressing into legalist "policy-making" frameworks and reductionist logics of liberal versus conservative and because the Democratic Party had become the party of neoliberalism.

To that end, the New York General Assembly issued a Port Huron–style statement, the "Declaration of the Occupation of New York City," that listed several of the events and issues that gave rise to the movement—the bailout of big banks, generalized workplace inequality, legislative attacks on collective bargaining, animal cruelty, student debt, capital punishment, media control and misinformation, war, torture and colonialism, lack of investment in infrastructure and alternative energy, increasing costs of health care, corporate personhood, and so on. Like Port Huron, the statement was general and nonformulaic, but it did provide a grievance framework. The idea was not to make demands on a system that occupiers believed was illegitimate but rather to pinpoint specific social and political problems and explain why the movement was taking direct action to address them. After the New York City GA issued the statement, Keith Olbermann read it in full on the MSNBC cable television network, and local Occupys adapted and adopted it.

The GAs provided an important mode of political socialization and spaces of engagement for masses of disaffected Americans outside the political mainstream but had a particular set of challenges and limitations. GAs and spokescouncils did not always operate as bastions of inclusivity and participatory democracy, and some meetings became so process oriented that they resembled the bureaucratic "iron cages" the movement opposed.[28] Infighting and stalemates occurred more frequently at spokescouncils when working group representatives were vying for resources. In New York, the GA initially attracted close to a thousand people, but the numbers dwindled as the process became dominated by practical, internal issues of camp maintenance rather than broad-based political education and strategy.

After the closing of the camps, the trend worsened. Cliques formed and some GAs and spokescouncils devolved into yelling matches. When progressive groups with different organizational and political orientations attempted to stage alternative events, they were accused of co-opting the movement. The New York City GA periodically issued statements indicating whether or not it sanctioned a particular action or group, becoming a kind of sovereign authority with the power to approve or disapprove of certain activities. Occupy activists around the country complained that GAs were being controlled by facilitators. Others asserted that the process was too time-consuming and thereby alienated activists who had jobs, families, or other commitments. Some activists just wished that the GAs could engage in "normal" conversations with less "process." Such complaints were also common among occupiers in Madrid and London. According to one of the Indignados in Spain's 15m movement, the group Anonymous came to control much of what went on in the assemblies: "That's not true democracy. It's Anonymous democracy."[29]

The Cancer in Occupy?

Pundits and activists alike blame the devolution of OWS on the problem of (dis)order within the camps and GAs, the movement's failure to issue formal demands, and the seeming lack of strategy and direction, all of which, at some point or another, have been pinned on the movement's anarchist roots. In terms of accusation of disorder, members of the Occupy camp in New York did attempt to mitigate crime and assist mentally unstable people living there by developing noncoercive deescalation methods for dealing with aggression rather than ceding issues of mental health and social order to the authoritarian institutions the movement opposed. The suicide of a thirty-five-year-old protester at Occupy Vermont, drug overdoses at camps in Vancouver and Salt Lake City, sexual assault in Zuccotti Park, and the shooting of a man near Occupy Oakland brought heavy pressure from law enforcement and fed media reports that occupiers were ill equipped to deal with "real world" problems—or worse that they were lawless, disorderly, and unsanitary. New York Police Department officers were rumored to be directing homeless and intoxicated people to the camp, and increased negative reporting strained the movement's relationship to the media.

In addition to confronting the difficult social conditions that beset most urban environments, occupiers constantly faced threats from state forces. At Occupy Albany, police refused an order from the governor to disperse an Occupy crowd, reasoning that such a move could incite a riot that everyone would regret. The Occupy Philly camp was initially sanctioned by the mayor's office, which allowed tents, portable toilets, and amplification devices. But Albany and Philly were in the minority; most OWS camps existed in a constant state of siege.

In Zuccotti Park, for example, the encampment was surrounded by a multitude of police officers who routinely used pepper spray and physical force and arrested protesters in large numbers. Every week, Mayor Bloomberg would concoct reasons for clearing the camp—sanitation concerns or laws against the presence of tents or generators in public parks. After three months of failed attempts to manipulate the law and the local community board, Bloomberg used his executive power and police force to pull the plug on Occupy.[30] Early on the morning of November 15, he ordered a media blackout and shutdown of bridges leading into the city and authorized police and sanitation workers to raze the camp. Subsequent efforts to reoccupy—in Duarte Park, Union Square, and the financial district—were preemptively policed. Within this highly securitized environment, a small group of "black bloc" protesters staged a "Fuck the Police" march (following the example set by activists in Oakland) after an anarchist book fair in Greenwich Village. Some of these activists engaged in property destruction (they broke windows at a Starbucks) and were arrested for allegedly attacking police officers.

More intense forms of police violence took place at Occupy Oakland, which was transformed into a veritable war zone when police fired tear gas, stun grenades, and rubber bullets at crowds of peaceful occupiers in an attempt to clear their encampment. Many of the injured protesters had been shot in the back, and video from the raid showed a wheelchair-bound woman in a tear-gas haze. Iraq War veteran Scott Olsen was hospitalized in critical condition after police shot him in the head with a projectile at point-blank range. Amid widespread public outrage, Mayor Jean Quan attempted to defuse the situation with a YouTube apology and personal visit to the camp. Days later, the city became host to what was billed as the first general strike in decades, spurring solidarity protests around the country and shutting down the fourth-busiest container port in the United States. That demonstration was a bit of a mixed bag, however, as unions offered varying evaluations of the action and its utility.[31]

After the port closing, Quan again had law enforcement clear out the encampment, prompting the deputy mayor's resignation. Quan's legal adviser also quit, pointing to Oakland's history of police violence, which included a 2003 incident at the Oakland port in which police fired beanbags and wooden bullets at antiwar protesters. These acts were condemned by the United Nations and cost the city millions in settlements. City statutes mandate that weapons such as rubber bullets, beanbags, and flash-bang devices are not to be used for crowd control. In addition, failure to obtain a parade permit is not a sufficient basis to declare unlawful assembly.

In this context of escalating violence, smaller cadres of Occupy protesters engaged in property destruction and threw bottles at police, spurring a national debate among occupiers on the use of confrontational tactics in protest.[32] It also brought increased fear-mongering from mainstream media sources, which used the term *anarchist* pejoratively to describe any protester with a militant orientation or who dressed in all-black (the "black bloc"). Police and FBI also targeted anarchist groups and individuals associated with Occupy. Rumors of law enforcement questioning suspected anarchists in the lead-up to the May 2012 NATO Summit protests in Chicago, for example, and raids of activists' apartments and meetings spaces were confirmed during the trial of the NATO Three, self-described anarchists charged with possession of Molotov cocktails.[33] In Ohio, five young males who supposedly planned to blow up a bridge (but who may have been entrapped by FBI agents) were arrested in what the media labeled "the Ohio anarchist bridge-bombing plot."[34]

While corporate media, especially conservative outlets, were quick to deride Occupy as violent and criminal, one of the most vehement criticisms emerged from within the movement, with Chris Hedges's scathing critique of black bloc protesters as "the Cancer in Occupy" and as hooligans, petty vandals, and criminals.[35] Occupiers (and of course many anarchists) were incensed by the article, in part because Hedges had previously praised the militancy of Greek and Egyptian protesters who engaged in markedly more disruptive behaviors than their U.S. counterparts and in part because of various factual inaccuracies that echoed the dangerous, sensational reporting of Fox News and other corporate media.[36] I have witnessed firsthand protest events in the European context as well as those involving black blocs in the United States, and the former are much more confrontational.

Contrary to Hedges's account, the black bloc is not a particular group or organization; it is a tactic that is said to have originated with the European autonomist and militant squatter youth in the 1980s who were distinguished by their all-black clothing and masks. Black blocs are not necessarily composed of people who identify as anarchist, although the methods used may reflect anarchist principles. At Alterglobalization Movement protests in the United States, for example, black blocs tended to operate in "free association," converging only temporarily for particular events or actions and organizing nonhierarchically. Even when participants did not agree on tactics at a given moment, the black blocs featured a strong culture of tolerance and autonomy: each person was free to decide how and when to participate. However, the constitution of black blocs changes with each action and venue. Sometimes they do become involved in more direct confrontations with police, while at other times they participate in large-scale, peaceful marches or protect them from police attack. In short, members of black blocs embrace a diversity of tactics, many of which do not involve property destruction and civil or social disobedience.[37]

In addition to his misunderstanding of the black blocs and anarchism's role in OWS, Hedges's article raises fundamental questions regarding the viability of purely nonviolent direct action in the United States. He assumes that the legitimacy of American power structures rests on the consent of the people, yet time and time again, state actors used excessive force to limit nonviolent protesters' ability to assemble and express dissent. In November 2011, for example, University of California at Berkeley students and faculty, including poet laureate Robert Hass and his wife, were clubbed by police with truncheons while protesting budget cuts and tuition increases; at the University of California at Davis, police pepper-sprayed young college students peacefully staging a sit-in, sending two of them to the hospital and requiring eleven others to receive treatment for exposure.[38]

In both instances, police claimed that they had been surrounded by protesters and were acting in self-defense, but video images told a very different story. In fact, when video of the Davis event was broadcast worldwide, it drew enormous media attention and public consternation, in part because of the cavalier way in which police sprayed toxic agents on such a defenseless group of kids. (MSNBC's Chris Hayes said that it looked like the cops were spraying cockroaches.)[39] Such widespread outrage would seem likely to precipitate a change in the way the Occupy protests were being policed, but it did not. In fact, the UC chancellor who invited the police on campus got off with a simple apology, and despite multiple investigations, only a couple of officers were held accountable.[40]

Contrary to Hedges's prediction that civil disobedience is an effective way to tug at the heartstrings of the general public and pressure politicians, only a handful of those within Hedges's "structures of power" came to the defense of the Occupy movement. In fact, most efforts by local politicians to protect the occupiers were ignored, and most of the power holders directly involved in managing the protests defended the use of force as necessary for public order. Moreover, in the aftermath of the general clearing of the camps and street protests, countless occupiers were acquitted of charges, but only after they had been incarcerated and thus prevented from protesting. Occupiers' conflicts with police may have reinforced the movement's critique of the ongoing loss of public space as a consequence of privatization, but the pressure they exerted did not translate into a reclaiming of that space or any kind of institutional change. This lack of results, however, should be attributed not to any sort of "cancer" but rather to the violent nature of the American state and its mandate to protect the interests of Wall Street at all costs.

Conclusion

OWS may have entered with a bang and left with a whimper, but it did raise an important set of questions for future anticorporate movements and anarchism. First, can nonviolent tactics be used against powerful state and corporate forces that have seemingly limitless implements of violence at their disposal and that are recognized, at least by large segments of the population, as legitimate executors of that violence? The version of democracy that Hedges and liberal democrats defend is predicated on a relationship of legitimacy in which state actors are ultimately accountable to the people they claim to represent. But where does the possibility for egalitarian social change lie in a context in which violence inheres in the dominant power structures and the politics they engender? Where are the spaces of resistance and counterculture in a brutally revanchist city such as New York?

Second, how can such movements accommodate the diversity of actors found in New York and the United States? Anarchist-inspired movements have historically remained marginalized in mainstream culture, but OWS involved much larger numbers of people, many of whom had no experience in grassroots politics or any political framework through which to evaluate the significance of their activism. As the Alterglobalization Movement attests, cooperative deliberative bodies such as spokescouncils and GAs tend to be highly functional when constituted by people with long-standing commitments, affinities, and political experience. OWS's rapid growth resulted in part from the ease of organizing through social media, but Facebook and Twitter do not foster the kind of deep affinity that underpins robust countercultural communities and movements.

The consensus process used in spokescouncils and GAs enabled the construction and nurturing of affinity and stable interactions among individuals and heterogeneous groups. As conceived by OWS, however, the process ran the risk of rendering an inordinate amount of power to facilitators and individuals with axes to grind, thereby devolving into minority rule. Moreover, consensus, like any other process, can easily become a bureaucratic iron cage in which form becomes ideological and overtakes the political and social content of the movement. There is also the question of being sensitive to the organizational mores of unions and other kinds of groups with elected leaderships that have their own democratic processes. Occupy was sometimes good at that, and sometimes not. Unions also tend to bring significant resources and large constituencies, which leads to the question of whether it is just to position representatives of large groups on par with individuals with no organizational commitments. The point of leaderless or anarchist movements is to put all participants on equal footing, but not everyone brings the same sets of resources to the table, and some people are not accountable to constituencies. This issue requires more serious examination.

Despite the need for continued experimentation and fine-tuning, movements such as OWS demonstrate anarchist political organization's unique ability to connect disparate parts of the fragmented Left by creating spaces and structures for democratic capacity building and giving rise to forms of life based on the needs of real communities. As unions, students, artists, and everyday

New Yorkers continue to watch state and corporate power holders shape the city in the image of Wall Street, such connections will be crucial for moving forward and once again rising up.

Notes

1. OWS claimed the identity of the "99 Percent," a slogan based on the well-known statistic that by 2011, an elite 1 percent of the American population had come to own more than 40 percent of the nation's wealth. Joseph Stiglitz wrote on the qualitative implications of this quantitative disparity in his seminal article, "Inequality of the 1%, by the 1%, for the 1%," *Vanity Fair*, May 2011, http://www.vanityfair.com/news/2011/05/top-one-percent-201105.

2. See Dave Neal, "Anarchism: Ideology or Methodology?," September 17, 1997, www.spunk.org/library/intro/practice/sp001689.html; Andrej Grubacic, "Harvey on Anarchists and the State," *Anarchisms Listserv*; Noam Chomsky, *Chomsky on Anarchism*, ed. Barry Pateman (Edinburgh: AK, 2005), 18; David Graeber, *Fragments of an Anarchist Anthropology* (Chicago: Prickly Paradigm, 2004).

3. Murray Bookchin, "Anarchy and Organization: A Letter to the Left," *New Left Notes*, January 15, 1969, http://dwardmac.pitzer.edu/Anarchist_Archives/bookchin/leftletter.html.

4. Andrej Grubacic, "A Talk on Anarchism and the Left," 2005, http://www.zcommunications.org/znet/viewArticle/6404.

5. See Mikhail Bakunin, *Marxism, Freedom, and the State*, trans. K. J. Kenafick (London: Freedom, 1958).

6. See Saul Newman, "Anarchism, Marxism, and the Bonapartist State," *Anarchist Studies* 12:1 (2004); Tadzio Mueller, "Empowering Anarchy: Power, Hegemony and Anarchist Strategy," *Anarchist Studies* 11:2 (2003): 122–49.

7. Chomsky, *Chomsky on Anarchism*, 212–20.

8. See ibid., 118–30; David Graeber and Andrej Grubacic, "Anarchism; or, The Revolutionary Movement of the 21st Century," http://www.zmag.org/znet/viewArticle/9258.

9. Chomsky, *Chomsky on Anarchism*, 178.

10. Ibid.

11. Massimo DeAngelis, "Opposing Fetishism by Reclaiming Our Powers: The Social Forum Movement, Capitalist Markets, and the Politics of Alternatives," *International Social Science Journal* 56:182 (2004): 591.

12. *Anarchy* derives from ancient Greek, meaning "absence of a leader" or "without rulers."

13. See Michael Hardt and Antonio Negri, "The Fight for 'Real Democracy' at the Heart of Occupy Wall Street," *Foreign Affairs*, October 11, 2011, http://www.foreignaffairs.com/articles/136399/michael-hardt-and-antonio-negri/the-fight-for-real-democracy-at-the-heart-of-occupy-wall-street.

14. "Bloomberg to Cut More Than 6,000 Teaching Positions," CNN.com, May 6, 2011, http://www.cnn.com/2011/US/05/06/new.york.bloomberg.teachers/index.html.

15. Matthias Schwartz, "Pre-Occupied: The Origins and Future of Occupy Wall Street," *New Yorker*, November 28, 2011, http://www.newyorker.com/reporting/2011/11/28/111128fa_fact_schwartz.

16. Ray Sanchez, "More Than 700 Arrested in Wall Street Protest," October 2, 2011, http://www.reuters.com/article/2011/10/02/us-wallstreet-protests-idUSTRE7900BL20111002. Just days before the demonstration, JP Morgan Chase donated some $4.6 million to the New York Police Department. See "Is JP Morgan Chase Getting a Good Return on $4.6 Million 'Gift' to NYC Police (Like Special Protection from OccupyWallStreet)?," October 2, 2011, http://www.nakedcapitalism.com/2011/10/is-jp-morgan-getting-a-good-return-on-4-6-million-gift-to-nyc-police-like-special-protection-from-occupywallstreet.html.

17. Pete Donohue, Emily Sher, and Helen Kennedy, "TWU Blasts City for Putting Handcuffed Occupy Wall Street Protesters on Buses," *New York Daily News*, October 3, 2011, http://www.nydailynews.com/new-york/twu-blasts-city-putting-handcuffed-occupy-wall-street-protesters-buses-article-1.960059.

18. Colin Ward, "Anarchism as a Theory of Organization," *Anarchy* 52 (June 1965): 171–78.

19. Bookchin, "Anarchy and Organization," 1.

20. David Harvey, *The New Imperialism* (Oxford: Oxford University Press, 2003).

21. See Neil Smith, *The New Urban Frontier: Gentrification and the Revanchist City* (New York: Routledge, 1996). See also Neil Smith, "Giuliani Time," *Social Text* 57 (1998): 1–20.

22. See Gina Bellafante's analysis of the Bloomberg Administration in "A Mayor Who Puts Wall Street First," *New York Times*, August 16, 2013, http://www.nytimes.com/2013/08/18/nyregion/a-mayor-who-puts-wall-street-first.html?pagewanted=all&_r=0 . Also note that during the Occupy protests, Bloomberg claimed in a weekly radio address that the big banks were essential job creators, and not responsible for the financial crisis. He also said that most Wall Street traders struggle to make ends meet, with only $40–50,000 in a salary per year. The movement tried to stick him with the facts: job creators don't initiate mass layoffs, as Bank of America and Citigroup have, while issuing obscenely large bonuses to their execs. And, according to the state Comptroller's Office, workers in the securities industry in New York made an average of $311,000 in 2009.

23. Occupy camps in other locales also published papers, among them the *Occupied Chicago Tribune* and *Occupied Oakland Tribune*.

24. Gloria Goodale, "Bank Transfer Day: How Much Impact Did It Have?," *Christian Science Monitor*, November 7, 2011, http://www.csmonitor.com/USA/Politics/2011/1107/Bank-Transfer-Day-How-much-impact-did-it-have.

25. See Marina Sitrin, ed., *Horizontalism: Voices of Popular Power in Argentina* (Oakland, Calif.: AK, 2006). See also Michael Menser, "Disarticulate the State! Maximizing Democracy in 'New' Autonomous Movements in the Americas," in *Democracy, States, and the Struggle for Global Justice*, ed. Heather Gautney, Omar Dahbour, Ashley Dawson, and Neil Smith (New York: Routledge, 2009), 251–73.

26. In Zuccotti Park, protesters were forbidden to use tents and amplification devices, which led to the creation of the infamous "People's Mic," whereby people's voices were

used to amplify the words of presenters and facilitators. Each night, the New York City GA began with a "mic check." Facilitators would then run meetings with hundreds of attendees, usually for a couple of hours. Even though other camps permitted amplifying devices, the mic check became a signature of the movement, and occupiers around the country started to mic check at large demonstrations to announce and reach a consensus on impromptu protest actions as well as at smaller venues to interrupt public figures such as Barack Obama and Karl Rove.

27. David Graeber, "The New Anarchists," *New Left Review* 13 (January–February 2002), https://newleftreview.org/II/13/david-graeber-the-new-anarchists.

28. In *The Protestant Ethic and Spirit of Capitalism* (1905), Max Weber wrote about the bureaucratic iron cage of rationality, inherent in Western capitalist society, which traps people in systems based on efficiency and rational calculation.

29. Email exchange with a 15m occupier, October 10, 2011.

30. Bloomberg tried to discredit the Occupy camp in Zuccotti Park by claiming that it was unsanitary and disruptive. The local community board voted unanimously in favor of the camp but also issued a warning to the protesters regarding noise and sanitation. See Matt Sledge, "Occupy Wall Street Gets a Vote of Approval, and a Warning, from Community Board 1," *Huffington Post*, October 26, 2011, http://www.huffingtonpost.com/2011/10/26/occupy-wall-street-community-board_n_1031892.html. During a 2011 speech at MIT, Bloomberg declared, "I have my own army in the NYPD, which is the seventh biggest army in the world. I have my own State Department, much to Foggy Bottom's annoyance. We have the United Nations in New York, and so we have an entree into the diplomatic world that Washington does not have" (Hunter Walker, "Mayor Bloomberg: 'I Have My Own Army,'" *Politicker*, November 30, 2011, http://politicker.com/2011/11/mayor-bloomberg-i-have-my-own-army-11-30-11/).

31. Scott Morris, "Occupy Movement Plans Port Shutdown—Union Leaders Not All Supportive," *Berkeley Daily Planet*, December 9, 2011, http://www.berkeleydailyplanet.com/issue/2011-12-09/article/38970?headline=Occupy-Movement-Plans-Port-Shutdown—Union-Leaders-Not-All-Supportive—By-Scott-Morris-BCN-.

32. Jason Cherkis, "Did Police Raids against Occupy Oakland Break the Law?," *Huffington Post*, November 15, 2011, http://www.huffingtonpost.com/2011/11/15/police-raids-against-occupy-oakland-break-the-law_n_1095464.html.

33. Joel Handley, "New Documents Show FBI Targeted NATO Protesters," *In These Times*, January 21, 2015, http://inthesetimes.com/article/17555/exclusive_new_documents_show_fbi_spied_on_nato_protesters.

34. See Arun Gupta, "Cleveland Anarchist Bomb Plot Aided and Abetted by FBI," *Guardian*, November 28, 2012, http://www.theguardian.com/commentisfree/2012/nov/28/cleveland-anarchist-bomb-plot-fbi. See also Arun Gupta, "Has the FBI Launched a War of Entrapment against the Occupy Movement?," *Alternet*, May 24, 2012, http://www.alternet.org/story/155581/has_the_fbi_launched_a_war_of_entrapment_against_the_occupy_movement.

35. Chris Hedges, "The Cancer in Occupy," February 6, 2012, http://www.truthdig.com/report/item/the_cancer_of_occupy_20120206/.

36. Chris Hedges, "The Greeks Get It," May 24, 2010, http://www.truthdig.com/report/item/the_greeks_get_it_20100524/.

37. For an excellent discussion of these dynamics, see David Graeber's response to Hedges, *n+1 Magazine*, February 9, 2012, http://nplusonemag.com/concerning-the-violent-peace-police. See also the discussion on anarchist "diversity of tactics" in chapter 4 of Heather Gautney, *Protest and Organization in the Alternative Globalization Era* (New York: Palgrave Macmillan, 2012).

38. Robert Hass, "Poet-Bashing Police," *New York Times*, November 19, 2011, http://www.nytimes.com/2011/11/20/opinion/sunday/at-occupy-berkeley-beat-poets-has-new-meaning.html. See also "UC Davis' Pepper-Spray PR Appears to Backfire Badly," *CBS News*, April 17, 2016, http://www.cbsnews.com/news/student-group-wants-uc-davis-chancellor-to-quit-over-pepper-spray-pr/.

39. Chris Hayes, "Up! With Chris Hayes," MSNBC TV News Archive, November 19, 2011, https://archive.org/details/MSNBCW_20111119_120000_Up_W_Chris_Hayes.

40. The movement attempted to hold the police officers accountable through the spread of Internet memes and by publicly disclosing the officers' identities. Noel Randewich and Greg Lucas, "UC Chancellor Sorry for Pepper Spray Incident," Reuters, November 22, 2011, http://www.reuters.com/article/us-protests-davis-pepperspray-idUSTRE7AI0ZA20111122. See also Biran Nguyen, "University of California to Pay Nearly $1 Million in Deal with 21 Pepper-Sprayed UC-Davis Students," NBC News, September 26, 2012, http://usnews.nbcnews.com/_news/2012/09/26/14112860-university-of-california-to-pay-nearly-1-million-in-deal-with-21-pepper-sprayed-uc-davis-occupy-protesters.

Contributors

ALLAN ANTLIFF is an associate professor at the University of Victoria, Canada, where he also serves as director of the Anarchist Archive. He is the author of *Anarchist Modernism: Art, Politics, and the First American Avant-Garde* (2001), *Anarchy and Art from the Paris Commune to the Fall of the Berlin Wall* (2007), and *Joseph Beuys* (2014). He edited *Only a Beginning: An Anarchist Anthology* (2004) and serves as art editor for the interdisciplinary journals *Anarchist Studies* and *Anarchist Developments in Cultural Studies*.

MARCELLA BENCIVENNI is an associate professor of history at Hostos Community College/City University of New York, where she has taught since 2004. Her research focuses on the histories of im/migration, labor, and social movements in the modern United States, with a particular interest in the Italian American experience. She is the author of *Italian Immigrant Radical Culture: The Idealism of the Sovversivi in the United States, 1890–1940* (2011) and coeditor of *Radical Perspectives on Immigration* (2008). She has also published widely on topics related to the Italian diaspora and American radicalism and serves as editor of the *Italian American Review*. Bencivenni is currently at work on a biography of left-wing activist Carl Marzani, the first political victim of McCarthyism.

CAITLIN CASEY is a lecturer in Harvard University's History and Literature program and the Allston Burr Assistant Dean of Harvard College for Lowell House. She is currently exploring the global networks of American activists in the late 1960s and early 1970s. Her writing has appeared in *The Sixties: A Journal of History, Politics, and Culture* and the *Atlantic Monthly*.

CHRISTOPHER J. CASTAÑEDA is a professor of history at California State University, Sacramento. He is the author of "'Yours for the Revolution': Cigar Makers, Anarchists, and Brooklyn's Spanish Colony, 1878–1925," in *Hidden Out in the Open: Spanish Migration to the United States (1875–1930)*, ed. Phylis Cancilla Martinelli and Ana Varela-Lago (forthcoming) and is the coeditor of *River City and Valley Life: An Environmental History of the Sacramento Region* (2013). He is currently working on a coedited volume about transnational Hispanic anarchists.

ANDREW CORNELL is a visiting assistant professor of American studies at Williams College. He is the author of *Oppose and Propose! Lessons from Movement for a New Society* (2011) and *Unruly Equality: U.S. Anarchism in the Twentieth Century* (2016).

HEATHER GAUTNEY is an associate professor of sociology at Fordham University. She is the author of *Protest and Organization in the Alternative Globalization Era* (2012) and the coeditor of *Democracy, States, and the Struggle for Global Justice* (2009) and *Implicating Empire* (2003). She writes for news media outlets including the *Washington Post* and CNN.

TOM GOYENS is an associate professor of history at Salisbury University in Maryland. His research focuses on immigrant anarchism in the United States. He is the author of *Beer and Revolution: The German Anarchist Movement in New York City, 1880–1914* (2007) and is the editor of Helene Minkin's memoir, *Storm in My Heart: Memories from the Widow of Johann Most* (2015). His articles on anarchism and social space have appeared in *Social Anarchism* and *Rethinking History: The Journal of Theory and Practice*. He is currently working on a biography of Johann Most.

ANNE KLEJMENT is a professor of history at the University of St. Thomas. A specialist in twentieth-century social history, she is the author of several monographs and articles on Dorothy Day and the Catholic Worker, and she and Nancy L. Roberts are coeditors of *American Catholic Pacifism*, winner of the 1997 Pax Christi USA Book Award.

ALAN W. MOORE has written on artists' groups, cultural economy, and self-organized occupied social centers. He worked with the artists' group Colab and helped start the cultural center ABC No Rio. He is the author of *Occupation Culture:*

Art and Squatting in the City from Below (2015) and coeditor with Alan Smart of *Making Room: Cultural Production in Occupied Spaces* (2015). He is also a contributor to Julie Ault, ed., *Alternative Art New York, 1965–1985* (2002); Blake Stimson and Gregory Sholette, eds., *Collectivism after Modernism* (2007); and Clayton Patterson, Joe Flood, and Alan W. Moore, eds., *Resistance: A Radical Political and Social History of the Lower East Side* (2007).

ERIN WALLACE is an independent scholar and musician from Vancouver Island, Canada. In 2013, she completed a master's degree in art history from the University of Victoria, receiving a Governor General's Academic Medal for her thesis on Gordon Matta-Clark. She currently resides in Berlin, where she teaches English and organizes creative activities for children living in refugee shelters.

KENYON ZIMMER is an assistant professor of history at the University of Texas at Arlington. He has published numerous articles and book chapters on transnational radical history and is the author of *Immigrants against the State: Yiddish and Italian Anarchism in America* (2015). He is also the coauthor of *Michele Centrone, tra vecchio e nuovo mondo: Anarchici Pugliesi in difesa della libertá spagnola* (2012) and is coeditor of *Cold War Crossings: International Travel and Exchange across the Soviet Bloc, 1940s–1960s* (2014). He is currently working an a transnational history of America's deportees from the post–World War I Red Scare.

Index

Abarno, Frank, 68
ABC No Rio, 1, 216; and anarchists, 208, 209–10, 216; and artists, 204–5, 206–7; and the city, 214–15; and commercialism, 205–6, 207–8; founding of, 201; management of, 213; and punks, 209, 210–12, 214; and space, 202, 203, 214, 215, 216; and squatters, 202, 208
Abello, Manuel Martínez. *See* Martínez Abello, Manuel
Abend Tsaytung, Di, 41
Academia, La, 84
Acierno, Lou, 206, 210, 212–13
Action Committee for Immediate Defense (ACID), 173
Adbusters, 225
L'Adunata dei Refrattari, 63, 64, 65–66, 69, 71, 72, 125, 126, 139
Agostinelli, Diva, 126, 131, 132, 133, 137, 142
AIDS, 207, 218n20
Albasi's grocery, 59
Albert, Stew, 165
Alchemical Theatre, 219n28
Alexander II of Russia, 34
Algarín, Miguel, 204
All-America Anti-Imperialist League, 104
Allegra, Pietro, 62

Allied Productions, 203
Alpert, Anne Clark, 180, 192
Alpert, Hollis, 192
Alphabet City, 188
Alter-globalization movement, 229, 234, 236
Altgeld, John Peter, 83
Alva, Freddy, 211
Am-Shal Group, 123
Amalgamated Clothing Workers Union, 59, 123
America (magazine), 105
American Federation of Labor (AFL), 113, 125
Amerikanische Arbeiter-Zeitung, 23, 24
L'Anarchia, 67
L'Anarchico, 58, 65
anarchism: and art, 7; components of, 2–3, 6; definition of, 2–4, 6–9, 222–24; divisions of, 5, 22; as label, 6; periodization of, 3; and revolution, 7
Anarchist, Der, 24
anarchist conference, international (1893), 84
Anarchist Switchboard, 209
anarchists, deportation of. *See* deportation of anarchists

Index

anarchist women, 12, 19, 24–25, 31n63, 40, 60
anarchosyndicalism: and Cuban separatists, 92; defined, 82; *El Despertar* and, 78, 82, 85–88; and immigrant workers, 96; mentioned, 47, 125, 222; Tresca and, 62, 127; *Vanguard* and, 124
Anderson, Laurie, 196–97
Angiolillo, Michele, 61, 89
Angry Arts Week, 165–66, 190
Anonymous, 225, 229, 231
antifascism, 70, 71. *See also* Solidaridad Internacional Antifascista
Antilles, 93
AntiPigMilitia, 173
Antliff, Allan, 6, 7
Antolini, Ella, 68
Arbayter Fraynd, Der, 34, 36, 37, 44
Arbayter Fraynd Group, 37
Argentina, 3, 44, 84, 229
Árgüelles y López (cigar workshop), 86
Ark, The, 150
Arrigoni, Enrico, 63–64
Artaud, Antonin, 6; and Living Theatre, 152–53, 154–55, 156, 157; and Matta-Clark, 182, 190–91, 192, 193, 197
Artists Against the Expressway, 187
Artists and Writers Protest, 190
Art Workers Coalition, 190
Asian Americans for Equality (AAFE), 215
Autonomedia, 209, 213, 217n3
Autonomists, 24, 31n58
Avrich, Paul, 4, 56
L'Avvenire, 62, 65

Bachmann, Moritz, 15
Bäcker-Zeitung, 82
Bad Newz, 209
Baginski, Max, 23
Baird, Peggy, 103
Bakunin, Mikhail, 3, 7, 22, 33, 36, 44, 78, 125, 223
Baldwin, James, 128
Bank of America, 228, 238n22
Bank Transfer Action, 228
Barcelona, 4; bombing in (1893) 37; Esteve in, 77, 84; Krax City Mine(d) conference in, 216; periodicals in, 79, 80, 81, 82, 83; prison in, 89

Barcia Quilabert, Luis, 79
Baronio, Ninfa, 61
Barre, Vt., 62
Barrios-Paoli, Lillian, 215
Batterham, Forster, 104
Baynard, Ed, 188
Beat Generation, 137, 138
Beck, Julian, 6, 7, 137, 142, 149; and Artaud, 153, 191; and *The Brig*, 154–55, 156–57; and Cherry Lane Playhouse, 146; and *The Connection*, 150, 152, 154; and Goodman, 143, 144, 145, 147; and pacifism, 144, 145, 146, 149, 153, 155–56
Becker, Maurice, 102
Bellow, Saul, 127
Bencivenni, Marcella, 5
Bender, Thomas, 9
Bennett, Clif, 129
Berkeley, 122, 137, 234
Berkman, Alexander, 24, 33, 35, 36, 38, 123; autonomists, 22; and Frick, 21, 22, 39, 43; and Haymarket, 21; and Most, 23, 34
Berneri, Camillo, 60, 71
Berneri group, 60
Bettelheim, Bruno, 127
Biennio Rosso, 70
Billionaire Marches, 228–29
black bloc, 232–33, 234
Black Mask, 165, 166, 171
Black Mountain College, 191
Blackout Books, 203, 213–14
Black Power movement, 162, 165, 168
Blanqui, Auguste, 22
Bloomberg, Michael, 225, 227, 232, 238n22, 239n30
Bloombergville, 225
Blowdryer, Jennifer, 207
Bluestein, Abe, 123–24, 129
Bluestockings, 1
Boas, Franz, 127
Bologna, Anthony, 225
bombings, 55, 68–69, 175n2; and anarchists' image, 21; in Chicago (1886), 5, 20, 35, 80; in Frankfurt (1883), 16–17; by officials, 105; planned, 68, 126, 233; in Spain, 37, 89; on Wall Street (1920), 54–55, 68
Bookchin, Murray, 163, 164, 222
Borden Milk, 113

Index

Borghi, Armando, 70
Borsodi, Ralph, 134, 135, 139
Bortolloti, Artillio, 124, 125
Boulez, Pierre, 191
Bovshover, Joseph, 35, 39, 43
Brandfackel, Die, 31n58
Brandon, Jorge, 204–5
Brassens, Georges, 6
Brecht, Berthold, 191
Brel, Jacques, 6
Bresci, Gaetano, 55, 93, 94
Bresci Group, 58, 59–60, 68, 94
Bronx: Goodfriend, 122; Italians in, 59, 70, 71; Jewish anarchist in, 43; Matta-Clark in, 182, 183, 184–86, 189, 193, 194, 195; squatting in, 208; Why? group, 123; Wieck in, 129
Bronx Casino, 27
Brookfield Office Properties, 225
Brooklyn, 5, 59, 60; Italian anarchists in, 126; Spanish anarchists in, 77, 78, 79, 80, 83, 84, 90, 92, 94, 96; streetcar strike in (1895), 85. *See also* Bushwick, Brooklyn
Brooklyn Bridge, 225
Brooklyn Heights, 78
Brooklyn Labor Lyceum, 20
Brown, Kenneth, 154
Brustein, Robert, 152
Buber, Martin, 135, 150
Buda, Mario, 54–55, 62, 68
Buenos Aires, 48, 64
Bugout Society (punk band), 210
Buhle, Paul, 3
Bullet squat, 208
Bullshit, Mike, 210, 211
Burns, Lucy, 103
Bushwick, Brooklyn, 59, 69, 126
Byrnes, Thomas F., 26

Cafiero, Carlo, 58, 65
Cage, John, 6, 149, 191
Cahan, Abe, 40, 46
Calley, William, 190
Calvert, Greg, 169–70
Caminita, Ludovico, 68
Campos, José C., 78–79, 80, 82, 89, 95; and Cuba, 87, 92
Camus, Albert, 127
Canada, 44, 45, 93, 106
Cánovas del Castillo, Antonio, 55, 61, 89
Cantine, Holley, 127, 130, 135, 146
Carbone, Carmine, 68
Carillo, Donato, 70
Carl Sahm Club, 5
Carnot, Marie François Sadi, 55
Caro, Robert, 185
Carr, Cynthia, 205
Casey, Caitlin, 6
Castañeda, Agustín, 87, 90–91, 99n71
Casteleiro, José, 81
Castelli, Leo, 187
Castrucci, Paul, 214
Catello, Elvira, 60
Catholic Association for International Peace, 114
Catholic Peace Fellowship, 115
Catholic Worker, 106, 107, 108, 120n55, 143; anarchopacifism and, 113, 115; circulation of, 108
Catholic Worker movement, 5, 6, 9, 106–17, 128, 131, 137, 143, 149; and farming communities, 112
CBGB's, 203, 210, 211
Chaikin, Joseph, 41
Challenge (journal), 142
CHARAS community center, 188, 204, 208, 218n15
Chase Manhattan Bank, 187, 228
Chase Manhattan Plaza, 225
Chavez, Cesar, 113
Cherry Lane Playhouse, 146, 147
Chicago, 5, 84, 85, 128, 132, 186, 192; Day in, 100, 101, 104; Democratic National Convention in, 170, 178n51; German anarchists in, 15, 17, 20, 24; IWW and, 27; Jewish anarchist in, 38, 39; Maurin in, 106; NATO summit protests in, 233. *See also* Haymarket Affair
Chicago Seven, 170
Chimes, Winchester, 206–7
Chomsky, Noam, 223
Christo, 197
Christodora building, 208
Christy, Liz, 188
Chumbawamba, 6
Ciancabilla, Giuseppe, 57

cigar makers, 80, 86–87, 89, 90, 92–93, 94, 96; factories, 77, 80, 81, 85, 86; and strikes, 78, 85, 86, 87–88
Cigar Makers' International Union (CMIU), 90, 92–93
Circolo di Studi Sociali, 59
Circolo Libertario, 59
Circolo Volontà, 60
Círculo de Anarquista, 83
Círculo de Estudios Sociales, 89, 97n20
Círculo de Trabajadores, 92
Citibank, 228, 238n22
Civilian Public Service (CPS), 115, 130, 131
civil rights movement, 137, 164
Claramunt, Teresa, 78, 89
Clarendon Hall, 20, 82
Clark, Anne, 180, 192
Club Avanti, 59
Club Indipendente Bassa Città, 59
Clurman, Harold, 152
Cohen, Joseph J., 45, 46, 47
Cohn, Jesse, 4, 8
Cohn, Michael A., 35, 36, 45, 47
Colab, 202, 218n13
Cold War, 3, 109, 115, 116, 137, 148
Collaborative Projects (Colab), 202, 218n13
Collegiate Anti-Militarism League (CAML), 102
Columbia University, 102, 127, 129, 135, 137
COMA group, 209
Comitato Italiano pro Vittime Politiche, 71
Comité de Auxilios de Tampa, 87
commercialism, 147, 150, 204, 205–6, 207, 209, 210, 212
Committee for Nonviolent Revolution, 132
Common Ground, 173
Commonweal, 105
Commune festival, 20
communism, 5, 7; and Catholic Worker movement, 104, 105, 106, 107, 108, 110, 113, 114, 116; and Italian anarchists, 71; and Jewish anarchists, 45, 46, 47, 123; and McCarthyism, 133
Communist Party USA, 47, 104, 105, 106, 107, 123, 124, 131, 133
Comstock, Sarah, 25
Concordia Assembly Rooms, 20
Congress of Industrial Organizations (CIO), 113, 125

Congress of Racial Equality (CORE), 130
conscientious objectors (COs), 114, 115, 116, 128, 143
Contact II, 204
Cooper Union, 12
Cornell, Andrew, 5–6
counterculture, 138, 162, 163, 164, 165, 169, 236
Courbet, Gustave, 6
Courtney, Matthew, 206, 207, 210, 218n20
Coxey's Army, 85
Cramer, Peter, 203, 206, 210, 214, 218n20
Crass (punk band), 6, 212
Crawford, Jane, 187
Creek (Motherfucker), 165, 173, 177n23
Cronaca Sovversiva, 62, 67, 68, 69; suppression of, 67
Cross Bronx Expressway, 185
C Squat, 216
CUANDO, 208
Cuba, 3, 64, 80, 84, 88, 90, 92, 94
Cuba Libre, 78, 87, 89, 92
Cultura Obrera group, 64
Cultura Proletaria, 125
Cunningham, Merce, 149
Czolgosz, Leon, 41, 93

Dada, 180, 212
Daily Worker, 107
Daly, Richard, 178n51
Danbury Federal Penitentiary, 129, 130, 131
D'Andrea, Virgilia, 70
Darrow, Clarence, 71
Day, Dorothy, 8, 100–105, 108, 109, 143; and anti-militarism, 101–2, 103, 109, 113–16; and Catholicism, 100, 101, 104, 105, 108, 109, 112, 116–17; and communes, 112; and communism, 104–6; as editor, 106; and Maurin, 106; and unions, 112–13
Day Book, 101
Dead Kennedys (punk band), 6
de Beauvoir, Simone, 127
Defensa, La, 86, 87, 90
Delabar, August, 82
Delfino, Albina, 70
De Ligt, Bart, 131
Dellinger, David, 130, 131, 132, 137, 143, 170
del Valle, Adrián, 84, 88, 89, 92
democracy, participatory, 164, 171, 231

Department of Housing Preservation & Development (NYC), 202, 214, 215
deportation of anarchists: Goldman, 5, 134; Italians, 58, 62, 63, 67, 68, 69, 70, 126
Derecho á la Vida, 97n20
de Silver, Margaret, 127
Despertar, El, 5, 77, 82–83, 92, 93, 94, 95; on Bresci, 93–94; closing of, 78, 96; on Cuba, 87, 88; dispute covered by, 91; on Most, 82; in Paterson, 90, 95; on Spain, 88, 89; on strikes, 85, 86, 87, 92–93; subscription base of, 80–81, 90
Deutsche, Rosalyn, 208
DeWeiss, Dan, 128, 133
Di Paolo, Bill, 216
Diggers, The, 164–65, 176n7
DiGia, Ralph, 130, 131
Dimon, Jamie, 229
Dingle, Okra P., 206
Direct Action, 132
Diritto all'Esistenza group, 59, 61
Doctrina Anarquista-Socialista, 96
Do-It-Yourself (DIY), 181, 211, 212, 229
Dolgoff, Esther, 124, 125
Dolgoff, Sam, 124, 125
Domani, Il, 69
Donny the Punk, 209, 219n27
draft, resistance to, 129–31, 132
Drury, Victor, 5, 15
Duarte Park, 232
Duchamp, Marcel, 6, 180
Duncan, Robert, 128, 132
Durio, Isabel, 78
Dwarves, The (punk band), 210

Ealham, Chris, 4
East Harlem, 58, 59, 60, 68
East Village, 202, 203, 205–6, 208
East Village Eye, 205
East Village Other, 163, 173, 174
Edelstadt, David, 34, 35, 36, 38, 39
Eisenman, Peter, 182, 183, 194
Elia, Roberto, 69
Elisabeth of Austria, 55
Ellsberg, Robert, 116
Emmicke, William, 202
Englander, Steven: at ABC No Rio, 203, 210, 212–13, 214, 215, 216, 220n46; other activities of, 209, 217n3

Epson, Bill, 177n29
L'Era Nuova, 61, 65, 68; suppression of, 67
Eresia, 63, 64
Esclavo, El, 86–87, 88
Escuela Moderna. *See* Modern School
Esenwein, George, 89
Espionage Act (1917), 102
Esteve, Pedro, 77, 89, 93, 96; and Cuba, 84, 88, 90; as editor, 77, 90, 93, 96; family of, 5, 94; as speaker, 5, 27, 84, 85
Esteve, Sirio, 94
Exposition internationale du Surréalisme, 180

Fabrizi, Oreste, 70
Falangists, 109
Fanon, Frantz, 165
Fasci Siciliani, 57
fascism, 70, 71, 114, 124, 125, 126, 129, 134
Fascist League, 71
Fatti di Maggio, 57
Fedeli, Ugo, 64
Federal Bureau of Investigation (FBI), 69, 115, 233
Felicani, Aldino, 58
Fellowship of Reconciliation, 106, 115, 128, 130, 148
feminism, 5, 25, 60, 138
Fernández, Anita, 81
Fernández, Antonio, 91
Fernández, Modesto, 81
Ferré, Léo, 6
Ferrer Center, 40, 43, 68, 123
Ferrer i Guàrdia, Francisco, 40, 65
Ferrero, Vincenzo, 57, 58
Festa della Frutta, 61
Fielden, Samuel, 83
Fillmore East, 172–73, 175
Finch, Roy, 137
Fleigler, Bessie, 124
Fleigler, Franz, 124, 125
Flint sit-down strike, 113
Flower Power, 168
Flynn, Elizabeth Gurley, 62
FOOD, 181, 188, 197
Food Not Bombs, 212
Forverts, 40, 41, 43, 46
Foucault, Michel, 138, 195
Four Freedoms, 114

Francis of Assisi, saint, 112
Franco, Francisco, 114
Frank, Herman, 33, 37
Fraye Arbeter Shtime, 8, 33, 37, 39, 41, 42, 43, 44, 46, 47, 123; circulation of, 41, 42, 45, 46, 48; and communism, 45; on labor unions, 38, 40; on propaganda by the deed, 41; style of, 40
Fraye Arbeter Shtime Group, 43, 48
Fraye Gezelshaft, Di, 39, 41
Fraye Gezelshaft Clubs, 41, 43
Free Workers' Center, 46
Freedom (newspaper), 126
Freedom Group, 126
Freiheit, 8
Freud, Sigmund, 127, 133, 134, 192
Frick, Henry Clay, 21, 39
Führer, Wenzel, 19
Fuhse, Fritz, 19
Fuller, Buckminster, 188

Galileo Club, 126
Galleani, Luigi, 57, 62, 64, 67, 68, 69, 126; and *Cronaca Sovversiva*, 62; deportation of, 63
galleanisti, 63, 64, 67, 68, 69
Gallo, Firmino, 61
Gallo, William, 67
Gandhi, Leela, 145
Gandhi, Mohandas, 111, 116, 129, 130, 131, 146
Garbage Action (Motherfuckers), 171
García, Juan, 91
Garcia y Pando (cigar workshop), 86
Gautney, Heather, 6
Gelber, Jack, 150–51, 152
general assemblies (GAs), 7, 224, 225, 226, 229, 231, 232, 236, 239n26
General Strike for Peace, 154, 160n77
Genn, Sally, 123
George, Carl, 204
Germania Assembly Rooms, 9, 20, 93
Ghetto Brothers, 184
Ginsburg, Allen, 138
Girault, Jean, 89
Girouard, Tina, 193
Gitlin, Todd, 171
Giuliani, Rudolph, 203, 227
Glen Gardner, N.J., 132

Global Day of Rage, 228
Gold, Mike. *See* Granich, Irwin
Goldhagen, Eric, 216
Goldman, Emma, 33; and Catholic Workers, 100; deportation of, 134; and Haymarket, 5, 21, 35; and Most, 8, 16, 22, 25, 31n63; in New York, 24, 27; and Russia, 44, 45; in Toronto, 124. *See also Mother Earth*
Goldman, Robert, 201, 202, 203
Goldman Sachs, 228
Gomez, Manuel (Charles Phillips), 105, 118n20
Gompers, Samuel, 90
Gooden, Carol, 189
Goodfriend, Audrey, 6, 8, 122, 129, 139; and Jewish anarchists, 123; in San Francisco, 132, 133, 137; and Why? Group, 124, 127, 131, 135, 142
Goodman, Paul, 7, 144, 145, 149, 152; influence of, 128, 143–44; and Reich, 133; and theater, 146, 147, 148, 149–50, 155, 156; and Why? Group, 128, 131, 132, 135
Goodman, Percival, 135
Gordon, Uri, 182, 194
Gori, Pietro, 57
Gosciak, Josh, 204
Gozzoli, Virgilio, 70
Graeber, David, 138, 230, 240n37
Graham, Bill, 172
Graham, Robert, 7
Granda, J., 91
Grand Central Palace, 5
Granich, Irwin, 102, 105, 118n10
Grateful Dead, 172
Grave, Jean, 78, 88
Great Depression, 9, 47, 105, 106, 221
Greco, Calogero, 70
Green Guerillas, 188
Greenwich Village, 102, 137, 146, 185, 186, 187, 233
Greenwich Village Society for Historic Preservation, 1
Greie, Johanna, 30n30
Grido degli Oppressi, Il, 65
Grido della Folla, Il, 67
Grieg, Michael, 128, 133, 137
Grieg, Sally, 128, 133, 137, 142

Index

Group of Feminist Propaganda, 60
Grubacic, Andrej, 223
Grupo Parsons, 80, 82, 83, 85, 94
Gruppo Emancipazione della Donna, 60
Gruppo Socialista-Anarchico Rivoluzionario, 58–59
Guabello, Alberto, 67
Guerra (cigar workshop), 86
Guerrilla Art Action Group, 190
Guglielmo, Jennifer, 4, 60

Habraken, N.J., 195
Hänsch, Clara, 31n59
Hapgood, Hutchins, 39, 42, 43
Harlem, 40, 41, 43, 44, 108, 129, 146, 228
Harvey, David, 227
Hass, Robert, 234
Hasselmann, Wilhelm, 23
Havana, 79, 80, 81, 82, 90, 92, 93
Havel, Hippolyte, 103
Haymarket Affair, 5, 20–21, 35, 36, 78, 80, 83, 94
Hedges, Chris, 234, 235, 240n37
Heinzen, Karl, 26
Hennacy, Ammon, 116, 128, 132
Herridge, Francis, 152
Hillquit, Morris, 102
Hiroshima bombing, 149
homelessness, 9; and Catholic Worker movement, 108, 109, 111; and Lower East Side, 173, 181, 204, 208, 209, 232
Homestead strike (1892), 21, 85
homosexuality, 134, 143, 203, 205, 207, 219n27
Hoover, J. Edgar, 115
Horowitz, Irving, 3
houses of hospitality, 108, 109–11, 113, 143, 149
Housing Act (1949), 185
Howe, William, 26
Howland, Becky, 201, 202, 203
Huasipungo (punk band), 212
Hugo, John J., 120n58
Hummel, Abraham, 26
Huneker, James Gibbons, 19

Ibsen, Henrik, 66
Ideal, El (group), 83

immigration, 5
Improvisors Network, 209
Industrial Workers of the World. *See* IWW
Institute for Architecture and Urban Studies, 182, 184
Insurgence (punk band), 212
insurrection. *See* propaganda by the deed
international anarchist conference (1893), 84
International Ladies' Garment Workers' Union, 40, 59
Intesa Libertaria, 64
In Zikh, 42
Irving Place Hall, 123
Isca, Ida, 70
Isca, Valerio, 69–70
Italian anarchists, 5; divisions among, 61–63
Italian Chamber of Labor, 59
Italian Socialist-Anarchist-Revolutionary Group Carlo Cafiero, 58
IWW, 27, 41, 46, 62, 78, 96, 101, 102, 104, 124

Jackson, Thelma, 154
Jacobs, Jane, 187
Jacquerie, 68
Jaffa, Joseph, 36
Japanese internment, 115
Jefferson Airplane, 172, 175n6
Jencks, Charles, 183
Jerez uprising, 89
Jesus Chrust (punk band), 212
Jewish Anarchist Federation, 45, 48, 123
John XXIII (pope), 116
Jones, Jeff, 163, 177n29
Joplin, Janis, 172
Jovenes Anarquistas, 97n20
Judd, Donald, 6, 187
Judd, Julie, 187

Katts, Moyshe, 35, 36, 38, 39, 43, 45
Katzman, Allen, 173
Kennel, Phillip, 19
Kepler, Roy, 130, 132
Key West, 80, 93
kibbutzim, 135
Klejment, Anne, 5
Koch, David, 229
Koch, Ed, 202

Kohout, Henry, 29n26
Korean War, 145
Kosuth, Joseph, 196
Koven, David, 124, 127, 128, 132, 133, 137, 138
Krause, Martha, 30n30
Krax City Mine(d) conference, 216
Kristal, Hilly, 210–11
Kristallnacht, 183–84
Kropotkin, Peter: and communist-anarchism, 22, 61; and Day, 101, 103, 108, 116; and *mutual aid*, 224; writings of, 36, 78, 88, 112, 124, 143; and WWI, 5, 45; and Yanovsky, 37
Kurzenknabe, Ernst, 82

Labriola, Arturo, 67
La Guardia Place, 187
Lamantia, Phillip, 128, 150
La Plaza Cultural Garden, 181, 188, 192, 197
Lavin, Maud, 181, 194
Lawrence strike (1912), 62
Leib, Mani, 42
Leo XIII (pope), 112
Levy, Carl, 57
LeWitt, Sol, 197
Liberation, 137, 143
Liberator, The, 104
Libertarian Book Club, 70, 71, 209
Libertarian Circle, 132
Libertarian Press, 132
Libertarian Socialist League, 142
Liberti, Guy, 72
Liberty, 29n26
Liberty House, 173
Liebknecht, Wilhelm, 28n4
Liesin, Abraham, 41
Lincoln Brigade, 114
Lincoln Center, 171–72
Lismar Lounge, 210
Little Italy, 56, 62, 66, 70, 187
Living Theatre, 6, 7, 115, 143, 147, 157, 191; and authorities, 148–49, 154, 155; in Europe, 156; influence of, 157, 164; location of, 146, 147, 150, 219n28; performances of, 146, 151, 153, 154, 155
Loisaida, 204. *See also* Lower East Side
London, England, 5, 194, 231; Freedom Group in, 126; Galleani in, 62; German anarchists in, 14, 15, 22, 24, 77; Jewish anarchists in, 34–35, 36, 37, 44, 48
London, Jack, 101
Loomis, Mildred, 134, 135
Lorenzo, Anselmo, 89
Lott, August, 19
Love and Rage, 212, 214
Lower East Side, 1, 4, 123, 166, 167, 169, 175, 178n53, 209, 214, 216; ABC No Rio in, 201, 207, 208, 210, 211, 216; and Catholic Worker movement, 100, 101, 109, 143; German anarchists in, 12, 14; homelessness and, 173, 181, 204, 208, 209, 232; Italian anarchists in, 60; Jewish anarchists in, 33, 34, 35, 36, 40, 43, 47, 48; Matta-Clark in, 188, 192; Motherfuckers in, 161, 163, 165–66, 171, 173, 174. *See also* Loisaida; squatters; Tompkins Square
Lower East Side Patrol, 173
Ludlow, Robert, 116
Ludlow massacre, 68
Luis, Roman, 39

MacDonald, Dwight, 127, 128
MacDonald, Nancy, 127
Mac Low, Jackson, 128, 156
MacNair, Andrew, 183
Madrid, 231
Magliocca, Michele, 70
Magliocca, Sebastiano, 70
Mailer, Norman, 127
Malatesta, Errico, 37, 57, 61, 92
Malina, Judith, 6, 7, 137, 142, 145, 146, 156; and Artaud, 153, 191; and *The Brig*, 154–55, 156, 157; and *The Connection*, 150–51, 152, 154; and Goodman, 143, 144, 146–47, 149–50; and pacifism, 115, 144, 145, 146, 147, 155–56; and police, 148–49
Manhattan Clock Tower, 192
Manhattan Lyceum, 59
Martello, Il (group), 60
Martello, Il (publication), 62, 124; circulation of, 65; suppression of, 67
Martí, José, 87–88
Martínez Abello, Manuel, 80, 81
Martínez-Campos, Arsenio, 89
Marx, Karl, 3, 22, 36, 44, 116, 223
Marxism, 2, 3, 128, 133, 134, 197, 223

Index

Maryfarm, 112
Maryson, Jacob A., 35, 43, 45
Masses, The, 102, 103, 104
Matta, Roberto, 180
Matta-Clark, Gordon, 6, 9, 180, 183, 186–88, 195–97; and Artaud, 190–93; and graffiti, 188–89; and South Bronx, 182, 184–86, 194; and violence, 181–82, 184, 194, 197
Mattick, Paul, 128
Maurin, Peter, 100, 106, 108, 109, 111–12
May Day, 61, 107
Mazur, Karl, 24
MC5, 6, 172
McCarthyism, 133
McCormick, Carlo, 205, 218n13
McCullough, John, 26
McKinley, William, assassination of, 26, 41, 93, 94, 95
Mecca Normal (punk band), 209
Meehan, Sean, 209
Mégy, Edmond, 5, 15
Mella, Ricardo, 78
Merlino, Francesco Saverio, 57
Mexico, 3, 54, 67, 84, 102, 129, 215
Michels, Tony, 4
Mills, C. Wright, 127
Milstein, Cindy, 138
Minkin, Helene, 24, 25, 26
Minor, Robert, 104
Modern School, 40, 65, 123. *See also* Ferrer Center
Mohegan, N.Y., 70
Moisseiff, Leon, 33, 39, 47
Montjuïc prison, 89
Moore, Alan W., 4, 6
Morales, Frank, 208
Morea, Ben, 163, 164, 165, 166, 167, 168, 169, 170, 172, 174
Moro, Joseph, 67
Moses, Robert, 182, 185, 186, 187, 195
Most, Johann, 4, 8, 12, 14, 16, 22, 34, 37, 82; childhood of, 13; death of, 5, 27; as editor, 14, 15, 23–24, 25, 26, 28n6; influence of, 16, 37, 38, 82; on propaganda by the deed, 5, 14, 15, 16–17, 21, 29n19, 39; relationships of, 5, 22, 24, 25, 31n59; as speaker, 5, 12, 14, 16, 19, 22, 34, 85; on trial, 26, 28n7
Most, John, Jr., 25

Most, Lucifer, 26
Mother Earth, 41
Motherfuckers. *See* Up Against the Wall Motherfucker (UAW/MF)
Mounier, Emmanuel, 111
Murdoch, Rupert, 229
Museum of Modern Art, 190, 206
Museum of Reclaimed Urban Space (MoRUS), 216
Mussolini, Benito, 67, 70, 71
Muste, A. J., 128, 130, 137, 139
My Lai Massacre, 190

Nacional, La (club), 83
Naeve, Lowell, 130, 131, 132
Nardini, Mary, 68
National Endowment for the Arts, 206, 218n15
National Labor Relations Act (1935), 125
National Maritime Union, 113
National Woman's Party (NWP), 103
Native Americans, 168
Neebe, Oscar, 83
Needle, The, 138
Neill, A. S., 137
Neither East nor West project, 217n3
Netter, A. Jacob, 36
Netter, Anna, 35, 36, 39
Nettlau, Max, 37, 77
Neumann, Osha, 161, 165, 166, 167, 170, 171, 172, 174, 175
Neve, Johann, 22, 31n49
Newark, N.J., 59, 129; African Americans in, 165, 166; riots in (1967), 165, 166
New England Anzeiger, 23
New Jersey Arbeiterzeitung, 23
New Left, 6, 8, 122, 162, 169, 216, 230
Newman, Barnett, 6, 187
New Masses, 105
Newsreel (collective), 167, 171, 174
New York Anarchist Book Fair, 204
New York Call, 101, 118n12
New York City, 8, 9. *See also* Bronx; Brooklyn; Lower East Side
New York Emergency Act, 149
New Yorkers Against Budget Cuts, 225
New York Stock Exchange, 221
New York University, 35, 187

253

New York World, 26
Nietzsche, Friedrich, 19
Nixon, Richard, 190
No Conscription League, 118n10
Nomad, Max, 41
nonviolence, 5, 40, 235; Catholic Workers and, 103, 106, 108, 111, 113, 114, 116, 117, 143; Living Theatre and, 144; Occupy and, 221, 222, 234; rejection of, 168, 170; of war resisters, 129, 130, 131, 132
Norse, Harold, 147, 150
Nott, Charles Cooper, 69
Novatore, Il, 63
Nuevo Ideal, El, 92
Nuova Civiltà, La, 59
Nuyorican Poets Café, 204
Nuyoricans. *See* Puerto Ricans

O'Brien, Jim, 171
Occoquan Workhouse, 103–4
Occupied Wall Street Journal, 228
Occupy Harlem, 228
Occupy Wall Street, 1–2, 216, 237n1; and anarchism, 221–22, 226–27, 229–31, 233, 236; disorder of, 232, 234; growth of, 228–29; and police, 232–33, 234–35, 240n40; and public space, 227; and social media, 229, 236
Olbermann, Keith, 231
Oller, Cayetano, 89
Olsen, Scott, 233
Onslow-Ford, Gordon, 180
Oppenheim, Dennis, 184
Orange Valley, NJ, 59
L'Ordine, 69
Organización de los Torcedores de Tabaco Habano de las Cuidades de New York y Brooklyn (aka La Defensa), 86, 87, 90
Orr, Fly, 210, 213
Ortiz (cigar workshop), 86
Ottanelli, Fraser, 71
Owen, William C., 82

Pacifica Radio, 132, 138
pacifism, 123, 131
Pallás Latorre, Paulino, 89
Palmeiro, Manual, 91
Palmer, A. Mitchell, 67, 69. *See also* Red Scare
Palmer, Bob, 209
Palmer, Robin, 169, 174
Parsons, Albert, 80
Parsons Group. *See* Grupo Parsons
participatory democracy, 164, 171, 231
Partisan Review, 127
Pason, Greg, 212
Paterson, N.J., 9, 60, 93, 95; Italian anarchists in, 55, 58, 59, 61, 62, 67, 94; Jewish anarchists in, 38; Spanish anarchists in, 90
Patria (newspaper), 87
Patterson, Clayton, 4, 219n23
Paul, Alice, 103
Paul VI (pope), 116
Pax, 114, 115
Payne, Roz, 167
Peacemakers, 143, 146, 148
Pearl Harbor, 114
Peck, Jim, 130, 131
Peña, Sandalio, 91
Pennsylvania Station, 195
Pentagon, 169–70
People's House, 59
People's Kitchen, 228
People's Library, 228
Perkoff, Stuart, 137
Perlin, Terry, 7
Pereira, Merced, 81
Pernicone, Nunzio, 55, 68, 71, 72
Peterson, Elizabeth, 132
Petit, Abelardo, 81
Peukert, Josef, 22, 24, 31n49
Pfahler, Kembra, 204
Philly (artist), 203–4, 205
Phoenix, Ariz., 128, 132
Pioneers of Liberty, 35–37, 38, 39
Pirani, Alberico, 67
Pissaro, Camille, 6
Pius XI (pope), 109, 112
Plebe, La, 62
Polignani, Amedeo, 68
Political Art Documentation and Distribution Group (PAD/D), 205, 218n11
politics (journal), 127, 135
Pomex, Lee, 152
Port Huron statement, 164, 231
Powell, Adam Clayton, 130
Poylisher Yidl, Der, 34

Index

Prat, José, 78
prefigurative politics, 6, 9, 123, 138, 145, 167, 181, 197, 222–23
Productor, El, 79, 80, 81, 82, 83, 84
Progressive Miners of America, 129
Proletario, Il, 62
propaganda by the deed, 138, 142; and German anarchists, 14, 15, 16, 21–22; and Italian anarchists, 55, 56, 61, 68, 71, 125; and Jewish anarchists, 35, 37, 39, 41; and Spanish anarchists, 88–90, 93, 94, 95
Pruitt-Igoe public housing (St. Louis), 183
Psychodrama (group), 205
Pucciatti, John, 59
Puerto Rican Day, 184
Puerto Rican Independistas, 184
Puerto Ricans, 185, 195, 204, 208
punk, 6, 138, 203, 209, 210–12, 213, 214, 215, 216. *See also specific bands*
Punk Island festival, 212

Quakers, 106, 148
Quan, Jean, 233
queerness. *See* homosexuality
Questione Sociale, La, 65, 67, 90, 93, 94, 95
Quilabert, Luis Barcia. *See* Barcia Quilabert, Luis
Quintana, Gerardo, 89, 92, 95
Quintiliano, Luigi, 62, 71

racial segregation, 132
radical space. *See* space(s)
Raffuzzi, Maria, 60
Rainer, Dachine, 146
Rat, 163, 167, 174
Rauschenberg, Robert, 187, 197
Ravage, Marcus, 34
Reagan, Ronald, 206, 212, 218n15
Rebelde, El, 92
Reclaiming Project (Motherfuckers), 172–73
Reclus, Elisée, 78
Red Scare, 5, 67, 104
Refrattari, I, 60
Rehab collective, 206
Reich, Wilhelm, 128, 133–34, 137
Rensselaer Polytechnic Institute, 137
Resistance (publication), 122, 132, 133, 135, 137; and Living Theatre, 142, 143, 149, 152

Resistance Group, 7, 134, 137, 144, 146
Retort, 127, 128, 130, 135, 146
Rexroth, Kenneth, 127, 128, 132, 133, 147, 150
Richards, Mary Catherine, 152, 191
Rimbaud, Penny, 212
Riscossa, La, 67
Risveglio, Il, 59
Rivas, Bimbo, 204
Rivington School group, 208
Rivolta degli Angeli, La, 63
Road to Freedom group, 64, 70
Robinson, Neil, 211
Robinson, Walter, 205, 218n13
Rocca, Massimo (Libero Tancredi), 63, 67
Rockefeller, David, 187, 190
Rockefeller, John D., 68
Rocker, Rudolf, 25, 70, 125
Roda, Maria, 5, 60, 90; and Esteve, 5, 84, 90; on marriage, 85
Rodriguez, Angel, 89
Rogers, Dorothy, 124, 125, 126, 142
Roig y Ramos, Enrique, 80
Rolle, Giovanni, 95
Roodenko, Igal, 132
Roosevelt, Eleanor, 187
Rosenfeld, Morris, 36
Rosselli, Carlo, 71
Rothko, Mark, 6
Rubin, Emily, 218n15
Russell, Saunders, 150
Russian Revolution (1917), 5
Rustin, Bayard, 130, 137

Sacco, Nicola, 62, 67, 72
Sacco-Vanzetti case, 54, 69, 71, 104
Sacco-Vanzetti Defense Committee, 58
Sale, Kirkpatrick, 178n45
Sallitto, Dominick, 58, 70, 72
Salsedo, Andrea, 69
Samá y García y Vega (cigar workshop), 86
Samoa (musician), 205
Sanchez, Pablo, 95
San Francisco: communal home in, 132–33, 137; Day in, 100; Diggers in, 164; earthquake in (1906), 100; Ferrero in, 57; Gelber in, 150; Motherfuckers in, 175; raid in, 29n19; *Why?* and, 128
San Francisco Mime Troupe, 176n7

255

Sartin, Max (Raffaele Schiavina), 64, 68, 72, 126
Schiavina, Raffaele (Max Sartin), 64, 68, 72, 126
Schirru, Michele, 71
Schmidt, Michael, 7
School of Living, 134, 135
Schultze, Moritz, 19
Schumann, Max, 210
Schwab, Justus H., 1, 2, 4, 12, 15
Schwab, Michael, 83
Schwab's saloon, 9, 10n2, 13, 19
Scribbler's Club, 101
SDS (Students for a Democratic Society). *See* Students for a Democratic Society (SDS)
Second Vatican Council, 116
segregation, racial, 132
Sennett, Richard, 186, 189
sexism, 24–25, 72, 174, 203, 211
Shafrazi, Tony, 190
Shalom Aleichem Houses, 123
Shea, David, 206
Signac, Paul, 6
Simons, Rayna, 101
Sinclair, Upton, 101
Singer, Tim, 211
Situationists, 138, 212
Smith, Neil, 208, 227
Snyder, Gary, 138
Socialist, The, 212
Socialist Party of America, 131
Sociedad de Torcedores Habano, 90–91, 92
Society for Proletarian Sexual Politics, 133
Society of Havana Cigar Rollers, 90–91, 92
SoHo, 180, 187, 188
Solidaridad Internacional Antifascista, 128, 137, 144
Solotaroff, Hillel, 35, 43
South Bronx, 182, 184, 186, 189, 193, 194, 195, 208
space(s): and anarchists, 2, 8–9, 19, 20, 60, 61, 167–68, 170, 172, 173, 175n5, 208, 212, 216, 223; and Occupy, 225, 227, 231; public, 56, 107, 181, 182, 186, 187, 188, 216, 235; and theater, 154, 193
Spanish-American War (1898), 78, 87, 89, 92
Spanish anarchists, 5

Spanish Civil War, 3, 47, 60, 71, 109, 114, 124, 138, 164
Spanish Refugee Aid Committee, 127
Speed, John Gilmer, 19
Spellman, Francis, 109, 166
Squat or Rot (record label), 211
squatter(s), 206, 209, 216, 220n47, 224, 234; Brandon as, 204; in East Village/Lower East Side, 202–3, 208, 210, 214, 217; meetings of, 213; moving out, 215; and punk music scene, 212, 213, 214
Stami, Cesare, 63
Staten Island, 20, 104, 112
Stelton, N.J., 70, 123, 124
Stern, Susan, 161
Stiglitz, Joseph, 237n1
Stirner, Max, 19, 63, 64
St. Marks Place, 161, 173, 209
St. Patrick's Cathedral, 68, 108, 166
strikes. *See specific strikes or strikers*
Student Nonviolent Coordinating Committee (SNCC), 166
Students for a Democratic Society (SDS): break-in at West Village office of, 173; and Motherfuckers, 163, 164, 169–70, 171; New Left and, 162, 230; rallies organized by, 166, 177n29; on U.S. college students, 178n45. *See also* Weather Underground
Sturmvogel, 31n58
suffrage movement, 103–4, 118n16, 118n18
syndicalism, 3, 7, 27, 37, 40, 125. *See also* anarcho-syndicalism

Tallmer, Jerry, 152
Tampa, 58, 80, 84, 86, 87, 88, 90, 92, 93
Tampa Aid Committee, 87
Tancredi, Libero (Massimo Rocca), 63, 67
Tarrida del Mármol, Fernando, 89
Teamsters Union, 113
Testa, Jim, 210–11, 214
Thalia Theatre, 9, 59, 85
Thatcher, Margaret, 212
theater and performance, 7–8, 9, 60, 65, 71. *See also* Cherry Lane playhouse; Living Theatre; Thalia Theater
Times Up! group, 216–17
Timmermann, Claus, 31n58
Tivoli, N.Y., 112

Index

Tlatelolco Square massacre, 215
Tobocman, Seth, 204
Todo para Todos, 97n20
Tolstoy, Leo, 66, 101, 108, 127
Tompkins Square, 2, 12, 127, 173, 202, 204, 209; riot (1988), 202, 209
Transit Workers Union Local 100, 225
Travis (Motherfucker), 165, 177n23, 177n33, 178n53
Tresca, Carlo, 60, 70, 125, 127; arrested, 68; as editor, 62, 65, 124; and IWW, 62–63; and Sacco-Vanzetti case, 71
Trevens, Amanda, 214
Trombetta, Domenico, 67
Tudor, David, 191
Turcato, Davide, 56
Tytell, John, 143

UAW/MF. *See* Up Against the Wall Motherfucker (UAW/MF)
Umberto I of Italy, 55, 93, 95
Underground Press Syndicate, 176n12
unemployment councils, 105
Union 8, 129, 130
Unión de Torcedores, 78
Union Square, 38, 106; Brandon at, 204; *Catholic Worker* sales at, 107; Day and, 102, 117; Occupy movement and, 232. *See also* Irving Place Hall; Solidaridad Internacional Antifascista; Vanguard Juniors
United Farm Workers, 113
Up Against the Wall Motherfucker (UAW/MF), 6, 7, 161, 162, 170, 172, 175, 175n6, 176n12; and anarchism, 163–64; and art, 167; and counterculture, 164–65; founding of, 165–66; and Lower East Side, 171–74; and race, 168; and SDS, 164, 171; and violence, 168–69; and women, 174. *See also* Angry Arts Week; Creek (Motherfucker); Travis (Motherfucker)
Urales, Federico, 89

Valdinoci, Carlo, 68, 69
vandalism, 182, 185, 188, 194–95
van der Walt, Lucien, 7
Vanguard, 124, 125, 139, 142
Vanguard Group, 124, 125
Vanguard Juniors, 124, 129

Vannucci, Delfina, 220n46
Vanzetti, Bartolomeo, 54, 57, 58, 62, 69
Varhayt, 36
Varon, Jeremy, 163
Vattuone, John, 70
Veblen, Thorstein, 134
Vecoli, Rudolph, 72
Vesuvio restaurant, 59
Vidler, Anthony, 181
Vienna, 5, 64
Viennese Actionists, 205
Vietnamese National Liberation Front, 169
Vietnam War: artists and, 166, 190; Catholic Workers and, 116; Day on, 115; draft resisters and, 129; Morea on, 165; Motherfuckers and, 162, 169, 172, 175
Village Voice, 149, 152, 205, 211
violence: anarchists and, 20, 55, 56, 69, 78, 88, 93, 144, 153, 164, 167, 168, 172–73; and art, 181, 182, 190, 191, 194–95, 197; by police, 20, 66, 170, 233, 235; and punks, 211. *See also* nonviolence; propaganda by the deed
Vorse, Mary Heaton, 105, 106

Walden School, 137
Walker, Scott, 224–25
Walker Commission, 178n51
Wallace, Erin, 6
Wall Street, 188, 225, 226, 227, 228; bombing (1920) on, 54–55, 68
War?, 102
War Commentary, 126
Ward, Colin, 182, 194
War Resisters League (WRL), 115, 130, 131, 143, 148, 149
Washington, D.C., 15, 85, 101, 103, 105, 114
Washington Square Outdoor Art Exhibit, 189
Washington Square Park, 187
Washington Square Village, 187
Washington Street Hall, 83
Waters, Jack, 203, 204, 206, 210, 214, 218n15, 218n20
Weather Underground, 161, 175n2
Webster Hall, 59
Weinberg, Chaim, 16
Weissmann, Henry, 82

Westenberg, Carol, 150–51
West Hoboken, N.J., 59
West Village, 173
Whitney Museum of American Art, 187
Why? (publication), 122, 124, 127, 135, 142, 143; and Goodman, 128; and Italian anarchists, 126; name change of, 132, 142; and WWII, 125, 128, 129, 130. See also *Resistance* (publication)
Why? Group, 6, 123, 124, 127, 128, 135, 139; name change of, 132; and radical pacifism, 131; and Reich, 133, 134; and WWII, 126
Why?/Resistance Group, 7, 122, 138, 139
Wide Open Cabaret, 206–7
Wieck, David Thoreau: and draft, 129, 130, 131, 132; and *Resistance*, 132, 133, 135, 1936, 1937, 139 Williams, Paul, 149
Wiesinger, Franz, 19
Williams, Vera, 149
Williams, William Carlos, 150
Williamsburg, Brooklyn, 59
Wilmann, Helene, 30n30
Wilson, Robert, 192
Wilson, Woodrow, 103
Winchevsky, Morris, 34
Wirth, Louis, 134
Wobblies. *See* IWW
Wölky, Carl, 19
women. *See* anarchist women
Woodcock, George, 3–4

Woodstock festival, 127, 170
Workman's Circle, 123
World's Columbian Exposition (1893), 84
World Trade Center, 225
World War I, 5, 66–67; and antiwar protests, 102; and Italian anarchists, 66–67; US entry into, 101
World War II, 6, 114–15; and anarchists, 125, 128; US entry into, 124
Worst, The (punk band), 212

Yanovsky, Saul, 5, 27, 33, 34, 35, 36, 37, 40, 44, 47, 48; as editor, 33, 36, 37, 39, 41, 42, 45, 46; and Russia, 45
Yevzerov, Katherina, 35, 43
yidishkayt, 44, 48
Yippies, 165, 169, 173
Yonkers, 59
Young Communist League, 129
Young Eagles, 123, 124
Yunge, Di, 42
Yuppiecide (punk band), 212

Z, Bob, 209
Zarrella, Joseph, 114
Zimmer, Kenyon, 4, 5, 65
Zola, Émile, 66
Zuccotti Park, 1, 2, 221, 225, 227, 228, 232, 238n26, 239n30
Zukunft, Die, 23
Zum groben Michel (bar), 24

The University of Illinois Press
is a founding member of the
Association of American University Presses.

Composed in 10.75/13 Arno Pro
with DIN 30640 Std display
by Kirsten Dennison
at the University of Illinois Press

University of Illinois Press
1325 South Oak Street
Champaign, IL 61820-6903
www.press.uillinois.edu